ROCK MUSIC SCHOLARSHIP

**Recent Titles in
the Music Reference Collection**

Keyboard Music of Black Composers: A Bibliography
Aaron Horne, compiler

Salsa and Related Genres: A Bibliographical Guide
Rafael Figueroa, compiler

A Conductor's Repertory of Chamber Music: Compositions for Nine to Fifteen Solo Instruments
William Scott, compiler

Opera Mediography: Video Recordings and Motion Pictures
Sharon G. Almquist, compiler

American Fuging-Tunes, 1770–1820
Karl Kroeger, compiler

Classical Singers of the Opera and Recital Stages: A Bibliography of Biographical Materials
Robert H. Cowden

Rock Stars/Pop Stars: A Comprehensive Bibliography, 1955–1994
Brady J. Leyser, compiler

The Johnny Cash Record Catalog
John L. Smith, compiler

Thesaurus of Abstract Musical Properties: A Theoretical and Compositional Resource
Jeffrey Johnson

Song Finder: A Title Index to 32,000 Popular Songs in Collections, 1854–1992
Gary Lynn Ferguson, compiler

Musical Anthologies for Analytical Study: A Bibliography
James E. Perone, compiler

A Guide to Popular Music Reference Books: An Annotated Bibliography
Gary Haggerty

ROCK MUSIC SCHOLARSHIP

An Interdisciplinary Bibliography

JEFFREY N. GATTEN

Music Reference Collection, Number 50

GREENWOOD PRESS
Westport, Connecticut • London

Library of Congress Cataloging-in-Publication Data

Gatten, Jeffrey N.
    Rock music scholarship : an interdisciplinary bibliography / Jeffrey N. Gatten.
        p. cm.—(Music reference collection, ISSN 0736-7740 ; no. 50)
    Includes bibliographical references and indexes.
    ISBN 0-313-29455-0 (alk. paper)
        1. Rock music—Instruction and study—Bibliography. I. Title. II. Series.
ML128.R6G37   1995
016.78166—dc20   95-36391

British Library Cataloguing in Publication Data is available.

Copyright © 1995 by Jeffrey N. Gatten

All rights reserved. No portion of this book may be reproduced, by any process or technique, without the express written consent of the publisher.

Library of Congress Catalog Card Number: 95-36391
ISBN: 0-313-29455-0
ISSN: 0736-7740

First published in 1995

Greenwood Press, 88 Post Road West, Westport, CT 06881
An imprint of Greenwood Publishing Group, Inc.

Printed in the United States of America

The paper used in this book complies with the Permanent Paper Standard issued by the National Information Standards Organization (Z39.48-1984).

10 9 8 7 6 5 4 3 2 1

Dedicated to

Carolyn J. Radcliff
Jennifer R. Gatten
Megan E. Gatten

Contents

Preface	ix
Introduction	xi
Communication	1
Articles	1
Chapters	14
Books	18
Dissertations	19
Education	25
Articles	25
Chapters	38
Books	39
Dissertations	40
Ethnomusicology	45
Articles	45
Chapters	56
Books	62
Dissertations	64
Films and Videos	65
History	67
Articles	67
Chapters	75
Books	78
Dissertations	96
Films and Videos	97

Literature and the Arts	99
Articles	99
Chapters	109
Books	110
Dissertations	115
Films and Videos	117
Music	119
Articles	119
Chapters	130
Books	135
Dissertations	143
Films and Videos	148
Politics	151
Articles	151
Chapters	157
Books	163
Dissertations	166
Films and Videos	167
Psychology	169
Articles	169
Chapters	190
Books	190
Dissertations	191
Religion	197
Articles	197
Chapters	203
Books	205
Dissertations	206
Films and Videos	206
Sociology	207
Articles	207
Chapters	231
Books	241
Dissertations	246
Films and Videos	248
Author Index	249
Subject Index	261

Preface

For forty years, rock and roll music has dominated American popular culture. A powerful force in contemporary society, rock music is a multi-billion dollar industry. Scholars have studied the sociological, psychological, and political impact of rock music on such diverse aspects of modern culture as censorship, violence, performing arts, fashion, literature, women's issues, diversity, and ethnomusicology. Commanding the attention of researchers in numerous fields of study, rock music scholarship is an interdisciplinary phenomenon that saturates both the humanities and the social sciences.

Scholarship is defined here as any work that provides a serious treatment of the subject with the intent to inform, enlighten, educate, or add to the body of knowledge on rock music. A subtle difference exists between rock music scholarship and rock music criticism. I've ignored this subtlety on occasion while making selections for inclusion in this work. However, readers will find that most items are primarily interpretive and analytical, rather than merely descriptive or just factual. This, then, excludes most news publications which report on current events but do not attempt to provide analysis (e.g., *Time*, *Newsweek*, *People*), popular or mass market biographies and histories, fanzines (e.g., *Rolling Stone*, *Spin*, *Creem*, *Musician*), popular fiction, record reviews, and juvenile works. There are exceptions when a piece serves to illuminate scholarly discourse. This is particularly true for selected trade journals that are important to a discipline's scholarly communication process (e.g., the fields of education and music). Finally, scholars should note that published interviews are excluded due to space limitations, but they are a tremendous source for oral histories.

Chapters in this work are organized into subject disciplines. Journal articles, book chapters, books, dissertations, and films and videos are included when appropriate. Each entry includes bibliographic information applicable to the physical format. Annotations are written to provide clear descriptive explanations of content. Each entry is numbered sequentially and identified in the author and subject indexes by the entry number. The detailed indexes are designed to serve as the primary locating tools for this work.

In compiling and annotating scholarly resources for this publication, no attempt was made to distinguish between the terms "rock" and "rock and roll." While some scholars have made of point of defining "rock and roll" chronologically as existing only from the mid-1950s to the mid-1960s and "rock" as evolving sometime shortly thereafter, I have used the term "rock" as a description of most popular music from the mid-1950s to the present. Defining rock music precisely is problematic because it is a subgenre of popular music while itself containing many subgenres. Clearly, definitions of popular music in the 1990s include both rock music and country music as separate genres, but it gets a bit more ambiguous after that. Is rap music a subgenre of rock or its own genre? If the Sex Pistol's punk music is a subgenre of rock music, then is Brian Eno's ambient music? I believe these questions are best answered by the scholars who undertake the study of rock music. I have simply tried to be more inclusive than exclusive in making selections for this book, and readers will find information on a variety of musical genres.

Rock music scholarship is a rapidly growing area of study for which bibliographic control can be difficult to establish due to its interdisciplinary and elusive nature. This annotated bibliography is intended to facilitate research and study by students, scholars, teachers, librarians, music industry and record company executives, the news media, and anyone seeking scholarly information about rock music. This work will fill an obvious need in the collections of academic and public libraries.

I would like to extend grateful acknowledgement to Carolyn J. Radcliff for invaluable assistance and advice; Alicia S. Merritt of Greenwood Publishing for encouragement and enthusiasm; and Kent State University Libraries and Media Services for providing the support to complete this work, especially the interlibrary loan and circulation staff members who accommodated my extraordinary needs.

Introduction

Rock music scholarship strives to explore and explain the musical genre's role as a dominant force of modern culture. This book presents an impressive testimony to the significance of rock music in contemporary society. Certain themes of socialization processes, mass communication effects, political agendas, and artistic merits emerge as a result of the interdisciplinary approach.

For example, rock music is viewed as a socializing agent that facilitates symbolic expression and conveys meaning to audiences, especially to adolescents. James Lull argues that the effects of rock music are experienced at the physical, emotional, and cognitive levels. Rock music is gratifying to adolescents due to strong socialization messages. These messages are embedded in both the lyrical content and the moods created by the music. Because adolescents attempt to reject traditional agents of socialization, the importance of rock music in this regard may increase.

Some debate centers around whether the socialization power of rock music is dependent upon audience reception. Cristina Bodinger-deUriarte asserts that certain rock music can be so powerful a motivating art form that its alternative messages are absorbed and confronted by the audience. In fact, rock may serve as an essential element in the adolescent ceremony of rebellion, in which the audience uses the music for ritualized alienation and the creation of community. Claims are made that rock music functions to socialize youth, not to alternative subcultures, but to mainstream consumerism through the celebration of taste and fashion. Others conclude that audiences are not passive receivers of the values transmitted through rock music. Several scholars contend that audiences prefer to listen to lyrics that reinforce existing values and beliefs, rather than create new meaning.

Sex and violence are two controversial issues associated with socialization and rock music. Simon Frith and Angela McRobbie state that sexuality is a construct of rock music. However, a major dispute is the extent to which adolescents can identify or understand references to sexual or deviant lyrical themes. Jill Rosenbaum and Lorraine Prinsky claim that their subjects tended to interpret lyrics literally, ignoring symbolism and metaphors. Other studies suggest that the amount of sexual content in lyrics has increased across time, but occurs less in rock music than in other genres, such as country music and soul music. Still others insist that themes of uncontrolled sexual abandon are intentionally used to increase record sales.

Various musical genres evoke particular socialization models. For example, rap music often represents obsession with materialism and sexual desire, expressing an urban ideology. Heavy metal music preference among adolescents is associated with higher aggression, lower guilt, increased sex-role stereotyping, and elevated negative attitudes toward women. Punk rock music is associated with violence through its articulation of rebellion without any meaningful alternative vision.

Perhaps the greatest amount of attention given to sex and violence in rock music is through the analysis of music videos. Some scholars claim that music videos detract from song lyrics and reduce the emotional responses to songs. However, most studies support the notion that exposure to violent rock music videos can increase aggressive attitudes and behavior toward females, although most aggression in videos is directed towards males. Further content studies of music videos show a high level of sexism directed at women, although music videos have fewer and shorter scenes of sex and violence compared to prime-time television. Christine H. Hansen and Ranald Hansen demonstrate that preference for music videos is positively related to sexual content, but negatively related to violent content.

While music videos are often examined for scenes of sex and violence with attention given to the effects on adolescents, other issues such as race, gender, and peer group are studied as well. Jane Brown, Kenneth Campbell, and Lynn Fisher discovered that African-American adolescents are more likely to watch videos for instruction on how to dance and on fashion. They are also more likely to think about the meaning of lyrics and to desire to be like some of the characters portrayed. This suggests that African American youths are more likely to use mass media to derive meaning. Lisa Lewis observes that selected female performers, such as Cyndi Lauper and Madonna, attempt to connect with the female audience by constructing references to consumer girl culture through appropriation of traditional male space and celebration of female expression.

Music videos also serve as examples of postmodern art, having abandoned the lyrical narrative as a source for visual content. George Lipsitz contends that music videos are postmodern because they merge icons and images from diverse contexts to provide both a coherence and a confusion of mythology. Music videos can assist with the development of visual literacy because of the need to decode thickly layered images in a nonlinear narrative. However, some scholars view rock music videos as less an artistic formation of culture and more a product of commercial advertising. Interestingly, adolescents are able to recognize and evaluate music video presentations designed to influence behavior, attitudes, and values.

The portrayal and representation of women is another important aspect of the study of rock music socialization. Images of women in rock lyrics have changed over time from goddesses or girls-next-door to sex objects. Predominant subjective male worldviews are often accepted as objective fact. While female musicians traditionally have been a minority, there does appear to be an increasing prominence of female rock bands since the mid-1980s. Alan Stewart contends that women musicians are making declarations of independence directly through lyrical content and indirectly through composition, performance, and the use of unexpected extremes, such as violence and language.

Death and suicide are two socio-political issues that are often associated with rock music, especially the genre of heavy metal. Scholars have approached these topics in several ways. One method is to study adolescent attitudes, beliefs, and music preferences that may serve as indicators of suicidal behavior. Another approach is to conceptualize death as one form of adolescent rebellion recognized by the youth culture. A third method is to investigate the expression of death in song lyrics as a communicative source of contemporary societal views on death.

Satanism is a topic often connected with death and suicide studies. Controlled studies investigate the power of suggestion in the perception of satanic messages, which are sometimes claimed to exist as backward messages in rock music recordings. Michael Walker explores the issue of backward messages and concludes that individuals cannot understand these messages either consciously or unconsciously (i.e., there is no biological utility in being able to understand backward messages) and that subliminal stimulation does not cause behavioral changes. However, the rock group Judas Priest was sued for intentionally placing subliminal messages in a song that was associated with suicide attempts. Ozzy Osbourne also has been in court regarding a suicide allegedly resulting from two of his recordings. While these cases are typically debated as First Amendment issues, some scholars are concerned that basic legal rights may evaporate if satanism is believed to be a real cause of social problems.

Censorship emerges as an issue from the First Amendment arguments, evoking discourse on parental sovereignty, industry self-regulation, obscenity, children's rights, and the test of a clear and present danger. The formation of the Parents Music Resource Center (PMRC) in the mid-1980s is often cited and discussed as a significant event in the history of rock music censorship. The PMRC heavily promoted the concept of warning labels and ratings for records. Scholars question the validity of PMRC theories on rock music as a cause of social problems. Lorraine Prinsky and Jill Rosenbaum argue that adults are more likely than adolescents to be able to interpret lyrics because metaphor perception is dependent upon metacognitive knowledge. Therefore, warning labels or ratings may function to educate adolescents to themes of which they were previously unaware. Additional problems identified with assigning warning labels to records include the need to make value judgments, and interpreting art in ways that may differ from those intended by the artists.

Censorship issues, court cases, U.S. Senate hearings, and payola scandals all represent components of a larger discourse on the political nature of rock music. Controversy rages over the political function of rock music. Similar to the socialization issues, debate centers on whether it is possible to control the production and consumption of rock music when, and if, the meaning is dependent upon the audience. Building on the theories of Theodor Adorno, scholars argue that the music industry has succeeded in negating the rebellious nature of rock music through repetition, mass production, and marketing. John Orman explores the political messages of rock music that support specific social movements, establish particular worldviews, or propagandize. He concludes that rock music is a leisure activity and has rarely had any political influence on audiences. Thaddeus Coreno asserts that rock music will express rebellion, alienation, individualism, and protest only as long as it produces profitable results. Simon Frith claims that rock music does not exist as an independent art form free from economical conditions and its ideological impact is dependent upon the marketplace.

Rock music as art and the aesthetics of rock are two additional points of contention among scholars. Bruce Baugh questions whether there can be an aesthetics of rock music based upon traditional standards. He argues that rock music must be critiqued by standards unique to the genre, based primarily on performance and the effect on the body. Meanwhile, others claim that because rock music is a recorded medium, it has truly unique artistic qualities. Technology is often cited as having the biggest impact on rock aesthetics, primarily through the use of new methods of recording (e.g., digital) and new instruments (e.g., synthesizer). Peter Wicke defines rock music as art made from the contradictory elements of mass culture and individual creativity. It differs from other art forms because value and meaning are determined through a collective experience.

Interdisciplinary research requires scholars to approach topics from several areas of knowledge. The purpose of this work is to provide links among the various forms of scholarship used to decipher and comprehend rock music. It is an attempt to provide organization to a wide body of research that shares a common theme. In doing so, it is hoped that future studies will be better informed and thus provide greater insight into this particular expression of the human experience.

Communication

ARTICLES

1.   Aufderheide, Pat. "Music Videos: The Look of the Sound." *Journal of Communication* 36, no. 1 (1986): 57-78.
   Claims that music videos offer "an environment, an experience, a mood." Insists that music videos are commercials, having eliminated any distinctions between commercials and programs. Comments on the abandonment by music videos of the song's lyrical narrative. Describes music videos as postmodern art, made from a commercial culture structured on dreams and desire. Videos perpetuate a world without social identity and "invent the world they represent."

2.   Berry, Venise T. "Rap Music, Self Concept and Low Income Black Adolescents." *Popular Music and Society* 14 (1990): 89-107.
   Studies 115 black adolescents, between thirteen and eighteen years of age, to better understand the uses made of rap music. Argues that there is a "complex interaction" between lower socio-economic status and popularity of rap music. Concludes that rap music serves as a mechanism for enhancing positive self-concepts.

3.   Brown, Jane Delano. "Race and Gender in Rock Video." *Social Science Newsletter* 70, no. 2 (1985): 82-86.
   Describes the visual content of music videos with regard to roles of sex and race. Uses content analysis to study 112 music videos. Videos were coded "for sex and race ratios among lead performers, for portrayal of sex roles, and for antisocial behaviors, sexual behaviors, and mood." Discovers that music videos are dominated by white male performers. Compared to prime-time television, music videos have fewer scenes of sex and violence. Notes some difficulties in applying to rock music videos content analysis designed for traditional television programming. For example, scenes in music videos are noticeably

shorter than in regular television programs. Suggests that for videos, it would be reasonable to attempt to measure the combined effects of the visuals and the music.

4.   Brown, Jane D., and Kenneth Campbell. "Race and Gender in Music Videos: The Same Beat but a Different Drummer." *Journal of Communication* 36, no. 1 (1986): 94-106.

Notes that women and blacks remain in the minority with regard to visibility on MTV. Samples music videos from both MTV and the Black Entertainment Television (BET) channel. Discusses possible reasons why videos by black performers are not widely shown on MTV, a situation that results in fewer diverse images of race and gender.

5.   Brown, Jane D., and Laurie Schulze. "The Effects of Race, Gender, and Fandom on Audience Interpretations of Madonna's Music Videos." *Journal of Communication* 40, no. 2 (1990): 88-102.

Begins by claiming that informed readings of texts "cannot predict the meanings that will be made by audiences in social situations different from those of the academic critic." Also, content analysis can provide a count of certain overt acts, but will not indicate how the acts are interpreted by the various audiences. Attempts to rectify these problems by considering race, gender, and familiarity with respect to interpretation of music videos by adolescent audiences. Utilizes two videos by Madonna, *Papa Don't Preach* and *Open Your Heart*, as examples of portrayed sexuality. Discusses results in terms of blacks and whites, males and females, and those who like and dislike Madonna.

6.   Brown, Jane D., Kenneth Campbell, and Lynn Fisher. "American Adolescents and Music Videos: Why Do They Watch?" *Gazette* 37, no. 1-2 (1986): 19-32.

Explores the different uses made of music videos by different groups of adolescents. Randomly samples 1029 adolescents by administering questionnaires regarding media use patterns and preferences. Results indicate that almost 80% of the sample watch music videos, with more than one-third watching daily. Finds significant racial and gender differences in the use of music videos. African American adolescents are more likely than other adolescents to watch music videos for instruction on how to dance and for instruction on fashion. They are also more likely to think about the meaning of song lyrics and to desire to be like some of the characters portrayed. Suggests that African American adolescents are more likely than others to use mass media for a "source of information about their lives." Females are more likely than males to watch for purposes of dancing, fashion, and listening to lyrics. Using the uses and gratifications model, concludes that African Americans and females are those most likely to be affected by music videos.

7. Brown, Mary Ellen, and John Fiske. "Romancing the Rock: Romance and Representation in Popular Music Videos." *Onetwothreefour* 5 (1987): 61-73.

Investigates the appeal of rock music videos to female audiences through the utilization of a feminine narrative, the romance. Studies two videos: A-Ha's *Take on Me*, and Madonna's *Material Girl*. Claims that the two videos offer a sense of power to female audience members through fantasy and representation. States that the videos are fantasies that assert women's right to control their own representation.

8. Cantor, Joanne R., and Dolf Zillmann. "The Effect of Affective State and Emotional Arousal on Music Appreciation." *Journal of General Psychology* 89, no. 1 (1973): 97-108.

Tests the effect of varying the affective and emotional states of subjects on subsequent music appreciation. Sixty college students (thirty-two males, twenty-eight females) were exposed to four film segments: positive hedonic tone, negative hedonic tone, low excitatory potential, and high excitatory potential. After being exposed to the film segments, subjects were asked to rate musical selections by Doris Troy. Results indicate that "prior stimulation can indeed exert pronounced effects on the appreciation of music," suggesting that a communicator can manipulate an audience by sequencing "the affect-inducing and excitation-producing segments of his message."

9. Chesebro, James W., Davis A. Foulger, Jay E. Nachman, and Andrew Yannelli. "Popular Music as a Mode of Communication, 1955-1982." *Critical Studies in Mass Communication* 2 (1985): 115-135.

Analyzes the top fifteen records of each year from 1955 to 1982. States that popular music is repetitive, physical, and artistic. Classifies each song as ironic, mimetic, leader-centered, romantic, or mythical. Classifications are based on two elements: 1) the intelligence of the central character in relation to the audience's intelligence, and 2) the ability of the central character to control situations in relation to the audience's ability to control. For ironic communication, the central character is less intelligent and less able to control situations than the audience. For mimetic communication, the central character is equal to the audience. For leader-centered communication, the central character is more intelligent than the audience but equal in terms of control. For romantic communication, the central character is relatively more intelligent and more able to control situations than the audience. For mythical communication, the central character is far superior than the audience in both intelligence and control. Results lead to labeling the 1950s as the decade of "innocence," the 1960s as "exploration," the 1970s as "frustrated idealism," and the 1980s as "pragmatism." Identifies five eras based on the content of popular music: 1) 1955-1959 is the era of "interpersonal romance," 2) 1959-1964 is "dynamic equilibrium," 3) 1965-1976 is "ironic leadership," 4) 1974-1979 is "ironic romance," and 5) 1980-1982 is "pragmatic skepticism." Concludes that popular music reflects American attitudes and demonstrates "an increasingly ironic perspective of human relationships."

10.   Christenson, Peter. "The Effects of Parental Advisory Labels on Adolescent Music Preferences." *Journal of Communication* 42, no. 1 (1992): 106-113.

Examines whether parental advisory labels on record albums, cassette tapes, and compact discs will act as incentives or deterrents for adolescents to purchase these materials (i.e., forbidden-fruit versus tainted-fruit). Subjects of the study were 145 public middle school students, grades six through eight, ages eleven to fifteen, ninety-five percent white, and socio-economically diverse. Subjects were exposed to labeled and unlabeled music. Results indicate that there is no evidence that parental advisory labels will act as incentives to acquire labeled items.

11.   Cuthbert, Marlene. "Cultural Autonomy and Popular Music: A Survey of Jamaican Youth." *Communication Research* 12, no. 3 (1985): 381-393.

Surveys 300 Jamaican youth (ages twelve to eighteen, forty-five percent male) in 1983 to discover whether socio-economic status would correlate with musical preference for Reggae music. Results indicate this to be the case. Discusses briefly the historical development of Reggae music. Preferences were examined with regard to listening, dancing, favorite singers, significance of lyrics, and location for listening. The higher the socio-economic status, the greater the preference for foreign rock music performers.

12.   Denski, Stan. "One Step Up and Two Steps Back: A Heuristic Model for Popular Music and Communication Research." *Popular Music and Society* 13 (1989): 9-21.

Asserts that critical scholarly writing on rock music has emerged from a base of 1960s journalists who are "atheoretical and unfocused." Contends that this form of rock music writing has essentially expended its usefulness. Presents a sociological model with macro and micro levels designed for continuing scholarly investigation into rock music. Suggests ways in which scholars can better communicate their work to music listeners and practitioners.

13.   Desmond, Roger Jon. "Adolescents and Music Lyrics: Implications of a Cognitive Perspective." *Communication Quarterly* 35, no. 3 (1987): 276-284.

Probes the relevance of cognitive research methodologies to policy debates surrounding the regulation of rock music. Provides principles, based on cognitive psychology, for governing how adolescents may receive and assimilate messages from rock music lyrics. Builds on the assumptions that lyrics are not texts studied by listeners, that lyrics are redundant, that a single song's lyrics are heard repeatedly during a given day, and lyrics are like poetry because the content may be "metaphoric, symbolic, and not easily accessible to a casual listener." Explores the issues of lyric comprehension, memory, and backward masking. Promotes the need for basic research to inform policy decisions given that "there is not much evidence for specific learning from lyrics."

14. Doherty, Thomas. "MTV and the Music Video: Promo and Product." *Southern Speech Communication Journal* 52, no. 4 (1987): 349-361.

Describes the development of MTV and the consequences for television in general. Observes that MTV has prospered due to "market research, saturation airplay, and changes in the institutional and technical structures of television itself." Attributes the success of MTV to the synthesis of rock music and the commercial power of television.

15. Frith, Simon. "Critical Response." *Critical Studies in Mass Communication* 3, no. 1 (1986): 74-77.

Responds to Lawrence Grossberg's article "Is There Rock After Punk?" Criticizes Grossberg for suggesting "that youth is somehow the privileged bearer of the postmodern condition." Agrees that punk rock challenged rock music and this challenge is part of the postmodernism discussion.

16. Glausser, Wayne. "Gotta Revolution, 1987: Grace Slick, Paul Kantner, and *Volunteers of America*." *Popular Music and Society* 12, no. 2 (1988): 45-53.

Compares and contrasts the rhetorical perspectives of Grace Slick and Paul Kantner in 1987, with special attention to Jefferson Airplane song *Volunteers of America*. Concludes that Slick and Kantner are both motivated by a combination of political consciousness and nostalgia.

17. Grossberg, Lawrence. "Is There Rock After Punk?" *Critical Studies in Mass Communication* 3, no. 1 (1986): 50-74.

Attempts to define a conceptual framework for exploring the social and political significance of rock music. Begins by defining rock music as a "mode of functioning." Discusses rock music as affective empowerment, punk rock as a watershed phenomenon, and the resulting deconstruction of youth. Claims that one can only begin to understand rock music by examining the ways in which it empowers by articulating a youth culture. Contends that a three dimensional geography (youth, pleasure, attitude) defines the unity and continuity of the rock music culture. Youth is celebrated via risk, instability, and change. Pleasure is emphasized through the affirmation of sexual desire. Attitude is defined by image and style. Describes the deconstruction of youth as a result of the commercialization of fashion and of rock music, a depressed economy, shifting cultural focus from youth to middle-aged baby boomers, increasing conservatism, and new technologies that replace rock music as means of leisure activities. Questions whether rock music can continue to empower. Also published in *On Record: Rock, Pop, and the Written Word* edited by Simon Frith and Andrew Goodwin.

18.   Grossberg, Lawrence. "Reply to the Critics." *Critical Studies in Mass Communication* 3, no. 1 (1986): 86-95.

Replies to the critical responses by Simon Frith, Greil Marcus, and Stephen L. Nugent to his article "Is There Rock After Punk?" Clarifies that the meaning of empowerment is the politics, and not the description, of an experience.

19.   Grossberg, Lawrence. "*I'd Rather Feel Bad Than Not Feel Anything at All*: Rock and Roll, Pleasure and Power." *Enclitic* 8, no. 1-2 (1984): 94-111.

Points out that even though much has been written about rock music, there is little understanding about how audiences "select, appropriate and make use of a limited set of available media messages." Claims that traditional discourses on rock music have taken one of two tracks: 1) attack rock music as being a manipulative commodity, or 2) compare rock music to art. Offers a postmodern interpretation that positions rock music as discourse and as a source of empowerment.

20.   Hansen, Christine Hall, and Ranald D. Hansen. "Schematic Information Processing of Heavy Metal Lyrics." *Communication Research* 18, no. 3 (1991): 373-411.

Studies undergraduate students to test schematic processing of lyrics from heavy metal songs. Examines lyrical themes such as sex, suicide, violence, and the occult. High and low cognitive loads were tested. It was expected that low load would result in better lyric recall, comprehension, and content extraction. Argues that schematic processing can affect the ease and type of information processing, as well as the impact and future use of the information. Places past research into perspective given that lyrics can be processed schematically.

21.   Hansen, Christine Hall, and Ranald D. Hansen. "The Influence of Sex and Violence on the Appeal of Rock Music Videos." *Communication Research* 17, no. 2 (1990): 212-234.

Conducts two experiments to test a number of hypotheses on the effects of sex and violence in rock music videos. Purpose of the studies is to explain the conventional wisdom that sex and violence are in rock music videos because they "sell." Previous research indicates that, in reality, "sex may sell, violence may or may not, and sex and violence together will not." Results show that preference for both the music and the visuals is positively related to sexual content, that preference is negatively related to violent content, and that preference is negatively related to the combination of sexual and violent content. Explanation is provided in terms of excitation-transfer theory. Concludes that sexual content does sell, but may have a curvilinear impact. Violent content does not sell.

22. Harmon, James E. "Meaning in Rock Music: Notes Toward a Theory of Communication." *Popular Music and Society* 2 (1972): 18-32.

Contends that music, as an art form, is a "cognitive force that can help bring the latent to the surface." Notes that this does not mean that music invokes certain behaviors. Rather, the appeal of certain music may be dependent upon the extent to which it reinforces existing attitudes. Bemoans the lack of a comprehensive theory of communication that would prevent rock music from being viewed as "demonology." Offers that the communication theories of Kenneth Boulding can be applied to reach an understanding of rock music, especially in terms of cultural change.

23. Kalis, Pamela, and Kimberly A. Neuendorf. "Aggressive Cue Prominence and Gender Participation in MTV." *Journalism Quarterly* 66, no. 1 (1989): 148-154,229.

Argues that aggressive behavior in rock music videos may not be as considerable as commonly criticized. Studies the content of music videos. Sample consisted of fourteen hours of randomly selected MTV content. Aggressive cues were contained in nine percent of the total video time. Forty percent of the sample videos did not contain aggressive cues. Contrary to popular criticism, findings show that aggression was depicted three and one-half times more towards males than females. When females were depicted as aggression initiators or recipients, they were more likely than males to be shown in close-up shots, possibly resulting in more attention being centered on the event.

24. Kaplan, E. Ann. "History, the Historical Spectator and Gender Address in Music Television." *Journal of Communication Inquiry* 10, no. 1 (1986): 3-14.

Begins with a discussion of how contemporary film theory replaced the notion of history as objective truth. Applies this concept and related theories to an analysis of MTV. Surveys a variety of modes depicted on MTV, including romantic, socially conscious, nihilist, classical, and postmodernist. Considers these modes in relationship to predominant MTV themes of authority and love/sex. Concludes by questioning how the nature of postmodernism, radical or coopted, is represented by MTV.

25. Kemp, Jim. "'Normalizing' an Epidemic." *Christianity and Crisis* 48, no. 10 (1988): 227-229.

Criticizes the mass media for creating a media culture in which AIDS is represented as a dichotomy of guilt versus innocence. Claims that at stake is the issue of "who controls the vocabulary of associations attached to the disease." This distracts from the real issue of controlling an epidemic by casting sufferers of AIDS as heroes or villains. Discusses various media portrayals of AIDS, including television, cinema, and rock music. States that rock musicians on the whole have not made a very strong effort to realize their potential for reaching adolescents with "the safer-sex message in a sex-positive context." Rather, one of the traditional underlying messages of rock music, that of "unrestrained sexual abandon," continues to be used to sell records.

26.   Lampman, Richard A. "The Metaphysics of Automated Rock Radio." *Popular Music and Society* 7, no. 3 (1980): 159-164.

Claims that the metaphysics of automated radio programming of rock music is one of product that "points to the total cooption of rock's rebellious and celebratory nature." Rock music becomes simply a product offered in exchange for advertising. States that there is no communication because there is no context in which the communication occurs. Compares this radio programming format to television, "offering an impersonal service and demanding nothing from the listener in return."

27.   Lipsitz, George. "A World of Confusion: Music Video as Modern Myth." *Onetwothreefour* 5 (1987): 50-60.

Submits that in order to view music videos as modern mythology, one must accept the medium as "a vehicle for both coherence and confusion." Describes music videos as the "quintessential postmodern art" by fusing "icons and images from diverse contexts." Argues that music videos can present social evils, such as sexism and racism, as natural phenomena or they can present oppression as inherently bad. Concludes that the myth is a means of domination. However, to be effective it must be ambiguous and available to contradictory interpretations. Music videos can function as a "powerful locus of criticism and reflection."

28.   Lull, James T., Lawrence M. Johnson, and Carol E. Sweeny. "Audiences for Contemporary Radio Formats." *Journal of Broadcasting* 22, no. 4 (1978): 439-453.

Constructs demographic profiles of audience types by radio station formats. Seeks to identify the most relevant demographic variables associated with radio station formats. Uses six station formats for analysis: Top Forty (best selling records), Beautiful Music (easy listening), Middle of the Road (light rock, oldies), Live Progressive Rock (extended play of a variety of album selections), Automated Rock (pre-recorded with little announcing), and All News (no music). Examines demographic factors of sex, age, marital status, education, geographic stability, dwelling type, residence ownership, and subscriptions received. Discovers that age and education are the "fundamental demographic criteria for determining format distinctness." Notes that contrary to the stereotyped image, Top Forty listeners are not mainly adolescents. Rather, almost one-half of the Top Forty listeners studied were married and over one-half owned their residences.

29. Lull, James. "On the Communicative Properties of Music." *Communication Research* 12, no. 3 (1985): 363-372.

Discusses rock music as an instrument that serves to facilitate the adolescent socialization process. Argues that the effects of rock music are experienced at the physical, emotional, and cognitive levels. Claims that music is communication because it facilitates symbolic expressions in dyadic, small-group, and large social settings. Rock music is the primary medium for conveying socialization themes to adolescents. It exposes one to alternative values and lifestyles that may be in opposition to mainstream dominant culture media messages. Also discusses MTV in terms of both negative and positive socialization effects. Concludes that music as communication has rarely received scholarly attention because to adults it is a background medium, whereas with adolescents it is used to find meaning.

30. Marcus, Greil. "Critical Response." *Critical Studies in Mass Communication* 3, no. 1 (1986): 77-81.

Responds to Lawrence Grossberg's article "Is There Rock After Punk?" Claims that Grossberg's cultural theory is flawed because it does not derive from specific artifacts. Contends that "any cultural theory must both inform and illuminate not just whatever large questions it poses, but whatever minute artifacts it appropriates along the way." Concludes that Grossberg's theory does not provide a different way of viewing the world.

31. Nugent, Stephen L. "Critical Response." *Critical Studies in Mass Communication* 3, no. 1 (1986): 82-85.

Responds to Lawrence Grossberg's article "Is There Rock After Punk?" Discounts a number of Grossberg's points, including the notion that the consumerism of rock music is exclusively associated with the youth culture. Observes that it is very difficult to determine exactly what is rock music and, therefore, difficult to assign value to the significance of punk rock as a point of departure.

32. Orlova, Irina. "Notes From the Underground: The Emergence of Rock Music Culture." *Journal of Communication* 41, no. 2 (1991): 66-71.

Assesses the state of rock music in the Soviet Union since the 1985 legalization of an already active rock music culture. Depicts the development of Soviet rock music as a pre-1985 underground activity and notes how this affected its evolution. Prior to 1985, musicians had complete artistic control over their products. Poor music production equipment led to a greater emphasis on lyrics "to carry much of the music's meaning." Post-1985 sees both Soviet and foreign rock music becoming integrated into television and radio programming. Rock music now functions primarily as entertainment.

33. Perterson-Lewis, Sonja, and Shirley A. Chennault. "Black Artists' Music Videos: Three Success Strategies." *Journal of Communication* 36, no. 1 (1986): 107-114.

Notes that black musicians and performers have created visual images in music videos that are designed to cross physical and social barriers. Three strategies are identified. Self-presentation is discussed in terms of impression management. Disassociation and neutralization are reviewed. Concludes that black performers may change their musical styles, may abandon old audiences for new ones, or may attempt to include new audiences by broadening their appeal.

34. Roe, Keith. "Swedish Youth and Music: Listening Patterns and Motivations." *Communication Research* 12, no. 3 (1985): 353-362.

Reports the results of a study of 509 Swedish adolescents, ages eleven to fifteen, during 1976, 1978, and 1980. Purpose of the study was to investigate the social role of music as a group phenomenon. Discovered a "relationship between amount of peer orientation and type of music preferred." Three distinct types of music preference surfaced: punk/rock/new wave, popular, and classical/jazz/folk. Concludes that listening motivations were "more physical and emotional than cerebral."

35. Rouner, Donna. "Rock Music Use as a Socializing Function." *Popular Music and Society* 14 (1990): 97-107.

Studies the media effects of rock music as related to cognition. Assumes that mass media are used differently depending upon exposure, reliance, and involvement. Observes that adolescents find rock music gratifying. Speculates that the gratification is related to rock music's messages about adult socialization, including sexuality, identity, values, and beliefs.

36. Sherman, Barry L., and Joseph R. Dominick. "Violence and Sex in Music Videos: TV and Rock 'n' Roll." *Journal of Communication* 36, no. 1 (1986): 79-93.

Attempts to provide descriptive information about music videos, to offer comparative information on the method of delivery of music videos (i.e., cable only, cable and broadcast, broadcast only) in relation to the extent of sexual and violent content, and to generate baseline data for a study of effects on audiences. Conducts a content analysis of music videos and concludes that they are "violent, male-oriented, and laden with sexual content." Suggests a cultivation analysis as a next logical study.

37. Simpkins, John D., and Jack A. Smith. "Effects of Music on Source Evaluations." *Journal of Broadcasting* 18, no. 3 (1974): 361-367.

Evaluates the effect of background music in audio messages based on audience preferences for certain types of music. Subjects were forty undergraduate students who had indicated they most preferred rock music and least preferred country music. Three thirty-second "radio" messages were presented: 1) verbal message only, 2) verbal message with country music background, and 3) verbal message with rock music background. Results indicate that the presence of the most preferred music (rock music) has little impact on the credibility of the message. However, the presence of the least preferred music (country) has a negative impact on the credibility of the music. Concludes that background music does affect audience evaluations of messages negatively if the background music is not preferred by the audience.

38. Singletary, Michael W. "Some Perceptions of the Lyrics of Three Types of Recorded Music: Rock, Country and Soul." *Popular Music and Society* 9, no. 3 (1983): 51-63.

Explores the idea that music teaches, and examines the nature of what is being taught. Subjects were 185 undergraduate students who were asked to evaluate one of three genres of music: rock, country, and soul. Measured specific characteristics: style, comprehensibility, social/psychological characteristics, and the extent to which sex is a lyrical theme. Results show that rock music has "greater lyrical sophistication, using more semantic devices, employing more subtle and complex ideas, and employing more social comment." Observes that rock music contained significantly more social commentary, but significantly less sexual content than country music and soul music.

39. Snow, Robert P. "Youth, Rock 'n' Roll, and Electronic Media." *Youth & Society* 18, no. 4 (1987): 326-343.

Establishes a relationship among the youth culture that emerged in the 1950s, rock music, and electronic media. Media communications establish and maintain rock music youth culture. Notes that as communication strategies change (e.g., from radio to music television), meanings also change for the youth culture.

40. Stratton, Jon. "Between Two Worlds: Art and Commercialism in the Record Industry." *Sociological Review* 30 (1982): 267-285.

Attempts to map a series of aesthetic presuppositions through which journalists and critics analyze rock music. Contends that rock music critics are able to reconcile art and capitalism because they are not economically tied to the music industry. Rather, they are obligated economically to connect with their readership.

41. Sun, Se-Wen, and James Lull. "The Adolescent Audience for Music Videos and Why They Watch." *Journal of Communication* 36, no. 1 (1986): 115-125.

Considers the patterns of exposure to, and motivations for viewing, music videos in regard to race, gender, peer group, and attitudes toward school among adolescents. Subjects were 603 high school students in San Jose, California.

Conducted a factor analysis of motivations for viewing music videos. Results suggest that motivational statements for watching television or listening to music do not adequately represent motivations for viewing music videos.

42. Tankel, Jonathan David. "The Practice of Recording Music: Remixing as Recoding." *Journal of Communication* 40, no. 3 (1990): 34-46.

Outlines the practice of remixing sound recordings as a recoding process. Suggests "consequences of that practice for the construction and consumption of popular music." Discusses the "sonic" and the "grain" of recording. Traces the history of remixing recordings and its impact on rock music. Argues that current technology for remixing allows for a "collaborative creative enterprise without end" given that a recording of a particular song may be remixed and re-released into the market. This creates aesthetic dilemmas, much like the colorization of motion pictures, and calls into question the definition of artifact.

43. Theberge, Paul. "Musicians' Magazines in the 1980s: The Creation of a Community and a Consumer Market." *Cultural Studies* 5, no. 3 (1991): 270-293.

Asserts that as new musical technologies have developed, the number of magazines devoted to music and musicianship has increased. Claims that these consumer magazines contribute to a sense of community among musicians who face a growing complexity of technology related to music production. Comments on the magazine publishing industry and the reliance of musicians on this mediated form of interaction for communicating information. Notes that the publishers of these magazines believe that they not only represent trends in the music industry, but also contribute to, and inform, the development of the trends. Discusses the advertising function of consumer magazines and concludes that magazines aimed at musicians function to create both a community and a market.

44. Vincent, Richard C., Dennis K. Davis, and Lilly Ann Boruszkowski. "Sexism on MTV: The Portrayal of Women in Rock Videos." *Journalism Quarterly* 64, no. 4 (1987): 750-755,941.

Analyzes 110 music videos from MTV to examine the portrayal of sex roles. Studies the "social context in which sex roles are presented and the function of performer in the portrayal of women." Utilizes a four-item ordinal scale with the following levels: condescending, keep-her-place, contradictory, and fully-equal. Results indicate that sexism is fairly high in the portrayal of women in music videos, with over one-half of the videos rated as "condescending." Concludes it is revealing that music videos "perpetuate social norms so effectively" given that they are produced by an industry that promotes itself as being progressive.

45. Vincent, Richard C. "Clio's Consciousness Raised? Portrayal of Women in Rock Videos, Re-Examined." *Journalism Quarterly* 66, no. 1 (1989): 155-160.

Updates a study conducted eighteen months earlier to determine if there have been any changes in the portrayal of women in music videos. Using the same methodology as in the previous study, results indicate "that sexism still is fairly high in music videos." Mentions one notable change from the previous study in that the extent of sexism varies by the gender of the performer. Questions the "socializing effect such life portrayals have on audiences" and claims a passive attitude within the rock music video industry.

46. Walker, James R. "How Viewing of MTV Relates to Exposure to Other Media Violence." *Journalism Quarterly* 64, no. 4 (1987): 756-762.

Examines the relationship between viewing MTV and perceived violence in society and between viewing MTV and viewing other television violence. Subjects were more than 200 adolescents. Results show that there is an inverse relationship between MTV viewing and exposure to other television violence. Subjects who were "above average in MTV viewing, tended to be below average in the viewing of other types of violent content." Concludes that although previous content analysis research directed at MTV has indicated a high amount of violence in music videos, it may be that this violence is not consequential.

47. Wells, Alan. "Images of Popular Music Artists: Do Male and Female Audiences have Different Views?" *Popular Music and Society* 12 (1988): 1-17.

Probes the images of rock musicians and pop stars as perceived by 108 college students (sixty-three males, forty-five females). Results suggest common agreement regarding image content, suggesting that the music industry is successful in projecting certain images. Notes variations by gender with regard to image acceptance and reaction. Males were hostile to images that females interpreted as sexy, but females did not display the same reaction for images that males found to be sexy. Concludes that although the received image may be common among females and males, the reactions vary by gender.

48. Wicke, Peter. "Young People and Popular Music in East Germany: Focus on a Scene." *Communication Research* 12, no. 3 (1985): 319-325.

Offers an explanation of the popularity of western rock music in the German Democratic Republic (GDR). As a medium of cultural communication, rock music in East Germany has not disrupted the national fabric despite its tendency to provide an international cultural perspective. Calls for rock music in the GDR to be promoted as more than a consumable import product. Advocates rock music as a potential legitimate expression of adolescent cultural and political communication.

49.   Wolfe, Arnold S. "Rock on Cable: On MTV: Music Television, the First Video Music Channel." *Popular Music and Society* 9, no. 1 (1983): 41-50.

Describes MTV, its goals, programming, and demographics. Looks at the history of the relationship between rock music and television. Presents the debate surrounding the potential value and likely commercial success of music videos.

50.   Zillmann, Dolf, and Norbert Mundorf. "Image Effects in the Appreciation of Video Rock." *Communication Research* 14, no. 3 (1987): 316-334.

Reports on a study in which both sexual and/or violent images were inserted into a rock music video. The video was reviewed by 100 subjects (fifty male and fifty female undergraduates). Anticipates results from two different theoretical models: excitation-transfer theory and attribution theory. Results show that the sexual stimuli increased music appreciation in both males and females, with a "tendency for the involvement of violent stimuli to have a similar effect." A combination of both sexual and violent stimuli did not increase music appreciation. The addition of sexual stimuli resulted in the music being more sensual for the males. However, the absence of the stimuli resulted in the music being more sensual for the females. Concludes that the two predictive theoretical models are valid, but discusses where the models fail.

CHAPTERS

51.   Denski, Stan W. "Music, Musicians, and Communication: The Personal Voice in a Common Language." In *Popular Music and Communication*. 2nd ed., edited by James Lull, 33-48. Newbury Park, Calif.: Sage, 1992.

Looks at interviews with rock musicians in order to explore how musicians describe music as a form of communication. Identifies five themes for categorizing the communicative nature of music. "Magical" describes the idea that music flows through the musician, originating from some unknown source. "Social" describes music designed to communicate purpose and function related to political and societal issues. "Personal" describes music that communicates emotional situations at the individual level, with strong emphasis on the lyrical content. "Formal" describes an emphasis on the artistic and technical merits of composition and presentation over textual messages. "Adult" describes communication regarding mature themes as opposed to youthful themes of alienation and rebellion. The 'Adult' theme is most notable among older rock musicians.

52.   Denski, Stan, and David Sholle. "Metal Men and Glamour Boys: Gender Performance in Heavy Metal." In *Men, Masculinity, and the Media*, edited by Steve Craig, 41-60. Newbury Park, Calif.: Sage, 1992.

Uses "performative theory of gender" to examine the constructions and representations of masculinity in heavy metal music. Links three broad areas of concern: 1) the idea that gender differences can be understood in terms of "culturally transmitted codes of performance," 2) the concept that audiences participate actively in media consumption, and 3) the notion that rock music is increasingly fragmented. Concludes that audiences can decode media, but questions to what extent the process is liberating or empowering. Heavy metal music's "appropriation of feminine gender signs fails to offer a meaningful challenge" to the traditional masculine roles.

53.   Grossberg, Lawrence. "Rock and Roll in Search of an Audience." In *Popular Music and Communication*. 2nd ed., edited by James Lull, 152-175. Newbury Park, Calif.: Sage, 1992.

Stresses the history of rock music as a set of images: "musical and visual, live and recorded, personal and public, of performers and fans, of youth and adults, of fun and rebellion." Presents rock music as a unique form of mass communication, responsible for socializing adolescents to consumerism, celebrating "the evanescent quality of taste and fashion," and undermining "notions of quality and historical transcendence." Associates rock music with communication theory due to its emphasis on message and audience. Asserts that individual identities are the construction of social relationships created by communicative messages. Describes the postmodern conditions that created rock music.

54.   Hanna, Judith Lynne. "Moving Messages: Identity and Desire in Popular Music and Social Dance." In *Popular Music and Communication*. 2nd ed., edited by James Lull, 176-195. Newbury Park, Calif.: Sage, 1992.

Demonstrates that dance is a nonverbal form of communication that can express emotions and assert gender, ethnic and socio-economic status, and political identity. Communication in dance occurs through shared assumptions. Dance functions to serve pleasure, emotional release, and identity establishment. Provides a historical perspective on dance and presents dance as cultural capital. Uses rap music to illustrate social and political expression through dance.

55.   Hayward, Philip. "Music Video, the Bicentenary (and after)." In *From Pop to Punk to Postmodernism: Popular Music and Australian Culture From the 1960s to the 1990s*, edited by Philip Hayward, 160-171. North Sydney, Australia: Allen & Unwin, 1992.

Considers music videos as text. Examines a series of videos associated with the Australian Bicentenary. Looks at videos by Not Drowning Wave, The Go Betweens, Midnight Oil, Yothu Yindi, and Star Club.

56.   Horton, Donald. "The Dialogue of Courtship in Popular Songs." In *On Record: Rock, Pop, and the Written Word*, edited by Simon Frith and Andrew Goodwin, 14-26. New York: Pantheon Books, 1990.

Conducts a content analysis of song lyrics to determine the functions of language in popular song lyrics. Argues that lyrics are a rhetorical device that "may promote a sense of identity."

57.   Lewis, Lisa A. "Consumer Girl Culture: How Music Video Appeals to Girls." In *Television and Women's Culture: The Politics of the Popular*, edited by Mary Ellen Brown, 89-101. London: Sage, 1990.

Argues that women performers Cyndi Lauper and Madonna focus on, and connect with, adolescent females by constructing references to "consumer girl culture" through their music videos and fashion styles. They accomplish this through the use of "access signs" and "discovery signs." Access signs are those in which traditional male space is appropriated by females. Discovery signs are those in which references to female expression are celebrated. Concludes that the "textual strategies of female performers can cohere with female spectators' cultural experience to create a powerful correspondence between text and audience."

58.   Lull, James. "Popular Music and Communication: An Introduction." In *Popular Music and Communication*. 2nd ed., edited by James Lull, 1-32. Newbury Park, Calif.: Sage, 1992.

Serves as an overview and introduction to a collection of essays by various authors. Establishes two theoretical assumptions: 1) participants in popular music communication "act willingly and imaginatively," and 2) structural circumstances influence communicative capacities. Discusses the role of popular music as a commodity constructed to fit within a normative culture as well as a means of expressing protest. Touches on the decline in popularity of rock music in favor of rap music and more mainstream popular music. Covers the impact of technology on creating distance between the music producers/performers and audiences. Argues that music videos represent a new medium different from traditional television and radio. Also reviews world music and the internationalization of popular music. Explores the physical, emotional, cognitive, personal, and social levels of music as communication. Finally, presents dance as a form of empowerment.

59.   Rex, Idena. "Kylie: The Making of a Star." In *From Pop to Punk to Postmodernism: Popular Music and Australian Culture from the 1960s to the 1990s*, edited by Philip Hayward, 149-159. North Sydney, Australia: Allen & Unwin, 1992.

Examines the career of the female performer Kylie Minogue as the "new pop woman." Discusses the performer's music popularity in terms of her television popularity through an exploration of her various self-inventing processes. Kylie Minogue uses meaning to construct a "star" image for the public.

60. Rothenbuhler, Eric W., and Tom McCourt. "Commercial Radio and Popular Music: Processes of Selection and Factors of Influence." In *Popular Music and Communication*. 2nd ed., edited by James Lull, 101-115. Newbury Park, Calif.: Sage, 1992.

Asserts that popular music is "designed to meet the needs of the radio industry rather than individual consumers or the culture at large." Describes the music industry system of which the radio is a component. Discusses how station formats are used to provide standardized predictability in order to maintain listeners (i.e., consumers). Details the process of decision making regarding the music that gets played on the radio. Concludes that as a result of its organization and function, the radio industry discourages "significant stylistic innovation in popular music and the communicative potential that such creative endeavors would produce."

61. Schwichtenberg, Cathy. "Music Video: The Popular Pleasures of Visual Music." In *Popular Music and Communication*. 2nd ed., edited by James Lull, 116-133. Newbury Park, Calif.: Sage, 1992.

Explores "the various facets of music video within a cultural context that accounts for commercial constraints as well as audience enablement." Provides a history of the relationship between popular music and television and the eventual development of MTV. Music video genres are identified as performance, narrative, and conceptual. Analyzes the content of Madonna's video *Cherish* with attention to the theme of female pleasure. Discusses audience interpretation of Madonna videos. Purpose is to present context, form, interpretation, and audience as affecting the production and experience of music videos.

62. Sherman, Barry L., and Laurence W. Etling. "Perceiving and Processing Music Television." In *Responding to the Screen: Reception and Reaction Processes*, edited by Jennings Bryant and Dolf Zillman, 373-388. Hillsdale, N.J.: Lawrence Erlbaum Associates, 1991.

Serves as a review of the literature related to music television. Begins with a review of the contributions of rock music and the radio in the formation of a youth culture. Turns to a discussion of marketing practices aimed at the youth culture and the subsequent emergence of MTV and its marketing strategies. Follows with an examination of rock music video production techniques. Concludes by examining audience responses to music television. Comments on behavioral effects, especially in relation to the portrayal of women, and enculturation effects of music videos.

63.   Stewart, Alan D. "Declarations of Independence: The Female Rock and Roller Comes of Age." In *Beyond Boundaries: Sex and Gender Diversity in Communication*, edited by Cynthia M. Lont and Sheryl A. Friedley, 283-298. Fairfax, Va.: George Mason University Press, 1989.

Observes the rise in prominence of female rock performers during the 1970s and 1980s as demonstrating a declaration of independence. States that the declarations take two distinct forms: direct and indirect. Direct declarations are found in the lyrical content of songs. Indirect declarations are found in music composition, performance, cooption of previously recorded male-oriented material, and use of unexpected extremes (e.g., violence, language, topics). Concludes that this phenomenon parallels the larger women's movement in society and that rock music is a dominant communicative aspect of popular culture. Focuses on Genya Raven, Chrissie Hynde, Marianne Faithfull, Robin Lane, and Patti Smith.

64.   Stockbridge, Sally. "Rock Video: Pleasure and Resistance." In *Television and Women's Culture: The Politics of the Popular*, edited by Mary Ellen Brown, 102-113. London: Sage, 1990.

Asserts that audiences extract meaning from rock music videos that may not be intended by the artists. Three major factors of performer-audience relationship are investigated: performance, direct address, and fantasy. Nine specific videos are studied.

BOOKS

65.   Dunne, Michael. *Metapop: Self-Referentiality in Contemporary American Popular Culture.* Jackson: University Press of Mississippi, 1992.

Investigates the phenomenon of self-referentiality in popular culture. Discusses television, motion pictures, comic strips, country music, music videos, and rock music. Surveys numerous rock songs to illustrate various mechanisms of self-referential treatments. Discusses how the performer can create a shared experience with the audience in order to make self-referential lyrics succeed. Notes that audiences are fully aware that mass media representations are not reality. Concludes that performers encourage audiences to recognize the mediated aspect of popular culture.

66.   Jones, Steve. *Rock Formation: Music, Technology, and Mass Communication.* Newbury Park, Calif.: Sage, 1992.

Examines the role of technology in shaping rock music. Claims that each technological advance in the production of music contributes to the evolution of music creation. Observes the emergence of a new type of music composer, the performer-programmer who understands the operating systems of such technology as the synthesizer. Provides a history of sound recording and its role in enhancing the "collective memory" of the culture. Discusses issues surrounding copyright and digital technology.

67.   Laing, Dave. *One Chord Wonders: Power and Meaning in Punk Rock.* Milton Keynes, England: Open University Press, 1985.
   Questions assumptions about punk rock music and its status as a major unique event in the history of rock music. Provides both a historical presentation of punk rock and an exploration of its meaning. Examines the ways in which punk music created meanings, what the meanings were, and how those meanings were used by consumers of punk rock. Uses semiology as a method of analyzing all of the signs (i.e., lyrics, music, performance) associated with popular music as a communication device. Concludes with a discussion of class, politics, and pleasure. Speculates that punk rock was a paradoxical movement with far reaching effects. Includes a chronology and a discography.

DISSERTATIONS

68.   Burns, Gary Curtis. "Utopia and Dystopia in Popular Song Lyrics: Rhetorical Visions in the United States, 1963-1972." Ph.D. Northwestern University, 1981. *Dissertation Abstracts International* 42: 1839A.
   Studies the top-twenty records from 1963 to 1972 to determine the existence of dramatic action patterns. Lyrics are classified with regard to "overall mood" (utopian or dystopian) and depiction of social relationships: family, community, society, individualism. Concludes that chronological patterns of rhetorical visions do occur in lyrics.

69.   Clark, Alan Randall. "A History of American Exploitation Films, 1954-1989." Ph.D. Bowling Green State University, 1990. *Dissertation Abstracts International* 51: 3932A.
   Describes the history and function of exploitation films and offers possible reasons for the popularity of this genre. Identifies the major elements in exploitation films as sex, violence, action, and rock music. Utilizes theories developed by Bela Balazs, Siegfried Kracauer, and Hugo Munsterberg.

70.   Denski, Stan Walter. "An Examination of Popular Music Preferences and Functions by the Contemporary Popular Music Audience." Ph.D. Ohio University, 1990. *Dissertation Abstracts International* 51: 2189A.
   Utilizes survey methodology to analyze and map the framework of popular music preferences and functions among the college student audience. Surveyed 448 undergraduate students to study gender differences with regard to music preference and music function as well as the possible connections between the two.

71.   Dinkelacker, James Walter. "Distinguishing Radio Audience Segments by Format Preferences in the Multichannel Programming Environment: A Multidimensional Approach." Ph.D. Michigan State University, 1982. *Dissertation Abstracts International* 43: 3743A.

Develops a methodology for distinguishing radio audience segments by format preferences. Uses multidimensional scaling (MMDS) paired comparison measurements. A MMDS instrument was created by scaling five radio station formats: rock, jazz, Top 40, easy listening, and country & western. Also included a radio listening diary and questions regarding self-concept, consumer behavior, and radio program preferences.

72.   Doll, Susan M. "Elvis Presley: All Shook Up. The Effect of Ideology and Subculture on Star Image." Ph.D. Northwestern University, 1989. *Dissertation Abstracts International* 51: 320A.

Studies the career of Elvis Presley as an American popular culture icon. Based on Richard Dyer's work on "star" analysis that focuses on how meaning is conveyed to an audience through image rather than through art. Elvis Presley's career is divided into three stages, each centered around a specific image which the author contends was intentionally constructed. Claims that an image was replaced only after it had outlived its usefulness.

73.   Henderson, Ian Clark. "Rock Goes Pop: Rock Music, Post-Modernism and Popular Culture." Ph.D. Southern Illinois University at Carbondale, 1991. *Dissertation Abstracts International* 53: 348A.

Responds to a detected end to the genre of rock music by placing it in a postmodern context. Focuses on three aspects of rock music: punk rock, rap music, and music videos. Punk rock is explained as a "carnival of ambiguity." Rap music is offered as the "humanization of technology, exemplified in the redefinition of authenticity." Music videos are presented as being "exemplary of the practice of postmodern communication."

74.   Jones, Steven George. "Rock Formation: Popular Music and the Technology of Sound Recording." Ph.D. University of Illinois at Urbana-Champaign, 1987. *Dissertation Abstracts International* 49: 7A.

Examines the changing relationships in the production of rock music due to technological advances. Looks at the effects of technology on the composition and production of music. Interviews professional and amateur musicians, producers, and engineers. Discusses issues such as the effects of the musical equipment industry's product decisions, the changing relationships among the individuals involved in music production, and the possible subtle, but profound, effects of technology on music composition itself. Also addresses copyright and access to music.

75. Kowieski, Richard E. "A Descriptive Analysis of the Vernacular Lexicon of Black and White Students at Ohio University in Relation to Rock Music." Ph.D. Ohio University, 1978. *Dissertation Abstracts International* 39: 5208A.

Explores similar and different uses of slang terms among black and white students with regard to rock music. Subjects were 200 college students (110 blacks, 100 whites). Concludes that slang associated with rock music is the result of acculturation. However, results also show "an intimate reciprocity between language, culture, experience and rock music, that resist acculturation." Discusses rock music as creating "culture-bound" experiences articulated through the use of slang.

76. Nowell, William Robert, III. "The Evolution of Rock Journalism at the *New York Times* and the *Los Angeles Times*, 1956-1978: A Frame Analysis." Ph.D. Indiana University, 1987. *Dissertation Abstracts International* 48: 1045A.

Presents the evolution of journalistic attention to rock music from 1956 to 1978 provided by two major daily newspapers, the *New York Times*, and the *Los Angeles Times*. Analyzes the coverage of three rock music phenomena: Elvis Presley, the Rolling Stones, and the Sex Pistols. Argues that each of these acts "in successive decades challenged the dominant cultural values that mass media generally supports." While acknowledging that the news frames have evolved from generally negative to generally positive, asserts that appropriate critical standards have not been developed for journalistic coverage of rock music. Offers the works of Theodor Adorno, Herbert Marcuse, and Raymond Williams as sources for appropriate critical standards.

77. Outwin, Christopher Maxwell. "The Effect of Anti-Drunk-Driving Television Public Service Announcement's Style, Theme, and Level of Threat on an Eighteen to Twenty-Four Year Old Audience's Cognitive, Motivational, and Attitudinal Response." Ed.D. Boston University, 1987. *Dissertation Abstracts International* 48: 1047A.

Studies the effectiveness of various production styles and themes utilized in television anti-drunk-driving public service announcements. Subjects were 143 community college students between the ages of eighteen and twenty-four. Results indicate that the weakest theme was the association to rock music and rock music performers, while the strongest was threat of death.

78. Reading, Joseph Donald. "Tears of Rage: A History, Theory, and Criticism of Rock Song and Social Conflict Rhetoric, 1965-1970." Ph.D. University of Oregon, 1980. *Dissertation Abstracts International* 41: 4542A.

Investigates the use of rock songs as rhetorical devices in relation to social criticism and political protest. Applies theories of rhetoric to selected songs from the late 1960s. Notes that songs advocating views on particular social issues appeared in the context of judicial, legislative, and ceremonial rhetoric. Argues that songs are a means for a performer to create unity around a given issue. Discovers that one of the most important rhetorical images in rock music is that of the outlaw as hero, victim, and martyr. Claims that these images of outlaws create an "essential impulse to revolution."

79. Schafer, Carol A. "The Mediated Self: Tragedy and Heroism in Late Twentieth Century United States." Ph.D. University of Texas at Dallas, 1993. *Dissertation Abstracts International* 54: 737A.

Focuses on the life of John Lennon as a study on the self-creation of the hero figure. Combines the theories of tragedy as a dramatic genre and ambivalence as a psychological concept. Contends that Lennon's construction of "the legend of his life" is an example of contemporary tragedy. Examines the self-mediated image of Lennon's life through the use of music, film, interviews, and event manipulation that was both text and performance.

80. Scheibel, Dean Frederick. "Organizational Communication Cultures and the Social Worlds of Local Rock Music." Ph.D. Arizona State University, 1991. *Dissertation Abstracts International* 52: 1132A.

Proposes the empirical application of theoretical social world concepts to a study of discourse. Studies the construction of a local rock music "world" through communicative processes. Specifies nine perspectives: music educators, manufacturers, presenters, consumers, conditioners, musicians, diffusers, dealers, and sound mixers. Analyzes the musicians' perspectives as organizational communication. Describes certain communicative processes (e.g., auditions, practices, recording sessions) as "patterns of meaning and expectations."

81. Semmel, Keith David. "The Pepperland Perspective: A Study in the Rhetorical Vision of the Beatles 1962-1970." Ph.D. Bowling Green State University, 1980. *Dissertation Abstracts International* 41: 2831A.

Investigates rock music as a rhetorical device of persuasion. Utilizes the methodological construct of Ernest Bormann regarding the identification of fantasy themes, fantasy types and resulting rhetorical vision. Specifically studies the lyrics of songs by the Beatles. Identifies seven themes: invitation to love, reaffirmation of love, love gone bad, entrapment, celebration of the rock culture, social commentary, and fantasy characterization/narrative. These themes are encompassed by three fantasy types: romantic, social, and expressionistic. Describes the resulting rhetorical vision as the "Pepperland Perspective" which is "a uniquely optimistic vision in a reality of pessimism."

82. Storm, Gary Bruce. "An Analysis of Progressive FM Radio." Ph.D. State University of New York at Buffalo, 1982. *Dissertation Abstracts International* 43: 2823A.

Discusses the relationship between progressive FM radio and popular music. Explores the "the aesthetics of music and the exigencies of the music industry."

Employs theories of culture by William S. Burroughs, Norman Mailer, and others. Notes the failure of mass media to reach their potential as educational tools.

83. Stover, Sherri Elliott. "Adolescent Perceptions of Music Television: What is the Message?" Psy.D. Antioch University, 1991. *Dissertation Abstracts International* 52: 1740B.

Examines the effects of music videos on adolescent attitudes and behaviors by interviewing adolescents. Results indicate that adolescents consciously process information about aggression, health, and social issues contained in music videos. Adolescent perceptions of music videos are dependent upon personal values and beliefs. Adolescents are not fully aware of the effects of repeated exposure to music video messages in altering personal attitudes and beliefs.

84. Tumas-Serna, Jane Anne. "An Investigation of the Primitive in Rock and Roll Performance: Steps Toward a Cultural Approach to the Analysis of Mass Media Texts." Ph.D. Ohio University, 1987. *Dissertation Abstracts International* 49: 163A.

Studies rock music in order to "provide a theoretical framework for deciphering" the performance text. Uses semiotics to perform a text analysis of performance. Contends that the use of the body in rock music performance results in the label of primitive. Concludes that the primitive performance text is central to rock music's "cultural expression" and does not mean that it is culturally inferior.

Education

ARTICLES

85.   Bell, Michael L., and Marilyn Droke. "The Blues Jazz Bluegrass Country & Western Soul Rock Experience." *Music Educators Journal* 67, no. 8 (1981): 52-53.

Presents the results of a survey of 167 southwest Missouri music educators. Assesses the variables of years of teaching experience, teaching level (i.e., elementary, junior high, high school), area of primary assignment (i.e., vocal, instrumental), type of school (i.e., urban, rural), and musical styles taught. Results indicate a heterogeneous sample of teachers. Rock music follows folk and jazz music with regard to the frequency of inclusion in the curriculum. Teachers indicated that they expect rock music to be the most popular musical genre among students.

86.   Binkley, Robert. "The New Rock and Music Education." *Music Educators Journal* 55, no. 9 (1969): 31-33.

Emphasizes the need for music educators to embrace the philosophy of Marshall McLuhan, who states that the individual is affected through the content and form of communication. Contends that teachers cannot force students to be objective about rock music as has been done with the teaching of traditional music. Suggests that rock music has value to be explored, even if that value is different from "good" music. States that teacher authority in the classroom is only meaningful to the extent that a student "incorporates it into his perceptual world."

87.   Blanchard, B. Everard. "The Effect of Music on Pulse-Rate, Blood Pressure and Final Exam Scores of University Students." *Journal of Sports Medicine and Physical Fitness* 19 (1979): 305-308.

Considers the effect of auditory background music on the pulse-rate, blood pressure, and academic achievement of college students. Subjects were 254 college students (124 males, 130 females) between the ages of twenty and thirty-one, tested while taking final exams. Subjects were divided into three groups: 1) no music, 2) rock music, and 3) classical music. Notes that the groups exposed to background music "displayed excellent recuperative activity of the heart." Concludes that the results of the study indicate that background music does act as factor in critical thinking because the groups that listened to background music earned higher grades on the exams. Music also minimizes the "nervous states of students while taking an examination." Suggests that colleges and universities may be causing hypertension.

88.   Butchart, Ronald E., and B. Lee Cooper. "Perceptions of Education in the Lyrics of American Popular Music, 1950-1980." *American Music* 5, no. 3 (1987): 271-281.
   Promotes the idea of examining rock music lyrics as artifacts representative of the youth culture. Studies the lyrics of 200 songs that deal with the topic of education in order to determine opinions of the educational system. Discovers descriptions of an educational system that is "dehumanizing, irrelevant, alienating, laughable, isolating, and totally unworthy." These images remain consistent across time. Concludes that the system is unlikely to change, despite the fact that the school is a social place that is central to adolescent self-perceptions.

89.   Caywood, Carolyn. "Presumed Influence." *School Library Journal* 39, no. 6 (1993): 44.
   Discusses the widespread belief that selected music is psychologically dangerous for adolescents. Calls for librarians to be responsible in building a library's music collection by being aware of parents' concerns. Encourages discussion between parents and children regarding the meaning of rock music lyrics and the expression of values. Concludes that adults must respect the right of adolescents to cultivate their own tastes.

90.   Chilcoat, George W. "The Images of Vietnam: A Popular Music Approach." *Social Education* 49, no. 7 (1985): 601-603.
   Observes that, until the Vietnam conflict, the wars involving the United States of America have produced popular songs that served to promote national unity. However, the Vietnam War produced popular music that "polarized public opinion for nearly a decade." Organizes songs related to the Vietnam War into broad themes, including attitudes toward war, battle/soldiers, the draft, peace, establishment/government, and related domestic events. Categorizes specific songs under each theme as either anti-war (folk/rock) or pro-war (country-western). Includes a list of recommended classroom activities and a bibliography.

91.   Cooper, B. Lee. "Exploring the Future Through Contemporary Music." *Media & Methods* 12 (1976): 32-35,61.

Recommends the use of rock music lyrics to teach students about the future and one's ability to direct personal destiny. Provides lesson plans for the following topics: generation gaps, technological change, political participation, freedom, civil liberties, aging and death, and utopias.

92.   Cooper, B. Lee. "Mick Jagger as Herodotus and Billy Joel as Thucydides?: A Rock Music Perspective 1950-1985." *Social Education* 49, no. 7 (1985): 596-600.

Presents rock music lyrics as oral history. Contends that rock music represents a multitude of idea and value fragments in an "ever-changing audio collage." Compares rock music lyrics to "remnants in an Indian burial mound" awaiting reconstruction by an archeologist. Notes some limitations to using lyrics for a complete picture of social values. These include the brevity of any one composition, the commercial purpose of a composition which limits extreme deviant expressions, and the relatively short shelf-life. Also, the intent and actual effect of rock music can be different. Provides examples of song titles and associated recording artists that can be used as teaching tools for the following themes: authority, military, public education, railroads, politics, racism, conformity, worker alienation, and urban unrest.

93.   Cooper, B. Lee. "Music and the Metropolis: Lyrical Images of Life in American Cities, 1950-1980." *Teaching History* 6 (1981): 72-84.

Argues that rock music lyrics "assemble attitudes, ideas, events, and values" that can assist history students in defining the urban experience. Notes that lyrics utilize elements of "biography, fantasy, memory, illusion, fact, and folklore" to communicate ideas. Presents several lesson plans that can be used to teach about urbanization in relation to such topics as social decline, the African American experience, and the male experience.

94.   Cooper, B. Lee. "Popular Records as Oral Evidence: Creating an Audio Time Line to Examine American History, 1955-1987." *Social Education* 53, no. 1 (1989): 34-40.

Presents a chronology of social and political events from 1955 through 1987 organized into a chart that includes historical events, historical figures, and relevant song titles and their performing artists. Argues that social science teachers want and need new methods of engaging students in the study of social history. Claims that songs from the rock music era serve as an oral history of "social trends, economic issues, and regional fads." Notes that the social topics covered in rock songs are diverse and include war, civil rights, the women's movement, and urban strife.

95. Cooper, B. Lee. "Social Concerns, Political Protest, and Popular Music." *The Social Studies* 79, no. 2 (1988): 53-60.

Notes the contributions of David Pichaske in promoting the use of rock music lyrics in the classroom as an instructional device. States that rock lyrics "constitute an oral battlefield" of social and political issues. Presents a "bibliographic" or discographic essay on images in rock music related to political protest and social critique. Covers the period from 1960 through 1985. Includes a table of dates, historical events, and relevant recordings.

96. Cooper, B. Lee. "Sounds of the City: Popular Music Perspectives on Urban Life." *International Journal of Instructional Media* 8, no. 3 (1980/81): 241-254.

Suggests five topics and more than 100 recordings that teachers can use to have students investigate various aspects of the urban experience.

97. Cooper, B. Lee, and Laura E. Cooper. "Commercial Recordings and Cultural Interchanges: Studying Great Britain and the United States, 1943-1967." *International Journal of Instructional Media* 19, no. 2 (1992): 183-189.

Describes American influences on British culture through the exportation of American rock music to Great Britain during the 1954-1963 period. Notes that the 1964 British invasion of the Beatles and the Rolling Stones suddenly reversed this exchange, resulting finally in an equilibrium after 1967. Offers a discography and a bibliography designed to assist history teachers in illustrating this Anglo-American cultural exchange.

98. Cooper, Laura E., and B. Lee Cooper. "Exploring Cultural Imperialism: Bibliographic Resources for Teaching about American Domination, British Adaptation, and the Rock Music Interchange, 1950-1967." *International Journal of Instructional Media* 17, no. 2 (1990): 167-177.

Serves as a bibliography documenting American dominance over the British rock music culture and the turning of the tide with the British invasion beginning in 1964. Organizes the literature into the following categories: America's embracing of rhythm and blues 1950-1959, British reception of American cultural imperialism 1950-1963, cultural imperialism at its zenith 1960-1964, British assimilation and adaptation 1962-1967, American reaction 1964-1967, the Beatles' reversal of cultural imperialism 1967, and discographies on American and British recordings 1950-1967. Claims that the Beatles' album *Sgt. Pepper's Lonely Hearts Club Band* essentially ended American cultural imperialism.

99. Cutietta, Robert A. "Popular Music: An Ongoing Challenge." *Music Educators Journal* 77, no. 8 (1991): 26-29.

Notes that twenty years after the Tanglewood Symposium (1967), rock music has been included widely in music education curriculum for all the wrong reasons. Rock music is a "bait-and-switch technique" used to capture the attention of students only to the ends of teaching about classical music. Bemoans the fact that rock music has been adapted to marching bands and twenty soprano choirs singing in unison. Challenges music educators to teach and perform rock music as it is written and intended.

100. Cutietta, Robert A. "Using Rock Videos to Your Advantage." *Music Educators Journal* 71, no. 6 (1985): 47-49.

Describes two types of music videos, visual music (e.g., *Leave It* by Yes) and visual lyrics (e.g., *Hello* by Lionel Ritchie). Argues that music videos are effective classroom tools and can be used to generate discussion regarding "modulations, harmonic accents, and harmonic tension." Mentions various observations about rock music structure made by students as a result of analyzing music videos. Explains the author's experience of working with students to make a music video. Claims the process resulted in necessary discussions about "form, tonality, accents, harmonic rhythm, and meter."

101. Dubin, Fraida. "Pop, Rock, and Folk Music: An Overlooked Resource." *Englisch* 10, no. 3: 109-113.

Advocates using rock, popular, and folk music to teach English as a second language. Unlike other mass media, music is not viewed as authoritarian and is widely embraced. Organizes the selection of materials into phonological, grammatical patterns, and semantics. Phonological elements include internal sound changes, rhythms, and regional and ethnic sounds. Grammatical patterns include repetition, substitution, and internal pattern rearrangements. Semantics include narratives, actions, concepts, and themes.

102. English, Helen W. "Rock Poetry, Relevance, and Revelation." *English Journal* 59, no. 8 (1970): 1122-1127.

Explains the author's experience at offering a contemporary poetry class that focused on rock music lyrics. Notes that some students are not able to approach poetry analytically, even though they have emotional responses to poetry. Itemizes goals of the course as teaching students to: listen, appreciate poetry, explore feelings, and express feelings. Discusses the evolution of student responses to the course as it progressed.

103. Fowler, Charles B. "The Case Against Rock: A Reply." *Music Educators Journal* 57, no. 1 (1970): 38-42.

Disputes three arguments commonly used to exclude rock music from public school music education. The first argument is that rock music is aesthetically inferior. Acknowledges that one should be able to recognize a good performance from another and that there will be individual preferences. However, to claim that rock music is inferior is Euro-centric and ignores rock music's own sophistications of "aesthetics, sociology, theory, technique, and terminology." States that music educators should not position themselves as selectors of proper tastes. Teachers should be nurturers and not exemplars. The second argument is that rock music is physically and morally damaging. Notes that simply because rock music is often played at high volumes does not mean that the music is bad. Claims that this particular problem dates back generations before rock music. As for morality, states that rock music is a manifestation of our culture and its elimination would not eliminate immorality or social evils. The third argument is that rock music is easily acquired in the vernacular and, therefore, time in school should be devoted to other forms of musical expression. Contends that the "teaching of English does not proceed from the motivation of Shakespeare" and teachers must provide an understanding of the role of a subject matter in contemporary society. Concludes that music educators are interpreters of the present, not conservers of the past.

104.   Fox, Sidney. "From Rock to Bach: Youth Music on Our Terms." *Music Educators Journal* 56, no. 9 (1970): 52-55.

Suggests a means of engaging students in the study of music by introducing the musical elements from selections of rock music and then tracing those elements backwards through time. Outlines a methodology for students to listen to melody, harmony, form, rhythm, timbre, and mood in rock music and then similar compositions from earlier genres of the twentieth century and then from classical compositions. Argues that lectures and facts are incidental information. Contends that teachers should focus on the aural elements "unencumbered by the verbal or visual blocks."

105.   Gass, Glenn. "Why Don't We Do It in the Classroom?" *South Atlantic Quarterly* 90, no. 4 (1991): 729-736.

Claims that rock music is a "vital musical form and cultural force" and this is why universities now teach it as history and culture. Argues in support of teaching about rock music's role in society as part of higher education because it embodies the "dreams, values, experience, and worldview" of each new generation. Points to heavy metal music and rap music as examples of rock's continuing ability to challenge the status quo. Also published in the book *Present Tense* edited by Anthony DeCurtis.

106.   Goldsen, Rose K., and Azriel Bibliowicz. "Plaza Sesamo: 'Neutral' Language or 'Cultural Assault?'." *Journal of Communication* 26, no. 2 (1976): 124-125.

Remarks on the production of the Spanish language version of the television show *Sesame Street* designed for Latin America. Discusses the sociological and ideological questions raised when an attempt is made to produce the show "neutrally" with regard to cultural issues. Notes that the music utilized for production was rock music and not Latin American music. Questions whether the goal of neutrality actually results in a cultural assault on 22 million pre-school children. This is one of several articles appearing in this issue of the journal that deal with *Sesame Street*'s context in the global community.

107. Graebner, William. "Teaching 'The History of Rock 'n' Roll'." *Teaching History* 9, no. 1 (1984): 2-20.

Describes in detail the author's teaching of a college course on the history of rock music. Attempts to give students an appreciation of the links between social and cultural history and rock music. Organizes the course content into the following segments: The Postwar Era 1947-1957, From Sputnik to the Kennedy Assassination 1957-1963, The Age of Expectations the 1960s, and Disillusion in the 1970s. Concludes that "rock music is a remarkable mirror of American history and culture."

108. Graham, David B. "Using Audiotapes for Instruction and Assessment: La Musique C'est Quelque Chose de Magique." *Language Association Bulletin* 40, no. 3 (1989): 1,3-6,27.

Contends that "awareness and communication of feelings and emotion is what the business of second language teaching is about." Suggests incorporating rock music into the teaching of foreign languages in order to establish a direct connection with students and maintain their attention. Rock music recorded in foreign languages can help to present cultural issues and highlight colloquial pronunciations.

109. Hale, Tony. "Teaching Poetry Through Rock Music." *English in Education* 5, no. 1 (1971): 15-22.

Professes that rock lyrics can be used as a bridge to more conventional poetry. Argues that students should realize that poetry is alive. Contends that it is the responsibility of the teacher to encourage taste and selectivity among students. Uses numerous examples of rock lyrics to explore various themes.

110. Harvey, John. "A Saucerful of Secrets: Contemporary Music as a Basis for Original Writing." *English in Education* 6, no. 1 (1972): 49-55.

Suggests that rock music can be used for more than teaching about poetry. It can be used to develop creative writing skills. Offers examples of poetry written by students after being exposed to selected rock music. Prescribes a methodology for classroom implementation.

111. Herberger, Rainer. "The Degree of Attractiveness to 15-Year-Old High School Students in the German Democratic Republic (GDR) of Different Styles, Genres, and Trends of Contemporary Music: Results of a Factor Analysis." *Bulletin of the Council for Research in Music Education*, no. 91 (1987): 70-76.

Seeks to solve problems encountered when introducing new music to students. Attempts to identify which styles, genres, and trends are attractive to the age group being studied. Subjects were seventy-three males and sixty-nine females, all fifteen years of age. Eighteen musical samples were played and subjects were asked to rate the selections. Selections ranged in style and included rock music. Results indicate that students' interest in studying new music is dependent upon the attractiveness of the music. However, other styles were not completely rejected, particularly if elements of sound effects, modern jazz, and symphonic music were present. Finally, males were found to "have a stronger affinity to rock music" and females demonstrated "greater interest in pop music."

112.   Heussenstamm, Frances K. "I Dig Rock n' Roll Music: A Counselor's Listening Guide." *School Counselor* 18, no. 3 (1971): 198-203.

Attempts to provide school counselors with a guide to the important adolescent political, social, and aesthetic issues explored in rock music compositions. Itemizes and provides lyrical examples of conformity, rebellion, ritual, retreat, innovation, materialism, conflict, self-identity, social roles, pressure, hypocrisy, divisiveness, and love as common rock music themes.

113.   Hoffman, Paul Dennis. "Using Rock Music to Teach History." *OAH Magazine of History* 1, no. 1 (1985): 10-11.

Suggests using rock music to teach history to high school students. Explains the author's nine years of experience using rock music in the classroom. Remarks that history is then seen as a "living, changing force."

114.   Kuzmich, John, Jr. "Popular Music in Your Program: Growing with the Times." *Music Educators Journal* 77, no. 8 (1991): 50-55.

Presents a case-study of a nontraditional method of introducing rock music performance into a high school music education curriculum.

115.   LaVoie, Joseph C., and Betty R. Collins. "Effect of Youth Culture Music on High School Students' Academic Performance." *Journal of Youth and Adolescence* 4, no. 1 (1975): 57-65.

Reports on an investigation into the effects of rock music on high school students with regard to reading comprehension and retention of factual content. Subjects were 356 high school students (207 males, 149 females) randomly assigned to one of three groups: no music, rock music, and classical music. Each subject was given one topic to study (literature, mathematics, physical science, or social science). Comprehension was measured immediately, the next day, and three days later. Results indicate that rock music interferes with comprehension and retention regardless of the topic being studied or the level of difficulty. Speculates that rock music interferes because it contains reward value for adolescents in that it consists of informational value and represents peer identification. Classical music does not have much reward value for adolescents.

116.   Lindsay, Brian. "The Blues\Rock Group Biography." *Humanities Journal* 8, no. 1 (1974): 17-18.

Comments that rock music shapes many aspects of one's lifestyle, including language, dance, fashion, and interior design. Proposes a *Blues\Rock Group Biography* project designed to function as a tool for moving students beyond typical appreciation to "solid shores of intellectual and aesthetic involvement." Proclaims that popular culture provides topics of natural curiosity for teaching students to be researchers. Specifically, the *Blues\Rock Group Biography* project has six major elements: 1) the student selects an established blues or rock music group, 2) the student develops a discography for the music group, 3) the student compiles a bibliography of books, articles, and record reviews of the group, 4) the student writes a biography of the music group based on the discography and the bibliography and includes one's own opinions about the group's overall contribution to music, 5) the final project should be between five and ten pages, and 6) the instructor should allow six to eight weeks for completion of the project. Warns that the popular press is often no more than a publicity outlet and that students will include fact and fiction indiscriminately in their projects.

117. Linton, David S. "Rock & the Media." *Media & Methods* 13, no. 2 (1976): 56-59.
Promotes the idea of using rock music lyrics in the classroom to examine the ways in which contemporary music comments on mass media and, consequently, itself.

118. Little, Jim. "Pop and Rock Music in the ESL Classroom." *TESL Talk* 14, no. 4 (1983): 40-44.
Promotes the idea of using rock music to teach English as a second language. Observes that regardless of the native language, English language rock music has a universal appeal that "cuts across cultural and linguistic boundaries." Suggests that rock music as a teaching device can provide variety, increase motivation, and be used as "an effective mnemonic." Reviews the literature to synthesize an appropriate approach to using rock music in the classroom. Notes that selections should be meaningful to students and slow enough for comprehension. Lyrics should be clearly enunciated, and colloquialisms, slang, and vulgarities should be avoided. Specifically, rock music can be used to introduce opposition (e.g., *Hello Goodbye* by the Beatles), conditional statements (e.g., *If Not for You* by Bob Dylan), past tense (e.g., *Rocky Raccoon* by the Beatles), and the imperative (e.g., *Love Me Tender* by Elvis Presley). Concludes that the use of rock music can make the course content more relevant and personal to students.

119. Love, Randolph D. "Design and Teach a Popular Music Course." *Music Educators Journal* 77, no. 8 (1991): 46-49.
Lists and discusses materials and techniques for starting a popular music education course. Includes a bibliography of suggested resources and recommended classroom projects.

120.   Luskin, Bernard J. "A Portable Course with Pop Culture." *New Directions for Community Colleges* 3, no. 4 (1975): 9-16.

Outlines the development of an interdisciplinary humanities course created for community colleges. Employs popular culture artifacts, including rock music, designed to capture the interests of students. The goal is to engage students through the use of familiar icons and then lead them to an appreciation and understanding of the arts through a historical perspective. Assumes that after the experience of this course, one will "cease to define himself and his reality solely in terms of a job or material goals."

121.   MacCluskey, Thomas. "Peaceful Coexistence Between Pop and the Classics." *Music Educators Journal* 65, no. 8 (1979): 54-57.

Reviews ten years of incorporating rock music into the music education classroom. Claims that those instructors who have not embraced the use of rock music in the curriculum are not convinced of popular music's educational value, are unfamiliar with the various styles of rock music, or are biased against rock music. Notes a lack of commitment in higher education to updating music teacher educational programs to insure that rock music is included in the core curriculum.

122.   Miller, D. Merrily. "Effects of Music-Listening Contingencies on Arithmetic Performance and Music Preference of EMR Children." *American Journal of Mental Deficiency* 81, no. 4 (1977): 371-378.

Investigates whether contingent reinforcement with a preferred type of music listening would "differentially increase arithmetic performance of educable mentally retarded (EMR) children and whether this contingent reinforcement would influence preference for that reinforcer." Analysis shows that significant differences exist between contingent reinforcement and no-reinforcement conditions. Significant differences also exist between the control and experiment groups during the contingent reinforcement phases. Contingencies do not influence music preference.

123.   Morse, David E. "Avant-Rock in the Classroom." *English Journal* 58, no. 2 (1969): 196-200,297.

Coins the late 1960s evolution of poetic lyrics in rock music as "avant-rock." Claims that avant-rock "clearly challenges the traditional notions of what is literature." Recommends a method for introducing avant-rock lyrics into an English literature course.

124.   Mowsesian, Richard, and Margaret R. Heyer. "The Effect of Music as a Distraction on Test-Taking Performance." *Measurement and Evaluation in Guidance* 6, no. 2 (1973): 104-110.

Tests whether music would act as a distracting element with regard to academic performance of high school students. Subjects were 167 tenth grade students, each assigned to one of five groups: rock music, folk music, classical-instrumental, classical-vocal, and a control group. Subjects were administered three standardized tests. Results show that the presence of music did not affect academic performance, regardless of musical genre. Subjects had indicated a preference for rock music, but the mean scores for the rock music group were not significantly different from the other groups. Speculates that because background noise is common, it may be incorrect to assume that background music will adversely affect academic performance.

125. Mueller, Jean W. "Rock 'n' Roll Heroes: Letter to President Eisenhower." *Social Education* 49, no. 5 (1985): 406-408.

Reproduces a March 1958 handwritten letter to President Eisenhower asking that Elvis Presley not be given a standard military haircut. Suggests how the letter can be used as a teaching device to engage students in the study of history. Offers ideas on studying American culture of the 1950s, debating current military registration laws, and expressing opinions and concerns to elected officials. Places Elvis Presley and the letter in the context of the time period.

126. Mullikin, Colleen N., and William A. Henk. "Using Music as a Background for Reading: An Exploratory Study." *Journal of Reading* 28, no. 4 (1985): 353-358.

Questions the effects of auditory background on reading comprehension. Tested forty-five students (nine each from grades four through eight) who had at least an average reading ability on the Metropolitan Achievement Test. Subjects were approximately fifty-percent male, fifty-percent female, and one-third black. Subjects were exposed to three types of auditory background conditions: 1) no music, 2) classical music, and 3) rock music. Results indicate that classical music produced the highest level of reading comprehension while the rock music condition produced the lowest. Concludes that the nature of auditory background does affect reading comprehension and that no music is better than rock music. Acknowledges that there can be a great deal of variation within a musical genre and more research is required. Also warns of the possibility of a novelty effect in which the positive influence of classical music would decline if used frequently.

127. Murphey, Tim. "English Through Music: A Sheltered Subject Matter Language Course." *Bulletin CILA* 46 (1987): 95-100.

Describes a course offered in Switzerland designed to improve English language competence. The class was taught entirely in English, but the subject matter was popular, folk, rock, and classical music. Krashen's hypothesis that "students acquire language by receiving comprehensible input" (messages that they understand) served as the basis for the course. The messages can be about any topic as long as the comprehension level is appropriate. Notes that by focusing on the subject matter, and not the language, there was a relatively equal encounter with regard to the information "stock" of any one individual.

Concludes that language courses should be taught for a specific purpose and that "effective natural communication does not exist without relevant information being exchanged."

128.   Newsom, Sarah Duncan. "Rock 'n Roll 'n Reading." *Journal of Reading* 22, no. 8 (1979): 726-730.

   Recounts a method developed by the author to motivate adolescents in a remedial reading course. Incorporates rock music lyrics and recordings to overcome problems of attitude and motivation. Insists that this method is successful because the vocabulary of rock lyrics is simple and repetitive. Notes that the unit even encourages independent reading. Also reviews the literature on the appeal of rock music to students and on music as a learning aid.

129.   Pendergast, Joseph S. "Nachleben Is Where You Find It." *Classical Journal* 83 (1988): 323-325.

   Recommends the use of classical myth by rock groups as a device for engaging students in the study of the impact of the ancient world on modern culture. Mentions works by Led Zeppelin, Iron Maiden, and Steely Dan. Comments on Rush's song *Cygnus X-1* which utilizes characters from ancient mythology and has a total of 154 verses, thus emulating mythical stories.

130.   Poovey, Mary. "Cultural Criticism: Past and Present." *College English* 52, no. 6 (1990): 615-625.

   Argues, to illustrate cultural criticism, that teachers of college English should embrace rock music because not to do so will further make "institutionalized education seem even more irrelevant to our students' past experiences and extra-curricular lives." Claims that cultural criticism changes the nature of the questions we ask as well as the answers that are considered to be adequate and relevant.

131.   Ramsey, Joseph, and C. Lamar Thompson. "The Initiation Theme in Adolescent Literature." *Clearing House* 52, no. 5 (1979): 210-213.

   Calls for the use of multiple unconventional literary genres to present the theme of initiation when teaching literature to adolescents. Defines adolescent initiation as having the following characteristics: loss of youth, awareness of inner change, sexual confusion, isolation, conflict, and escapism. Uses the example of rock music as a possible alternative instrument for engaging adolescents in the learning process. Argues that rock music often speaks to alienation and rejection of adult values. Specifically highlights the rock operas *Jesus Christ Superstar* and *Tommy* as examples of "the initiation pattern." Cautions that attention must be given to "possible sub-themes which might prove to be dangerous" (e.g., sexually explicitness, violence).

132. Robinson, Deanna Campbell. "Rock Around the World: Music and Youth Culture." *Momentum* 16 (1985): 14-18.

Stresses the emerging international youth culture in which youth identify more with a global culture than with their own culture. Attributes the global culture to the international distribution of rock music. Discusses the contrasts between locally produced cultural music and international rock music in terms of the economics of multinational record companies and various governmental policies regarding radio programming. Suggests that generation gaps between youth and the establishment may be a result of "extensive use and identification with generational-exclusive cultural products during the period of youth" which vary from country to country.

133. Segreto, Anna. "Teachers, Leave Those Kids Alone." *Journal of Teaching Writing* 8, no. 1 (1989): 31-39.

Discusses the introduction of the music video concept into the realm of teaching poetry. The author read poetry to a class while the students "closed their eyes and pretended to see a television screen." Notes that the students did not just visualize the poem, but they also formed interpretations immediately just as the author had noticed her daughters doing while watching MTV. The students saw images and reflected upon those images, thus creating meaning. Students were also shown the Pink Floyd film *The Wall*, which was used to generate creative writing exercises.

134. Shrader-Frechette, K. "Introducing Philosophy Through Folk and Rock." *Teaching Philosophy* 1, no. 3 (1976): 243-251.

Suggests the use of folk and rock music lyrics to motivate beginning philosophy students. Describes the author's experience in creating an assignment in which students had to write a paper based on the philosophies expressed in folk and rock music lyrics. Required that the papers discuss the social, political, ethical, or religious philosophy expressed in the lyrics. Requested that three concepts be included: the composer's philosophy, examples of lyrics, and an evaluation. Argues that contemporary music is not always philosophical. Folk music and rock music help to frame a culture of social rebellion. Considers that lyrics are often not "epistemologically critical and precise." Concludes that folk and rock music can serve as a starting point, but not the norm, for teaching philosophy. Once students have an interest in clarifying certain positions, then classical philosophical texts can be introduced.

135. Smith, Ben A., and Charles W. Davidson. "Music and Achievement." *Journal of Social Studies Research* 15, no. 1 (1991): 1-7.

Assesses the effects on student learning of four different conditions of auditory background during independent study. Subjects were thirty-seven seventh grade students (fourteen females, twenty-three males; twenty-two blacks, fifteen whites). Subjects were randomly assigned to four groups. The first group was exposed to rock music. The second group listened to classical music. The third group heard easy listening music. The fourth group studied without background music. Initial results show that there were no significance differences among the four groups with regard to academic performance. Further manipulation of the data indicates that classical music may have a more positive effect than no music.

136.   Smith, Stuart. "Rock-Swim in It or Sink." *Music Educators Journal* 56, no. 5 (1970): 86-87,141-142.

Identifies a "crisis of relevance" in music education. Blames the crisis on parents and teachers refusing to abandon a Euro-centric "aristocratic orientation" towards music. Notes that rock music is based on an anti-hero attitude that rejects pretension and promotes juxtapositions and discontinuity. Discusses the role of mass media.

137.   Thompson, Dick. "Plugging into Pop at the Junior High Level." *Music Educators Journal* 66, no. 4 (1979): 54-59.

Suggests a detailed junior high school music curriculum designed to engage students. Includes an outline for teaching rock music history that incorporates other musical genres by discussing their influences on rock music. Describes the components of a performance lab, an independent listening lab, an electronic lab, and a multimedia lab.

CHAPTERS

138.   Farmer, Paul. "Examing Pop." In *Pop, Rock and Ethnic Music in School*, edited by Graham Vulliamy and Ed Lee, 56-70. Cambridge: Cambridge University Press, 1982.

Focuses on music education in Great Britain. Suggests a way in which popular music can be incorporated as a CSE level course.

139.   Grossberg, Lawrence. "Teaching the Popular." In *Theory in the Classroom*, edited by Cary Nelson, 177-200. Urbana: University of Illinois Press, 1986.

Describes the author's attempts to teach rock music as cultural history and his resulting theories. Uses rock music to "illustrate certain pedagogical and interpretive strategies." Discusses the conflicts in credibility between being a scholar and a fan. Details the crisis of multiple interpretations of musical events and the problems associated with the text being not internally determined, but rather temporal and individualized. Wrestles with how popular culture can best be defined and taught. Offers a three-stage strategy: 1) describe the structures of response, 2) deconstruct the fan's phenomenological response, and 3) create the contexts "within which the relations between fans and music acquire affective and political functions."

EDUCATION

BOOKS

140. Cooper, B. Lee. *Images of American Society in Popular Music: A Guide to Reflective Teaching.* Chicago: Nelson-Hall, 1982.

Presents discussions and resources that will allow one to use popular music when teaching about contemporary American society. Focuses on a reflective methodology that is more concerned with the meaning of music to the individual audience member as opposed to the intended meaning of the composer or performer. Organizes the work into three major sections: 1) Popular Music in the Classroom, 2) Popular Music as a Mirror of American Society, and 3) Popular Music and the Librarian. Includes an annotated bibliography of discographies, a recommended popular music collection for a library, and reviews of selected recordings that can be used as instructional resources.

141. Cooper, B. Lee. *Popular Music Perspectives: Ideas, Themes, and Patterns in Contemporary Lyrics.* Bowling Green, Ohio: Bowling Green State University Popular Press, 1991.

Promotes the idea that teachers should consider the possibilities of using lyrics to teach about contemporary society. Contends that popular recordings are oral history. Claims that lyrics contain "sociopolitical imagery" that explain contemporary society. Like an archeologist, one can construct a social reality from the lyrical "fragments" representing a "multiplicity of ideas and values." Focuses on specific ideas, themes, and patterns in order to illustrate social change, human interaction, technology, and intellectual development. Ideas conveyed through lyrics are organized into categories of education (ridicule and condemnation), railroads (technological and social change), and rebels and outsiders (frustration and isolation). Themes surveyed include: automobiles (social mobility), Christmas (social institutions), death (lifecycles), food and drink (prosperity), and telephones (social being). Contains numerous discographies and a selected, but extensive, bibliography.

142. Rubin, Nathan. *Rock and Roll: Art and Anti-Art.* Dubuque, Iowa: Kendall/Hunt, 1993.

Offers a chronological survey of major rock music styles and musicians. Designed to assist in the teaching of music appreciation. Defines anti-art as being like Dadaism in that the focus is on "chance means." Focuses on the differences between African and European musical influences. Traces the origins of rock music in African music, country music, blues, and rhythm and blues. Chapters discuss early rock musicians, the British invasion, folk rock, psychedelic rock, art rock, guitarists, heavy metal music, avant-garde music, glitter rock, punk music, reggae, new wave, disco, and grunge. Appendices include suggested classroom activities, a discography, bibliography, chronology, glossary, and index.

DISSERTATIONS

143. Crandall, Dorothy Jean. "The Relationship Between Teenage Preference for Rock Music and Their Attitude Toward Education, Church, and Family." Ed.D. Brigham Young University, 1984. *Dissertation Abstracts International* 45: 1032A.

Seeks to establish a relationship between "the amount of time teenage students listen to rock music and their grade level, educational achievement, level of education desired, their relationship with their parents and their attitude toward traditional Judeo-Christian ethical standards." Employed survey methodology to sample 182 high school students from Morristown, New Jersey, and Ventura, California. Determines that there are no significant relationships between any of the variables. Concludes that rock music is a universal phenomenon among adolescents and therefore does not serve as an indicator of religious or social alienation.

144. Criner, Clyde, III. "Black Music: Three Instructional Modules and Resource Materials for Urban Education." Ed.D. University of Massachusetts, 1981. *Dissertation Abstracts International* 42: 1042A.

Introduces three instructional modules for music education aimed at assisting curriculum development for urban schools. Contends that music education must include the unique musical experiences contributed by African Americans. Presents a discography of more than 1,000 records with brief historical sketches and descriptions used to construct three instructional modules: rhythm, melody, and harmony. Asserts that: 1) a need exists for African American music resource materials, 2) the availability of such resources will reinforce self-motivation, 3) education about African American music will motivate study and appreciation of all music, and 4) successful music education must be sensitive to student needs.

145. Degregoris, Christina Nicole. "Reading Comprehension and the Interaction of Individual Sound Preferences and Varied Auditory Distractions." Ph.D. Hofstra University, 1986. *Dissertation Abstracts International* 47: 3380A.

Argues that previous research on auditory distraction has led to contrasting conclusions. Examines "the interaction of individuals' sound preferences and their performance on a reading comprehension task with varied auditory distractions present." Uses five acoustical situations to test fifty-eight adolescents with definite sound level preferences as determined through a learning style inventory. The five environments were: 1) pre-taped contemporary music at 95 dB, 2) pre-taped schoolroom noise consisting predominately of talking at 75 dB, 3) quiet at 60-62.25 dB, 4) pre-taped contemporary music at 75 dB, and 5) pre-taped schoolroom noise consisting predominately of talking at 95 dB. Reveals acoustical setting as "the sole variable responsible for significant differences" in reading comprehension scores.

EDUCATION

146. Franklin, James Leo. "The Effects of Rock Music on the Reading Comprehension of Eighth-Grade Students." Ph.D. University of Iowa, 1976. *Dissertation Abstracts International* 37: 7597A.

Tested fifty-four eighth grade students with regard to differences in reading comprehension under three conditions: high intensity rock music, low intensity rock music, and no music. Results indicate that rock music, at either high or low intensity, will not affect significantly the reading comprehension of persons in this age group who listen to music while reading or studying. Concludes that frequency of listening to rock music while reading makes no difference in reading comprehension. Notes that there were no differences among the groups of students in their opinions of whether rock music was helpful for studying or whether it affects concentration while studying.

147. Fromm, Mark Lawrence. "The Effects of Music Upon the Values of Compliant and Non-compliant Adolescents." Ph.D. University of Colorado at Boulder, 1981. *Dissertation Abstracts International* 42: 1488A.

Determines the effects of three different types of music conditions (rock music, classical, no music) on the self-reported values of compliant and non-compliant adolescents. Ninety compliant adolescents were randomly assigned to one of those music condition groups of thirty persons per group. The same was done with the ninety non-compliant adolescents. Instruments used included the Gordon Survey of Personal Values and the Gordon Survey of Interpersonal Values. Results indicate no significant differences among the compliant adolescents' groups. Among non-compliant adolescents and between compliant and non-compliant groups there are some significant differences, but none related to rock music.

148. Gerver, Robert. "The Effects of a Certain Type of Mathematics Simulation on the Attitude, Achievement, Attendance and Punctuality of Ninth-Grade Remedial Mathematics Students." Ph.D. New York University, 1990. *Dissertation Abstracts International* 51: 1539A.

Investigates the effects of an applied simulation theory for mathematics education on ninth-grade remedial mathematics students. Utilized a particular START (Simulations That Address Remedial Teaching) program, *Sound Foundations*, in which each student is assigned the role of a rock group manager in order to illustrate the dependency of the rock music industry on mathematics. The program was conducted in twelve New York City suburban school districts with a sample of twenty-five teachers, thirty-five classes, and 326 students.

149. Grandy, Larry Howard. "Collegiate Non-Music Major Courses in Jazz and Rock: A Curriculum Development." D.M.A. Arizona State University, 1988. *Dissertation Abstracts International* 49: 1087A.

Surveys faculty members nationwide to determine higher education course offerings in jazz and rock music for non-music majors. Attempts to identify "teaching strategies, materials, objectives, resources, course content, and course construction" as well as professional backgrounds of the instructors in order to develop a syllabus for such a course.

150. Helfrich, David Charles. "The Effect of Rock Music, Controlled for Tempo and Volume, on Disabled Readers in Remedial Reading Classes." Ph.D. University of Georgia, 1973. *Dissertation Abstracts International* 34: 3024A.

Explores the effects of rock music played during remedial reading instruction for students in grades four through six. Claims that previous research in this area has not given attention to the precise control of music by volume and tempo. Forty-five remedial reading students were divided into three groups: no background music, fast instrumental rock music, and slow instrumental rock music. All three groups attended twenty-four 30-minute sessions over twelve weeks. Results show that improvements in reading were approximately the same for all three treatment groups.

151. Johnson, Jackie Lavaree. "A Use of Music to Reduce Discipline Problems in an Inner-City Junior High School." Ed.D. United States International University, 1985. *Dissertation Abstracts International* 46: 1861A.

Investigates the possible function of music as a behavior modification device. Three groups of junior high school students in Los Angeles, California were tested. The first group listened to rock music as background sound during classes. The second group listened to Baroque music as background sound and the third group did not listen to any music as background sound. Results indicate that "the presence of music but not the type of music affects the number of occurrences of inappropriate behaviors in the classroom." Student behavior was better in the classrooms where background music was introduced.

152. Markert, Louis Francis. "The Use of Poetry as a Tool in Career Counseling." Ph.D. University of California, Los Angeles, 1980. *Dissertation Abstracts International* 41: 109A.

Contends that literature, especially poetry, can stimulate high school students to think about vocational opportunities. Tests whether poetry, including rock music lyrics, can function as a values clarification technique and "evoke and modify feelings and attitudes about work" by exploring values. Argues that values are critical in thinking about self-identity and career choices. Subjects were 142 high school students randomly assigned to one of three groups: valuing process based on poetry, valuing process based on career guidance films, and a control group. Results indicate that the two experimental groups performed better that the control group in their ability to consider values as part of vocational planning. Concludes, based on students' reactions and as evidenced by the poetry they wrote, that there is reason to believe "a counseling technique that engages the poetic sense for the purpose of forwarding career growth" will stimulate students to think about vocations.

153. Patton, Nancy Dale Walker. "The Influence of Musical Preference on the Affective State, Heart Rate, and Perceived Exertion Ratings of Participants in Aerobic Dance/Exercise Classes." Ph.D. Texas Woman's University, 1991. *Dissertation Abstracts International* 52: 2858A.

Studies the influence of music preference and familiarity on mood, heart rate, and exertion of twenty female students in aerobic exercise classes. Results indicate that there are no significant relationships between preference or familiarity with rock and popular music and the above variables. Notes that instructor enthusiasm and support were considered to be more important to the subjects than music preference or familiarity.

154. Schultze, Helen Jacquin. "The Effects of Concurrent Musical Task on Lexical Decision Performance in Reading Disability." Ph.D. University of California, Los Angeles, 1986. *Dissertation Abstracts International* 47: 2100A.

Investigates disabled readers to determine whether music could reduce the interference of right hemisphere predominant processing of reading in left hemisphere verbal processing. Tested disabled and nondisabled readers under three music conditions: classical music, soft rock music, and no music. Results indicate that soft rock music does facilitate left hemisphere performance for both disabled and nondisabled readers.

155. Weisskoff, Rita Seiler. "The Relationship of Pop/Rock Music to Children's Task Performance and Continuing Motivation in Language Arts Instruction." Ph.D. University of Connecticut, 1981. *Dissertation Abstracts International* 42: 537A.

Compares two learning conditions, music and no music, in regard to task performance and continuing motivation. Subjects were 201 fourth and sixth grade students, who were given instructional language arts packages with music lyrics. Subjects were organized into two groups, those who heard a recording of the song from which the lyrics were taken and those who heard the instructor read the lyrics aloud. No relationship was found between music condition and task performance. A significant relationship was found between music condition and continuing motivation.

Ethnomusicology

ARTICLES

156. Anderson, Stephen. "No-Wave Nihilism." *Atlantic* 255, no. 6 (1985): 94-95.
Covers the emergence of "no wave" music in the late 1970s as a rejection of punk music and the marketable version of punk known as new wave music. Describes no wave music as the "dark unconscious of rock."

157. Aquila, Richard. "*Not Fade Away*: Buddy Holly and the Making of an American Legend." *Journal of Popular Culture* 15, no. 4 (1982): 75-80.
Defines Buddy Holly's cult status in terms of "the American character." Outlines several factors that contribute to the legendary status of Holly. First, he died at the peak of his career, leaving a legacy of recordings that would represent his total work. He died a complete success without ever having the opportunity to fail, thus being remembered as a totally successful artist. Second, the quality of his work was excellent, inspiring other musicians for years to follow. Third, his physical appearance was typical, not extraordinarily handsome, and he was from a middle-class background. Millions of aspiring youths could identify with him. Fourth, his death left a vacuum of original talent in the music industry that was not filled for some time. Fifth, he died a dramatic death. Concludes that the continuing popularity of Buddy Holly is a result of the American tendency to value excellence and creativity. It illustrates America's infatuation with the underdog hero figure.

158. Calder, Jeff. "Living by Night in the Land of Opportunity: Observations on Life in a Rock & Roll Band." *South Atlantic Quarterly* 90, no. 4 (1991): 907-937.
Relates the actual experiences of the author and his rock group, the Swimming Pool Q's. Remarks on the culture of the rock music industry from a musician's perspective, including touring and recording. Also published in the book *Present Tense* edited by Anthony DeCurtis.

159.　Cooper, B. Lee. "Johnny Rivers and Linda Ronstadt: Rock 'n' Roll Revivalists." *JEMF Quarterly* 18, no. 67-68 (1982): 166-177.

Summarizes the phenomenon of contemporary musicians recording songs that were hits previously for other singers. Offers several explanations based on the notion of the known commodity. An already familiar song may be used to launch the career of a new artist. Established artists may use familiar songs in order to highlight their own unique style of performance and interpretation. A third reason may be an artist's desire to pay tribute to the original performer. Finally, some songs are re-recorded by the original artist in order to offer yet another interpretation. Focuses on Johnny Rivers and Linda Ronstadt as examples of two artists who have been extremely successful at capitalizing on the concept of cover versions.

160.　DeCurtis, Anthony. "Introduction: The Sanctioned Power of Rock & Roll." *South Atlantic Quarterly* 90, no. 4 (1991): 635-647.

Surveys rock music in the 1980s and contrasts the period to the 1960s. Begins with the death of John Lennon and continues through punk music, Michael Jackson's *Thriller* album, MTV, the Parents' Music Resource Center (PMRC), Live Aid, world music, and rap music. Concludes that the 1960s can serve as more than nostalgia by providing alternative lessons to 1980s' individualism. Also published in the book *Present Tense* edited by Anthony DeCurtis.

161.　Emblidge, David. "Down Home With The Band: Country-Western Music and Rock." *Ethnomusicology* 20, no. 3 (1976): 541-552.

Studies the music of The Band and describes the group's unashamed merging of country music and rock music styles. Notes that their music has a "homemade quality that is noticeable in its simplicity." Focuses on, and reproduces the lyrics of, three songs: *Rag Mama Rag*, *The Night They Drove Old Dixie Down*, and *King Harvest*. *Rag Mama Rag* illustrates the group's instrumental versatility. *The Night They Drove Old Dixie Down* demonstrates the narrative form typical of their songs. *King Harvest* presents an example of the group's overall effectiveness at aesthetics. Explains the popularity of The Band's music in terms of escapism from urbanization and sentimentalism.

162.　Friedlander, Paul. "The Rock Window." *Tracking: Popular Music Studies* 1 (1988): 42-51.

Excerpts the chapter on research design from the author's dissertation. Describes the "Rock Window" as a model for organizing research into the "text" of rock music. Identifies four elements: music, lyrics, artist history, and social context.

163. Gonzalez, Juan-Pablo. "Hegemony and Counter-Hegemony of Music in Latin-America: The Chilean Pop." *Popular Music and Society* 15, no. 2 (1991): 63-78.

Emphasizes the relationship between society and music. Suggests that culture shapes music and that music creates "social and cultural reality." Focuses on the Chilean musical styles of art music, Nueva Cancion, and rock music. Contends that rock music started in the United States playing a counter-hegemony role, but was quickly transformed through commercialism and "integrated into the hegemonic system." Thus, when rock music was introduced into underdeveloped countries it was a culturally imperialistic hegemonic force. Contends that while rock music in Chile began by reinforcing United States ideology, it has since contributed to a cultural independence and regained its counter-hegemonic role. Uses the Chilean rock group Los Prisioneros to illustrate how rock music provides an ideological platform framed by class and generation. Also discusses the music group Fulano and their fusion of various Chilean musical styles.

164. Groce, Stephen B., and John A. Dowell. "A Comparison of Group Structures and Processes in Two Local Level Rock 'n' Roll Bands." *Popular Music and Society* 12, no. 2 (1988): 21-35.

Compares the group structures and processes of two local-level rock groups: a copy group, and an original music group. One author was a member of the copy group, The Copy Cats, and the other author was a member of the original music group, Curious Cargo. Compares and contrasts the two groups in terms of "four essential features of social groups." The first feature is that of goal orientation. Notes that The Copy Cats' primary goal was to earn money while Curious Cargo desired an outlet for creativity. The second feature is that of cohesiveness. The Copy Cats had a lower level of cohesiveness than Curious Cargo. The third feature is that of social norms. The Copy Cats norm was efficiency while Curious Cargo's norm was quality. The fourth feature is that of dimensions of differentiation. Here differentiation was greater where the goal was financial (i.e., with The Copy Cats). Concludes that these four features all relate to the level of success obtained by a rock group.

165. Groce, Stephen B., and Margaret Cooper. "Just Me and the Boys? Women in Local-Level Rock and Roll." *Gender & Society* 4, no. 2 (1990): 220-229.

Interviews fifteen local-level female musicians in two cities in order to explore audience reactions and female musicians' interactions with male musicians. Results show that the female musicians believe they are objectified by audiences and by male musicians as a result of being compelled to behave and dress in overtly sexual ways during performances. They do not see themselves as being taken seriously as musicians or as being part of the decision-making process in male dominated rock groups. In some cases, female musicians were paid less than male musicians.

166. Hamm, Charles. "Rock 'n' Roll in a Very Strange Society." *Popular Music* 5 (1985): 159-174.

Recounts in detail the different receptions that were provided rock music in South Africa during the 1950s. White audiences struggled with the issues of youthful rebellion and confrontation between adolescents and adults over the harmful effects of rock music. The black community met rock music with indifference. South African blacks perceived rock music as a product of white society because the early recordings released in South Africa were by white performers.

167. Harding, Deborah, and Emily Nett. "Women and Rock Music." *Atlantis* 10, no. 1 (1984): 60-76.

Analyzes the role and portrayal of women in rock music. Explores the history of female performers and sexism in the rock music industry. Studies the images of women in rock music through representation in lyrics and portrayal on album covers. Lyrical content reveals two general images of women, erotic and nurturing, each with a good side and an evil side. Discusses male domination in the industry and the limited access for females. Provides a feminist perspective and suggests that "the relationship between gender and sexuality, economics, and symbolic languages including music are little understood."

168. Holden, Stephen. "Pop Nostalgia: A Counterrevolution." *Atlantic* 255, no. 4 (1985): 121-122.

Bemoans the advent of nostalgia themes in contemporary rock music. Attributes the phenomenon to "the disintegration of the rock culture's sense of itself as a monolithic, progressive movement" and refers to punk music as rock's "first generational schism."

169. Keller, Susan Etta. "Jamming on the Jersey Shore: A Community of Rock Musicians in Asbury Park, Its Formation and Traditions." *New Jersey Folklife* 13 (1988): 39-48.

Proposes that the fascination with the Asbury Park, New Jersey music scene is based on a belief that "the community of Jersey Shore musicians shared unique and special experiences." Examines the important role of the Upstage nightclub that functioned as headquarters for musicians in the late 1960s. Notes how the sense of community was established and how the community dispersed. Comments on attempts to re-establish the community in the Stone Pony nightclub while under the focused attention of the mass media.

170. Kruse, Holly. "Subculture Identity in Alternative Music Culture." *Popular Music* 12, no. 1 (1993): 33-41.

Explores the formation of identity through subculture membership by studying the alternative music subculture in Champaign, Illinois. Acknowledges that subcultures can be defined by certain forms of "musical consumption," but contends that subculture formations are also a result of race, gender, and socioeconomic status. Argues that alternative music allows members to define boundaries and reject definitions imposed by mainstream culture.

171.   Kuwahara, Yasue. "I'm So Glad I'm Living in the U.S.A.: Chuck Berry's America." *Popular Music and Society* 13, no. 4 (1989): 17-34.
 Explores several dichotomies that surface in the songs written by Chuck Berry. Discusses Berry's deliberate use of place names and social icons (e.g., automobiles, school) that ensured rock music's status as an American art form that celebrates American culture. Notes the image of the automobile as a symbol of freedom, status, and urbanization. Examines Berry's use of California to represent the promised land and the realization of the American dream. Studies the contrast in Berry's lyrics between school (boredom) and rock music (fun). Finally, brings these dichotomies to an analysis of the contradictions between Chuck Berry the fun-loving rock musician and Chuck Berry the conservative American.

172.   Larkey, Edward. "Austropop: Popular Music and National Identity in Austria." *Popular Music* 11, no. 2 (1992): 151-185.
 Studies rock music in Austria in terms of consumption, imitation, de-anglicization, and re-ethnification. Traces in detail the history of Austrian rock music. Argues that "Austropop" is a "hegemonically-determined symbol and boundary-setting mechanism" that selects which music will become part of the culture thus constituting a national identity.

173.   Levy, Claire. "The Influence of British Rock in Bulgaria." *Popular Music* 11, no. 2 (1992): 209-212.
 Attributes the emergence of Bulgarian rock music to the influences of British rock, as opposed to American, of the 1960s. Claims that given the time period, British rock represented a group activity (e.g., Beatles) compared to the individualism of American rock music (e.g., Elvis Presley). Also, British rock music at that time represented a new musical style that was being appreciated worldwide. Asserts that Bulgarian rock groups adapted British sounds to create a Bulgarian rock tradition.

174.   Lewis, George H. "Ghosts, Ragged but Beautiful: Influences of Mexican Music on American Country-Western & Rock 'n' Roll." *Popular Music and Society* 15, no. 4 (1991): 85-103.
 Discusses the influences of Mexican music on country music and rock music. Traces the rock influences starting with Buddy Holly. While Holly's overall style was rockabilly with its strong country music roots, his guitar playing style is attributable to Mexican influences. Mentions the significance of the direct Mexican impact of Ritchie Valens and Los Lobos. Refers to the Mexican music

styles that appear in the works of Bob Dylan, Neil Young, and Jimi Hendrix. Concludes that the influences of Mexican music styles on rock music have been both tremendous and largely ignored.

175. Light, Alan. "About a Salary or Reality? Rap's Recurrent Conflict." *South Atlantic Quarterly* 90, no. 4 (1991): 855-870.

Remarks on the state of rap music in the early 1990s. Explores rap music's rise as a viable popular music form once it had developed closer connections to rock music. Offers the Beastie Boys' *Licensed to Ill* album as an example. Studies the resulting backlash represented by Public Enemy's recordings that explicitly rejected ties to rock music. Also discusses the geography of rap music and the nature and content of the lyrics. Also published in the book *Present Tense* edited by Anthony DeCurtis.

176. Manuel, Peter. "Ideology and Popular Music in Socialist Cuba." *Pacific Review of Ethnomusicology* 2 (1985): 1-27.

Explores attitudes toward various genres of popular music in Cuba. Notes a "frequent lack of consistency between Marxist theories of art, Cuban cultural policy as explicitly stated, and policy as actually practiced." Observes that although rock music is not produced in Cuba, it is consumed widely. Cuba's mass media provide a considerable outlet for rock music. Attributes this attention to the music's popularity and to an attempt to compete for audiences with Florida stations and Voice of America broadcasts. Argues that there is a belief among some that the socialism of Cuba is so strong that it can maintain its integrity in the face of foreign influences such as rock music. Also discusses Cuban dance music, salsa music, the cancion romantica, and the nueva trova. Concludes that rock music is the dominate popular music in Cuba. Socialism has had little effect on the various genres of popular music, probably because of its working class origins. Cuban socialist cultural policy has been more tolerant than one would expect.

177. Manuel, Peter. "Marxism, Nationalism and Popular Music in Revolutionary Cuba." *Popular Music* 6, no. 2 (1987): 161-178.

Observes that popular music in Cuba is dominated by rock music from the United States. Attributes the popularity of rock music in Cuba to the genre's ties to the working class. Concludes that the political revolution in Cuba has had little effect on popular music styles. Updates and revises an earlier version of this article that appeared in volume two of *The Pacific Review of Ethnomusicology*.

178. Mayer, Gunter. "Popular Music in the GDR." *Journal of Popular Culture* 18, no. 3 (1984): 145-158.

Presents various forms of popular music found in the German Democratic Republic (GDR), including jazz, schlager (e.g., easy listening), and rock.

Discusses the various elements of rock music in the GDR, such as blues music, folk music styles, and socially critical lyrics. Notes the 1983 founding of the Centre for Popular Music, dedicated to documenting popular music in the GDR.

179.   McAllester, David P. "New Perspectives in Native American Music." *Perspectives of New Music* 20, no. 1-2 (1981/1982): 433-446.

Discusses the evolution of Native American music. Notes the incorporation of Anglo styles and influences. Suggests that rock music is incorporated into Native American music in order to appeal to the youth. In doing so Native American composers demonstrate their ability to function in the popular mainstream while promoting traditional Native American cultural values.

180.   Mitchell, Tony. "Mixing Pop and Politics: Rock Music in Czechoslovakia Before and After the Velvet Revolution." *Popular Music* 11, no. 2 (1992): 187-203.

Reviews the historical role of rock music in Czechoslovakia. Discusses the significance of Frank Zappa and Lou Reed to the Czech counterculture. Recounts the history of rock music in Czechoslovakia, with special attention paid to the Plastic People. Updates the Prague music scene since 1990. Projects that the political role of rock music in Czechoslovakia will decline now that the Eastern bloc Communist regimes have collapsed.

181.   Murray, James Briggs. "Understanding and Developing Black Popular Music Collections." *Drexel Library Quarterly* 19, no. 1 (1983): 4-54.

Provides an overview and history of various black music genres, including work songs, spirituals, gospel, blues, rhythm and blues, rock, soul, funk, fusion, disco, Caribbean, and African music. Discusses cover songs of the 1950s and the rise of Motown. Makes recommendations for library collections, including methods, organization, and preservation.

182.   Mutsaers, Lutgard. "Indorock: An Early Eurorock Style." *Popular Music* 9, no. 3 (1990): 307-320.

Focuses on a rock music style that evolved in Holland during the 1960s and is now known as Indorock. Indorock was performed by Indonesians who migrated to Holland. Indorock musicians were popular in Germany at the same time as the Beatles and other Merseybeat groups invaded Hamburg. Reviews the musical elements of the Indorock style and discusses the impact of the genre.

183.   O'Grady, Terence J. "Rubber Soul and the Social Dance Tradition." *Ethnomusicology* 23, no. 1 (1979): 87-94.

Details the musical structure of each song appearing on the Beatles album *Rubber Soul*, which demonstrates a subtle, yet significant, departure from earlier Beatles compositions. Claims that previous songs by the Beatles which experimented only with harmony, melody, and instrumentation. On *Rubber Soul* experimentation reaches new heights and the music "is no longer primarily concerned with expediting the dance," which is to say that it did not follow rock music conventions. Notes heavy country music and folk music influences. Claims that greater experimentation was possible because the Beatles' status was such that any recording by them would be a commercial success. Argues that *Rubber Soul* paved the way for future experimentation.

184. Palmer, Robert. "The Church of the Sonic Guitar." *South Atlantic Quarterly* 90, no. 4 (1991): 649-673.

Provides a detailed history of the electric guitar and the musicians primarily responsible for its centrality to rock music. Gives particular attention to Muddy Waters and his early Chess Records recordings and to Sam Phillips' Sun Records. Presents Guitar Slim as the "patron saint of our Church of the Sonic Guitar." Concludes with a profile of Ike Turner's contributions. Also published in the book *Present Tense* edited by Anthony DeCurtis.

185. Pearson, Anthony. "The Grateful Dead Phenomenon: An Ethnomethodological Approach." *Youth & Society* 18, no. 4 (1987): 418-432.

Argues that by examining the phenomenon of the Grateful Dead subculture, sociologists can learn more about the "cognitive processes by which all social life is generated" and about how social realities are constructed and maintained. Concludes that the Grateful Dead experience is not learned rationally or absorbed simply as a result of membership in a subculture. The result is a socially based experience which is not socially determined.

186. Pekacz, Jolanta. "On Some Dilemmas of Polish Post-Communist Rock Culture." *Popular Music* 11, no. 2 (1992): 205-208.

Points out some of the problems for rock music's survival in Poland when associated with sudden political change. Discusses wide-spread illegal piracy of recordings due to an end to censorship and outdated copyright laws. Notes that the overall Polish music industry suffers from blurred distinctions between capitalism and crime.

187. Perrone, Charles A. "Changing of the Guard: Questions and Contrasts of Brazilian Rock Phenomena." *Studies in Latin American Popular Culture* 9 (1990): 65-83.

Traces the historical development of rock music in Brazil. Observes that rock music's biggest influence has been in the area of style rather than "direct imitation." Discusses the significance of the 1985 *Rock in Rio* concert that solidified rock music as a "major cultural force among Brazil's urban youth." Explores issues related to authenticity, resistance, motivation, and originality in Brazilian rock music. Notes that to understand the role of rock music in Brazilian culture, one must recognize the "interplay between material and mental dimensions."

188. Ramet, Pedro, and Sergei Zamascikov. "The Soviet Rock Scene." *Journal of Popular Culture* 24, no. 1 (1990): 149-174.

Provides a history of the growth of rock music in the Soviet Union. Notes that prior to 1986 there was a strong distinction between official and unofficial rock music. Reports that policies regarding rock music are reflective of larger policy issues and that the "liberalization in the sphere of music closely paralleled liberalization in other spheres." Observes that after many years of imitating Western genres, rock music in the Soviet Union is now "developing autonomously" although not in isolation. Therefore, Soviet rock music is richer and more diverse than ever. Questions whether the liberalization of rock music in the Soviet Union will negatively affect the music because a defining characteristic of the past has been the unofficial music's political edge. Includes an annotated list of the major Soviet rock groups. Also includes a chronological chart of Soviet rock music history, dividing the evolution into six stages: Early Pre-Beatles Developments (1950s - 1963), Imitative Rock (1963 - late 1960s), Emergence of Indigenous Styles (late 1960s - mid 1970s), Search for Ethnic Roots (late 1970s), Diversification (late 1970s - 1985), and Liberalization (1985 - present).

189. Regev, Motti. "Israeli Rock, or a Study in the Politics of 'Local Authenticity'." *Popular Music* 11, no. 1 (1992): 1-14.

Attempts to place Israeli rock music in the context of having local authenticity in that it reflects and expresses local culture. Profiles Israeli rock musicians who have incorporated rock music aesthetics with elements of traditional Israeli music. Places the notion of local authenticity into a theoretical construct. Includes a selected discography of Israeli rock music.

190. Rubey, Dan. "Voguing at the Carnival: Desire and Pleasure on MTV." *South Atlantic Quarterly* 90, no. 4 (1991): 871-906.

Suggests that music videos can assist in the development of visual literacy because "decoding these densely packed visual texts requires attention and imagination." Videos bring to the forefront, without dichotomizing, issues of gender and race that are not present on the radio. Discusses the amount of heavy metal music presented on MTV and the history surrounding the issue of black musicians on MTV. Focuses much attention on the topic of visual pleasure, especially as presented in the videos by female performers. Also published in the book *Present Tense* edited by Anthony DeCurtis.

191. Santino, Jack. "The Spirit of American Music: *Nobody Ever Told Me It Was the Blues*." *Journal of American Culture* 5, no. 4 (1982): 20-26.

Writes on the defining moment when rock music began. Attempts to convey a sense of the interconnectivity of various American music genres. Illustrates the continuous and cyclical nature of musical genres. Describes the mutual influences of folk, blues, rhythm and blues, country, popular, and various ethnic musics in the early formation of rock music.

192. Shumway, David R. "Rock & Roll as a Cultural Practice." *South Atlantic Quarterly* 90, no. 4 (1991): 753-769.

Notes that rock music is difficult to define as a genre. Offers that it is better to think of rock music in terms of cultural practice. In addition to the music, one must also consider the associated behaviors of the performers and the audience. Uses Elvis Presley as an example. Argues that the performers are the primary texts of rock music, but the audience contributes to the production nevertheless. Also published in the book *Present Tense* edited by Anthony DeCurtis.

193. Skvorecky, Josef. "Hipness at Noon: Communism's Crusade Against Jazz and Rock in Czechoslovakia." *New Republic* (1984): 27-35.

Describes in detail the history of jazz and punk rock music in Czechoslovakia and the early 1980s "witch hunt" aimed overtly at the punk movement, but also covertly at jazz music.

194. Smith, Martha Nell. "Sexual Mobilities in Bruce Springsteen: Performance as Commentary." *South Atlantic Quarterly* 90, no. 4 (1991): 833-854.

Explores the meaning of Bruce Springsteen's "conflicting and ambiguous sexual expressions." Analyzes Springsteen's music videos with regard to homoerotic images. Specifically examines six videos from the *Bruce Springsteen Video Anthology / 1978-88*: *Born to Run*, *Brilliant Disguise*, *Tunnel of Love*, *One Step Up*, *Tougher Than the Rest*, and *Spare Parts*. Suggests that Springsteen highlights the limitations of stereotyped sexuality. Also published in the book *Present Tense* edited by Anthony DeCurtis.

195. Smith, Paul. "Playing for England." *South Atlantic Quarterly* 90, no. 4 (1991): 737-752.

Focuses on the 1990 recording *World in Motion* by New Order as the official theme song for England's World Cup soccer team. Considers the political and social environment in Great Britain during 1990. Claims that the song was an "abortive attempt to represent a certain kind of populist nationalism" and was an example of subculture forms being manipulated as part of the military-industrial complex. Also published in the book *Present Tense* edited by Anthony DeCurtis.

196. Stigberg, David K. "Foreign Currents During the 60s and 70s in Mexican Popular Music: Rock and Roll, the Romantic Ballad and the Cumbia." *Studies in Latin American Popular Culture* 4 (1985): 170-184.

Concentrates on the influences of North American music styles on Mexican popular music. Uses the genres of the romantic ballad, the dance music known as cumbia, and rock music as examples. Observes the impact of 1960s North American and British music styles on Mexican culture, including fashion, youth ideology, counterculture, and the drug culture. Notes that by the mid-1970s, other genres had come into favor in Mexico, reducing the significance of rock music.

197.   Szemere, Anna. "Some Institutional Aspects of Pop and Rock in Hungary." *Popular Music* 3 (1983): 121-142.
   Examines the relationship between rock music and related institutions in Hungary in terms of problems associated with "autonomy and self-expression." Explores the connections between the cultural policy of "show business" and rock music. Claims that intelligent rock music was never allowed to develop because commercial pop music was promoted by an "aristocratic and ill-coordinated cultural policy" tied to an equally bad media policy and outdated political, legal, and financial systems. Concludes that the increasing attention paid to rock music is not based on its inherent value, but on its "mass effect, which can be controlled or exploited for particular purposes."

198.   Trosset, Carol. "Welsh Communitas as Ideological Practice." *Ethos* 16, no. 2 (1988): 167-180.
   Uses the rock opera *Y Mab Darogan (The Foretold Son)* to illustrate the anthropological notion of communitas. Communitas is a mental image of a homogeneous society with an "intense emotional experience of social unity." Outlines the appeals of ideology to the audience regarding Welsh identity. Examines the ability of the performance structure to evoke communitas. The rock opera's musical style, historical subject, lyrical appeal, and performance context are offered as evidence of communitas identity.

199.   Vila, Pablo. "Argentina's Rock Nacional: The Struggle for Meaning." *Latin American Music Review* 10, no. 1 (1989): 1-28.
   Describes the social movement in Argentina known as "rock nacional" which is based on the youth culture's rock music. Rock nacional developed in the 1960s in parallel with other worldwide youth movements that utilized rock music as a main means of communication and cohesiveness. Unlike in the United States, rock nacional disassociates itself from the mainstream culture but also from its own current manifestation in order to develop new youth identities. Therefore, it is always "open to the construction of new meanings." Provides a history of the genre and concludes that the foundation of rock nacional as a musical genre is its "struggle for meaning."

200.   Wallis, Roger, and Krister Malm. "Sain Cymru: The Role of the Welsh Phonographic Industry in the Development of a Welsh Language Pop/Rock/Folk Scene." *Popular Music* 3 (1983): 77-105.
   Explores the rise and struggle of the music industry in Wales. Discusses the "electrification process" and the reactions evoked. Mentions the rise of punk

and new wave bands in South Wales. Notes trends in the use of the Welsh language when performing and the difficulty of gaining access to venues for live performances.

201.   Zion, Lawrence. "The Impact of the Beatles on Pop Music in Australia: 1963-66." *Popular Music* 6, no. 3 (1987): 291-311.
Describes the response to the Beatles in Australia during their first tour of the country. Also discusses British immigrants and the Beatles-inspired rock groups that followed.

CHAPTERS

202.   Bahry, Romana. "Rock Culture and Rock Music in Ukraine." In *Rocking the State: Rock Music and Politics in Eastern Europe and Russia*, edited by Sabrina Petra Ramet, 243-296. Boulder: Westview Press, 1994.
Assesses the history of rock music in Ukraine and its effects on the culture. Identifies four stages in the history of Ukrainian rock music. The first stage was the first wave of rock music in the early 1960s and included recordings of the Beatles and Rolling Stones made from Voice of America radio broadcasts. The second stage was represented by government censorship and control in the wake of the 1968 invasion of Czechoslovakia. Rock performers had to belong to state-approved Vocal Instrumental Ensembles and English language lyrics were restricted. The third stage emerged near the end of the 1970s and began to reflect world music influences. The fourth stage is defined as beginning in the wake of the Chernobyl nuclear power plant disaster. Notes that the rock music cultural centers are Kiev and Lviv. Discusses numerous rock music performers. Includes an appendix profiling major Ukrainian rock groups from 1986 to 1991.

203.   Berry, Venise. "Redeeming the Rap Music Experience." In *Adolescents and Their Music: If It's Too Loud, You're Too Old*, edited by Jonathon S. Epstein, 165-187. New York: Garland, 1994.
Explores rap music issues related to sex, violence, and racism. Contends that black music has always been a "communicative response to the pressures and challenges" within the African American community. Defines rappers as "empowered storytellers" articulating an urban ideology and forcing public debate on cultural issues. Compares the context of rap music as a manifestation of rebellion to that of punk and heavy metal music.

204.   Castles, John. "Tjungaringanyi: Aboriginal Rock." In *From Pop to Punk to Postmodernism: Popular Music and Australian Culture from the 1960s to the 1990s*, edited by Philip Hayward, 25-39. North Sydney, Australia: Allen & Unwin, 1992.
Presents the history of, and influences on, Aboriginal music as its developed over the last one hundred years. Focuses on the Aboriginal rock music that

developed during the 1980s as a merging of traditional and contemporary sounds. Discusses the problematic music of the group Midnight Oil.

205. Decker, Jeffrey Louis. "The State of Rap: Time and Place in Hip Hop Nationalism." In *Microphone Fiends: Youth Music & Youth Culture*, edited by Andrew Ross and Tricia Rose, 99-121. New York: Routledge, 1994.
   Attempts to account for the rise of black nationalism in rap music. Contends that rap music represents a nationalism based on a "collective challenge to the consensus logic" of U.S. nationalism. Compares and contrasts the hip hop nationalism of the 1990s to the black nationalism of the 1960s. Discusses sexism in rap music and Afrocentricity.

206. Flores, Juan. "Puerto Rican and Proud, Boyee!: Rap Roots and Amnesia." In *Microphone Fiends: Youth Music & Youth Culture*, edited by Andrew Ross and Tricia Rose, 89-98. New York: Routledge, 1994.
   Reports on the experiences of Puerto Ricans in rap music. Observes that for Puerto Ricans to participate in rap music they must undertake cultural negotiation. Notes that Puerto Ricans have been involved with rap music from its earliest beginnings. Traces the history of Puerto Ricans' roles in rap music and their anonymity once the genre became popular in the media.

207. Ford, Larry. "Geographic Factors in the Origin, Evolution, and Diffusion of Rock and Roll Music." In *The Sounds of People and Places: Readings in the Geography of American Folk and Popular Music*, edited by George O. Carney, 255-270. Lanham, MD: University Press of America, 1987.
   Illustrates the concept of cultural diffusion by tracing the geographic evolution of rock music. Examines the notion of cultural hearth which is the contribution of a particular geographic culture to the development of new cultural traits. Diffusion is the spread of new cultural traits. Identifies Appalachia, the Mississippi Delta, New York City, Philadelphia, Kansas City, Cleveland, Detroit, Chicago, Nashville, New Orleans, Memphis, Southern California, and San Francisco as cultural hearths. Attributes diffusion to migration and mass media objectification. Also appeared in *The Journal of Geography* (vol. 70, November 1971).

208. Gaines, Donna. "The Local Economy of Suburban Scenes." In *Adolescents and Their Music: If It's Too Loud, You're Too Old*, edited by Jonathon S. Epstein, 47-65. New York: Garland, 1994.
   Focuses on suburban youth and their alienation. Describes the emergence of informal social organizations and subcultures within this context. Often, social organization is centered around a music genre that defines specific "practices and processes." Concentrates on the "hardcore" scene with its associated music groups and fanzines. Observes that suburban youth create their own music scenes in order to isolate themselves from the larger culture and to survive the "teenage wasteland."

209. Garofalo, Reebee. "Popular Music and the Civil Rights Movement." In *Rockin' the Boat: Mass Music and Mass Movements*, edited by Reebee Garofalo, 230-240. Boston: South End Press, 1992.

Discusses the role of rock music in the Civil Rights Movement. Notes that most people associate only folk and protest music with civil rights. Traces the history of the relationship between music and the Civil Rights Movement. Observes how rock music became more central to the movement as the notion of black power became more radical.

210. Gottlieb, Joanne, and Gayle Wald. "Smells Like Teen Spirit: Riot Grrrls, Revolution and Women in Independent Rock." In *Microphone Fiends: Youth Music & Youth Culture*, edited by Andrew Ross and Tricia Rose, 250-274. New York: Routledge, 1994.

Probes the historically hidden role of women in rock music, the increasing prominence of female grunge rock bands, relationships among "performance, gender, and sexuality," feminism, and aesthetics. Contends that contemporary female musicians (i.e., riot grrrls) share a punk aesthetic of minimalism, amateurism, and rawness.

211. Green, Archie. "Austin's Cosmic Cowboys: Words in Collision." In *'And Other Neighborly Games:' Social Process and Cultural Image in Texas Folklore*, edited by Richard Bauman and Roger D. Abrahams, 152-194. Austin: University of Texas Press, 1981.

Recounts the rise of the term "cosmic cowboy" in the 1970s to describe the "considerable degree of interaction among the vernacular and popular forms - musical, graphic, and literary." Purpose of the chapter is to contribute to the understanding of the cowboy figure as hero and anti-hero. Traces the history of various interpretations of the cowboy myth to provide background for an exploration of the Austin, Texas music scene of the early 1970s. Notes that a fusion of country and rock music emerged in Austin during this period. Examines the growth of the phenomenon best described as a country-rock culture. Discusses in detail the history, impact, and significance of the song *Cosmic Cowboy* by Michael Murphey. Also mentions works by Kinky Friedman and Guy Clark.

212. Hebdige, Dick. "Style as Homology and Signifying Practice." In *On Record: Rock, Pop, and the Written Word*, edited by Simon Frith and Andrew Goodwin, 56-65. New York: Pantheon Books, 1990.

Attempts to resolve the paradox of the punk culture's ability to symbolize chaos only because the "style itself was so thoroughly ordered." Concludes that subcultures are defined not only by objects or content, but also by the practices that give meaning to the content.

213.   Kan, Alex, and Nick Hayes. "Big Beat in Poland." In *Rocking the State: Rock Music and Politics in Eastern Europe and Russia*, edited by Sabrina Petra Ramet, 41-53. Boulder: Westview Press, 1994.

Discusses the history of rock music in Poland. Notes that the rock music scene has always experienced a relative openness among communist countries. Profiles several influential Polish rock groups. Focuses on the punk rock movement in Poland.

214.   Keyes, Cheryl L. "'We're More than a Novelty, Boys': Strategies of Female Rappers in the Rap Music Tradition." In *Feminist Messages: Coding in Women's Folk Culture*, edited by Joan Newlon Radner, 203-220. Urbana: University of Illinois Press, 1993.

Traces the history and sources of rap music, including "foresisters" Moms Mabley and Millie Jackson. Focuses on contemporary female rap performers. Observes that female rappers must appropriate male performance aesthetics and overcome sexual stereotypes. Notes that women rappers address issues of female empowerment, acceptance, and recognition.

215.   Kotarba, Joseph A. "The Postmodernization of Rock and Roll Music: The Case of Metallica." In *Adolescents and Their Music: If It's Too Loud, You're Too Old*, edited by Jonathon S. Epstein, 141-163. New York: Garland, 1994.

Describes the heavy metal group Metallica as the "prototypical rock and roll band of the contemporary 1990s period." Discusses the relationship between Metallica and their fans and the importance of the "lyrical narrative." Demonstrates that heavy metal music is "culturally pervasive." Notes that heavy metal music displays postmodern attributes for the following reasons, among others: 1) it is no longer limited to a working-class male adolescent audience, 2) its meaning is "an open horizon," and 3) it reflects moral ambiguity.

216.   Lipsitz, George. "Chicano Rock: Cruising Around the Historical Bloc." In *Rockin' the Boat: Mass Music and Mass Movements*, edited by Reebee Garofalo, 267-280. Boston: South End Press, 1992.

Considers the history of popular music among the Mexican American community in Los Angeles, California. Discusses the impact and significance of Ritchie Valens, Frankie 'Cannibal' Garcia and the Headhunters, and the rock group Los Lobos. Explores the connections between Mexican American culture and various periods of rock music history.

217. Lipsitz, George. "Land of a Thousand Dances: Youth, Minorities, and the Rise of Rock and Roll." In *Recasting America: Culture and Politics in the Age of Cold War*, edited by Lary May, 267-284. Chicago: University of Chicago Press, 1989.

Considers the rolls of rock music in the cultural interactions within urban America in the post-World War II period. Utilizes the recording of *Land of a Thousand Dances* by the Mexican American rock group Cannibal and the Headhunters as a point of entry into a discussion of rock music as a social force. Focuses on the Mexican American community of East Los Angeles, California and the role of music, class, and ethnicity in collective memory. Notes the enormous popularity of native Ritchie Valens and his synthesis of Mexican folk music and rock music. Claims that the ethnic and class interactions found in urban environments of the 1940s and 1950s are being destroyed, but desire to recall those heterogeous times is responsible for the nostalgia of the late 1970s.

218. Lont, Cynthia M. "Women's Music: No Longer a Small Private Party." In *Rockin' the Boat: Mass Music and Mass Movements*, edited by Reebee Garofalo, 241-253. Boston: South End Press, 1992.

Focuses on women's music through a historical presentation of the genre. Discusses the political and cultural nature of women's music. Explores the growing interest in women's music by the mainstream market and questions the cooption of the genre by major record companies.

219. Lull, James. "Thrashing in the Pit: An Ethnography of San Francisco Punk Subculture." In *Natural Audiences: Qualitative Research of Media Uses and Effects*, edited by Thomas R. Lindlof, 225-252. Norwood, N.J.: Ablex, 1987.

Attempts to explain the punk subculture in San Francisco, California, by means of symbolic interaction and social processes. Notes that punks are distinguished among themselves based on preferences for particular punk music bands. Discusses the punk lifestyle in terms of food, school, religion, money, drugs, gender relations, and enemies. Observes that punk music is the "primary aspect of the subculture" and that it reinforces lifestyle choices of subculture members. Comments on live punk music, the performer-audience relationship, thrashing, and use of mass media. Devotes some attention to skinheads.

220. Oglesbee, Frank W. "Lady as Tiger: The Female Hero in Rock." In *Heroines of Popular Culture*, edited by Pat Browne, 158-182. Bowling Green, Ohio: Bowling Green State University Popular Press, 1987.

Assesses the repressive nature of "rebellious" rock music towards women. Discusses the concept of the female hero historically and in contemporary society. Focuses on girl groups, Janis Joplin, Grace Slick, Suzi Quatro, Patti Smith, Joan Jett, Pat Benatar, Annie Lennox, and Cyndi Lauper. Concludes that contemporary female rock musicians serve as suitable role models because they are not larger than life, but are intelligent and talented.

221. Perry, Steve. "Ain't No Mountain High Enough: The Politics of Crossover." In *Facing the Music: A Pantheon Guide to Popular Culture*, edited by Simon Frith, 51-87. New York: Pantheon Books, 1988.

Remarks on the phenomenon of "crossover" where black musicians have hits on the popular music charts. Articulates two anti-crossover positions: 1) the aesthetic sellout in which black musicians abandon the black musical traditions in favor of a whiter sound, and 2) the politics of black nationalism in which "the erosion of racial barriers in the production, distribution, and consumption of black music poses an economic threat" to the black music market. Focuses on the writings of Nelson George, black music columnist for *Billboard*. Provides a history of the racial dynamics of rock music in America. Concludes that black music continues to be underrepresented, but it "presents black people and black art on a larger scale and in more humanizing terms than any other facet of mass culture."

222. Ramet, Sabrina Petra, Sergei Zamascikov, and Robert Bird. "The Soviet Rock Scene." In *Rocking the State: Rock Music and Politics in Eastern Europe and Russia*, edited by Sabrina Petra Ramet, 181-218. Boulder: Westview Press, 1994.

Chronicles in detail the history of rock music in the Soviet Union. Questions whether Russian rock music will continue to be vital now that it is not political. Updates a previous version of this essay that appeared in the publication *Journal of Popular Culture* (vol. 24, no. 1, Summer 1990). At that time, author Ramet was publishing under the name of Pedro Ramet.

223. Sardiello, Robert. "Secular Rituals in Popular Culture: A Case for Grateful Dead Concerts and Dead Head Identity." In *Adolescents and Their Music: If It's Too Loud, You're Too Old*, edited by Jonathon S. Epstein, 115-139. New York: Garland, 1994.

Analyzes Grateful Dead concerts as secular rituals. Describes the "mythical nature of Dead Head unity" with respect to shared meanings and identity. Argues that the collective identity of Deadheads is based more on the ritual of the group's concerts than on a shared appreciation of their music. Notes that the concert setting allows the reinforcement of values that symbolically create the myth model. Contends that music does not create youth subcultures, but rather reflects them. Deadheads and other subcultures that are reflected in rock music (e.g., heavy metal) are centered on concert ritual.

224. Survilla, Maria Paula. "Rock Music in Belarus." In *Rocking the State: Rock Music and Politics in Eastern Europe and Russia*, edited by Sabrina Petra Ramet, 219-241. Boulder: Westview Press, 1994.

Probes the relationship between rock music and the cultural expression of identity in Belarus. Observes that language, themes, and traditional references are essential components of Belarusian rock music. Focuses on the Miensk rock group Mroja in order to illustrate stylistic elements of Belarusian rock music.

225. Willis, Paul. "The Golden Age." In *On Record: Rock, Pop, and the Written Word*, edited by Simon Frith and Andrew Goodwin, 43-55. New York: Pantheon Books, 1990.

Attempts to describe the use of rock music by a subculture. Draws parallels between characteristics of a Great Britain motorcycle subculture and the genre characteristics of rock music. Argues that there is a symbolic connection between lifestyle and the musical forms that provide or reinforce meaning. Concludes that there is "a profound inner connection with a life-style."

226. Yoffe, Mark. "Hippies in the Baltic: The Rock and Roll Era." In *Cross Currents: A Yearbook of Central European Culture*, edited by Ladislav Matejka, 157-176. Ann Arbor: Department of Slavic Languages and Literatures of the University of Michigan, 1988.

Describes the ways in which rock music unified 1970s Baltic hippies from Latvia, Lithuania, and Estonia despite historical ethnicity and mutual hatred. Rock music is presented as providing spiritual solidarity. Discusses the religious significance of the rock opera *Jesus Christ Superstar*, the problems that Soviet-controlled governments and the press faced in attempting to assimilate and control rock music, and the existence of official Vocal Instrumental Ensembles (VIAs). Highlights composer Imant Kalninsh as one of the most popular rock musicians of the era. Reviews the role of rock festivals as a major unification force. Contends that the primary contribution of the hippies was their exertion of a humanistic influence into Soviet society.

227. Zook, Kristal Brent. "Reconstructions of Nationalist Thought in Black Music and Culture." In *Rockin' the Boat: Mass Music and Mass Movements*, edited by Reebee Garofalo, 254-266. Boston: South End Press, 1992.

Argues that there is a black nationalist ideology that informs rap music. Claims that rap music is an offensive, as opposed to defensive, political and cultural gesture. Defines black nationalism as "a desire for cultural pride, economic self-sufficiency, racial solidarity, and collective survival." Provides a brief history of rap music. Places rap music into a larger context of the cultural expressions of nationalism.

BOOKS

228. Cohen, Sara. *Rock Culture in Liverpool: Popular Music in the Making*. Oxford: Clarendon Press, 1991.

Concentrates on two bands in Liverpool, England, as being representative of the relationship between art and society. Explores the tensions between creativity and capitalism. Demonstrates the way in which the male dominated culture of rock groups perceives both commercialism and women as threats to creativity, solidarity, and existence which in turn affects performance, production, and marketing. Presents a history of the Liverpool rock music scene. Focuses on the social factors existing in the two case-study rock groups, the efforts required to maintain a rock group, and an analysis of public performances and strategies for success. Observes the musicians' "aesthetics and conceptualization of music" and their personal tensions and contradictions with other members of the rock groups. Denies the superficiality of rock music by presenting it as a cultural force with tangible meaning tied to social, economic, and political reality with geographical, historical, and ideological characteristics.

229.   DeCurtis, Anthony, ed. *Present Tense: Rock & Roll and Culture.* Durham: Duke University Press, 1992.

Attempts to address, through various essays by a variety of authors, the question of how the meaning of rock music changes across time. Assumes that rock music is "created in a social context" and that "critical writing can be a means of exploring broader questions about life in the culture at large." Strives to present a mixture of journalism and scholarship with "theoretical, speculative, technical, and practical approaches" to the subject. Originally published as *South Atlantic Quarterly* volume 90, issue number 4, in 1991. The book version of the publication benefits from having a single subject index to all of the essays.

230.   Prendergast, Mark J. *The Isle of Noises.* New York: St. Martin's Press, 1990.

Details the significance of rock music in Ireland and the international influences of numerous Irish rock performers. Devotes an entire chapter to Van Morrison. Also focuses on U2 and gives special attention Bob Geldof and his *Live Aid* efforts.

231.   Ryback, Timothy W. *Rock Around the Bloc: A History of Rock Music in Eastern Europe and the Soviet Union.* New York: Oxford University Press, 1990.

Depicts rock music in the Soviet Union since 1985 as the figurative and literal "sound track of the Gorbachev revolution." Prior to this time, rock music endured thirty years of unfavorable policies as result of being labeled subversive. Claims that rock music "debunked Marxist-Leninist assumptions about the state's ability to control its citizens." Chronicles the entire history of rock music in the Soviet Union and the rest of Eastern Europe, beginning in the early 1950s. Discusses the wave of Beatlemania that swept the Soviet Union and Eastern Europe, as well as the eventual political backlash. Covers the Soviet Ministry of Culture's formation of the Vocal Instrumental Ensembles. Devotes separate chapters to the punk movements in Hungary and in Poland. Concludes that the current state of rock music reflects the realization of the democratic process in socialist countries. Includes a chronology of rock music in the Soviet Union and Eastern Europe.

232. Shank, Barry. *Dissonant Identities: The Rock 'n' Roll Scene in Austin, Texas.* Hanover, N.H.: University Press of New England, 1994.

Argues that rock music performance "functions as a process of identity-formation." Uses the Austin, Texas music scene as a contextual setting for identity formation. Notes that the nature of the Austin music scene has changed over time, becoming more aligned with the national music industry, thus altering the musical aesthetics and resulting identities. Presents a history of the Austin music culture, from cowboy music to hillbilly, from country rock to punk. Theorizes about the postmodern nature of music performance.

233. Stapleton, Chris, and Chris May. *African Rock: The Pop Music of a Continent.* New York: Dutton, 1990.

Covers a wide range of urban African rock music genres (e.g., juju, chimurenga, benga, township pop). Presents the development of African rock music as a series of musical fusions. Notes the two-way influences of Western culture and African music. Includes a discussion on the African recording industry.

DISSERTATIONS

234. Bayton, Mavis Mary. "How Women Become Rock Musicians." Ph.D. University of Warwick, 1989. *Dissertation Abstracts International* 51: 3254A.

Examines thirty-six female rock musicians in the United Kingdom using interview techniques. Probes both the social constraints on females that result in few women rock musicians and the associated variables that allow one to overcome these restraints. Models the development of female rock groups. Investigates feminist musicians' career strategies.

235. Cohen, Sara. "Society and Culture in the Making of Rock Music in Merseyside." Ph.D. University of Oxford, 1987. *Dissertation Abstracts International* 50: 721A.

Attempts to study the "relationship between creativity and commerce through description and analysis of the processes of musical production." Provides a case-study focused on two bands from Liverpool, England. Considers both the influence of a commercial environment and the socio-economic conditions of Liverpool. Contends that previous research lacks microsociological analysis.

236. Fenster, Mark Andrew. "The Articulation of Difference and Identity in Alternative Popular Music Practice." Ph.D. University of Illinois at Urbana-Champaign, 1992. *Dissertation Abstracts International* 53: 2144A.

Explores the processes by which alternate musical genres form and survive, and their social significance. Concentrates on the articulation of differences such as race, social class, sexual preference, and taste. Provides a theoretical argument for a "processual model to account for the cultural and economic context for the production and reception" of alternate genres. Discusses the music industry's control over musical genres, and presents three case-studies to document "difficulty and social and cultural significance of such practices." One case-study is the emergence of homosexual punk fans as a dispersed community. A second case-study is the development of a bluegrass music industry. A third case-study is a survey of diverse publications' (e.g., mainstream, radical) reactions to rap music.

237. Friedlander, Paul David. "A Characteristics Profile of Eight 'Classic Rock and Roll' Artists, 1954-1959: As Measured by the *Rock Window*." Ph.D. University of Oregon, 1988. *Dissertation Abstracts International* 49: 652A.

Utilizes the *Rock Window*, a research model that divides data into four categories: music, lyrics, artist history, and social context. Samples eight artists based on success, creativity, and legacy: Chuck Berry, Fats Domino, the Everly Brothers, Bill Haley, Buddy Holly, Jerry Lee Lewis, Little Richard, and Elvis Presley. The sample divides into two categories: early and late periods. The early period sample shows rhythm and blues patterns dominated by saxophone music with lyrics concentrating on romance, adolescence, sex, and rock music. The late period sample shows emphasis on guitar music with lyrics concentrating almost exclusively on romance.

238. Gay, Leslie Clay, Jr. "Commitment, Cohesion, and Creative Process: A Study of New York City Rock Bands." Ph.D. Columbia University, 1991. *Dissertation Abstracts International* 52: 3763A.

Studies the rock group as a musical and social phenomenon in New York City with regard to the relationships of the individuals to the group, group cohesion, and the music composition process. Utilizes participant observation, interviews, and content analysis techniques of data collection. Observes that there are "patterns of communication and interaction" and "shared conventions and practices." Argues that individuals gain validation and status from rock group participation and that the group requires a high degree of commitment. The life of the individual participant is centered on the activities of the rock group. Music composition is viewed as a "communal, oral process."

FILMS AND VIDEOS

239. *Don't Look Back.* D. A. Pennebaker, dir. Leacock-Pennebaker Films, 1967.

Documents Bob Dylan's 1965 tour of England. Captures Dylan at the height of his reign.

240.   *The Great Rock 'n' Roll Swindle.* Julien Temple, dir. Virgin Films, 1980.

Documents Malcolm McLaren's management of the Sex Pistols within the context of the punk rock movement.

241.   *Wattstax.* Mel Stuart, dir. Columbia Pictures, 1973.

Captures the concert held in the name of the Los Angeles, California neighborhood known as Watts. Includes numerous African American performers and leaders.

History

ARTICLES

242. Allan, Blaine. "The Rolling Stones Era." *Queen's Quarterly* 92, no. 2 (1985): 265-276.

Differentiates among the numerous books in which the history of the Rolling Stones is chronicled. Categorizes the books as follows: picture books, journalistic histories, biographies, reports of tours, and insider stories. Notes that the Rolling Stones "express a narcissism that draws public attention."

243. Bayles, Martha. "Hollow Rock & the Lost Blues Connection." *Wilson Quarterly* 17, no. 3 (1993): 10-29.

Describes the decline of rock music into a mere expression of "unsettling emotions" of anxiety, lust, anger, and aggression. Compares this decline to the history of blues music. Focuses specifically on the mid-1960s merge of blues and rock music as expressed in the music of Cream, Jimi Hendrix, and Janis Joplin. Traces the musical, social, and political history of blues music and its relationship to popular music. Observes that the emergence of rock/blues music began in Great Britain in reaction to the commercial popular music of the Beatles and other British invasion era groups. Contends that rock musicians of that era, especially the Rolling Stones, "bludgeoned the spirit of the blues" in their "treatment of the erotic" and the "relationship between performer and audience." Discusses the early 1970s evolution of heavy metal music and themes of eroticism and satanism. Connects these themes back to blues music which is perennial and offers a "hope for an imminent improvement in the quality" of contemporary popular music.

244. Bindas, Kenneth J., and Craig Houston. "*Takin' Care of Business*: Rock Music, Vietnam and the Protest Myth." *Historian* 52, no. 1 (1989): 1-23.

Questions why rock musicians during the 1960s were, for the most part, silent on the subject of the Vietnam War. Notes the minimal number of rock songs from that era addressing the war. Documents the anti-establishment nature of rock music and the commercial nature of the rock music industry. Contends that because rock music was anti-establishment, it was also viewed as being anti-war. Further, post-1960s rock songs about the Vietnam War add to the myth that social activism, anti-war attitudes, and rock music have a symbiotic relationship. Record sales from the period indicate that songs about alienation and love sold well, but Vietnam War songs did not. As for the few anti-war recordings that were produced, the themes are analyzed and it is noted that specific references to the Vietnam War were avoided. Concludes that rock music during this period remained apolitical because the target audience was apolitical, despite the romantic revisionism of hippies as social reformers.

245. Burks, John. "Songs & Sounds of the Sixties." *American Libraries* 3, no. 2 (1972): 122-133.

Surveys the music industry of the 1960s in an attempt to predict where rock music is headed in the 1970s. Features Jim Morrison, Janis Joplin, Jimi Hendrix, and the Rolling Stones. Includes a list of selected important records and publications.

246. Burton, Thomas L. "Rock Music and Social Change, 1953-1978." *Loisir et Societe / Society and Leisure* 8, no. 2 (1985): 665-683.

Considers the evolution of rock music during its first twenty-five years. Attempts to show how rock developed in "form and style, and how it reflected broad socio-cultural trends and conditions." Organizes the discussion into three distinct stages. The first stage was the Struggle for Acceptance (1953-1959) in which rock music emerged as a fusion of rhythm and blues and country music. Its appeal was basic and emotional in a society that was seeing the beginnings of a youth culture. Society's first response was trying to control and suppress the music, then to coopt it. The second stage was Acculturation and Assimilation (1958-1970) in which a successful fusion with folk music opened the possibilities of other musical experimentation. Plus, the British invasion firmly established the prominence of the musical group. This reflected the wider social experimentations of the 1960s found in the drug culture and the sexual revolution. Society became more receptive to rock music, despite an increasing political content. The third stage was Diversification and Fragmentation (1968-1978) in which more distinct and numerous rock music styles developed. This, too, was reflective of increased fragmentation in society, partly as a result of the market economy and the targeting of consumers.

247. Cooper, B. Lee. "Examining a Decade of Rock Bibliographies, 1970-1979." *JEMF Quarterly* 16, no. 62 (1981): 95-101.

Offers a list, with selected annotations, of fifty-five bibliographic sources on rock music published between 1970 and 1979. Divides the citations into two sections, annotated and not annotated. Considers the items included in the annotated list to be the more important resources.

248. Denisoff, R. Serge. "*Teen Angel*: Resistance, Rebellion and Death-Revisited." *Journal of Popular Culture* 16, no. 4 (1982): 116-122.

Reviews a number of songs from the early 1960s with the common theme of death, or "teenage coffin" songs. Argues that these songs can be interpreted "within the framework of Camus' thesis on the nature of rebellion." In the lyrics of these songs, adolescents are in conflict with their expected social status. Death is a form of rebellion.

249. Denisoff, R. Serge, and William Romanowski. "Katzman's *Rock Around the Clock*: A Pseudo-Event?" *Journal of Popular Culture* 24, no. 1 (1990): 65-78.

Describes the making of the Sam Katzman film *Rock Around the Clock* as a cultural event. Explains how the film was made to profit from the success of the film *Blackboard Jungle* featuring the Bill Haley recording of *Rock Around the Clock*. Publicity accompanying the release of the film created a climate of fear accented with overblown and inaccurate accounts of violence at the showings. The result was that the film, advertised as "telling the story of rock," became a central tenet in the history of rock music because society pointed to it as an illustration of the corrupting force of rock music.

250. Garofalo, Reebee, and Steve Chapple. "From ASCAP to Alan Freed: The Pre-History of Rock 'n' Roll." *Popular Music and Society* 6 (1978): 72-80.

Provides a history of the conditions that led to the rise of rock music in the mid-1950s. Covers the battles over music publishing between ASCAP and BMI. Describes the growth and changes in the radio industry, the effects of population migrations, and the impact of technological advances.

251. Goldman, Albert. "The Emergence of Rock." *New American Review* 3 (1968): 118-139.

Explores the history of rock music and the associated development of the youth culture. Claims that rock music is developing from popular culture into real art by "pushing toward higher levels of imaginative excellence." Attributes the process to two conditions: the assimilation of fine art themes through the mass media, and the exploitation of popular culture by artists. Focuses on the music of the Beatles and the Doors. Concludes by questioning who would be the wiser as a result a discussion of music between John Lennon and John Cage.

252. Hamm, Charles. "The Fourth Audience." *Popular Music* 1 (1981): 123-141.

Discusses the relationships between ethnic groups, socioeconomic status, subcultures and audiences. Disputes the notion that rock music has changed dramatically from its mid-1950s beginnings. Contends that punk rock and new wave music are only the latest manifestations of the same instrumentation and text that first defined early rock music. Notes that tin pan alley, rhythm and blues, and country music had very discrete audiences prior to the 1950s. Rock music combined elements of all three musical genres, resulting in universal appeal. However, subsequent subgenres of rock music, except perhaps for disco, have not gained the same amount of appeal across ethnic and socioeconomic groups.

253. Hill, Trent. "The Enemy Within: Censorship in Rock Music in the 1950s." *South Atlantic Quarterly* 90, no. 4 (1991): 675-707.

Deals with the issue of censorship of rock music and associated sociological explanations of why rock music is viewed as an easy target for censors. Recounts the various explanations offered regarding rock music's threatening status in the 1950s. First, the beat of rock music was linked to sexual behavior and negative ideology. Second, the roots of rock music were based in black culture and, consequently, created fear among the white middle-class. Third, rock music evoked a fashion of delinquency with images of blue jeans, leather jackets, and motorcycles. Explores censorship in terms of power, beginning with a case-study of Elvis Presley. Discusses two series of hearings held in the 1950s: 1) the 1958 hearings on royalties, and 2) the 1960 payola hearings. Also published in the book *Present Tense* edited by Anthony DeCurtis.

254. Ingham, Peter, and Toru Mitsui. "The Search for Sweet Georgia Brown: A Case for Discographical Detection." *Popular Music* 6, no. 3 (1987): 273-290.

Attempts to sort out the truth among the various historical versions of the Beatles' very first recording sessions, backing singer Tony Sheridan. Confusion exists with regard to the actual recording dates, who was performing, and what songs were recorded. Concludes that those recording as the Beatles were John Lennon, Paul McCartney, George Harrison, and Pete Best, and not Stuart Sutcliffe, on June 22-24, 1961. Also includes a list of the songs recorded and a discussion regarding many versions of some of the songs that have served to confuse the issue.

255. Jarrett, Michael. "Concerning the Progress of Rock & Roll." *South Atlantic Quarterly* 90, no. 4 (1991): 803-818.

Offers an alternative history of rock music grounded on a theory other than conventionalization (which does not account for innovation). Presents an alternate means of interpreting conventionalization "that involves an investigation of decomposition as an agent capable not only of organizing information, but of generating a formula for the discovery or invention process." Claims that conventionalization is the compost that permits popularization as well as aberrant interpretations. Provides as examples the four "revolutionary moments" in the history of rock music when something new grew from the compost: 1) Elvis Presley and Little Richard, 2) Bob Dylan and the Beatles, 3) the Sex Pistols and the Clash, and 4) Public Enemy and De La Soul. Also published in the book *Present Tense* edited by Anthony DeCurtis.

256. Kelly, William P. "Running on Empty: Reimagining Rock and Roll." *Journal of American Culture* 4, no. 4 (1981): 152-159.

Comments on the trend in recent rock music films, television shows, and stage productions to address the historical elements of rock music. Unlike earlier productions of this nature, the current trend is not to deal with the art's contemporary status, but rather to engage in historical revisionism. Claims the past is being distorted in order to meet the needs of the present. Points to such films as *The Buddy Holly Story, American Hot Wax, I Wanna Hold Your Hand*, and *The Last Waltz* among others as examples of this phenomenon. Argues that *The Last Waltz* especially provides order from chaos by summarizing a rock group's career as if it were a narrative.

257. Leepson, Marc. "Rock Music Business." *Editorial Research Reports* 1, no. 22 (1977): 435-452.

Presents the history of rock music from an economic perspective. Notes that from its beginning rock music has been a commodity aimed at adolescents. Covers the full spectrum of revenue generation from rock music, including record sales, guitar sales, and concert revenues. Discusses the important role of the radio market and the various payola scandals that have occurred. Explains the confluence of country music and rhythm and blues, resulting in rockabilly and the rise of Elvis Presley. Conveys the influences of the Beatles. Describes the two types of record companies, independents and majors. Details the impact of the recession in the early 1970s. Offers some thoughts on the future of rock music.

258. Lewis, Jon. "Punks in LA: It's Kiss or Kill." *Journal of Popular Culture* 22, no. 2 (1988): 87-97.

Analyzes the ideology of the punk rock movement in Los Angeles, California during the late 1970s. Discusses its "symbiotic relationship" to mainstream rock music and casts punk rock as "a curious blend of anarchy and anomie." Asserts that punk was the "celebration of resignation." Suggests that two films are the most representative of the essence of the punk rock scene: Alex Cox's *Repo Man* and Penelope Spheeris' *The Decline of Western Civilization*. Unlike mainstream rock music, punk did not offer escapism. Rather, it offered a ritual of self-destruction.

259. McDonald, James R. "Censoring Rock Lyrics: A Historical Analysis of the Debate." *Youth & Society* 19, no. 3 (1988): 294-313.

Examines the history of rock music censorship in an attempt to evaluate assertions about its harmful effects made by the Parents Music Resource Center (PMRC). Surveys scholarship on the influences of rock music lyrics and considers how it may contribute to debates on censorship. Details the rise of the PMRC and the associated mid-1980s Senate hearings. Concludes that the PMRC operates on emotionalism, not intellectualism.

260.   McGilligan, Patrick, and Mark Rowland. "Reelin' and Rockin'." *American Film* 15, no. 12 (1990): 28-31.

Summarizes the history of rock music in the motion picture industry, from *Blackboard Jungle* to the present. Organizes the discussion by genre (e.g., rock documentaries, rock biographies).

261.   Mooney, Hugh. "Disco: A Music for the 1980s?" *Popular Music and Society* 7, no. 2 (1980): 84-94.

Provides a history of disco music. Attempts to explain why disco music grew to be so popular in the 1970s. Describes disco music as worldly with a satiny musical texture and rehearsed precision. Speculates on the future of this musical genre.

262.   Peterson, Richard A. "Why 1955? Explaining the Advent of Rock Music." *Popular Music* 9, no. 1 (1990): 97-116.

Attributes the rise of rock music in the mid-1950s to six factors that affect the production of culture: law, technology, industry, organization, occupations, and market. Discusses copyright law, patent law, and FCC regulations of the 1950s. Notes that the technological development of television changed the nature of radio programming which starting looking for cheap programming such as playing records. This, in turn, lead to numerous independent record companies searching for new sounds to meet an "unsatiated market demand."

263.   Ramet, Pedro. "The Rock Scene in Yugoslavia." *Eastern European Politics and Societies* 2, no. 2 (1988): 396-410.

Remarks on the history and current state of rock music in Yugoslavia, including the influences from the West. Notes that the absence of any significant control by the Yugoslavian government over rock music has resulted in the depolitization of the music. However, some musicians attempt to mobilize audiences on ecology issues and do occasionally speak to political issues. Regardless, rock music is still viewed primarily as a socializing agent.

264.   Rauth, Robert. "Back in the U.S.S.R. - Rock and Roll in the Soviet Union." *Popular Music and Society* 8, no. 3-4 (1982): 3-12.

Presents a history of rock music in the Soviet Union, beginning in the late 1950s. Discusses attempts to ban and domesticate rock music. Touches on the influences of radio, the underground rock movement, tours of the Soviet Union by Western musicians, and the "explosion" of disco music onto the Soviet music scene. Notes that rock music in the Soviet Union affects fashion, language, and beliefs. Rock music also demonstrates the Soviet Union's infatuation with Western culture. Contrasts the impact of rock music in the Soviet Union with other Eastern European countries where rock music is less regulated.

265. Redd, Lawrence N. "Rock! It's Still Rhythm and Blues." *Black Perspective in Music* 13, no. 1 (1985): 31-47.

Probes the history of rock music in order to determine when and why rock music became identified as something other than rhythm and blues music. Focuses on Alan Freed's promotion of rhythm and blues as rock and roll music. Observes that Bill Haley's contribution to rock music is overstated. Notes that Haley's recording of *Rock Around The Clock* was a cover version of an earlier recording by black performer Sonny Dae. Contends that Bill Haley's version only became famous because of the film *Blackboard Jungle*. Finally, views Elvis Presley as an "after-the-fact personality." Concludes that there is no difference between rhythm and blues and rock music, except that rock music is based on the music industry's marketing practices which have negative economic consequences for black musicians.

266. Romanowski, William D., and R. Serge Denisoff. "Money for Nothin' and the Charts for Free: Rock and the Movies." *Journal of Popular Culture* 21, no. 3 (1987): 63-78.

Provides a detailed history of the relationship between rock music and the motion picture industry. Begins with a discussion of rock exploitation films starting with *Blackboard Jungle*. Follows with commentary on the Beatles' early films which gave a respectability to the genre. The Beatles' films were followed by ones in which rock music complemented the storyline. Notes that rock music documentaries were the next development in the evolution, followed by rock musicals. Focuses on the rise of the rock music film soundtrack as a strategic development within the music/film industry.

267. Rosenberg, Neil V. "Bluegrass, Rock and Roll, and *Blue Moon of Kentucky*." *Southern Quarterly* 22, no. 3 (1984): 66-78.

Presents the various relationships that emerged between early rock music and bluegrass music. Notes that one audience response to rock music was to reject rockabilly as a diluted form of country music in favor of the more pure bluegrass sound. Observes that musicians attempted to synthesize bluegrass and rock music, especially in the development of rockabilly music. Demonstrates that it is professionally risky for career musicians to be too closely tied to any single musical genre or to suddenly change genres.

268. Shaw, Arnold. "Researching Rhythm and Blues." *Black Music Research Journal* (1980): 71-79.

Attempts to sort the confusion surrounding the relationship of rhythm and blues to rock music. Argues that the unquestionable historical influence of rhythm and blues on rock music has been often ignored or even disparaged. States that "chronologically, sociologically, or esthetically" rhythm and blues is not rock music, but historians have typically not understood the differences. Concludes that rapport between black and white adolescents promoted by rhythm and blues music should not be undervalued.

269. Sorrell, Richard S. "'My Life was Saved by Rock & Roll': Personal Reflections on the Age of Rock Music." *Popular Music and Society* 15, no. 1 (1991): 81-89.

Presents the author's personal history with rock music as defined by key events and performers (e.g., Elvis Presley, the Beatles, Bob Dylan, MTV) from the 1950s through the 1980s. Suggests that the current controversies surrounding 2 Live Crew mimic the controversies that surrounded Elvis Presley. Concludes that rock music keeps being re-invented by each new generation.

270. Starr, S. Frederick. "The Rock Inundation." *Wilson Quarterly* 7, no. 4 (1983): 58-67.

Provides a history of the development of rock music in the Soviet Union. Discusses the development in the 1960s of an underground commerce devoted to supplying electric guitars and amplifiers to the public. Notes that the combination of public demand and "ineffectual official opposition" led to a "complex and efficient organizational network" of entrepreneurs who financed, organized, and promoted rock music. Describes the events that created the government controlled rock music industry, resulting in a two-tiered system of official and unofficial rock performers.

271. Thorton, Sarah. "Strategies for Reconstructing the Popular Past." *Popular Music* 9, no. 1 (1990): 87-95.

Provides strategies for historians attempting to study rock music as popular culture: listing, personalizing, canonizing, and mediating. Lists four criteria for assigning historical significance to popular culture events: sales, biographical interest, acclaim, and media event. Applies these concepts to the study of disco music for illustrative purposes.

272. Von Meier, Kurt. "The Background and Beginnings of Rock and Roll." *Art International* 13, no. 8 (1969): 28-38.

Traces the early history of rock music from a detailed and well-footnoted perspective. Focuses on, but is not limited to, lyrical content as a self-documenting history, and the societal and musical confluences that resulted in a rock music culture. Includes a lengthy discography of rhythm and blues songs that influenced and shaped early rock music.

273. Welch, Richard. "Rock 'n' Roll and Social Change." *History Today* 40 (1990): 32-39.

Describes the birth of rock music in the 1950s as more than a musical phenomenon. It was also the trigger for sweeping social change, paving the way for desegregation, the mainstreaming of black musicians, and "social and political upheavals of the sixties." Begins by describing the 1950s adolescent as rejecting previous popular culture, evidenced in films such as *City Across the River*, *The Wild One*, and *Rebel Without a Cause*. Discusses Alan Freed, but moves quickly into a presentation of Sam Phillips' Sun Records. Concentrates on Sun Records' three biggest artists: Elvis Presley, Carl Perkins, and Jerry Lee Lewis. Claims that these artists personified "the very image of rock 'n roll itself" and were primarily responsible for the "injection of black musical influences" into mass culture.

274. West, Cornel. "On Afro-American Popular Music: From Bebop to Rap." *Black Sacred Music* 6, no. 1 (1992): 282-294.
Provides a history of black popular music in America, from bebop and jazz to soul and rap. Discusses the role and influence of Motown Records and its reflection of a stable, upwardly mobile black culture. Chronicles the mid-1970s rise of George Clinton and funk's expression of "blackness." Describes the uniqueness of Michael Jackson as the "musical dynamo of his generation." Observes that rap music is a "paradoxical cry of desperation and celebration of the black underclass."

275. Zion, Lawrence. "Disposable Icons: Pop Music in Australia, 1955-63." *Popular Music* 8, no. 2 (1989): 165-175.
Notes that rock music in Australia was largely the result of American influences. Rock music arrived in Australia from America as a packaged confluence of black and white musical styles for which no local equivalent existed. Explores the cultural barriers to rock music in Australia. Discusses the role of the music industry in constraining local talent. Observes that for Australians, being creative in early rock music was "like writing poetry in a foreign language."

CHAPTERS

276. Ashley, Stephen. "The Bulgarian Rock Scene Under Communism (1962-1990)." In *Rocking the State: Rock Music and Politics in Eastern Europe and Russia*, edited by Sabrina Petra Ramet, 141-163. Boulder: Westview Press, 1994.
Summarizes the history of rock music in Bulgaria. Observes that the cultural isolation of Bulgaria has resulted in rock music being viewed as a "foreign product to be copied and imitated but rarely to be created anew." Bulgarian rock musicians have not been able to create an independent culture or market due to the lack of technology and the strength of governmental opposition.

277. Barnes, Ken. "Top 40 Radio: A Fragment of the Imagination." In *Facing the Music: A Pantheon Guide to Popular Culture*, edited by Simon Frith, 8-50. New York: Pantheon Books, 1988.
Begins with a history of radio programming, starting in 1953 with the birth of the Top 40 format. Explains that advertisers discovered in the 1950s that adolescents "controlled the leisure-time choices of their entire families." By the mid-1960s, the LP developed as something more than a collection of

independent songs and, consequently, FM radio provided for the birth of Album-Oriented Rock (AOR) stations. Other station formats developed in the 1970s, such as Adult Contemporary and Disco. Offers a glossary of station formats, including AOR, classical, comedy, country, easy listening, jazz, new age, religious, sports, talk, and urban contemporary. Discusses the reasons for, and the benefits and disadvantages to, having so many different station formats. The major reason is marketing.

278.   Breen, Marcus. "Magpies, Lyrebirds and Emus: Record Labels, Ownership and Orientation." In *From Pop to Punk to Postmodernism: Popular Music and Australian Culture from the 1960s to the 1990s*, edited by Philip Hayward, 40-54. North Sydney, Australia: Allen & Unwin, 1992.
 Depicts the history of record companies in Australia and the conflict between major record companies and the independent labels. Comments on the struggle of the Australian music industry to maintain a national identity while competing in a global market.

279.   Frith, Simon. "The Industrialization of Popular Music." In *Popular Music and Communication*. 2nd ed., edited by James Lull, 49-74. Newbury Park, Calif.: Sage, 1992.
 Provides a historical context for understanding the dichotomy between music as expression and music as commodity. Traces in detail the development of the music and recording industries with a focus on the close ties between economic conditions and technological innovations. Includes a discussion on the impact of magnetic tape and the politics of technology.

280.   Frith, Simon. "Popular Music 1950-1980." In *Making Music: The Guide to Writing, Performing, And Recording*, edited by George Martin, 18-48. New York: Quill, 1983.
 Serves as an introduction to a book edited by George Martin on writing, performing, and recording music. Frith covers the full range of rock music's history, including rhythm and blues, the British invasion, folk rock, punk rock, the role of the guitar, the history of recording, and synthesizers. Concludes that rock music is a history of tensions between individual expression and the music industry, as well as between art and capitalism. Each chapter in the rest of the book is written by an established person from the music industry (e.g., musician, composer, engineer). The entire work is heavily illustrated.

281.   McClary, Susan. "Same As It Ever Was: Youth Culture and Music." In *Microphone Fiends: Youth Music & Youth Culture*, edited by Andrew Ross and Tricia Rose, 29-40. New York: Routledge, 1994.
 Traces the history of constraints against, and fears of, new youth music, starting with Plato. Contends that critics fail to realize that the means of manipulation in music resides in its ability to affect the body.

282. McGregor, Craig. "Growing Up (uncool): Pop Music and Youth Culture in the '50s and '60s." In *From Pop to Punk to Postmodernism: Popular Music and Australian Culture From the 1960s to the 1990s*, edited by Philip Hayward, 89-100. North Sydney, Australia: Allen & Unwin, 1992.

Remarks on the history of rock music in Australia and its relationship to the continent's youth culture. Discusses the conflict between adapting musical styles from Great Britain and the United States as opposed to establishing and maintaining a national identity through indigenous rock music. Describes the Australian surf music scene and the development of Australian country music.

283. Potts, John. "Heritage Rock: Pop Music on Australian Radio." In *From Pop to Punk to Postmodernism: Popular Music and Australian Culture from the 1960s to the 1990s*, edited by Philip Hayward, 55-67. North Sydney, Australia: Allen & Unwin, 1992.

Consists of a history of rock music on Australian radio. Discusses the notion of "heritage" rock music programming which is "a construction of rock history which creates a smooth lineage from the 1960s to the 1990s." Comments on the exclusive nature of heritage rock music that is often defined by the music of white male performers, thus not including punk, disco, heavy metal, funk, or rap music. Traces the relationship between Australian radio and rock music that has led to the popularity of heritage rock programming.

284. Stockbridge, Sally. "From Bandstand and Six O'Clock Rock to MTV and Rage: Rock Music on Australian Television." In *From Pop to Punk to Postmodernism: Popular Music and Australian Culture from the 1960s to the 1990s*, edited by Philip Hayward, 68-85. North Sydney, Australia: Allen & Unwin, 1992.

Recounts the history of rock music on Australian television. Comments on the Australian television shows *Countdown*, *Bandstand*, and *Rock Around the World*, among others. Discusses the influence of MTV. Pays particular attention to the "conventions and diversity in programming and attempts to make local interventions in spite of outside, mainly US domination."

285. White, Avron Levine. "Popular Music and the Law - Who Owns the Song?" In *Lost in Music: Culture, Style and the Musical Event*, edited by Avron Levine White, 164-189. London: Routledge & Kegan Paul, 1987.

Contends that copyright law as it relates to songwriting and recordings has "imposed considerable constraints on the working habits" of musicians. Discusses several legal cases related to the ownership and commercial control of popular music. Specifically dealing with rock music was the case of Clifford Davis Management Ltd and WEA Records regarding Fleetwood Mac. Clifford Davis sought to prevent the release of the Fleetwood Mac album *Heroes are Hard to Find* in Great Britain. Also reviews a case involving the Troggs in which the rock group attempted to switch management while under an existing management contract to Larry Page. Presents another case involving the Kinks and Larry Page. All cases presented illustrate attempts by management to ensure profit by controlling a musician's product. However, courts have been increasingly sympathetic to artists with regard to the extent that their "intellectual property can be taken in exchange for capital."

286.   Wicke, Peter. "The Role of Rock Music in the Political Disintegration of East Germany." In *Popular Music and Communication*. 2nd ed., edited by James Lull, 196-206. Newbury Park, Calif.: Sage, 1992.
   Describes how East German musicians helped prepare the political groundwork that eventually led to the fall of East Germany and reunification. Rock music was one of the few ways in which meaningful political discourse was able to occur. Outlines Erich Honecker's strategy to divide and censor the music community. Rather than dividing the community, the effect was to create a solidarity among musicians. Bemoans the fact that reunification has resulted in a "flood of commercial popular culture that has swept in from the west" and has ignored East German musicians. Includes the full text of the September 18, 1989, document outlining the musicians' positions on political and cultural matters.

BOOKS

287.   Aquila, Richard. *That Old Time Rock & Roll: A Chronicle of an Era, 1954-1963*. New York: Schirmer Books, 1989.
   Presents an overview of the first rock music era from 1954 to 1963. Organized into three major sections: Part One -- Rock & Roll's First Decade; Part Two -- Themes, Topics, and Hit Records; and Part Three -- The Performers, A to Z. Part One provides a history of rock music, reviews different rock styles, and attempts to place rock music of the era into a cultural context. Discusses the strong influence of rhythm and blues as well as how film and television served as catalysts in popularizing rock music. Provides an analysis which concludes that early rock music actually demonstrates that adolescents and their parents were more alike than different. Part Two consists mainly of lists of songs organized into themes (e.g., parties, love and courtship, surfing, teenage rebellion, religion, gender, ethnic and racial stereotypes, money). Part Three, the largest section, is an alphabetical encyclopedia of "virtually every performer. . . who made the charts between 1954 and 1963."

288.   Bane, Michael. *White Boy Singin' the Blues*. New York: Penguin Books, 1982.
   Establishes a history of black music and cultures that merged into, and influenced, rock music. Subtitled as "the black roots of white rock." Chapters include: Roots -- The African Connection, What Happened in Memphis, White Man's Blues, The Ubangi Stomp, Smiling Through The Sixties, Icons,

Bulldozing the Niggers, and The Reaction. Takes a broad, sweeping look at the history of contemporary music. Profiles the major performers. A detailed index provides immediate access to specific persons, groups, songs, and events.

289. Belsito, Peter, and Bob Davis. *Hardcore California: A History of Punk and New Wave.* Berkeley, Calif.: The Last Gasp of San Francisco, 1983.

Combines the visual with the written word to present a history of punk rock and new wave music in Los Angeles and San Francisco. Attempts to bring a chronological perspective to the events and the ever changing music scenes between 1977 and 1983. Includes several hundred photographs, mostly black and white.

290. Belz, Carl. *The Story of Rock.* 2nd ed. New York: Oxford University Press, 1972.

Emphasizes the history of rock music as an art form as opposed to a social or political forum. The first chapter introduces rock music as folk art. The second chapter starts by surveying musical styles that contributed to the formation of rock music. The specific contributions of Bill Haley and Elvis Presley are highlighted. Radio as a rock medium is explored, with special attention to Alan Freed. The third chapter follows the expansive nature of rock music as it evolves into sub-genres such as rockabilly and surf music and moves into the medium of television. Chapter four focuses on the British invasion, the impact of Bob Dylan, the revival of rhythm and blues, and the San Francisco scene. Finally, chapter five explores the commercialization of rock music. Includes as appendices a bibliographical essay and a selected discography.

291. Broven, John. *Rhythm and Blues in New Orleans.* Gretna, La.: Pelican, 1983.

Documents the musical traditions of New Orleans, Louisiana. Devotes one section to rock music in New Orleans between 1955 and 1959. Concentrates on the music of Little Richard and Fats Domino. Discusses the role and significance of record companies (e.g., Specialty Records, Chess Records) operating in New Orleans during this period. Reviews the impact of the small group of musicians that formed the "studio band." Also covers the clubs, promotions, disc jockeys, and musicians' union.

292. Brown, Charles T. *The Rock and Roll Story: From the Sounds of Rebellion to an American Art Form.* Englewood Cliffs, N.J.: Prentice-Hall, 1983.

Attempts to provide a "complete history of rock and roll." Begins by identifying and defining the various music genres that contributed to the rise of rock music, including black slave music, jazz (i.e., cakewalk, ragtime, stride, Dixieland, boogie-woogie), blues, and country music. Devotes early chapters to biographical and stylistic discussions of Bill Haley and Elvis Presley. Observes that the late 1950s and early 1960s was a transitional stage for rock music when the genre expanded and developed. Explains the 1960s in terms of the Beatles, the California sound, and acid rock. Comments on the influence of technological developments (e.g., amplifiers, microphones, synthesizers). Uses the Rolling Stones, The Who, and Elton John as examples of post-Beatles British rock music. Discusses the genre and performers of folk rock. Also touches on jazz-rock, funk, disco, punk, and new wave music. Contains numerous photographs of rock performers.

293. Budds, Michael J., and Marian M. Ohman, eds. *Rock Recall: Annotated Readings in American Popular Music from the Emergence of Rock and Roll to the Demise of the Woodstock Nation.* Needham Heights, Mass.: Ginn Press, 1993.

Compiles numerous writings about, and from, the first two decades of rock music. Emphasizes first-person accounts by rock performers and influential persons from behind the scenes. Attempts to present various "sources, styles, views, and topics." Arranged chronologically, chapters cover most of the significant historical figures and events from Bill Haley to Altamont. Organized to cover the 1950s, teen idols, Motown, folk rock, soul music, the British invasion, and psychedelic rock. Original sources range from book-length historical and biographical treatments to articles from *Rolling Stone* magazine, the *New York Times*, and *Variety*.

294. Burchill, Julie, and Tony Parsons. *'The Boy Looked at Johnny.' The Obituary of Rock and Roll.* Boston: Faber and Faber, 1987.

Observes and comments on the punk rock movement, primarily in Great Britain. Originally published in 1978, traces the history of punk music starting with Bob Dylan and California influences through the Sex Pistols' rise in England, ending with the Tom Robinson Band. Serves as a critical work of cynicism aimed at the entire rock music culture. Selected chapter titles include: Germs, Sex, Americans, Drugs, Girls, and Pearls and Scum.

295. Busnar, Gene. *It's Rock 'n' Roll.* New York: Julian Messner, 1979.

Focuses on the early history of rock music, from 1954 through 1963. Begins with an analysis of the 1950s revival that occurred in the early and mid-1970s. Contrasts the 1970s nostalgia with the actual rock music scene of the 1950s. Discusses various rock music styles and representative musicians: northern band music (e.g., Bill Haley), New Orleans (e.g., Fats Domino, Little Richard), rockabilly (e.g., Carl Perkins, Elvis Presley, Jerry Lee Lewis, Buddy Holly, Everly Brothers), Chicago (e.g., Chuck Berry, Bo Diddley), vocal group (e.g., Platters, Drifters, Coasters), female vocal groups (e.g., Shirelles), soul (e.g., Ray Charles, Sam Cooke). Takes each year and describes rock music in the context of other "major events," such as politics, the arts, television, sports, fads, and fashion. Concludes with an interview with Bobby Robinson, producer and songwriter of the era. Includes numerous discographies.

296. Chambers, Iain. *Urban Rhythms: Pop Music and Popular Culture.* New York: St. Martin's Press, 1985.

Organizes the chronology of rock music into "moments" of upheaval and reactionary cultural struggle, from a British perspective. Touches on the phenomenon of popular music acting as a bridge between the public and private self. Rock music is viewed as a catalyst for transforming popular culture "into an imaginative conquest of everyday life."

297. Chapple, Steve, and Reebee Garofalo. *Rock 'n' Roll is Here to Pay: The History and Politics of the Music Industry.* Chicago: Nelson-Hall, 1977.

Starts with the premise that rock music is the most important expression of culture and "source of entertainment and values." Notes that the music industry is intimately linked to the rest of corporate America. Contends that rock music cannot be understood only as an "aesthetic process." It must also be analyzed in terms of capitalism and as an industry of culture. Explores the economic and political power of the music industry. Begins with a chronological examination of the evolution of record companies and the radio industry, with a special focus on Warner-Reprise Records and RCA Records. Observes the expansion of the industry through agents, managers, promoters, and the press. Discusses the "political character of the music industry." Studies the interrelated "ownership patterns" of the industry and other components of corporate America. Probes the relationships of the music industry to black performers and to women performers. Contains several charts and graphs illustrating the successes and trends of the music industry.

298. Charlton, Katherine. *Rock Music Styles: A History.* 2nd ed. Madison, Wis.: Brown & Benchmark, 1994.

Serves as a textbook for teaching rock music history in college. Provides a chronological arrangement of rock music styles. Covers blues, country, and gospel influences. Each chapter is devoted to a rock music style, such as folk rock, the British invasion, psychedelic rock, funk, art rock, jazz rock, glitter rock, heavy metal, punk rock, reggae, rap, and alternative rock. Discusses important performers and analyzes numerous selected recordings in terms of tempo, form, features, and lyrics. A chronology chart ties historical rock music events to larger social and political activities of the era. Includes a glossary.

299. Cohn, Nik. *Rock: From the Beginning.* New York: Stein and Day, 1969.

Surveys the history of a broad array of genres existing within rock music at the end of the 1960s. Chapters include: The Beginning, Bill Haley, Elvis Presley, Classic Rock, Highschool, Eddie Cochran, P. J. Proby, Britain, American 1960+, The Twist, Spectorsound, California, Soul, The Beatles, The Rolling Stones, R&B England, Bob Dylan, Folk Rock, London 1964-65, The Monkees, Love, The Who, and Superpop. For most chapters, a performer is highlighted in order to launch a discussion into broader issues related to the specific genre. For example, "The Monkees" chapter begins by presenting a brief synopsis of The Monkees, but quickly turns into a discussion of the commercialization of rock music.

300. Curtis, Jim. *Rock Eras: Interpretations of Music and Society, 1954-1984*. Bowling Green, Ohio: Bowling Green State University Popular Press, 1987.
Utilizes Marshall McLuhan's work to organize the history of rock music into three eras, designated by the birth of rock and roll (1954-1964), the British invasion (1964-1974), and the disco era (1974-1984). Each era is subdivided into two parts, innovation and assimilation. Defines the first era in terms of media influence (especially radio) on the youth culture, ethnic origins of performers, secularization of black music, and the importance of the electric guitar, with emphasis on Chuck Berry and Buddy Holly. Uses New York City, Philadelphia, Detroit, and Southern California to illustrate the geographical influences on rock music. Stresses the political environment and the major performers during the second era, including the Beatles, Bob Dylan, the Rolling Stones, and Bruce Springsteen. Discusses the relationship forged by rock music between high culture and popular culture. Also explores the late 1960s counterculture politics of rock music, the early 1970s theatrical elements of rock, and the emergence of heavy metal music. Places disco and punk music in their social contexts of the third era. Concludes with an analysis of Michael Jackson as child/man, man/woman, good/evil, singer/dancer.

301. Dannen, Fredric. *Hit Men: Power Brokers and Fast Money Inside the Music Business*. New York: Times Books, 1990.
Provides a detailed inside view of the business aspects and power plays within the music industry. Focuses on the key personalities, including promoters and especially record company presidents such as Walter Yetnikoff, Clive Davis, David Geffin, Neil Bogart, and Irving Azoff. Attempts to demonstrate the process of using rock music as a commodity to create profit.

302. Dawson, Jim, and Steve Propes. *What Was the First Rock 'n' Roll Record?* Boston: Faber and Faber, 1992.
Presents fifty recordings as possible candidates for the title of "first rock 'n' roll recording." Includes information for each recording regarding chart position, music genre, observations as to why it may be an important recording, how it was influenced and what it influenced subsequently, and the story behind the recording.

303. DeCurtis, Anthony, James Henke, and Holly George-Warren, eds. *The Rolling Stone Illustrated History of Rock & Roll: The Definitive History of the Most Important Artists and Their Music*. 3rd ed. New York: Random House, 1992.
Updates significantly the previous editions with the inclusion of fifteen new

essays and the revision of many of the other essays. As with previous editions, essays are written by prominent rock music journalists (e.g., Anthony DeCurtis, Jonathan Cott, Greil Marcus, Dave Marsh, Ed Ward, Lester Bangs, Nik Cohn, Ken Tucker, Robert Christgau). In addition to chapters on specific musicians and performers, presents topical essays on major themes such as rockabilly music, the payola scandal, the British invasion, soul music, folk rock, the San Francisco sound, bubblegum music, heavy metal, art rock, funk, reggae, MTV, and rap music. Each chapter includes a discography and black and white photographs. Published as a coffee-table sized book.

304. Duncan, Robert. *The Noise: Notes From a Rock 'n' Roll Era.* New York: Ticknor & Fields, 1984.

Offers a rambling social commentary spanning the 1960s, the 1970s, and continuing into the early 1980s. Begins. . . "My father always blamed it on the rock 'n' roll. The drugs, the sex, the faithless wild boys and girls obeying no authority and bearing no responsibility, playing havoc with America in a mindless quest for the good time they believed was owed them by the world. My father's not stupid." The term "the noise" refers to the arrival and upheaval caused by another culture. Contends that the 1970s represented the arrival, not the rejection, of 1960s values. This book is about "a people's search for new values with which to confront the radically new circumstances of postwar technological life."

305. Eliot, Marc. *Rockonomics: The Money Behind the Music.* New York: Franklin Watts, 1989.

Provides an insight into the business of rock music as a commodity. Discusses the full history of the production, marketing, and consumption of rock music for the sake of profit. Emphasizes the songwriters, managers, lawyers, record company executives, and promoters. Comments on the payola scandals, royalty scams, contract negotiations, lawsuits, mergers among conglomerates, and other economic factors behind the production of culture.

306. Ennis, Philip H. *The Seventh Stream: The Emergence of Rocknroll in American Popular Music.* Hanover, N.H.: Wesleyan University Press, 1992.

Relates art, commerce, and politics as three realms in which power flows as follows: "art validates money, money regulates politics, and politics defines art." Contends that the history of rock music is tied to commercial struggles over the control of music. Demonstrates that rock music emerges as a "seventh stream" from six other musical genres: popular music, black music, country music, jazz, folk music, and gospel music. Discusses the impact of technological developments.

307. Escott, Colin, and Martin Hawkins. *Good Rockin' Tonight: Sun Records and the Birth of Rock 'n' Roll.* New York: St. Martin's Press, 1992.

Traces the history of Sun Records and the associated recording artists who "would redefine the musical genres in which they worked." Elvis Presley, Johnny Cash, Carl Perkins, Roy Orbison, and Jerry Lee Lewis are some of the artists that recorded for Sun Records' founder, Sam Phillips.

308. Ewen, David. *All the Years of American Popular Music.* Englewood Cliffs, N.J.: Prentice-Hall, 1977.

Surveys American popular music in its totality, from 1620 forward. Contends that popular music is a result of social and political voices and therefore attention is given to the social norms, customs, and politics of various eras. Part Six and Part Seven span the periods from 1950 to the present, covering such topics as the impact of radio, television records, the rock revolution of the 1950s, the rise of protest music, and the genres of acid rock and black music. In addition to focusing on numerous specific musicians, relevant topics are discussed as well. For example, sections of chapters deal with the payola scandals, the social climate of the 1950s, the British invasion, women's liberation, and black power. Chapter titles include *Rock Around the Clock, Rebels with a Cause, Black Power - and Soul,* and *Today's Troubadours: The Performing Composer.*

309. Gaar, Gillian G. *She's a Rebel: The History of Women in Rock & Roll.* Seattle: Seal Press, 1992.

Chronicles the contributions that women have made to rock music. Explores "the many roles women have played in the development of the rock industry, both onstage and off." Contends that women's roles in the rock music industry are often overlooked or downplayed in historical accounts because women are seen as "an 'other' that deviates from a male norm." Another factor is that success in rock music is typically measured in commercial, rather than artistic, terms. This is problematic because women are viewed as not having the same commercial potential as male artists and therefore are not given as many opportunities to be successful. Examines, for selected well-known performers, the experiences faced by these female artists being in a "unique" position, thus illustrating the lack of realization of an ongoing women's tradition in rock music. Introduction written by Yoko Ono.

310. Gillett, Charlie. *The Sound of the City: The Rise of Rock and Roll.* New York: Outerbridge & Dienstfrey, 1970.

Identifies "the circumstances that produced rock and roll" and examines the meaning of its existence. Traces the immediate success of rock music from when it first emerged, the music from which it emerged, and the music that has emerged from it. Offers that for African American culture, the history of rock music follows Talcott Parsons' description of a minority group's process of achieving social acceptance: exclusion, then assimilation, then inclusion. Pays attention to the geographical characteristics that shape the various facets of rock music.

311.   Goldman, Albert. *Sound Bites.* New York: Turtle Bay Books, 1992.

Collects over thirty of the author's previous writings on rock music covering more than twenty years. Observes in the introduction that there is an obsession among youth with the rock music and culture of the 1960s. Organizes the essays into time periods by subject, not necessarily in the chronological order of writing. Topics include Elvis Presley, the Beatles, the Doors, the rock opera *Tommy,* Jimi Hendrix, blues music, Albert King, soul music, the Apollo Theater, Aretha Franklin, the Rolling Stones, the Altamont concert, Randy Newman, Tiny Tim, disco, and Michael Jackson.

312.   Goldstein, Richard. *Goldstein's Greatest Hits: A Book Mostly About Rock 'n' Roll.* Englewood Cliffs, N.J.: Prentice-Hall, 1970.

Collects numerous articles written previously by the author between 1966 and 1968 for such publications as *The Village Voice,* and *New York Magazine.* Claims that the essays are "immediate impressions" designed to capture moments in rock music history. Organizes the essays into chapters centered around broad categories.

313.   Grossman, Loyd. *A Social History of Rock Music: From the Greasers to Glitter Rock.* New York: David McKay, 1976.

Views the history of rock music from the perspective of hedonism. Attempts to place rock music "in the social scheme of things." Organizes the history of rock music into five eras: Before the Flood (1954-1963), the Coming of the New Rock (1964-1966), The American Reaction (1965-1967), Rock at its Zenith (1967-1972), and New Thrills for the Jaded Generation (1972-1975). Discusses rock music in the context of the cold war. Focuses on the impact of the British invasion, especially on fashion. Devotes a chapter to the star system, women in rock, and the impact of technological developments.

314.   Guralnick, Peter. *Feel Like Going Home: Portraits in Blues & Rock 'n' Roll.* New York: Outerbridge & Dienstfrey, 1971.

Profiles selected blues musicians in an attempt to provide a historical progression of the genre. The first two chapters place the history of blues music, and rock music as its extension, into context. Claims that rock music died with the beginning of the Philadelphia sound and American Bandstand. Blues music offered an alternative that was authentic. Selected chapters include: *Rock 'n' Roll Music: Growing Up and Coming Down, Boppin' the Blues: Sam Phillips and the Sun Sound,* and *Jerry Lee Lewis: Hang Up My Rock 'n' Roll Shoes.*

315. Hamm, Charles. *Music in the New World.* New York: W. W. Norton, 1983.

Covers the entire history of music in the United States. Chapter 20 is *The Age of Rock* and deals in detail with the history of rock music. Begins the chapter with a discussion of rock music as "interracial" music. Includes analysis of the musical style of rock music and its various genres (e.g., folk rock, Motown sound, San Francisco sound, disco) as well as the social and economic ramifications of rock music's various manifestations across the decades. Notes the cyclical evolution of rock music from 1950s' popular music to 1960s' "serious" music and back to 1970s' popular music.

316. Hatch, David, and Stephen Millward. *From Blues to Rock: An Analytical History of Pop Music.* Manchester, England: Manchester University Press, 1987.

Applies the concept of sociomusicology to the history of popular music in the twentieth century. Presents the history as a comparative analysis of musical structures within the context of sociology, social psychology, and linguistics. Starts with "country blues" music and the "positive relationships between black and white musical traditions." Analyzes the birth of rock music as a sociomusical event involving country music and rhythm and blues. Focuses on the importance of blues music to the developing styles of rock music in the 1960s. Devotes attention to black music styles and white influences on music genre definitions. Traces the decline of rock music in the 1970s and its rebirth through punk music and new wave. Contains an appendix that concentrates on musical structures of mode, tonal prevalence, and tonal sequencing.

317. Henry, Tricia. *Break All Rules!: Punk Rock and the Making of a Style.* Ann Arbor: UMI Research Press, 1989.

Studies the evolution of punk music "style," starting with the underground music of Lou Reed and the Velvet Underground. Claims that the key elements were themes of pessimism and offensive lyrical topics. Deals with the impact of the Velvet Underground's association with Andy Warhol. Traces the progression to glitter rock as manifested in the works of such performers as David Bowie and the New York Dolls. Asserts that the "punk aesthetic" was a dialectical response to glitter rock. Concentrates on the New York City nightclub CBGB and highlights performers Patti Smith, the Ramones, and the Television as early punk influences. Explores Malcolm McLaren's involvement in transplanting the New York City underground music into Great Britain's punk movement via the Sex Pistols. Describes the fashions, dance, and behavior of punks, including a discussion about fanzines and their value as primary source material for studying the punk movement. Draws parallels between punk music and the avant-garde arts, observing that both are reactions against traditional techniques and against the society in which they are produced. Notes distinctions between the two as well. Contains an appendix of sheet music for selected punk rock songs.

318. Hibbard, Don J., and Carol Kaleialoha. *The Role of Rock.* Englewood Cliffs, N.J.: Prentice-Hall, 1983.

Looks at rock music as a social force influencing directly the lives of the audience. Studies the relationship of rock music to the larger society. Examines symbols of "associations, images, and myths." Asserts that early rock music presented a new view of the world that defied the status quo. Focuses primarily on the 1960s and asserts that the "musical spirit" of that time period still exerts an influence. Discusses protest music, drug songs, love songs, the Beatles, Bob Dylan, and the Rolling Stones. For the 1970s, notes the "revolution dissolution" with the evolution of soft rock, art rock, disco, punk music, and new wave. Includes a discography arranged by rock music genres (e.g., rockabilly, folk rock, soul, art rock).

319. Hopkins, Jerry. *The Rock Story.* New York: Signet, 1970.

Depicts the history of rock music from the viewpoint of a contemporary observer, rather than a historian. Traces rock music from its rhythm and blues and country music roots through the British invasion to the late 1960s psychedelic acid phase. Discusses the related issues on the commercial side of the business, the role of radio, and the rock musician as an idol.

320. Jackson, John A. *Big Beat Heat: Alan Freed and the Early Years of Rock & Roll.* New York: Schirmer Books, 1991.

Details the career of Alan Freed, from the Moondog Coronation to the payola scandals. Provides insight into the early years of rock music and the workings of the music industry.

321. Jahn, Mike. *Rock: From Elvis Presley to the Rolling Stones.* New York: Quadrangle, 1973.

Presents a history of rock music from Elvis Presley to the Rolling Stones (circa 1972). Provides an essentially chronological arrangement with each chapter representing a calendar year anchored on performers, as opposed to events. Limits inclusion to performers who contributed to advancing rock music. Concludes with a chapter discussing the social meaning of rock music.

322. Kelly, Michael Bryan. *The Beatle Myth: The British Invasion of American Popular Music, 1956-1969.* Jefferson, N.C.: McFarland, 1991.

Attempts to correct the historical record regarding the overall impact of the Beatles on popular culture. Contends that many rock music historians are revisionists who promote the Beatle myth.

323. Kent, Jeff. *The Rise and Fall of Rock.* Alsager, England: Witan Book, 1983.

Presents a history of rock music as written and self-published by the author. Offers a critical analysis of rock music. Describes rock as the "folk music of western youth." Claims that the musical achievements of many rock composers equal those of classical composers and have had greater impact on society. Covers the full range of rock music styles and influences from pre-rock jazz and big band to soul, folk rock, bubblegum music, heavy metal, punk rock, and new wave. References over 1,800 performers and 3,000 records. Written mainly from a British perspective.

324.   Kozak, Roman. *This Ain't no Disco: The Story of CBGB*. Boston: Faber and Faber, 1988.

Describes the history of the CBGB nightclub in New York City. CBGB was the focal point of punk rock and new wave music. Focuses on the numerous performers that were showcased, including Blondie, the Talking Heads, the Television, Patti Smith, the Ramones, the Dead Boys, and the Shirts.

325.   Laing, Dave. *The Sound of Our Time*. Chicago: Quadrangle Books, 1970.

Begins with a history of the development of popular music, from folk music to minstrel shows to ragtime to jazz to Tin Pan Alley. Mentions the concept of promoting music as a commodity. Discusses the evolution of rock music as popular music in the 1950s and notes the key performers responsible for this phenomenon (e.g., Elvis Presley, Bill Haley, Chuck Berry, Everly Brothers, Buddy Holly). Touches on the impact of rock music in Great Britain and the consequential rise of the Beatles. Also recounts the influence of blues music in Great Britain and the resulting popularity of the Rolling Stones and The Who. Devotes a chapter to Bob Dylan's contributions to popular music, especially in regard to the subject content of songs. Closes by considering Frank Zappa and the Mothers of Invention as an example of social commentary in popular music. Frames the book theoretically around the works of Theodor Adorno, Ian Birchall, Roland Barthes, and Marshall McLuhan.

326.   Laing, Dave, Karl Dallas, Robin Denselow, and Robert Shelton. *The Electric Muse: The Story of Folk into Rock.* London: Methuen, 1975.

Traces folk music's history and influence on rock music, especially the folk revival of the early 1960s. Claims that folk rock musicians (e.g., Bob Dylan, Paul Simon, Joni Mitchell, Jackson Browne) rescued folk music from stagnation and injected it into the popular mainstream. Notes that as a result, folk music has been transformed into folk rock. Observes that rock music was also transformed or expanded from the confines of "the Tin Pan Alley pop philosophy" by folk music. Examines the phenomenon of folk rock in the context of twentieth century American culture, but also traces its parallel development in Great Britain.

327.   Leigh, Spencer. *Let's Go Down the Cavern.* London: Vermilion, 1984.

Presents the chronological history of the Merseybeat sound as it developed in Liverpool, England during the late 1950s and early 1960s. Sheds light on numerous musical groups other than the Beatles, but also provides insight into the musical culture that gave birth to the Beatles.

328.   Lydon, Michael. *Rock Folk: Portraits from the Rock 'n' Roll Pantheon.* New York: Dial Press, 1971.

Profiles selected rock music performers. Offers more than standard biographical information by attempting to give the reader "a sense of what rock 'n' roll is and where it came from."

329.   Marcus, Greil. *Mystery Train: Images of America in Rock 'n' Roll Music.* New York: E. P. Dutton, 1975.

Attempts to deal with rock music "not as youth culture, or counter culture, but simply as American culture." Writes selectively about performers who are risk takers. Deals with the issue of musician and audience forming a community. States that the audience will interpret the work of the performer in unpredictable ways and this interpretation creates community. Observes that the performer must strike a balance between conforming to the audience's image and expectations and developing new work which might alienate the existing audience. Explores these issues by profiling representative "ancestors" (i.e., Harmonica Frank and Robert Johnson) and the "selected inheritors" (i.e., The Band, Sly Stone, Randy Newman, and Elvis Presley).

330.   Marcus, Greil. *Ranters & Crowd Pleasers: Punk in Pop Music, 1977-92.* New York: Doubleday, 1993.

Collects more than sixty essays on punk music written by the author between 1977 and 1992. Claims to have "tried, in the moment, to write about what scared me, disgusted me, made me and so many other people feel privileged to be present when, in some nightclub now long gone, rumor turned to fact." Chapters are arranged chronologically.

331.   Marsh, Dave. *Louie Louie: The History and Mythology of the World's Most Famous Rock 'n' Roll Song; Including the Full Details of Its Tortured and Persecution at the Hands of the Kingsmen, J. Edgar Hoover's F.B.I., and a Cast of Millions; and Introducing, for the First Time Anywhere, the Actual Dirty Lyrics.* New York: Hyperion, 1993.

Approaches the history of the song *Louie Louie* as symbolizing the history of rock music. Contends that by exploring the meaning and context of *Louie Louie* one can address questions regarding the "high appeal of low art" and the meaning of contemporary culture. Claims that the song is a transcendent object. Asserts that the meaning of the song is dependent upon the person listening to it.

332.   Martin, Linda, and Kerry Segrave. *Anti-Rock: The Opposition to Rock 'n' Roll.* Hamden, Conn.: Archon Books, 1988.

Recounts the history of rock music censorship from 1953 to 1986. Organizes the discussion into three time periods: 1953-1962, 1963-1973, and 1974-1986.

Touches on all of the relevant issues, such as delinquency, explicit lyrics, Alan Freed and the payola scandals, fear of Communism, the drug culture, the loudness, satanism, the punk rock movement, the visual imagery of MTV, the Parents Music Resource Center (PMRC), sexual imagery, and vulgarity. Includes an extensive bibliography.

333.   McDonough, Jack. *San Francisco Rock: The Illustrated History of San Francisco Rock Music.* San Francisco: Chronicle Books, 1985.

Organizes the history of the San Francisco sound into three major sections. The first section, The Sounds of Flowers, presents a historical overview of the late 1960s music scene in the Haight-Ashbury. The second section, Lights of the City, focuses on the non-musician personalities that help establish the environment, such as Bill Graham, David Rubinson, and the psychedelic poster artists (with several color plates of rock poster art). Also includes in this section a discussion of the San Francisco recording studios, record companies, concert halls, and nightclubs. The final section, Anthems of the Sun, profiles numerous individual performers and music groups associated with San Francisco. Publication is well illustrated with both color and black and white photographs. Forward by Paul Kantner.

334.   Miller, Jim, ed. *The Rolling Stone Illustrated History of Rock & Roll.* New York: Rolling Stone Press, 1976.

Presents over seventy essays written by prominent authors and journalists (e.g., Robert Palmer, Jonathan Cott, Greil Marcus, Dave Marsh, Ed Ward, Robert Christgau, Nik Cohn, Peter Guralnick, Lester Bangs). In addition to chapters on specific musicians and performers, contains topical essays on major themes such as rockabilly, the payola scandal, the British invasion, soul music, the Motown sound, the San Francisco sound, folk rock, rock festivals, heavy metal, and rock films. Each chapter includes a discography and is well illustrated with black and white photographs. Published as a coffee-table sized book.

335.   Palmer, Robert. *A Tale of Two Cities: Memphis Rock and New Orleans Roll.* Brooklyn: Institute for Studies in American Music, Department of Music, School of Performing Arts, Brooklyn College, City University of New York, 1979.

Focuses on the contributions of Memphis and New Orleans to the development of rock music. Reinforces the importance of geographical factors on the early evolution of rock music. Highlights the New Orleans jazz and rhythm and blues musicians (e.g., Fats Domino, Professor Longhair) and their styles. Concentrates on the Memphis contributions of Sam Phillips' Sun Records and Elvis Presley, along with Carl Perkins and Jerry Lee Lewis. Concludes that New Orleans gave rock music a musical style while Memphis provided performers with "spark."

HISTORY

336. Paraire, Philippe. *50 Years of Rock Music.* Edinburgh: Chambers, 1992.

Designed as a compact encyclopedia, this work consists mainly of 200 entries for musicians who have significantly contributed to the history of rock music. Arranged into five chronological sections, followed by a section devoted to black music. Each section begins with an essay discussing the major musical styles of the time. Concludes with a chapter on rock music in motion pictures.

337. Pattison, Robert. *The Triumph of Vulgarity: Rock Music in the Mirror of Romanticism.* New York: Oxford University Press, 1987.

Studies rock music as an element of "contemporary vulgarity" (popular culture) in an attempt to describe "the convergence of elite and mass cultures in our age." Argues that we live in a homogeneous society shared by similar elite and popular cultures, that romantic pantheism promotes vulgarity, and that the American democracy breeds romantic pantheism. Notes that rock music is appealing because it is vulgar and, therefore, one must defend vulgarity to justify an appreciation of rock music. Rock music glorifies youth while celebrating the self and universe through "the vulgar mode of feeling." Just as jazz replaced ragtime and rock replaced jazz, rock music will be replaced by increasingly vulgar music. Defends the notion that rock music lyrics are important, not incidental as many claim, by pointing out the rarity of instrumental rock songs. Notes that rock music lyrics provide an ideological consistency.

338. Pichaske, David. *A Generation in Motion: Popular Music and Culture in the Sixties.* New York: Schirmer Books, 1979.

Promotes the image of motion in describing the American culture of the 1960s. Contends that rock music is the "most accurate reflection of the generation in motion." Anchors the decade in its historical roots of the 1950s. Discusses the protest movement as articulated in folk rock music. Explores the concept of alternative lifestyles (e.g., drugs, hippies, black power). Devotes some attention to the transformation of rock music into art.

339. Pleasants, Henry. *Serious Music - and All That Jazz!: An Adventure in Music Criticism.* New York: Simon and Schuster, 1969.

Refers to ragtime, jazz, swing, bop, rhythm and blues, country and western, pop, and rock music as "a succession of Afro-American styles" in order to cast these genres as an "ideomatic phenomenon" in the evolution of Western music. The chapter *Rock and Pop* deals specifically with rock music. Reproduces the history of rock music in terms of its blend of rural black and rural white music elements, specifically rhythm and blues and country music. Discusses the evolutionary process of creating rock music as "appropriation-revitalization" in which white musicians appropriate elements of black music to create something new.

340. Pollock, Bruce. *Hipper than Our Kids: A Rock & Roll Journal of the Baby Boom Generation.* New York: Schirmer Books, 1993.

Contends that the first generation raised on rock music, the baby boomers, is hipper than previous and subsequent generations. Presents a free-wheeling tour of the history of rock music, questioning the place of "traditional" rock music in contemporary society and among aging baby boomers.

341. Pollock, Bruce. *When the Music Mattered: Rock in the 1960s.* New York: Holt, Rinehart and Winston, 1984.

Highlights selected musicians who represent a collective view of the 1960s from a unique vantage point. Argues that the 1960s was a period of contradictions and confrontations and that the intensity of the era "gave the music an added intensity." Each chapter profiles one or two musicians. Examples of chapters include: *The Urban Folk Scare* (Dave Von Ronk), *The Suburban Midcentury White Young America Blues* (Paul Simon, Roger McGuinn), *The Big Rock Candy Mountain* (Peter Tork), and *By The Time I Got To Woodstock* (John Sebastian).

342. Redd, Lawrence N. *Rock is Rhythm and Blues: The Impact of Mass Media.* East Lansing: Michigan State University Press, 1974.

Asserts that rhythm and blues music and rock music are the same music genre. Claims that mass media prevented the African American culture from receiving recognition for its musical contribution to popular American culture. Observes that mass media created and promoted a "false dichotomy." Discusses the cooption of rhythm and blues music through the radio (e.g., Alan Freed), cinema (e.g., *Blackboard Jungle*, *Rock Around the Clock*), and television (e.g., Elvis Presley). Includes interviews with B. B. King, Brownie McGhee, Dave Clark, Arthur Crudup, Jerry Butler, and Jessie Whitaker.

343. Reid, Jan. *The Improbable Rise of Redneck Rock.* Austin: Heidelberg, 1974.

Documents the emergent Austin, Texas music scene of the late 1960s and early 1970s. Mentions numerous musicians who contributed to the genre that the author labels "redneck rock."

344. Sander, Ellen. *Trips: Rock Life in the Sixties.* New York: Charles Scribner's Sons, 1973.

Attempts to capture the spirit of 1960s' rock music through personal anecdotes of prominent performers, including David Crosby, Cass Elliot, and Roger McGuinn. Includes a rock music taxonomy.

345. Savage, Jon. *England's Dreaming: Anarchy, Sex Pistols, Punk Rock, and Beyond.* New York: St. Martin's Press, 1992.

Chronicles in detail the rise of the punk rock movement in Great Britain. Concentrates on the Sex Pistols and the social, political, aesthetical, and cultural climate in which they evolved.

346. Schaffner, Nicholas. *The British Invasion: From the First Wave to the New Wave.* New York: McGraw-Hill, 1983.

Documents the history of the British rock music scene, beginning with the 1960s British invasion. Devotes entire chapters to the Beatles, the Rolling Stones, the Kinks, The Who, Pink Floyd, T. Rex, and David Bowie. Includes shorter profiles of 100 other British performers and musicians. Contains a list of all the U.S. Top 20 singles released by British artists from 1964 to 1980. Includes a chronology and a bibliography.

347. Sculatti, Gene, and Davin Seay. *San Francisco Nights: The Psychedelic Music Trip, 1965-1968.* New York: St. Martin's Press, 1985.

Provides a history of the San Francisco sound of the 1960s. Claims that the psychedelic rock movement, centered in San Francisco, resulted in greater artistic freedom for musicians. Attempts to present the spirit of the times while noting the major aesthetic and sociological influences. Mentions all of the major performers (e.g., Janis Joplin, Jefferson Airplane, Grateful Dead, Quicksilver Messenger Service) and touches on the international impact of the scene.

348. Selvin, Joel. *Summer of Love; The Inside Story of LSD, Rock & Roll, Free Love, and High Times in the Wild West.* New York: Dutton, 1994.

Chronicles the era of San Francisco's "Summer of Love" (1967) as it developed and withered, from 1965 to 1971. Provides a history of the Haight-Ashbury hippie movement. Focuses heavily on the rock musicians who were the primary players in establishing the San Francisco scene. Includes annotated lists of the rock groups and individuals who were key figures.

349. Shaw, Arnold. *Black Popular Music in America: From the Spirituals, Minstrels, and Ragtime to Soul, Disco, and Hip-Hop.* New York: Schirmer, 1986.

Offers a detailed history of black music. Includes a chapter dedicated to rhythm and blues and the rise of rock music through the "white synthesis" in the forms of cover recordings, rockabilly, British blues music, and surf music adaptations. Another chapter traces the evolution of soul music from gospel to the Memphis sound and to Motown. Devotes other sections to disco, funk, reggae, and rap music. Provides in each instance a description of the "white synthesis" which explains how black music was adopted or coopted to form another style.

350.   Shaw, Arnold. *The Rockin' '50s.* New York: Hawthorn Books, 1974.

Provides an extensive history of rock and popular music in the 1950s. Attempts to correct 1950s revivalists' images of the early rock years as bland, fun, and innocent. Frames the essays around the struggle to create a uniquely defined youth culture while facing resistance with "bans, arrests, lawsuits, not to mention actual physical destruction of recordings." Organizes the discussion into three sections: 1) Death of an Era Tin Pan Alley 1950-1953, 2) Upheaval in Pop 1954-1955, and 3) The Rock 'n' Roll Years 1956-1960. Includes interviews with selected personalities of the era. Concludes with a chapter devoted to the payola scandals.

351.   Stambler, Irwin. *Encyclopedia of Pop, Rock and Soul.* Revised ed. New York: St. Martin's Press, 1989.

Contains biographical information for most major rock music performers from Abba to the Zombies. Appendices include lists of the Recording Industry Association of America's gold and platinum record awards (1958-1988), the National Academy of Recording Arts and Sciences Grammy awards in selected categories, and the Academy of Motion Pictures Arts and Sciences nominations and awards (1958-1987). Also includes a bibliography.

352.   Szatmary, David P. *Rockin' in Time: A Social History of Rock and Roll.* 2nd ed. Englewood Cliffs, N.J.: Prentice-Hall, 1991.

Explores the social history of rock music. Places rock music in the context of influencing, and being influenced by, "major social transformations of the last forty years." Focuses on the significance of African American contributions, demographic and economic conditions (e.g., baby-boomers), technological advances (from the electric guitar to compact discs), and the growth of mass media. Examines the continuing theme of rebellion in rock music as it changed shape over the decades. Discusses the blues music influences of the early years and associated racism. Presents essays on Elvis Presley and the rockabilly sound, Dick Clark, payola, Don Kirshner, teen idols, girl groups, the California sound, Bob Dylan and the folk movement, the British invasion, the Motown sound, acid rock, soul music, protest music, heavy metal, disco, corporate rock, punk rock, the rise of music videos and MTV, Bruce Springsteen, and rap music.

353.   Taylor, Derek. *It was Twenty Years Ago Today.* New York: Simon and Schuster, 1987.

Chronicles the year 1967 in the framework of music, dominated by the Beatles' album *Sgt. Pepper's Lonely Hearts Club Band* and the Monterey International Pop Festival.

HISTORY

354. Tosches, Nick. *Unsung Heros of Rock 'n' Roll.* New York: Charles Scribner's Sons, 1984.

Profiles numerous lesser known musicians that contributed to the early development of rock music. Traces the emergence of rock music to the middle of World War II. Devotes each chapter to a single performer or group. Organizes the chapters in loose chronological order. Includes a detailed chronology from 1945 through 1955. Also includes discographies for the artists covered.

355. Troitsky, Artemy. *Back in the USSR: The True Story of Rock in Russia.* Boston: Faber and Faber, 1988.

Analyzes the Soviet Union's unfolding social revolution in terms of the history and development of Soviet rock music. Observes that under perestroika, noticeably few rock musicians attempt to test glasnost. Author claims to have not personally missed "a single important event or interesting character" related to Soviet rock music. Includes lists of selected recordings and films.

356. Trow, Michael-Arthur. *The Pulse of '64: The Mersey Beat.* New York: Vantage Press, 1979.

Presents a brief history of British rock music in the 1960s. Begins with the development of the Merseybeat sound in Liverpool, England.

357. Vassal, Jacques. *Electric Children: Roots and Branches of Modern Folkrock.* New York: Taplinger, 1976.

Concentrates on the folk rock movement and performers of the 1960s. Traces the origins of the folk movement through various ethnic groups. Singles out the influence of Woody Guthrie in creating the "urban folk revival." Devotes much attention to the musical career of Bob Dylan and those who followed in his footsteps. Organizes into two categories, America and Great Britain, discussions about the folk rock artists who emerged as a result of Dylan's success.

358. Ward, Ed, Geoffrey Stokes, and Ken Tucker. *Rock of Ages: The Rolling Stone History of Rock & Roll.* New York: Rolling Stone Press, 1986.

Divides an extremely detailed history of rock music into three eras: 1) the 1950s and before, 2) the 1960s, and 3) the 1970s and beyond. Each author tackles one era. Covers extensively the history of rock music in terms of its existence as music, culture, business, and mass media. Concentrates on the adaptability of rock music and its ability to survive events such as the payola scandals, the Altamont concert, and censorship attacks. Selected chapters focus on the counterculture, rock festivals, glitter rock, disco music, reggae, punk, and music videos.

359. Wenner, Jann S., ed. *20 Years of Rolling Stone: What a Long, Strange Trip It's Been.* New York: Friendly Press, 1987.

Presents selected articles originally published in *Rolling Stone* during the magazine's first twenty years. Attempts to provide an "impressionistic chronology" suggesting a social and political history of a rock music generation. The thirty-three articles range in topics from Haight-Ashbury to Woodstock to Kent State to the Sex Pistols to John Lennon's death to Michael Jackson.

360. Whitcomb, Ian. *After the Ball.* New York: Proscenium, 1986.

Recounts the history of popular music from ragtime to rock music. Describes the author's brush with rock stardom in a chapter titled *How I Became a Rock 'n' Roll Star.*

361. Whitcomb, Ian. *Rock Odyssey: A Musician's Chronicle of the Sixties.* Garden City, N.Y.: Dolphin, 1983.

Describes the author's brief experience as a rock star during the 1960s. Presents his personal history in relation to, and through, the history of rock music. Covers the full spectrum of 1960s rock music, from the British invasion through Woodstock.

DISSERTATIONS

362. Henry, Lucy Patricia. "Punk Rock: The Evolution of a Style." Ph.D. New York University, 1988. *Dissertation Abstracts International* 49: 2014A.

Locates the origins of punk rock music within the mid-1960s underground music of New York City. Traces the history of punk through the glitter rock movement of the early 1970s to "classic punk style in England between 1975 and 1979." Examines the music, style, performance, and philosophy of the genre. Includes such primary material as sheet music, lyrics, photographs, posters, and fanzines.

363. Pilskaln, Robert Joseph. "The Major Market Radio Station as a Component in the Political Economy of Rock and Roll." Ph.D. Case Western Reserve University, 1983. *Dissertation Abstracts International* 44: 2599B.

Analyzes the history of programming at five radio stations over a period of thirty-two years (1950-1982). Recounts the stations' influences on the marketing of rock music. Traces market developments, politics, and developments in the music industry as significant factors related to radio programming.

364. Worsley, John Ashton. "The Newport Jazz Festival: A Clash of Cultures." Ph.D. Clark University, 1981. *Dissertation Abstracts International* 42: 1287A.
   Contends that the history of the Newport Jazz Festival represents a microcosm of the "clash of cultures" during the 1950s and 1960s. One example of this clash was the 1958 performance by Chuck Berry which drew a younger crowd and protested the older middle-class jazz culture. Another example was the 1969 inclusion of rock music to again attract a larger younger audience, which resulted in violent confrontations. The Newport Jazz Festival "demonstrated clearly the cultural connections between traditional jazz music and middle class values and attitudes."

FILMS AND VIDEOS

365.   *History of Rock.* New York: Merit Audio Visual, 1988.
   Serves as a video history of rock music from the early rhythm and blues influences up through the late 1970s' punk and new wave era.

366.   *Rock and Roll: The Early Days.* Patrick Montgomery and Pamela Page, dirs. Archive Film Productions, 1984.
   Traces the early development of rock music as a fusion between rhythm and blues and country music.

Literature and the Arts

ARTICLES

367. Allan, Blaine. "My Springsteen Decade." *Queen's Quarterly* 93, no. 3 (1986): 558-580.
Surveys in detail the entire catalog of Bruce Springsteen's first seven albums: *Greetings from Asbury Park, N.J.*, *The Wild, the Innocent, and the E Street Shuffle*, *Born to Run*, *Darkness on the Edge of Town*, *The River*, *Nebraska*, and *Born in the U.S.A.* Asserts that Springsteen's work is an affirmation that rock music has not exhausted its possibilities. Notes that Springsteen's compositions explore working-class cultural icons (e.g., the automobile, factories). Springsteen writes songs about "people on the margin of US society."

368. Baker-White, Robert. "Crowds, Audiences, and the 'Liturgy of Irreverence': Rethinking the Altamont Concert as Participatory Theatre." *Studies in Popular Culture* 14, no. 2 (1992): 37-49.
Asserts that rock concerts represent situations in which audiences attempt to bring themselves closer to "theatrical authenticity." Considers the Altamont concert in terms of audience "participation, distance, and freedom." Discusses the rhetoric of Mick Jagger once violence erupted in the audience. Claims that the confrontation between the performers' stagecraft and the mindset of the audience at Altamont was a unique experience in participatory theater. Questions the extent to which rock music as participatory theater is liberating or constraining.

369. Bodinger-deUriarte, Cristina. "Opposition to Hegemony in the Music of Devo: A Simple Matter of Remembering." *Journal of Popular Culture* 18, no. 4 (1985): 57-71.
Examines the music of Devo. Focuses on the philosophy of socialized people and the ability of art to counter elements of socialization. Presents Devo's work as a "microcosm of collective consciousness." Art depicts the preoccupations of society and, therefore, has the ability for "radical change through the stimulation

of thought." Devo's music and presentation is designed to challenge current thinking and offer possible alternatives. Acknowledging a resistance to change, members of Devo believe that music works subliminally and cannot be entirely discounted or ignored. Regardless of audience receptivity, messages are absorbed and confronted. Argues that Devo's music can be a powerful motivating art form, designed to overwhelm satisfaction with the status quo.

370. Branscomb, H. Eric. "Literacy and a Popular Medium: The Lyrics of Bruce Springsteen." *Journal of Popular Culture* 27, no. 1 (1993): 29-42.

Stresses that Bruce Springsteen uses his albums, starting with *The River* and continuing through *Nebraska, Born in the U.S.A.*, and *Tunnel of Love*, as coherent arrays of "verbal statements and images" centered on a single concept, with each song serving as a chapter, and each album as a book. Contends that Springsteen is the "single most influential purveyor of literacy" in a typically non-literate culture. Notes that the sequencing of narrative segments into a hierarchy is a defining characteristic of literacy. Discusses the problems of centrality in a linear narrative, such as sequencing songs on an album so that the central idea is conveyed most effectively. Introduces the concept of anchor songs which serve to promote the central themes of a rock album. Examines each of the above Springsteen albums in order to identify the anchor songs and explain how they function. Explores the central themes of each album (e.g., *Nebraska* focuses on the "evil underbelly of American life and the resulting moral confusion"). Concludes that Springsteen uses language and music to communicate a vision.

371. Brinkmeyer, Robert H., Jr. "Never Stop Rocking: Bobbie Ann Mason and Rock-and-Roll." *Mississippi Quarterly* 42, no. 1 (1988/89): 5-17.

Remarks on the fictional works of author Bobbie Ann Mason. Notes that rock music "is everywhere in her fiction." Comments on a number of Mason's works to illustrate that she views her work as cultural expression in the same manner that rock music represents a form of cultural expression. Mason thinks that the primary purpose of her fiction is the same as that of rock music, to voice feelings that individuals are not always able to express. Fiction and rock music provide the audience with an understanding outside of their own. From that perspective, both are liberating. Mason uses rock music in her fiction as a "touchstone of characters' feelings about confronting the world." Rock music from the 1960s and early 1970s represents the concept of vision and is used by Mason to provide her characters with a catalyst of change.

372. Buchloh, Benjamin H. D. "From Gadget Video to Agit Video: Some Notes on Four Recent Video Works." *Art Journal* 45, no. 3 (1985): 217-227.

Analyzes the dramatic changes in the use of video technology as an art form from the 1960s to the present. Focuses on several projects, particularly Dan Graham's video "Rock My Religion" which explores the historical relationship between religion and rock music. Criticizes the videotape for ignoring the black working-class whose musicians created the foundation of rock music. Praises the videotape for presenting mass culture "from a high-cultural vantage point that is radically different from the traditional attitude of appropriation and quotation."

373.   Cameron, Dan. "The Lost Pop Artists." *Arts Magazine* 61 (1986): 86-89.
Comments on the special relationship between rock music and art. Contends that novelty record musicians of the 1950s and 1960s illustrate that the performer of pop music is not an artist, but an artwork. Observes that this notion is also reflected in contemporary performers such as Madonna.

374.   Camp, Charles. "Bad Blood: The Afterlife of Elvis Presley." *Appalachian Journal* 10, no. 1 (1982): 71-76.
Raises questions regarding the treatment of Elvis Presley and Southern culture in Albert Goldman's book *Elvis*. Discusses the enormous and continuing presence of Elvis Presley in contemporary popular culture. Goldman's book is viewed as an attack on the mythology of Elvis, yet ironically serves as testament "to the degree to which his life and work came to represent those aspects of American culture which are most basic, expressive, and eternal."

375.   Chenoweth, Lawrence. "The Rhetoric of Hope and Despair: A Study of the Jimi Hendrix Experience and the Jefferson Airplane." *American Quarterly* 23 (1971): 25-45.
Utilizes the lyrics of Jimi Hendrix and Jefferson Airplane in order to understand the rhetoric of "social withdraw or revolution." Defines rock music rhetoric as that which is "communicated not only through their lyrics but also their musical styles, album covers and stage presence." Labels the rhetoric as a mixture of hope and despair. States that although the specific messages in the recordings of Jimi Hendrix and Jefferson Airplane differ, both sets were "far more similar than different in their attitudes toward society, self-descriptions and goals." Concludes that their lyrics were ambivalent and contradictory, mainly due to paradoxes of cultural myths and social realities.

376.   Conrad, Robert C. "Bertolt Brecht's Dramatic Theories and Their Relationship to Rock Music: Another View." *University of Dayton Review* 7, no. 3 (1971): 103-110.
Counters an article by Douglas Milburn, Jr. that associates Brecht's epic theater with contemporary rock concerts. Argues that the audience response at rock concerts is emotional and primitive, not scientific and objective.

377. DeCurtis, Anthony. "The Product: Bucky Wunderlick, Rock 'n Roll, and Don DeLillo's *Great Jones Street*." *South Atlantic Quarterly* 89, no. 2 (1990): 369-379.

Discusses the novel *Great Jones Street* by Don DeLillo. Focuses on the nature of the main character, Bucky Wunderlick, a rock musician. Observes that a central theme in the book is the relationship of the main character to his audience. Notes that an important aspect in the novel is the notion that artists are objects of consumption. *Great Jones Street* portrays a society in which everyone and everything "is consumed or consumes itself" through "murder or suicide, exploitation or self-destruction."

378. Denisoff, R. Serge. "The 'Misadventures' of a Rock Film: Eddie and the Cruisers." *Popular Music and Society* 12, no. 3 (1988): 39-56.

Presents the history of the making of the rock film *Eddie and the Cruisers*. Focuses on the influences of the Asbury Park, New Jersey music scene and specifically Bruce Springsteen.

379. Dery, Mark. "Signposts on the Road to Nowhere: Laurie Anderson's Crisis of Meaning." *South Atlantic Quarterly* 90, no. 4 (1991): 785-801.

Reproduces an interview with Laurie Anderson which centers on the crisis of meaning in which traditional models of explanation seem to fail. Focuses on Anderson's *Empty Places* multimedia performance art piece. Also published in the book *Present Tense* edited by Anthony DeCurtis.

380. Doughty, Howard A. "Rock: A Nascent Protean Form." *Popular Music and Society* 2, no. 2 (1973): 155-165.

Attempts to show that rock music is not a tool of the 1960s counterculture. Rather, it is an aesthetic form. Argues that rock music is a Protean form in which the "disposability of artifacts, standards and ideals is not a threat but an assumption." Rock music will endure as a result of regression and progress, not as a logical function but through alteration and mutation.

381. Douglas, Ann. "Bruce Springsteen and Narrative Rock: The Art of Extended Urgency." *Dissent* 32, no. 4 (1985): 485-489.

Approaches the musical works of Bruce Springsteen as a narrative of American culture, evoking rock music's past while validating its future. Contends that the narrative, more so than the music, matters most to Springsteen. Argues that Springsteen's artistic output is aimed at America's "drive toward grotesquely commercial and heartbreakingly spiritual autobiography, its often frustrated impulse toward a complete account, the story of the neglected as well as the celebrated." Compares Springsteen to such writers as Kerouac. Claims that Springsteen's greatness lies within his understanding of the paradox of rock music and popular culture: "the quick but repeatable satisfaction of deep needs by expendable means."

382. Duxbury, Janell R. "Shakespeare Meets the Backbeat: Literary Allusion in Rock Music." *Popular Music and Society* 12, no. 3 (1988): 19-23.

Itemizes numerous accounts of literary allusions and quotes incorporated into rock music. Includes allusions to literary authors, novel titles, characters from novels, short story titles, drama titles, and poetry titles. Lists examples of direct literary quotes used in rock music lyrics. Also includes examples of rock concept albums and rock music videos. Speculates that the use of literary allusions and quotes may function in the same manner as musical "hooks" commonly found in rock music, to draw the attention of the audience "with a point of familiarity." Literary allusions may also lend respectability to rock music as a serious art form.

383. Evans, Paul. "Los Angeles, 1999." *South Atlantic Quarterly* 90, no. 4 (1991): 819-831.

Presents a work of fiction about rock music set in Los Angeles, California in 1999. Also published in the book *Present Tense* edited by Anthony DeCurtis.

384. Fransson, R. M. "Ovid Rox." *Classical Journal* 86 (1990/91): 176-182.

Compares three works by Ovid to selected contemporary rock music. Draws parallels between Ovid's "intoxication with Love" in *Amores* and Roxy Music's *Love is the Drug*. Claims that Paul Simon's *Fifty Ways to Leave Your Lover* resembles Ovid's *Remedia Amoris*. Notes that the song *The Fountain of Salmacis* by Genesis is derived from Ovid's *Metamorphoses*.

385. Gracyk, Theodore. "Romanticizing Rock Music." *Journal of Aesthetic Education* 27, no. 2 (1993): 43-58.

Criticizes those who contend that rock music is high art within the aesthetics of Romanticism and as such should be treated in the same fashion. Attacks Camille Paglia for asserting that rock musicians be treated as serious artists. Deconstructs each element of Paglia's argument, noting that the rebellion of rock's early heroes was simply adolescent in nature and had the plain goals of fame and fortune. Suspects that rock music created by a group of elite, sponsored musicians would not connect with the masses. Contends that rap lyrics have vitality "because they aren't composed by college students who have immersed themselves in great literature." Concludes that elitism has no place in popular culture and that Romanticism is not an appropriate model for appreciating rock music.

386. Grant, Barry K. "The Classic Hollywood Musical and the 'Problem' of Rock 'n' Roll." *Journal of Popular Film and Television* 13, no. 4 (1986): 195-205.

Raises the need for film genre criticism to be more closely tied to contemporary events. Remarks that without a knowledge of how mass media interact with the cinema, understanding of "film genres will remain artificially detached from the culture in which they thrive." Illustrates this point by examining the association between film musicals and rock music. Looks at the way in which rock music was at first antithetical to the film musical genre, but then quickly adapted. Notes the sudden decline in popularity of the musical during the mid-1950s and explains it in terms of relevance to movie goers. Offers that two strategies were adopted to fit rock music into the film musical genre: 1) utilizing themes of community, and 2) molding the images of rock stars (e.g., Elvis Presley). Makes references to numerous specific rock musicals.

387.   Green, Archie. "Kerry Awn's Soap Creek Saloon Calendars." *JEMF Quarterly* 16, no. 57 (1980): 24-35.

Attempts to bring attention to the musical genre of "country rock" as embodied in the musical culture of Austin, Texas. Uses the personal history and artwork of Kerry Awn to symbolize the local culture.

388.   Hinds, Elizabeth Jane Wall. "The Devil Sings the Blues: Heavy Metal, Gothic Fiction and 'Postmodern' Discourse." *Journal of Popular Culture* 26, no. 3 (1992): 151-164.

Contends that the advent of the Gothic novel in the late 1700s and the advent of heavy metal music in the late 1960s followed the same historical path. While retaining the outward form of the parents (i.e., the novel and rock music), both then rearranged the basic elements into new subgenres. Articulates how these subgenres succumbed to the commercial culture of the influences that they originally attempted to subvert.

389.   James, David E. "Rock and Roll in Representations of the Invasion of Vietnam." *Representations* 29 (1990): 78-98.

Probes the literary and cinematic treatments of the Vietnam War as rock music narratives through two "seminal" works: Michael Herr's novel *Dispatches* and the Hal Ashby film *Coming Home*. Traditional conventions were redefined through the "fundamentally contradictory nature of rock and roll, of its various forms of empowerment and pleasure and its equally various forms of repression." In *Dispatches*, rock music is used as a "ubiquitous tapestry" through its mention over forty times throughout the work. Rock music is used to relate and present the war as the experience of the American soldier, thus ignoring or reducing its other significances (e.g., colonialism, Vietnamese history). While a number of other Vietnam films are discussed, *Coming Home* is used to illustrate rock music's narrative power of transmitting specific information regarding time periods, social status, and irony.

390.   Larrick, Nancy. "Pop/Rock Lyrics: Poetry and Reading." *Journal of Reading* 15, no. 3 (1971): 184-190.

Stresses the value of utilizing rock music lyrics to introduce children to poetry and reading. Notes that rock lyrics illustrate "the power of first-person commentary in a rhythmical, conversational style." The lyrics place emotion above meaning which forces the audience to examine their own senses. Also, rock music lyrics contain themes not typically addressed in the school setting.

391. Lyons, Julie, and George H. Lewis. "The Price You Pay: The Life and Lyrics of Bruce Springsteen." *Popular Music and Society* 9, no. 1 (1983): 13-24.

Studies Bruce Springsteen's influence on popular culture. Examines Springsteen's musical influences, his impact, and the major themes of three of his albums. Contends that a significant aspect of Springsteen's work is his ability to assimilate early rock music styles into a contemporary sound. Springsteen produces music that is "a release, an escape, a hopeful means if not an end to triumph." Observes his concern for musical perfection over commercial success. Performs a content analysis of the albums *Born to Run*, *Darkness at the Edge of Town*, and *The River*. Includes a table of the major themes (i.e., release, beating the system, reality, working class, automobiles, love, and mystery women) represented on these three albums.

392. Marcus, Greil. "Liliput at the Cabaret Voltaire." *TriQuarterly* 52, no. 79 (1981): 265-277.

Associates the punk rock movement, specifically the Sex Pistols, with Dadaism. Notes that both Dada and punk are "part liberating prank and part desperate negation." Both deny their own histories as having betrayed them. Both contend that nothing is true and therefore everything is possible. Discusses the implications in a post-punk world, with attention to the group Liliput.

393. McConnell, Frank D. "Rock and the Politics of Frivolity." *Massachusetts Review* 12, no. 1 (1971): 119-134.

Discusses rock music in the context of literary fiction. Focuses on the "deliberately reductive versions" of language which are meant to "lead back to an expanded sense of the problematic reality of our language." Uses examples from the works of the Beatles and the Rolling Stones to illustrate the frivolity of contemporary literary criticism in a socio-political context. Contends that rock music "as a variety of imagination, like self-annihilative fiction, is probably incapable of handling or even assimilating the totally programmed anonymity of contemporary politics."

394. Milburn, Douglas, Jr. "Brecht and the Fillmores: Epic Theater and the Rock Concert." *University of Dayton Review* 7, no. 3 (1971): 93-102.

Argues that the revolutionary theater envisioned by Bertolt Brecht was premature, but is now manifested in psychedelic rock concerts and light shows. Contends that the counterculture has developed a unique theater form for "their own revolutionary needs." Summarizes the features of theater that Brecht was attempting to create. Draws parallels with rock concerts of the late 1960s and early 1970s. Claims that this new theatrical art form is very similar to Brecht's vision and is a "rather remarkable indication of the depth of Brecht's insight" into epoch.

395. Milburn, Douglas. "In reply." *University of Dayton Review* 7, no. 3 (1971): 111-113.
Asserts that the arguments put forward in a previous article regarding Brecht and modern rock concerts hold true despite a published rebuttal by Robert Conrad. Provides clarification.

396. Morse, David. "Plastic People." *Media & Methods* 6, no. 5 (1969): 42-44,52.
Deals with the image of phony personalities that appears in rock music lyrics with enough frequency to be considered "an archetype of our times." States that plastic is a successful metaphor because it paradoxically provides the freedom to "seal ourselves from our environment."

397. Nehring, Neil. "The Shifting Relations of Literature and Popular Music in Postwar England." *Discourse* 12, no. 1 (1989-1990): 78-103.
Explores youth subcultures in England that "arrived at a conscious understanding of the anarchistic possibilities in appropriating and recasting 'high' art." Studies the use of literature by subcultures to undermine cultural capital. Focuses on the literature of Colin MacInnes (*Absolute Beginners*), Anthony Burgess (A Clockwork Orange), and Graham Greene (*Brighton Rock*) in relation to the Rolling Stones (mods and teds) and the Sex Pistols (punks). Argues that the literary works amplified the messages of the music around which the subcultures formed.

398. Plasketes, George M. "Rock on Reel: The Rise and Fall of the Rock Culture in America Reflected in a Decade of 'Rockumentaries'." *Qualitative Sociology* 12, no. 1 (1989): 55-71.
Analyzes the rise and fall of the American youth culture of the 1960s as captured and represented on film. Compares and contrasts the narratives of the films *Monterey Pop*, *Woodstock*, *Gimme Shelter*, and *The Last Waltz*. Claims that the 1960s was a time in which rock music captured and presented an alternative social order. Rock music "addressed conflicts between freedom and responsibility, public and private obligations, community and individualism." States that the film *Monterey Pop* (1968) symbolized self-discovery, *Woodstock* (1970) demonstrated community, *Gimme Shelter* (1971) conveyed apocalypse, and *The Last Waltz* (1978) provided a conclusion. Concludes that in the 1980s, the rock film was replaced by the rock video, transforming a music culture into a visual culture.

399. Polan, Dana. "SZ/MTV." *Journal of Communication Inquiry* 10, no. 1 (1986): 48-54.

Suggests a need for theorists to examine the "socially effective power of aesthetic practices" as related to the effects of narrative and to the effects of the rejection of the narrative. Calls upon Barthes' *S/Z* as a literary example of postmodernism that parallels MTV. MTV highlights the aspect of rock music that allows its status as art to exist between "sense and non-sense, communication and noise, form and meaning."

400. Powe, Bruce W. "*The Tooth of Crime*: Sam Shepard's Way with Music." *Modern Drama* 24, no. 1 (1981): 13-25.

Begins with excerpts from a Patti Smith poem about Sam Shepard in which she describes his use of rock music to communicate immediacy, energy, and a notion of force. Discusses numerous Shepard plays, but focuses on *The Tooth of Crime* (his "ultimate" rock play) as being especially illustrative of his use of rock music. Shepard utilizes rock music in a variety of ways, including to structure speech patterns of characters. Rock music is also used to provide lyrical commentary on the work in progress, to communicate a character's emotion, and to establish moods.

401. Powell, Neil. "Is There a Poetry of Rock?" *Use of English* 26, no. 2: 102-107.

Argues that there is poetry to be found in the lyrics of rock music. Contends that rock music has an increasing effect on vocabulary and therefore urges the critical teaching of rock lyrics to students.

402. Ray, Robert B. "Tracking." *South Atlantic Quarterly* 90, no. 4 (1991): 771-784.

Builds an essay based on the premise that writing can be constructed in the same fashion as recorded music. Takes "six different tracks. . . conceived at different occasions (as recorded parts might be)" and presents a final mix, drawing heavily from rock music for a literary theme. Also published in the book *Present Tense* edited by Anthony DeCurtis.

403. Reichardt, Jasia. "The Art of Rock Music." *Architectural Design* 46 (1976): 634-635.

Acknowledges the art of Rick Griffin as representing and belonging to a "cultural stream." Griffin became popular in the 1960s for his psychedelic posters often designed to advertise rock music. Contends that Griffin's work is representative of the first time that art and music paralleled, where sounds and visuals drew strength from the other. The utilitarian function of the posters is offered as an explanation for their survival.

404. Reitinger, Douglas W. "Paint It Black: Rock Music and Vietnam War Film." *Journal of American Culture* 15, no. 3 (1992): 53-59.

Explores the use of rock music in Vietnam War films by Francis Ford Coppola and Stanley Kubrick. Coppola's *Apocalypse Now* merges rock music into the narrative themes of the film. Kubrick's *Full Metal Jacket* utilizes rock music to provide analogies for the film's subtexts. Both films provide metaphorical connections between sex and violence. Concludes that rock music themes paralleled the American experience of the Vietnam War.

405. Roos, Michael E. "The Walrus and the Deacon: John Lennon's Debt to Lewis Carroll." *Journal of Popular Culture* 18 (1984): 19-29.

Draws numerous parallels between the writings of Lewis Carroll and the songs of John Lennon. Notes that Lennon did not simply draw upon the images of Carroll, but re-cast those images. Compares Lennon's use of backward recordings to Carroll's use of backward images in *Through the Looking Glass*. Contends that an understanding of *Through the Looking Glass* is essential for understanding *Lucy in the Sky with Diamonds* and *I Am the Walrus*.

406. Scherzer, Joel. "Kerouac and the Big Beat." *Moody Street Irregulars* 15 (1985): 10.

Raises questions about author Jack Kerouac's relationship to rock music.

407. Schmid, Randy. "Thunder." *Weatherwise* (1989): 192-196.

Surveys the wide range of rock and popular music that contains references to some aspect of the weather.

408. Schwendener, Peter. "Popular Music and the Avant-Garde." *TriQuarterly*, no. 79 (1990): 199-206.

Critiques the book *Lipstick Traces* by Greil Marcus in terms of its statement on the avant-garde. Contends that Marcus attempts to establish links from rock music to Dadaism as a "meaningful criticism of modern life." Argues that a better comparison of Dadaism and rock music is that they are both "essentially expressions of boredom."

409. Shore, Michael. "Punk Rocks the Art World: How Does it Look? How Does it Sound?" *Artnews* 79, no. 9 (1980): 78-85.

Observes the phenomenon of cross-pollination among artists and musicians as a result of the punk rock movement. Describes a punk aesthetic that has emerged as a blend between the visual and performing arts.

410. Sullivan, Henry W. "Paul, John and Broad Street." *Popular Music* 6, no. 3 (1987): 327-338.

Contends that Paul McCartney's film *Give My Regards to Broad Street* is an unconscious portrayal of John Lennon and a re-enactment of Lennon's assassination. Supports this thesis by analyzing various scenes from the film

LITERATURE AND THE ARTS

and drawing parallels between Lennon and McCartney. Concludes that although the film was a commercial failure, it achieves "greatness in musical and dramatic terms."

411. Taylor, Denis. "Constructing the TV Drama Audience: A Case-Study of Channel 2's Sweet and Sour." *Australasian Drama Studies* 8, no. 1 (1986): 19-32.
   Chronicles the development of an Australian television show designed to attract an adolescent and young adult audience by integrating rock music into the format. The show was designed to use the characters' desires to form a rock group as an expression of seeking "personal and creative satisfaction."

412. Wells, John D. "Music Television Video and the Capacity to Experience Life." *Popular Music and Society* 9, no. 4 (1984): 1-6.
   Attempts to examine music television video as an art form. Comments on the commercialization of rock music and the consequences of market research, and their effects on music video as an art form. Speculates that the repetitive nature of mass media as illustrated by MTV will "lessen one's capacity to experience life in its fullest terms" because each repetition reduces the experience to a cliche.

413. "West Coast Graphics Face the Music." *Graphis* 28, no. 161 (1972/1973): 174-193,252,254.
   Describes the competitive market place for graphic arts in the design of album covers. Notes that the better cover designs are more than illustrations, they become cultural symbols.

CHAPTERS

414. James, David E. "The Vietnam War and American Music." In *The Vietnam War and American Culture*, edited by John Carlos Rowe and Rick Berg, 226-254. New York: Columbia University Press, 1991.
   Presents a content analysis of lyrics relating to the Vietnam War, with particular attention given to the theme of the American soldier. Asserts that the ideologies represented in lyrics "barometrically reflect the changes in the general public consensus." Looks in detail at both folk music and rock music. Notes the lack of Vietnam War representations in rock music of the late 1960s. Songs from that time period typically did not describe in any detail the meaning or experience of the War. Observes that early songs about war veterans portrayed them as being unstable. Discusses Bruce Springsteen's attempt in the song *Born in the U.S.A.* to distinguish between the veteran as a victim and the veteran as an aggressor. Comments on the song's intended purpose and subsequent interpretations.

415. Kaplan, E. Ann. "Whose Imaginary? The Televisual Apparatus, the Female Body and Textual Strategies in Select Rock Videos on MTV." In *Female Spectators: Looking at Film and Television*, edited by E. Deidre Pribram, 132-156. London: Verso, 1988.

Discusses the implications of the images of women as portrayed in music videos, especially on MTV due to its prominence as a medium that "at once embodies and then further develops major cultural changes." Conducts textual analyses of selected rock music videos by female performers, including Madonna, Cyndi Lauper, Donna Summer, Pat Benatar, Tina Turner, and Annie Lennox. Claims that MTV constantly comments on the "self" as related to "image." Warns that in the postmodern era, unlike earlier times when the "possibility of constructing other representations always existed," image becomes reality. Urges greater attention and examination by feminists.

416. McCaffery, Larry. "The Artists of Hell: Kathy Acker and 'Punk' Aesthetics." In *Breaking the Sequence: Women's Experimental Fiction*, edited by Ellen G. Friedman and Miriam Fuchs, 215-230. Princeton: Princeton University Press, 1989.

Links the aesthetics of Kathy Acker's novels to the punk rock movement. Argues that punk was the most significant artistic movement of the 1970s. Contends the Acker's work, like punk rock, produces a literary noise that openly defies tradition in an attempt to transcend repression and communicate alienation and frustration in ways that are troubling but cannot be denied. Claims that Acker shares with the punk subculture "an evident contempt and impatience with words that designate and describe rather than create." Moving beyond metaphor, Acker creates disorder (i.e., noise) in order to produce "a kind of antidiscourse of madness and sensual delirium."

BOOKS

417. Bruchac, Joseph. *The Poetry of Pop.* Paradise, Calif.: DUSTbooks, 1973.

Collects various writings by the author on the poetry of popular music. States that rock music era lyrics are more poetic than those of popular music of previous decades because rock music is born out of black music's suffering and folk music's hope. Analyzes the lyrical works and presentations of the Doors, Bob Dylan, the Beatles, the Impressions, and The Who (i.e., *Tommy*). Contains a chapter on African musical culture in Ghana.

418. Ehrenstein, David. *Rock on Film.* New York: Delilah Books, 1982.

Chronicles in detail the history of rock music in the cinema. Includes chapters organized by genres such as beach movies, soundtracks, and rockumentaries. Contains an appendix that is an annotated listing of motion pictures.

LITERATURE AND THE ARTS

419.   Errigo, Angie, and Steve Leaning. *The Illustrated History of the Rock Album Cover.* London: Octopus Books, 1979.

Presents a history of the art of rock album covers. Includes numerous full color illustrations. Starts with the use of album covers as marketing devices designed to sell a "face." Discusses how cover art evolved into selling images. Touches on selected subthemes such as sex and gimmicks. Devotes attention to the "art for art's sake" covers. Every subject is well documented with discussions of specific album covers.

420.   Fowlie, Wallace. *Rimbaud and Jim Morrison: The Rebel as Poet.* Durham: Duke University Press, 1994.

Compares and contrasts the poetry of Rimbaud and Jim Morrison. Draws parallels between their lives. Asserts that the "thirst of these two men for freedom, for adventure, and for self-expression appeals to the young and anyone who yearns for freedom and new beginnings." Argues that Jim Morrison was trying to articulate through his lyrics the dangers of complacency.

421.   Frith, Simon, and Howard Horne. *Art into Pop.* London: Methuen, 1987.

Explores the relationship between British musicians and their art school backgrounds. Hypothesizes that this experience provided British musicians with a sense of "style, image, self-consciousness" or "attitude" about commercialism. Attempts to derive explanations within a context of postmodernism.

422.   Grushkin, Paul D. *The Art of Rock: Posters from Presley to Punk.* New York: Abbeville Press, 1987.

Contains hundreds of pages of color illustrations representing thirty years of rock poster art, organized somewhat chronologically. Chapters titles are: Roots (1955-1965), The Psychedelic Years in San Francisco (1965-1971), The Psychedelic Years in Southern California and the Rest of the World (1965-1971), The Mainstream (1969-1987), and The New Music (1976-1987). Each chapter is divided into unique subsections devoted to specific musicians, cities, and topics (e.g., Backstage and Laminated Passes, Record Company Promotions, Early Rock Movies, Punk). Notes that during the early period from 1955 to 1965, most posters were created in the "boxing style" using woodblock and heavily emphasizing the words. This was followed by the late 1960s psychedelic period, characterized as flowery and vivid. Next was the 1970s corporate art with slick commercial graphics. In the late 1970s, with punk and new wave influences, poster art returned to a 1950s emphasis on "poster," as opposed to the 1960s emphasis on "art." Yet, it continued to offer its own unique aesthetics. Includes an extensive bibliography. Preface by Bill Graham.

423.   Loder, Kurt. *Bat Chain Puller: Rock & Roll in the Age of Celebrity.* New York: St. Martin's Press, 1990.

Collects articles written by the author for *Rolling Stone* magazine. Focuses on "people whose lives have been shaped by rock" or who have become part of the rock music culture. Concentrates on the concept of celebrity and career.

424.   Marcus, Greil. *Lipstick Traces: A Secret History of the Twentieth Century.* Cambridge: Harvard University Press, 1989.

Attempts to draw connections between the punk rock movement and avant-garde aesthetics. Claims that the punk rock movement was a continuing story about art and revolution. Discusses notions of transcendence in a critique of modern society from 1920s Dadaism to the Situationist International of the 1950s to the Sex Pistols of the 1970s.

425.   Marsh, Dave. *The First Rock and Roll Confidential Report.* New York: Pantheon Books, 1985.

Collects numerous essays from the publication *Rock & Roll Confidential*. Attempts to convey the meaning and power of rock music. Covers a wide variety of social and cultural aspects of rock music.

426.   Meltzer, R. *The Aesthetics of Rock.* New York: Something Else Press, 1970.

Comments on the aesthetics of rock music. Notes that rock music is the "only possible future for philosophy and art" and that through rock music, philosophy and art are interchangeable. Gives much attention to the Beatles, the Rolling Stones, and Bob Dylan.

427.   Mottram, Eric. *Blood on the Nash Ambassador: Investigations in American Culture.* London: Hutchinson Radius, 1989.

Collects various essays by the author representing studies of American culture. The chapter *Dionysus in America* is devoted to rock music. Describes rock music culture as an American art form with social and political implications that challenges traditional forms. Focuses on the rock festivals of Woodstock and Altamont.

428.   Neal, Charles. *Tape Delay.* Wembley, England: SAF, 1987.

Consists of numerous interviews with, and lyrics by, underground artists. Concerns "ideas and provocations that cannot adequately translate to the record market when the medium itself is founded wholly upon entertainment."

429.   Newland, Joseph N., ed. *No! Contemporary American DADA.* 2 volumes. Seattle: Henry Art Gallery, University of Washington, 1985.

Presents the companion publication to an exhibition of the same name. Rock music videos were included in the exhibition of artists who "present confrontational issues" with uncompromising stances.

LITERATURE AND THE ARTS

430. Peellaert, Guy, and Nik Cohn. *Rock Dreams.* New York: R&B, 1982.

Presents a series of original illustrations and commentary about rock music personalities. Attempts to capture the "dreams" of rock music at each developmental stage of the genre. Deals with rock music and "its myths, its heroisms and villainies; its triumphs and catastrophes. . . its landscapes, props and backdrops; its ironies, its cruelties and sentimentalities, its celebrations, its fetishes." Includes an introduction by Michael Herr.

431. Pichaske, David R. *Beowulf to Beatles: Approaches to Poetry.* New York: Free Press, 1972.

Accepts the notion that rock music lyrics are poetry. Includes rock poetry with traditional poetry in this anthology. Discusses words as meaning and as sound. Reviews various genres of poetry (e.g., ballads, elegies, complaints, sonnets).

432. Pichaske, David R. *The Poetry of Rock: The Golden Years.* Peoria, Ill: Ellis Press, 1981.

Presents essays on the poetry to be found in the lyrics of selected rock music performers. Includes the Beatles, the Rolling Stones, the Doors, The Who, Jefferson Airplane, Bob Dylan, Paul Simon, and Phil Ochs. Starts with a historical review of rock music poetry of the 1950s.

433. Russell, Ethan A. *Dear Mr. Fantasy: Diary of a Decade Our Time and Rock and Roll.* Boston: Houghton Mifflin, 1985.

Presents a photographic journal with accompanying text of numerous prominent rock music performers from the 1960s and 1970s. Emphasizes the Beatles and the Rolling Stones. Includes still excerpts from the last film footage taken of John Lennon shortly before his death. Ethan Russell seems to have been in all the right places at the right times, including in the studio with the Beatles, on tour with the Rolling Stones, and taking photographs for a Linda Ronstadt album cover. Contains color and black and white photographs.

434. Saleh, Dennis, ed. *Rock Art: Fifty-Two Record Album Covers.* Seaside, Calif.: Comma Books, 1977.

Collects fifty-two rock music album covers and presents them as graphic design art. Attributes the increased importance of album cover graphics to the mid-1960s increase in record sales competition. Points to the Beatles' album *Sgt. Pepper's Lonely Hearts Club Band* as the trigger event that sent album cover graphics into competitive high gear. Discusses some of the history of controversial covers as well as production complexities and questions of ownership.

435. *San Francisco Rock Poster Art.* San Francisco: San Francisco Museum of Modern Art, 1976.

Highlights San Francisco rock poster artists in this exhibition catalog from the San Francisco Museum of Modern Art. States that "poster art remains as a record of the consciousness of some of the most perceptive, intelligent, and creative youth of the 1960's." Organizes the presentation chronologically by artist in order to illustrate historical development and stylistic adaptations. The narrative places the posters within the context of the San Francisco hippie scene of the 1960s.

436. Sandahl, Linda J. *Rock Films: A Viewer's Guide to Three Decades of Musicals, Concerts, Documentaries, and Soundtracks 1955-1986.* New York: Facts on File, 1987.

Provides brief annotations for rock-related films produced between 1955 and 1986. Organizes the films into three sections: Musicals, Concerts and Documentaries, and Soundtracks. Musicals are films in which rock songs are incorporated into the plot and performed by characters in the drama. Concerts and documentaries are films of live concerts or films of musicians performing in some capacity, including working in recording studios. Soundtracks are films with rock music scores or with scores written or performed by rock musicians. Includes three indexes: film titles, names, and song titles.

437. Savary, Louis M., ed. *Popular Song & Youth Today.* New York: Association Press, 1971.

Presents selected rock music lyrics arranged topically. Contends that rock music offers commentary on values, lifestyles, and behaviors and confronts social issues such as injustice and alienation. Themes are organized into "images" as follows: Man and Woman, Relating, Alienation, Ways People Live, the World, and the Person.

438. Shore, Michael. *The Rolling Stone Book of Rock Video.* New York: Quill, 1984.

Explores the history of the relationship between visual images and musical sound. Discusses the aesthetics of rock music videos, how music videos are made, and promotional outlets for music videos. Includes a "diary" for the filming of the music video *Girls Just Wanna Have Fun* by Cyndi Lauper. Profiles several music video producers. Uses numerous examples to illustrate concepts and themes found in rock music videos.

439. Sinfield, Alan. *Literature, Politics, and Culture in Postwar Britain.* Berkeley: University of California Press, 1989.

Studies the literature, politics, and culture of postwar Great Britain. One chapter, "Making a Scene," deals directly with the influences of rock music on

British culture. Discusses the appropriation of rock music by "teddy boys" as a celebration of white American culture. Ties the rise of rock music and the adoption of jazz among intellectuals to British literary movements.

440.   Taylor, Paul. *Popular Music Since 1955: A Critical Guide to the Literature.* Boston: G. K. Hall, 1985.

Provides a "critical, bibliographical guide to the literature of contemporary popular music published in English since 1955." Observes that the literature of popular music is similar to the subject matter in that it is "an emerging art form struggling to be taken seriously." Attempts to be a comprehensive resource, listing over 1,600 monographs published between 1955 and 1984, regardless of availability. Includes information for over 200 periodical titles, but not for the articles within those periodicals. Each entry has full bibliographic information accompanied by a critical annotation. Organizes the literature into the following categories: general works (e.g., encyclopedia, histories, collected essays, bibliographies), social aspects (e.g., sociology, subcultures, religion, education), artistic aspects (e.g., aesthetics, musicology, photography), music industry (e.g., publishing, songwriting, record companies, radio, instruments), form (e.g., black music, folk, country, new wave), lives and works (i.e., biographies), fiction, and periodicals. Includes an extensive glossary and author, title, and subject indexes.

DISSERTATIONS

441.   Baker-White, Robert E. "Popular Theatre and Literary Text in Contemporary Drama: The Dialectic of Appropriation." Ph.D. Stanford University, 1990. *Dissertation Abstracts International* 51: 2566A.

Questions the effect of contemporary playwrights appropriating conventions of popular theater into their dramatic texts. In the context of rock music, Sam Shepard's *The Tooth of Crime* supplies a "view of the theatrical complexity generated when a drama rides principally on the performance energy of its own subject matter."

442.   Bodinger-deUriarte, Cristina Liegh. "The Impact of Artists' Perceptions on the Form, Content and Presentation of a Genre." Ph.D. Harvard University, 1989. *Dissertation Abstracts International* 50: 3062A.

Proclaims that, contrary to popular perception, an artist is "a culturally astute and self-aware actor purposively negotiating the forces of socialization from a relatively sophisticated view of the social process." Tests this notion using three genres: art rock, Dada, and Bahaus. States that an artist anticipates consciously social effect. Concludes that artistic expression and perception parallels exist "across temporal, regional and media boundaries" and demonstrates complex decision-making processes.

443.   Bourque, Darrell Jude. "Carbon Rites." Ph.D. Florida State University, 1981. *Dissertation Abstracts International* 42: 1133A.

Presents a collection of original poems. One of the major influences for the works is music, including rock music. Contends that music and dance are two forms of art "inherent in all ritual."

444.   Brown, William J. "*Lonesome Cowboy Bill*: The Western in the Later Fiction of William S. Burroughs." Ph.D. State University of New York at Buffalo, 1990. *Dissertation Abstracts International* 52: 161A.

Focuses on three novels by William S. Burroughs: *Cities of the Red Night* (1982), *The Place of Dead Roads* (1983), and *The Western Lands* (1987). Discusses the song, *Lonesome Cowboy Bill,* by the rock group the Velvet Underground and "the importance of rock 'n' roll music to Burroughs." Connects early 1970s changes in rock music to Burroughs. Also considers Burroughs' rock music recording made with Laurie Anderson in 1984 and comments on its connection to the three novels.

445.   Burk, Robert Eugene, Jr. "Reading Shepard and Lacan: A Dramaturgy of the Subject." Ph.D. University of Washington, 1986. *Dissertation Abstracts International* 47: 4236A.

Develops a theory based on the work of Jacques Lacan and applies it to selected works of Sam Shepard. Concepts include "the constitution and maintenance of the fictive self, including the mirror stage, metaphor and metonymy, and the manifestation of desire in the Oedipal narrative." In one chapter, the author examines Shepard's plays in which rock music is a theme.

446.   Kuwahara, Yasue. "The Promised Land: Images of America in Rock Music." Ph.D. Bowling Green State University, 1987. *Dissertation Abstracts International* 49: 855A.

Considers the myth of America as the promised land through a content analysis of images presented in rock song lyrics. Begins in the 1950s with the works of Chuck Berry who clearly reinforced the image of America as the promised land. During the 1960s, Bob Dylan and others questioned the validity of such a myth. The 1970s version of the myth was that of apathy. Bruce Springsteen revitalized the myth in the 1980s, contrasting it with reality. Concludes that the image of America as the promised land changes as society changes and that rock music is a powerful medium for perpetuating the myth.

447.   Laboissonniere, Barbara Rose. "A Study of Rock Music Videos as the Poetry of Secondary Orality." Ph.D. University of Rhode Island, 1989. *Dissertation Abstracts International* 50: 3590A.

Argues that rock music videos are primary poetry of secondary orality and that they are "physiological, mnemonic, and socio-normative entertainment." Investigates the development and transmission of oral poetry with regard to literary, print, and technological influences. Notes that primary oral poetry and rock music videos are both performed communication with specialized diction and formula conventions.

448.   Murphy, Kevin. "Far Rockaway." Ph.D. Florida State University, 1990. *Dissertation Abstracts International* 51: 4123A.

Presents an original novel about a rock music bass player who faces returning to his home town as someone who didn't make it as a rock musician. He must deal with the conflict between his dream of being a musician and the "mediocrity of his musical abilities." Other plot lines include a failed attempt to renew a romantic relationship and his desire to avoid his mother who wants him to abandon his dream.

449.   Viera, Maria. "Music Videos: The Dynamics of Ideology and Style." Ph.D. University of Southern California, 1986. *Dissertation Abstracts International* 48: 2998A.

Identifies three contexts in which to study music videos: institutional, aesthetic, and ideological. Defines institutionalization in terms of MTV programming and video production. Defines aesthetics in terms of music videos sharing characteristics of modernism and postmodernism. Define ideology in terms of production and consumption.

FILMS AND VIDEOS

450.   *The Poetry of Rock: A Reflection of Human Values*. Center for Humanities, 1975.

Studies rock music lyrics as poetry. Observes that across time rock music lyrics reflect changing social values.

451.   *Stop Making Sense.* Jonathan Demme, dir. Talking Heads Films, 1984.

Presents the Talking Heads in concert. More importantly, it is designed to be an art film.

Music

ARTICLES

452. Ballantine, Christopher. "Elite Music." *New Society* 14, no. 372 (1969): 779-780.
Suggests that avant-garde music has created a cultural vacuum that can be filled by rock music. Contends that rock music has increased its level of sophistication, is the only musical form to humanize technology, and appeals to modern intellects. Notes that the audience, unlike with avant-garde or New Music, is directly involved in the production and consumption of the art.

453. Baugh, Bruce. "Prolegomena to Any Aesthetics of Rock Music." *Journal of Aesthetics and Art Criticism* 51, no. 1 (1993): 23-29.
Questions whether there can be an aesthetics of rock music. Argues that rock music must be critiqued by its own standards which are "implicitly observed by knowledgeable performers and listeners" and that these standards are representative of the distinctiveness of rock music as a genre. Claims that it is not prudent to use traditional music aesthetics to evaluate rock music. Unlike other music genres, the performance of rock music is more important than the composition. Previous attempts to judge rock music by traditional measures resulted in musicians creating pretentious and excessive art rock and rock operas. Concludes that the aesthetics of rock music can be found in performance and measured by rhythm, loudness, and expressiveness as they affect the body.

454. Bergenfeld, Nathan. "It's All Music." *Clavier* 15, no. 6 (1976): 39-40.
Compares Paul McCartney's *Junk* to Henry Purcell's *Dido's Lament* in order to demonstrate similarities in Western composition styles throughout the ages. States that these two particular compositions use a similar "basso ostinato." Notes the use in both pieces of "chromaticism" which results in the expression

of "highly charged emotions." Stresses that common melodies and phrasing are not as important as similar constructions of bass lines, juxtaposition, and creating climaxes. Concludes that music is often universal and unchanging.

455. Bloomfield, Terry. "It's Sooner than You Think, or Where are We in the History of Rock Music?" *New Left Review*, no. 190 (1991): 59-81.

Rejects arguments formed in the postmodern analysis of rock music. Claims that society is only now in a modernist stage of rock music that started with punk rock, not with 1960s rock music that failed to challenge music as a commodity. Concludes that the end of rock music is not at hand and that the post-punk era demonstrates the "modernist tendency" to undermine "its status as commodity."

456. Brackett, David. "James Brown's *Superbad* and the Double-Voiced Utterance." *Popular Music* 11, no. 3 (1992): 309-324.

Studies the recording of *Superbad* by James Brown as a reflection of the differences between African American and European American use of "language, rhetorical styles and performances."

457. Breen, Marcus. "A Stairway to Heaven or a Highway to Hell?: Heavy Metal Rock Music in the 1990s." *Cultural Studies* 5, no. 2 (1991): 191-203.

Concentrates on the re-emergence of heavy metal music in the 1990s, focusing on the groups Metallica and Anthrax. Compares and contrasts current heavy metal music to the heavy metal sounds of the 1970s when the genre first evolved. Claims that contemporary heavy metal suffers from negative attitudes toward its earlier form. Categorizes heavy metal into subgenres of commercial/wimpy/glam/sleaze (e.g., Poison, Bon Jovi), mainstream (e.g., Stryper, AC/DC, Motley Crue, Iron Maiden), thrash (e.g., Megadeth, Slayer), and death (Metallica, Anthrax). Discusses the role and impact of MTV on marketing heavy metal music. Touches on the issues of satanism and violence in heavy metal lyrics.

458. Brittin, Ruth V. "The Effect of Overtly Categorizing Music on Preference for Popular Music Styles." *Journal of Research in Music Education* 39, no. 2 (1991): 143-151.

Explores the effect of overt categorizing of musical genres on music preference. Concludes that music preference "may be independent of classification taxonomies."

459. Browne, David. "You Can Look It Up: A Guide to Rock Reference Books." *High Fidelity* (1988): 67-69.

Provides a critical evaluative review of reference books devoted to rock music.

MUSIC

460.   Burns, Gary. "A Typology of 'Hooks' in Popular Records." *Popular Music* 6, no. 1 (1987): 1-20.

Presents a scheme for hook analysis of popular music. Examines how structural elements are manipulated by songwriters, performers, and producers through repetition, variation, and modulation. Identifies two textual elements controlled by the composer: music (rhythm, melody, harmony) and lyrics. Distinguishes performance elements as instrumentation, tempo, dynamics, improvisation, and accident. Labels production elements as sound effects, editing, mixing, channel behavior, and signal distortion. Shows how each of these elements can be manipulated to produce hooks. Presents an extensive section of examples from rock music. Encourages refinement and use of the typology to generate additional structural analyses of popular music.

461.   Clarke, Paul. "'A Magic Science': Rock Music As a Recording Art." *Popular Music* 3 (1983): 195-213.

Borrows the phrase "magic science" (used by Jimi Hendrix to describe his goal for rock music) in order to characterize the art of making rock music recordings. Notes that rock music evolved from the tradition of live performance music, but became an art (i.e., magic) through advances in recording technology (i.e., science). Argues that rock music recordings are a new manifestation of both performing arts and creative arts. States that in regard to artistic criticism, rock recordings cannot be considered against performing arts criteria because a recording is constructed to the artist's satisfaction prior to public scrutiny. However, creative art criticism is inappropriate when it reduces the recording to an artifact with literary analysis of the lyrics or compositional analysis of the score. Suggests an aural musico-linguistic critical approach that focuses on the aural interaction of the lyrics and the music to produce a criticism of rock music recordings as creative art. Lyrically, the language of rock music "falls somewhere between poetry and drama" because the words are meaningful only in the performing context. Uses as an example the Ian Dury song *Waiting for Your Taxi*.

462.   Compton, Todd. "McCartney or Lennon?: Myths and the Composing of the Lennon-McCartney Songs." *Journal of Popular Culture* 22, no. 2 (1988): 99-131.

Explodes the myth that John Lennon and Paul McCartney collaborated on most of the songs by the Beatles. Attempts to sort out the individual qualities that characterize the compositions of each. Includes a list of the songs credited to Lennon-McCartney with annotations designed to identify the "true" composer. Discusses the quality of their post-Beatles work and concludes that McCartney was more gifted as musical composer and Lennon as a lyricist.

463. Cutietta, Robert A., and Thomas Brennan. "Coaching a Pop/Rock Ensemble." *Music Educators Journal* 77, no. 8 (1991): 40-45.

Argues that it is better, for the sake of authenticity, to have several rock ensembles than attempting to have too many students in one group. Reviews each rock instrument (i.e., guitar, bass, keyboard, horns), its function, and sound.

464. Danielou, Alain. "Magic and Pop Music." *World of Music* 12, no. 2 (1970): 13-18.

Remarks on the use of musical elements such as tone, rhythm, and melody to create states of "mystic intoxication." Claims that the meaning of music is in its power to free one from rational bonds. Observes that rock and jazz music represent modern manifestations of primal musical traits that lead to a "communion with something mysterious and unknown." Cites the concluding funeral march in *Hair* as an example of a musical revolution.

465. Denisoff, R. Serge. "The Battered and Neglected Orphan: Popular Music Research and Books." *Popular Music and Society* 8 (1981): 43-59.

Provides a bibliographic essay on research into popular music. Organizes the discussion into six categories: 1) the music industry, 2) career management, 3) biographies, 4) technology, 5) history, and 6) on-the-road diaries. The bibliography is selective and extensive.

466. Denisoff, R. Serge. "Folk-Rock: Folk Music, Protest, or Commercialism?" *Journal of Popular Culture* 3, no. 2 (1969): 214-230.

Explores the nature of folk rock music, seeking to define it in the fusion of protest (folk) and commercial (rock) forms. Offers a history of folk rock music, noting Bob Dylan's leading role in creating the genre. Also discusses the influence of the Beatles. Seeks to explain the genre in terms of the exoteric (rock music) and the esoteric (folk music). Concludes that folk rock is not "overt protest in the historical sense," but is reflective of certain social goals while tied to commercialism.

467. Doruzka, Lubomir. "Protest through Popular Music." *World of Music* 12, no. 2 (1970): 19-31.

Focuses on two types of popular music that are capable of mobilizing political action, jazz and rock music. States that rock music has a history of appealing to nonconformist ideologies. This makes it an attractive vehicle for voicing protest.

468. Ferrara, Lawrence. "Music in General Studies: A Look at Content and Method." *College Music Symposium* 26 (1986): 122-129.

Proposes a general studies music course that focuses on rock music as a cultural metaphor in order to engage students in moving into other styles such as classical music. Prescribes the "responsive" methodology which is a commitment to allowing musical works to "show themselves in any way or dimension of meaning that might occur." Illustrates the methodology using the Moody Blues' album *Days of Future Past*. Claims that for a piece of music to be great, it must provide a "glimpse of the world."

469.   Fiori, Umberto. "Listening to Peter Gabriel's *I Have the Touch*." *Popular Music* 6, no. 1 (1987): 37-43.
Begins with a personal aesthetic evaluation of Peter Gabriel's song *I Have the Touch*. Identifies the lyrics as those of a typical classic rock song. Explores the ways that the melody and vocal choices provide commonplace expressions in the lyrics with emotion and multiple meanings. Provides an example of how the song was crafted to allow the listener to discern its many meanings without being too obvious. Asserts that such crafting belies the notion that rock music is created spontaneously. Rather, it results from a creative process in which a final version is reached only after various approaches are tried and altered. Discusses the lyrics in terms of fitting with the melody, vocal interpretation, and the more literary "artistic integration." Contends that the "speech acts" of the lyrics reflect the composer in both personally and symbolically. Concludes that popular music, unlike traditional western poetry, connects the listener with the composer at a basic human level.

470.   Flugrath, James M. "Modern-Day Rock-and-Roll Music and Damage-Risk Criteria." *Journal of the Acoustical Society of America* 45, no. 3 (1969): 704-711.
Analyzes sound levels of ten live rock music bands in order to determine if their amplified sound exceeds various established damage risk criteria (DRC). Determines that the actual intensity of live rock music is highly variable. Compensates by averaging numerous readings and concludes that due to a small standard deviation, live rock music can, in fact, be considered a form of "steady noise." Notes that the music does exceed "maximum permissible DRC" and is potentially harmful to hearing. Indicates that frequency of listening to live rock music would determine the amount of "noise trauma."

471.   Flugrath, James M., John A. Irwin, Basil N. Wolfe Jr., Betty Krone, and Mike Parnell. "Temporary Threshold Shift and Rock-and-Roll Music." *Journal of Auditory Research* 11, no. 4 (1971): 291-293.
Investigates the relationship between loud rock music and temporary threshold shifts in hearing. Follows through on previous research by concentrating on exposure time and recovery. Subjects were fifty-two males and eighty-six females, ranging in age from thirteen to twenty, attending weekly dances. Results indicate that females were more sensitive "both before and after exposure." Concludes that rock music does cause temporary threshold shifts and it should be possible to identify those for whom loud rock music might be particularly dangerous.

472. Geringer, John M., and Thomas Breen. "The Role of Dynamics in Musical Expression." *Journal of Music Therapy* 12, no. 1 (1975): 19-29.

Tests three hypotheses: 1) for both classical and rock music, a greater dynamic range will result in more musical expression, 2) dynamic changes are expressive "as a function of their context in the musical score," and 3) dynamic change is a factor of musical expression more so in classical music than in rock music. Subjects were 153 undergraduate students enrolled in an introductory music course for non-majors. Results indicate support for the first hypothesis as it relates to classical music, but not for rock music. Results support the second and third hypotheses. Notes that for rock music, minimal dynamic changes tend to "be more musically expressive." Suggests reasons why dynamic changes are not as significant in rock music. Variations in rock music tend to be in instrumentation, tempo, rhythm, and key changes.

473. Goertzel, Ben. "The Rock Guitar Solo: From Expression to Simulation." *Popular Music and Society* 15 (1991): 91-101.

Claims that the evolution of the guitar solo parallels the transformation of rock music from an expression of rebellion to stylized popular music. Grounds this theory in Jean Baudrillard's "analysis of the replacement of expression by simulation in popular culture." Argues that the early guitar solos expressed certain emotional realities, but they evolved with rock music into perversions of representative emotional reality. Next, guitar solos masked the absence of emotional reality, until finally there is no relation to emotional reality at all and no one cares.

474. Gridley, Mark C. "Clarifying Labels: Jazz, Rock and Jazz-Rock." *Popular Music and Society* 9, no. 2 (1983): 27-34.

Makes some observations regarding the similarities and differences among jazz, rock, funk, and jazz-rock. Notes that jazz and rock music share common roots but have followed divergent paths, noticeably in regard to the emphasis on lyrics. Focuses on the music groups Chicago, Ten Wheel Drive, and Blood, Sweat & Tears.

475. Hawkins, Stan. "Prince: Harmonic Analysis of *Anna Stesia*." *Popular Music* 11, no. 3 (1992): 325-335.

Utilizes the song *Anna Stesia* by Prince to study the extent to which harmony reflects "the ideological sentiments of the song." Examines in detail the harmonic and chord structures in order to determine the effects on the song's meaning.

476. Hey, Kenneth R. "I Feel A Change Comin' On: The Counter-Culture Image of the South in Southern Rock 'n' Roll." *Popular Music and Society* 5 (1977): 93-99.

Examines various musical elements and lyrical themes in Southern rock music. Concludes that the South is dependent upon the North which it rejects, creating a "negative cohesion."

477. Hojris, Mikael. "Rock Music with a Nordic Identity." *Nordic Sounds* (1986): 12-13.

Reproduces, in part, the author's remarks made at a Nordic rock music meeting. Discusses the role of rock music in the continuing process of Nordic integration. Calls for further strengthening of the Nordic rock music organizations in order to produce music built on common aesthetic and cultural policies.

478. Josephson, Nors S. "Bach Meets Liszt: Traditional Formal Structures and Performance Practices in Progressive Rock." *Musical Quarterly* 76, no. 1 (1992): 67-92.

Focuses in detail on the traditional structures and performance of progressive rock music. Looks at numerous contemporary recordings in terms of renaissance madrigal idioms, baroque idioms, and classical and romantic style variation structures. Notes that progressive rock "uses an impressive range of formal structures and harmonic techniques, coupled with an extensive employment of historical performance practices." Views progressive rock as an example of twentieth-century music that synthesizes avant-garde and popular styles.

479. Kamin, Jonathan. "Parallels in the Social Reactions to Jazz and Rock." *Black Perspective in Music* 3, no. 3 (1975): 278-298.

Utilizes a model developed by Neil Leonard regarding the reception of aesthetic "novelty" and a model developed by Richard Peterson regarding the popularization and dilution of jazz music to explore rock music's evolution from rhythm and blues. Demonstrates the generality of these models through their applicability to rock music. Admits that because jazz and rhythm and blues originated "from the sub-culture of an oppressed minority" the social responses may be similar. Article originally appeared in the *Journal of Jazz Studies* in 1974.

480. Killian, Janice N. "Effect of Model Characteristics on Musical Preference of Junior High Students." *Journal of Research in Music Education* 38, no. 2 (1990): 115-123.

Studies the "effect of modeling on the development of musical preference." Compares sex and race as variables in modeling. Subjects were 179 junior high school students (sixty-seven males, 112 females; 110 blacks, forty-five whites, and twenty-four Hispanics). Object of the study was the single recording of the song *We Are The World* by twenty-one rock music performers. Subjects were asked to rate their preferences for each performer. Subjects were then shown a videotape of the recording session and asked to select which solo they would prefer to sing. Analysis of the sex and race of the preferred performers and of the subjects show that subjects prefer same sex, same race models. Notes this tendency to be stronger among males than females. Discusses results in terms of music education.

481. MacCluskey, Thomas. "Rock in Its Elements." *Music Educators Journal* 56, no. 3 (1969): 48-51.

Explains musicologically the construction of rock music. Identifies four elements: rhythm, melody, harmony, and form. Notes that the rhythm is based on the same elements found in rhythm and blues and country music. Lists common melodic modes used in rock music composition: Ionian, Aeolian, Mixolydian, and to a lesser extent, Dorian. Explores the modal harmonic expressions of rock music. Finally, comments on the blues form influence.

482. Malm, William P. "Rock, Unpopular Pop and the Return of Poetry." *Decade* (1979): 35-37.

Reviews five features of popular music: topical, international, pluralistic, evanescent, and eclectic. Topical means that popular lyrics describe important issues of the times (emotional, political, sociological). International means each culture creates its own popular music. Pluralistic means that it transcends generations and socio-economic status. Evanescent means that trends come and go quickly. Eclectic means that rock music freely borrows from many other styles, mainly because it is not "hindered by a strong dogma." Concludes that popular music has value because it serves to provide meaning in a particular moment of history.

483. May, William V. "Musical Style Preferences and Aural Discrimination Skills of Primary Grade School Children." *Journal of Research in Music Education* 33, no. 1 (1985): 7-22.

Presents an article based directly on the author's Ph.D. dissertation. [See entry number 571 for annotation.]

484. Middleton, Richard. "'Play it Again Sam': Some Notes on the Productivity of Repetition in Popular Music." *Popular Music* 3 (1983): 235-270.

Studies the use of repetition in popular song composition, including those elements found in rock music. Offers explanations of the effects of repetition on the notion of pleasure, based on works of Guy Rosolato and Sigmund Freud.

485.   Mooney, Hugh. "Twilight of the Age of Aquarius?: Popular Music in the 1970s." *Popular Music and Society* 7 (1980): 182-198.

Attempts to assess in some detail the popular music of the 1970s. Covers the soft rock of the early 1970s, the disco years, punk music, and new wave. Focuses on the fusion of various musical genres.

486.   O'Grady, Terence J. "A Rock Retrospective." *Music Educators Journal* 66, no. 4 (1979): 34-45,94-107.

Presents a focused history of rock music in terms of its changing styles. Notes that the 1950s represented musical achievements that were "authentic but limited in scope." Describes the musical style of the Beatles and other British invasion groups as an "omnipresent" pop sound. Identifies "hard rock" music as that of the Kinks, The Who, and Tommy James. Devotes attention to other 1960s styles such as folk rock, the Motown sound, art rock, acid rock, and blues/jazz/rock fusions. Includes an annotated bibliography of selected books on rock music history. Also includes a selected discography.

487.   Paddison, Max. "The Critique Criticised: Adorno and Popular Music." *Popular Music* 2 (1982): 201-218.

Comments on the critique of popular music by Theodor Adorno. Notes that Adorno's theories on popular music are often dismissed, but there may be elements worth reviving. Uses the early works of Frank Zappa and the Mothers of Invention to illustrate Adorno's assertion that self-reflective popular music must both accept and reject its fate as commodity.

488.   Pearlman, Sandy. "Patterns and Sounds: The Uses of Raga in Rock." *Crawdaddy* 7 (1967): 5-10.

Observes the use of Indian (raga) music as a source of eclectic innovation for rock music. Discusses the assimilation of Indian music into the rock music mainstream through two means: 1) the appropriation of the sound, and 2) the adoption of the style and composition "in which musical texture and pattern become paramount." Concludes that rock music, through the assimilation of Indian music, is better able to express or invoke a particular state of mind than the literal text of lyrics.

489.   Pembrook, Randall G. "Exploring The Musical Side of Pop." *Music Educators Journal* 77, no. 8 (1991): 30-34.

Suggests that the determination as to whether popular music should be included in a music curriculum should be based on a "comprehensive musical analysis" of musical elements. Proposes a five element model to be used for music analysis: sound, harmony, melody, rhythm, and growth. Details each element and provides examples. Provides a sample analysis of Madonna's song *Cherish*.

490. Pembrook, Randall G. "A Stylistic Analysis of Selected Pop Songs, 1965-1984." *College Music Symposium* 27 (1987): 117-140.

Analyzes the "structure and elements" of selected rock music songs. Uses the top song for each of twenty years as identified through *Billboard* magazine's Hot 100 charts. Results indicate that the majority of songs are approximately three to four minutes in length, the melody is often not the emphasis of the composition, and eighteen of the twenty songs feature "even, simple subdivisions of the beat." Notes the common compositional and performance techniques among the twenty songs. Provides a number of tables itemizing meter, tempo, tonal center, melodic range, modulation, melodic vocabulary, harmonic vocabulary, major cadences, harmonic activity, and other elements. Also discusses changes in lyrical content across time.

491. Plasketes, George. "Like a Version: Cover Songs and the Tribute Trend in Popular Music." *Studies in Popular Culture* 15, no. 1 (1992): 1-18.

Assesses the nature and impact of cover songs and tribute albums. Provides a history of the concept of cover recordings. Notes that the current proliferation of cover recordings and tribute albums is typical of postmodernism with its repetition of "virtually everything into an exhaustive cycle of retreads." Discusses the commercial and charitable motivations for these recordings. Explains the motivations behind cover songs and tribute albums as being those of apprenticeship, homage, imitation, and interpretation.

492. Riley, Tim. "For the Beatles: Notes on Their Achievement." *Popular Music* 6, no. 3 (1987): 257-272.

Comments in detail on the various musical achievements of the Beatles. Claims that the Beatles integrated the best of what had come before them and influenced much of what followed. Discusses the influence of early rock music on the Beatles, the songwriting partnership of John Lennon and Paul McCartney, the musical interplay of the group as musicians, and their development as recording artists.

493. Root, Robert L., Jr. "A Listener's Guide to the Rhetoric of Popular Music." *Journal of Popular Culture* 20, no. 1 (1986): 15-26.

Proposes a paradigm for research into rock music and audience interactions. Identifies three elements of the paradigm: composition, performance, and response. Each element is "influenced by the other two: composition by the intention of the performance and the expectation of the response; performance by the nature of the composition and the expectation of the response; response by the nature of the composition and the execution of the performance." Further delineates each element by three factors. Composition is made of lyrics, arrangement, and melody. Performance is subject, speaker, and audience. Response is made of taste, occasion, and judgment. Uses numerous examples to illustrate how each factor of each element contributes to the rhetorical statement.

Also published as a chapter in the book *The Rhetorics of Popular Culture: Advertising, Advocacy, and Entertainment* by Robert L. Root (Greenwood Press, 1987).

494.   Salzman, Eric. "The Revolution in Music." *New American Review* 6 (1969): 76-96.
Covers the impact of recording technology on the creative process of music production. Notes that rock music represents the "acceptance of all modes of experience" and that in some cases it is "consciously synthetic art." Concludes that society is at the beginning of a new aesthetic experience.

495.   Schmidt, Mathias R. "The German Song-Writing Movement of the Late 1960s and 1970s." *Journal of Popular Culture* 13, no. 1 (1979): 44-54.
Surveys the history of popular music in Germany since World War II. Notes an increase in the use of German language lyrics and greater diversification in the popular music of Germany. Rock music, in particular, made a mid-1960s shift from English-language lyrics to German, mostly in an attempt to communicate explicit political messages.

496.   Souster, Tim. "Rock, Beat, Pop-Avant Garde." *World of Music* 12, no. 2 (1970): 32-43.
Distinguishes between commercial popular music and artistic rock music. Notes that rock musicians do their best work in live performances, with their recordings being poor representations of their artistry. Attributes enhanced artistic qualities of popular music to the use of technology. Illustrates specific concepts using the works of such performers as the Beatles, Jimi Hendrix, Cream, and the Velvet Underground.

497.   Taylor, Timothy D. "His Names was in Lights: Chuck Berry's *Johnny B. Goode*." *Popular Music* 11, no. 1 (1992): 27-40.
Demonstrates the ways in which Chuck Berry dealt with being an African American musician in the 1950s though an interpretation of the song *Johnny B. Goode*. Contends that Berry accessed three "powerful myths" shared by all Americans while maintaining elements of African American identity. The three myths are: genius, talent, and success. Claims that the story of Johnny B. Goode is somewhat autobiographical and that Berry continued the Johnny/Chuck theme through several other songs during his career. Discusses the musical structure of the song, derived from blues styles.

498.   Walser, Robert. "Eruptions: Heavy Metal Appropriations of Classical Virtuosity." *Popular Music* 11, no. 3 (1992): 263-308.
Discusses from a musicological perspective the influences of classical music on heavy metal music. Dismisses the use of classical elements in art rock as attempts at prestige. Contends that heavy metal music demonstrates a very selective appropriation of classical music and illustrates the finer elements of

such an appropriation. Focuses on Ritchie Blackmore, Eddie Van Halen, Randy Rhodes, and Yngwie Malmsteen. Bemoans the lack of respect afforded heavy metal musicians in the scholarly and popular press.

499. Whiteley, Sheila. "Progressive Rock and Psychedelic Coding in the Work of Jimi Hendrix." *Popular Music* 9, no. 1 (1990): 37-60.

Studies the relationship between the musical structures of compositions by Jimi Hendrix and the elements of the psychedelic movement to be found musically embedded in his works. Comments on the progressive elements of the musical structures in such songs as *Purple Haze*, *Hey Joe*, and *Love or Confusion*. Contends that the manner in which the songs are composed suggests knowledge of and experience with psychedelic drugs. Elements such as harmonies, lyrics, and melodies are secondary to effects of sound. Anchors Jimi Hendrix's style in the blues tradition.

500. Winn, James A. "The Beatles as Artists." *Michigan Quarterly Review* 23, no. 1 (1984): 1-20.

Follows the development of the Beatles as musical artists via their recordings. Argues that they were "self-consciously artistic makers of song." Contends that the Beatles were able to support an increasingly complex and creative process once they had stopped performing publicly, as evidenced by their subsequent work. Describes the collaborative songwriting/production process of John Lennon and Paul McCartney. Concludes that two current styles of rock music are "radical rejections" of the style created by the Beatles. Punk music reduces rock to theater while disco music reduces rock to muzak.

CHAPTERS

501. Bayton, Mavis. "How Women Become Musicians." In *On Record: Rock, Pop, and the Written Word*, edited by Simon Frith and Andrew Goodwin, 238-257. New York: Pantheon Books, 1990.

Raises and explores some of the issues confronting women rock musicians. Discusses learning to play instruments with or without formal classical training, singing, rehearsing, understanding jargon, songwriting, and developing a musician's identity. Observes that women may not be as committed to music as men, but are more emotionally committed than men to other members of their music group. Uses numerous quotes from female musicians to illustrate particular points.

502. Burnett, Michael. "Using Pop Music with Middle-School Classes." In *Pop, Rock and Ethnic Music in School*, edited by Graham Vulliamy and Ed Lee, 24-39. Cambridge: Cambridge University Press, 1982.

Offers an approach to explaining the construction of popular songs to adolescents. Discusses form, rhythm, chord sequences, riffs, melody, and the composition process. Contends that if adolescents understand and appreciate the musical composition process, then they will obtain greater enjoyment from listening to popular music and be more likely to try original composition themselves.

503.   Carson, Tom. "Rocket to Russia." In *On Record: Rock, Pop, and the Written Word*, edited by Simon Frith and Andrew Goodwin, 441-449. New York: Pantheon Books, 1990.

Discusses the album *Rocket to Russia* by the Ramones within the context of the punk movement. Observes that the Ramones "pushed their punk ironies to the limit." Concludes that the Ramones are a representation of American popular culture in that they are "devious, dumb, brilliant, and exhilarating."

504.   Chester, Andrew. "Second Thoughts on a Rock Aesthetic: The Band." In *On Record: Rock, Pop, and the Written Word*, edited by Simon Frith and Andrew Goodwin, 313-319. New York: Pantheon Books, 1990.

Asserts that the music made by the group The Band is the essence of rock music. Contends that this why their music has value without having significant lyrics, experimentation, or elements of other music genres. Claims that the aesthetic value of The Band's work is purely musical, which makes their work unique.

505.   Comer, John. "How Can I Use the Top Ten?" In *Pop, Rock and Ethnic Music in School*, edited by Graham Vulliamy and Ed Lee, 7-23. Cambridge: Cambridge University Press, 1982.

Provides methods of incorporating popular music into music courses designed for early adolescents. Divides the approach into "structured listening" and "reproduction" in order to provide an understanding reinforced with practice. Identifies the following elements to be studied in the classroom setting: melody, rhythm, harmony, lyrical content and form, and instrumentation. Presents three detailed examples to illustrate varied approaches: *Brown Girl in the Ring* by Boney M, *Mull of Kintyre* by Wings (Paul McCartney), and *Rat Trap* by the Boomtown Rats.

506.   Comer, John. "Rhythm and Percussion Work in Rock and Latin American Styles." In *Pop, Rock and Ethnic Music in School*, edited by Graham Vulliamy and Ed Lee, 40-55. Cambridge: Cambridge University Press, 1982.

Approaches the teaching of rhythm and percussion instrumentation to adolescents through the study of rock music and Latin American music. Argues that rhythm work is not easy and does not represent an inferior musical activity.

507. Comer, John. "Rock and Blues Piano Accompaniments." In *Pop, Rock and Ethnic Music in School*, edited by Graham Vulliamy and Ed Lee, 72-90. Cambridge: Cambridge University Press, 1982.

Offers that the learning of rock and blues piano playing is quite different from learning the classical music piano. Contends that the learning of African American musical styles requires an entirely different approach than that of classical training. Notes that sheet music is not a very useful tool for learning popular music styles. Suggests that the best approach is to become familiar with the idiom in order to develop an authentic playing sound.

508. Crawford, Paul. "The Central London Youth Project Music Workshop." In *Pop, Rock and Ethnic Music in School*, edited by Graham Vulliamy and Ed Lee, 214-224. Cambridge: Cambridge University Press, 1982.

Describes the Central London Youth Project as a youth club where music lessons are provided. Equipment and instruction are made available to young musicians, in recognition of the great interest among adolescents in music as a means of self-expression and creativity, and as an outlet for developing skills. Discusses the instruction, rehearsals, and performances by participants.

509. Gillett, Charlie. "The Producer as Artist." In *The Phonograph and Our Musical Life: Proceedings of a Centennial Conference*, edited by H. Wiley Hitchcock, 51-56. Brooklyn: Institute for Studies in American Music, Department of Music, School of Performing Arts, Brooklyn College, City University of New York, 1980.

Reproduces a conference presentation by the author in which he argues that a record producer can be as much of a contributing artist to a recording as the musicians. Illustrates various types of producers and the nature of their contributions to recordings. Discusses the evolution in rock music from the traditional bureaucrat record producer to the "Renaissance" producers to the "New Renaissance" producers to, finally, the artist as producer. Includes a transcript of the audience question-and-answer session that followed the formal remarks.

510. Goodwin, Andrew. "Rationalization and Democratization in the New Technologies of Popular Music." In *Popular Music and Communication*. 2nd ed., edited by James Lull, 75-100. Newbury Park, Calif.: Sage, 1992.

Assesses the impact and consequences of new technologies on the production of rock music. Utilizes the works of Max Weber, Walter Benjamin, and Theodor Adorno to discuss rationalization and democratization of modern music. Argues that new technologies associated with music production have had devastating results. Specifically, the sequencer, digital sampling, and MIDI (Musical Instrument Digital Interface) automate the production of music to its detriment.

511.   Goodwin, Andrew. "Sample and Hold: Pop Music in the Digital Age of Reproduction." In *On Record: Rock, Pop, and the Written Word*, edited by Simon Frith and Andrew Goodwin, 258-273. New York: Pantheon Books, 1990.

Debates whether new technologies affect musicologically the aesthetics of popular music. Observes that the most notable influences of technology have been the enhancement of dance music, not the development of new electronic or art music.

512.   Harron, Mary. "McRock: Pop as a Commodity." In *Facing the Music: A Pantheon Guide to Popular Culture*, edited by Simon Frith, 173-220. New York: Pantheon Books, 1988.

Details the strong relationship between rock music's intrinsic value and its market hype, from the 1950s to the 1980s. On one hand, the intrinsic value of rock music is used to manipulate the market for commercial gain. On the other hand, the value of music is entirely subjective and hype is just a part of the process. Attributes the tension between these two concepts to the fact that rock music serves as both a mass culture product and as an art form.

513.   Hughes, Walter. "In the Empire of the Beat: Discipline and Disco." In *Microphone Fiends: Youth Music & Youth Culture*, edited by Andrew Ross and Tricia Rose, 147-157. New York: Routledge, 1994.

Stresses that most African American musical styles typically receive criticism at first but are later accepted and recognized. Notes that one exception is disco music. Contends that continuing criticism of disco music is based on its association with male homosexuality. Explores this relationship in terms of disco music's resurgence in the early 1990s. Discusses the "process of dissolving musical, linguistic and narrative structures that disco dramatizes." Asserts that disco music's power is in the beat.

514.   Knight, Stewart. "Teaching Rock at the Basement Youth Club." In *Pop, Rock and Ethnic Music in School*, edited by Graham Vulliamy and Ed Lee, 225-240. Cambridge: Cambridge University Press, 1982.

Comments in detail on methods of teaching rock music to adolescents at a London youth club.

515.   Kruse, Holly. "In Praise of Kate Bush." In *On Record: Rock, Pop, and the Written Word*, edited by Simon Frith and Andrew Goodwin, 441-449. New York: Pantheon Books, 1990.

Contends that the music of Kate Bush "integrates intellectually challenging subject matter into complex and often experimental instrumental arrangements." Discusses the influences on Kate Bush and examines her work in detail.

516.   Laing, Dave. "Listen to Me." In *On Record: Rock, Pop, and the Written Word*, edited by Simon Frith and Andrew Goodwin, 326-340. New York: Pantheon Books, 1990.

Examines the uniqueness of songwriting and performance on selected Buddy Holly records. Studies the lyrical and musical structures, the vocal performances, the instrumental work, and the rhythm sections.

517.   McClary, Susan, and Robert Walser. "Start Making Sense! Musicology Wrestles with Rock." In *On Record: Rock, Pop, and the Written Word*, edited by Simon Frith and Andrew Goodwin, 277-292. New York: Pantheon Books, 1990.

Distinguishes between traditional and popular musicology. Notes that popular musicologists must deconstruct the premises of their classical discipline and create new premises for popular music. Compares the written score for traditional musicologists to the recorded performance for popular musicologists. Contends that in analyzing popular music there is often too much reliance on the lyrics alone or on semiotics. Suggests that the best way to critique popular music is to based the criticism on audience reaction.

518.   Michie, J. Allen. "Unchained Melody: Postmodernism and Twentieth-Century Music." In *Research in American Popular Music*, edited by Kenneth J. Bindas, 43-59. Carrollton, Georgia: West Georgia College, 1992.

Comments on the influences of postmodernism on contemporary music. With regard to rock music, claims that postmodernism was first expressed on the Beatles' albums *Sgt. Pepper's Lonely Hearts Club Band* and *The White Album*. Discusses the styles of Laurie Anderson and the rock group Sigue Sigue Sputnik. Observes that reggae music is postmodern in its effect if not in intent. Also discusses jazz and new music in the context of postmodernism.

519.   Newman, Joyce. "Rock and Ritual." In *La Musique et le Rie Sacre et Profane*, 273-285. Strasbourg, France: Association des Publications pres les Universites de Strasbourg, 1986.

Describes how rock music is the "most important musical movement of the second half of the twentieth century." Attempts to explain the development of rock music within the context of the rapid technological and sociological changes that have transpired since World War II. Examines the rock concert as a quasi-religious ritual. Concludes with a discussion of the musical elements of rock music composition.

520.   Riley, Vikki. "Death Rockers of the World Unite! Melbourne 1978-80 -- Punk Rock or No Punk Rock?" In *From Pop to Punk to Postmodernism: Popular Music and Australian Culture From the 1960s to the 1990s*, edited by Philip Hayward, 113-126. North Sydney, Australia: Allen & Unwin, 1992.

Gives an account of how the Melbourne, Australia music scene "positioned itself within the global dream" of the punk rock movement.

521. Santoro, Gene. "Rock: Kick Out the Jams." In *The Guitar: The History, the Music, the Players*, 158-201. New York: William Morrow, 1984.

Provides a history of the electric guitar with descriptions of styles, rock music genres, and specific musicians. Discusses the central instrument for rock music in terms of its use as a theatrical prop and as an image of sexuality. Organizes the chapter into essays on rockabilly, the West Coast sound, the blues revival in both the United Kingdom and the United States, the San Francisco sound, and L.A. rock. Includes entries for numerous rock guitarists and gives special attention to Jimi Hendrix's techniques. Also includes a discography of twenty-five albums that highlight the guitar as a rock instrument.

522. Walser, Robert. "Highbrow, Lowbrow, Voodoo Aesthetics." In *Microphone Fiends: Youth Music & Youth Culture*, edited by Andrew Ross and Tricia Rose, 235-249. New York: Routledge, 1994.

Observes that heavy metal musicians have appropriated and adapted styles from classical music, thus creating a guitar virtuosity. Notes techniques used by Eddie Van Halen, Ritchie Blackmore, Randy Rhodes, and Yngwie Malmsteen. Contends that their appropriations are based on affinities and are similar to adaptations made by J. S. Bach. Distinguishes heavy metal's use of classical music from that of art rock, which simply reflected and re-articulated the classical genre.

BOOKS

523. Bangs, Lester. *Psychotic Reactions and Carburetor Dung*. New York: Alfred K. Knopf, 1987.

Collects selected published and unpublished writings of Lester Bangs, influential rock music journalist. Greil Marcus, another influential writer, edits the work and provides an introduction. The detailed index demonstrates the breadth and scope of the writing.

524. Bennett, H. Stith. *On Becoming a Rock Musician*. Amherst: University of Massachusetts Press, 1980.

Outlines methodically the process of becoming a musician in the context of a local-level rock group. Discusses group dynamics, musical instruments, performance, mobility, and technology.

525. Bordman, Gerald. *American Musical Comedy: From Adonis to Dreamgirls*. New York: Oxford University Press, 1982.

Covers the genre of musical comedy in this second volume on the American musical theater. Chapter 13 deals specifically with rock music and the theater. Discusses, compares, and contrasts *Bye Bye Birdie*, *Hair*, *Your Own Thing*, *Grease*, and *The Wiz*. Notes that *The Wiz* differed from the other rock musicals due to its well developed plot, appeal to children, and lavish production.

526. Brooks, Tilford. *America's Black Musical Heritage.* Englewood Cliffs, N.J.: Prentice-Hall, 1984.

Covers virtually all genres of black music in America. Chapters are organized as follows: Black Music and Its Roots, Black Music Forms Before 1900, Black Music Forms After 1900, The Black Musician in American Society, and American Black Composers in the European Tradition. Each chapter is divided into genres. Specifically relevant here is the section titled Rhythm and Blues, Rock and Roll, and Soul. Special attention is given to Chuck Berry as "the most influential Black performer in early rock and roll." Discusses the emergence of soul music as an attempt by black musicians to "achieve cultural definition." Several other black artists are highlighted for their contributions, including Little Richard and Otis Redding. Focus is on the adaptation of rock music by white performers and the subsequent response of black musicians in developing genres more closely tied to traditional rhythm and blues.

527. Brown, Charles T. *The Art of Rock and Roll.* 2nd ed. Englewood Cliffs, N.J.: Prentice-Hall, 1987.

Treats rock music as a valid art form. Traces the history of rock music as it developed in Black culture, from slave music through jazz. Organizes the information chronologically and by genre. Explores the relationship of music as a reflection of and reaction to society. Identifies the elements of rock music as being nonverbal communication, melody, rhythm, harmony, lyrics, performance, reflection of values, and rebellion and escapism. The societal issues that influence rock music are given as politics, religion, class struggle, changing mores, and race. Selected chapters include: Listening Skills, The Sources of Rock, Broadening of Styles, Soul/Motown, Folk-Rock, English Rock, Art and Electric Rock, Country Rock, and Heavy Metal. Other chapters deal with specific artists (e.g., Elvis Presley, the Beatles) and other genres (e.g., disco, punk, new wave). Appendices include analyses of selected compositions, a glossary, a discography, and a bibliography. Illustrated with black and white photographs of selected performers.

528. Christgau, Robert. *Any Old Way You Choose It: Rock and Other Pop Music, 1967-1973.* Baltimore: Penguin Books, 1973.

Collects numerous writings by the author from his career as a rock music critic. Emphasizes that art is "contingent" and that rock music criticism should "invoke total aesthetic response." Articles first appeared in *Esquire, The Village Voice,* and *Newsday.*

529. Clifford, Mike, ed. *The Harmony Illustrated Encyclopedia of Rock.* 7th ed. New York: Harmony Books, 1992.

Serves as one of the more comprehensive encyclopedic reference guides to rock music, covering more than 900 performers. Entries are both biographical and evaluative. Discographies are included as well as many color photographs and illustrations. With each new edition, performers are added and deleted based upon the projected and realized longevity of their careers.

530. Doerschuk, Bob, ed. *Rock Keyboard.* New York: Quill, 1985.

Presents interviews with a number of prominent rock keyboardists who discuss their craft. Offers insights by the musicians into the various roles of keyboard instruments in rock music. Also provides technical information and analysis. Includes a foreword by Keith Emerson.

531. Downing, David. *Future Rock.* St. Albans, England: Panther Books, 1976.

Traces the works of musicians who have used rock music to explore various scenarios about the future. Labels the phenomenon as "future rock." Attempts to define the moment (circa 1965) when rock music began to "arise as a cultural expression of immense and profound change." Chapters include discussions of the recordings and influences of Bob Dylan, Lou Reed and the Velvet Underground, David Bowie, Jefferson Airplane and Jefferson Starship, and Pink Floyd. Also examines themes of apocalypse, science fiction, outer space, politics, love, relationships, and attitudes toward women as conveyed through lyrics. Other chapters focus on progressive music, the synthesizer and on country music's impact on rock music. Includes a discography of selected recordings.

532. Durant, Alan. *Conditions of Music.* Albany: State University of New York Press, 1984.

Discusses the aesthetics of music. Presents two case-studies, the madrigal and rock music. Notes that rock music is comprised of a variety of musical styles, artistic positions, and social meanings. Examines disco music as manifested in Jamaica, India, and the United States to illustrate that rock music is not a centralist universal language, but rather is asserted and defined based on geographical and temporal variables. Explores the imitation and appropriation of rock music across cultures and the conflict between music as capitalist product and music as social conflict. Covers the development of synthesizers and music videos, and speculates on the possible implications for rock music composition.

533. Felder, Rachel. *Manic, Pop, Thrill.* Hopewell, N.J.: Ecco Press, 1993.

Explores the nature of alternative music. Traces the origins to the late 1970s punk movement that rejected contemporary musical conventions. Claims that alternative music is postmodern in that it breaks the distinctions between high culture and popular culture. States that the music cannot be understood without examining audience behavior, college radio, independent record labels, and fanzines. Notes that the impact is "more about attitude than sales figures."

Establishes a number of alternative music subgenres and discusses the groups that fall into these categories. Attempts to address the significance of alternative music through a cultural, musical, and artistic analysis.

534.   Flanagan, Bill. *Written in My Soul: Rock's Great Songwriters Talk about Creating Their Music.* Chicago: Contemporary Books, 1986.

Collects numerous interviews by the author with rock music composers designed to better understand the process of songwriting. Explores sources of creativity (e.g., inspiration, hard work, the great beyond). Discusses such areas as personal lives and drug usage as related to songwriting. Focuses on musicians "whose songs could be performed on acoustic guitar without losing their sense or impact." Musicians selected for inclusion were those who follow the rock tradition that flows from Woody Guthrie and Leadbelly through Bob Dylan. Organizes the interviews into the following categories: Southern voices, heartland voices, London voices, penitents of the spirit, New York voices, California voices, and emigrants.

535.   Fletcher, Peter. *Roll Over Rock: A Study of Music in Contemporary Culture.* London: Stainer & Bell, 1981.

Delves into the acceptance of music from previous cultural milieus based on a greater understanding of past social circumstances. Considers the consequences for emotional responses to contemporary music. Organizes the presentation into three sections: 1) the history of western attitudes toward music, 2) the history of American and British attitudes toward popular music, and 3) an account of twentieth-century music founded in "the evolution of musical structures in the West since the Renaissance." Selected chapters include *The Path to Elitism, The Path to Chauvinism, Creating a Low-Brow, Cultural Cataclysm, Retreat into Ritual,* and *Devolution.*

536.   Hoffmann, Frank. *The Literature of Rock, 1954-1978.* Metuchen, N.J.: Scarecrow Press, 1981.

Provides bibliographic access to selected popular literature on rock music. Organizes entries primarily in chronological order, grouping related topics at the end of the book. Most entries are briefly annotated.

537.   Hoffmann, Frank, and B. Lee Cooper. *The Literature of Rock II, 1979-1983: With Additional Material for the Period 1954-1978.* 2 vols. Metuchen, N.J.: Scarecrow, 1986.

[See entry number 536.]

538.   Hoffmann, Frank W., and B. Lee Cooper. *The Literature of Rock, III, 1984-1990: With Additional Material for the Period 1954-1983.* Metuchen, N.J.: Scarecrow Press, 1994.

[See entry number 536.]

MUSIC

539. Landau, Jon. *It's Too Late to Stop Now: A Rock and Roll Journal.* San Francisco: Straight Arrow Books, 1972.

Collects various essays of the author in which he explores how to write about rock music. Examines specific recordings and performances in terms of a musician's larger body of work. Claims that "the criterion for art in rock is the capacity of the musician to create a personal, almost private, universe and to express it fully." Organizes the essays into the general categories of White Rock (e.g., Bob Dylan, the Beatles, the Rolling Stones), Rock Issues (e.g., rock as art, technology), Black Rock (e.g., Otis Redding, Wilson Pickett, Sly and the Family Stone), and Confessions of a Rock Critic. Includes a limited discography.

540. Madow, Stuart, and Jeff Sobul. *The Colour of Your Dreams: The Beatles' Psychedelic Music.* Pittsburgh: Dorrance, 1992.

Critiques, title by title, songs from the Beatles' psychedelic period. Discusses instrumentation and analyzes the musical quality and performance of each composition.

541. Marcus, Greil, ed. *Rock and Roll Will Stand.* Boston: Beacon Press, 1969.

Collects various essays that reflect on late-1960s rock music. Contributors are Marvin Garson, Greil Marcus, Mike Daly, Langdon Winner, Stewart Kessler, Steve Strauss, and Sandy Darlington.

542. Marsh, Dave. *Fortunate Son.* New York: Random House, 1985.

Collects numerous articles by the author about rock music that have appeared in a variety of publications, including *Creem*, *Rolling Stone*, and *Record*. Chapters are organized into themes, such as stardom, the music industry, mass media, politics, the punk rock movement, and black music.

543. Mellers, Wilfrid. *Angels of the Night: Popular Female Singers of Our Time.* Oxford: Basil Blackwell, 1986.

Organizes this study of female performers of popular music into three sections. The first section treats the development of blues, jazz, and gospel music in relation to the black female performers of those genres. The second section traces jazz, folk, and country music and their white female performers. The third section addresses the contemporary female singer in "search for social and creative identity in her New Edenic Garden." Includes a discography and a glossary of musical terminology.

544. Mellers, Wilfrid. *A Darker Shade of Pale: A Backdrop to Bob Dylan.* New York: Oxford University Press, 1985.

Examines the "nature and meaning" of Bob Dylan's mythical representation of a culture. The first part of the book explores the American musical heritage, primarily country and folk music, from which Bob Dylan's art emerges. The second part analyzes Dylan's works and their contributions to the cultural heritage from which they evolved.

545.   Moore, Allan F. *Rock: The Primary Text, Developing a Musicology of Rock.* Buckingham, England: Open University Press, 1993.
   Argues for a musicology unique to rock music because rock music serves unique purposes. Suggests specific elements for such a musicology. Contends that the rules of rock music are "culturally constructed" and that meaning and expression are mediated. Studies a number of rock music styles (e.g., progressive rock, art rock, punk). Discusses stylistic authenticity and aesthetics.

546.   Nassour, Ellis, and Richard Broderick. *Rock Opera: The Creation of Jesus Christ Superstar, from Record Album to Broadway Show and Motion Picture.* New York: Hawthorn Books, 1973.
   Chronicles the history of the rock opera *Jesus Christ Superstar*.

547.   Pavletich, Aida. *Sirens of Song: The Popular Female Vocalist in America.* New York: Da Capo, 1980.
   Discusses the role of women in popular music by examining the careers of a variety of selected individuals who have changed or reflected attitudes toward women. Argues that through singing, a woman can dominate by consent. Presents ideals about women that have been created by each popular music genre. Chapters include: 1) Rock-A-Bye, Baby, 2) Canaries, Frails, and Girl Singers, 3) Folk Madonnas, 4) Teen Angels, 5) Soul Sisters, 6) Rock 'n' Roll Women, 7) Chirps, Thrushes, and Nightingales, 8) Country Queens, 9) Women of Heart and Mind, and 10) Bye, Bye Baby.

548.   Podell, Janet, ed. *Rock Music in America.* New York: H.W. Wilson, 1987.
   Collects various essays about rock music. Examines rock music as a process of combining art and socialization. Claims that rock music absorbs diverse cultural traditions and then "recycles them in endless combinations" through the mass media. Organizes the presentation into three sections: the early impact of rock music, the cultural impact, and the music industry.

549.   Rimler, Walter. *Not Fade Away: A Comparison of Jazz Age with Rock Era Pop Song Composers.* Ann Arbor: Pierian Press, 1984.
   Focuses on the musical compositions, as opposed to the lyrics, of songwriters. Concentrates on selected popular music songwriters of the 1960s: John Lennon, Paul McCartney, George Harrison, Bob Dylan, Mick Jagger, Keith Richards, Paul Simon, Carole King, Eddie Holland, Lamont Dozier, and Brian Holland. Addresses whether the decline of these 1960s songwriters was inevitable by comparing them to selected popular songwriters of the 1930s: George Gershwin,

Jerome Kern, Richard Rogers, Irving Berlin, Cole Porter, and Harold Arlen. Discusses songwriting communities, partnerships, performance, lyrics, and productive longevity.

550.   Rorem, Ned. *Critical Affairs: A Composer's Journal.* New York: George Braziller, 1970.

Collects various writings by the author. One chapter, originally from the *New York Times*, is titled *Against Rock*. Argues that rock music is interesting as a social phenomenon and a commercial commodity, but not as music. Contends that rock music is neither art nor politics. Attacks rock music critics for only offering reactions to rock and not illuminating the music, for their product being only "pure enthusiasm," and for loosing objectivity. Notes the major problem with rock criticism is that "chaos cannot symbolize chaos."

551.   Ross, Andrew, and Tricia Rose, eds. *Microphone Fiends: Youth Music & Youth Culture.* New York: Routledge, 1994.

Collects essays originating from a conference at Princeton University in November, 1992. Explores the intense meanings attached to music by the youth culture. Argues that investment in, and the level of meaning attached to, rock music by the youth culture exceeds that of religion and all other organized activities. Chapters focus on rap music, heavy metal music, dance music, and rituals. [Selected chapters are annotated elsewhere in this volume.]

552.   Roxon, Lillian. *Rock Encyclopedia.* New York: Grosset & Dunlap, 1969.

Provides biographical entries for rock music performers. Also contains non-biographical entries for genres (e.g., acid rock, hot-rod music, soft rock) and related topics such as the electric sitar and rock musicals. Appendices include the *Cash Box* top albums (1960-1968), *Cash Box* top singles (1949-1968), and *Billboard*'s number one weekly hits.

553.   Schaefer, John. *New Sounds: A Listener's Guide to New Music.* New York: Harper & Row, 1987.

Focuses on the music genre of "new music." Devotes one chapter to the influence of rock music on new music. Notes the path of influence actually began with new music impacting on rock music through the early contributions of groups such as Pink Floyd, King Crimson, and Genesis. Claims that it has been only since the early 1980s that rock music has had any type of significant impact on new music, citing such artists as David Byrne, Brian Eno, and especially Laurie Anderson. Claims that rock music is the most effective means of increasing the popularity of new music, but composers need to avoid rock composition cliches.

554. Shaw, Arnold. *Dictionary of American Pop/Rock.* New York: Schirmer Books, 1982.

Professes to be a "style and semantic dictionary." States that it does not include biographical information about important individuals, but rather describes, analyzes, and evaluates each person's contributions. In addition to individuals, entries are included for musical genres and styles, instruments, awards (including lists of winners), associations, slang (e.g., Deadheads), and jargon (e.g., gig). Defines popular music as rock, pop, rhythm and blues, folk, country, blues, gospel, jazz, film, and theater. Includes cross-references and a detailed index.

555. Shaw, Arnold. *The Rock Revolution.* New York: Crowell-Collier Press, 1969.

Claims to examine rock music from a sociological, psychological, and aesthetic perspective. Discusses the recording studio as an integral part of the production of rock music. Traces the history of rock music from blues, rhythm and blues, and rockabilly. Devotes entire chapters to Bob Dylan, the Beatles, the British invasion, soul music, and the California sound. Notes that the main features of rock music are guitars, a reliance on technology, poetic and literary lyrics, experimentation with sound, greater artistic control by musicians over the production of records, fashion statements, the synthesis of other musical genres, and the rejection of romanticism in favor of ideology. Concludes that rock music continues to develop in complexity and has become worthy for listening in addition to dancing. Includes a glossary of rock music terms and a selected discography.

556. Stuessy, Joe. *Rock and Roll: Its History and Stylistic Development.* 2nd ed. Englewood Cliffs, N.J.: Prentice Hall, 1994.

Provides a textbook approach to the history of rock music as a series of musical styles. Organizes the presentation essentially in chronological order, starting with the music genres that formed rock music (i.e., country, rhythm and blues, popular music). Proceeds with a discussion of the major artists of the 1950s (e.g., Bill Haley, Elvis Presley, Little Richard, Fats Domino, Chuck Berry, Jerry Lee Lewis, and Buddy Holly). Notes the early 1960s era of surf music and dance music. Devotes an entire chapter to the Beatles and another chapter almost exclusively to the Rolling Stones. Also addresses folk rock, soul music, the Motown sound, the San Francisco Sound (e.g., Jefferson Airplane, Grateful Dead, Janis Joplin), jazz rock (e.g., Chicago, Blood Sweat & Tears), and art rock. Concluding chapters cover the 1970s (e.g., singer-songwriters, disco) and the 1980s (e.g., heavy metal music, rap, Michael Jackson, Bruce Springsteen, Madonna, U2, Guns N' Roses, Van Halen, Metallica). Each chapter concludes with a musical analysis of a representative style. Includes a discography and a bibliography.

DISSERTATIONS

557. Amos, Alvin Emanuel. "The use of Keyboard Instruments in the Religious Services of Selected Black Baptist Churches in Central Piedmont North Carolina." Ed.D. The University of North Carolina at Greensboro, 1987. *Dissertation Abstracts International* 48: 1348A.

Assesses the performance and training of keyboardists in relation to demographic factors. Sunday worship was tape recorded at twelve churches and the pastors and keyboardists completed a questionnaire and an interview. A keyboard performance summary table was constructed. Identifies the four most frequent styles: "as written," "classic gospel," "a cappella," and "jazz/blues." Notes that the prominent styles are gospel music and those borrowed from jazz and rock. Also notes that formal keyboard training is minimal.

558. Bennett, Hilton Stith. "Other People's Music." Ph.D. Northwestern University, 1972. *Dissertation Abstracts International* 33: 5832A.

Proposes a sociology of music based on a musical aesthetic. Identifies six categories of resources (personnel, instruments, practice site, transportation, gigs, and The Music) that provide a cultural definition of the rock music economy. Changes in musical ideas are associated with changes in resources.

559. Brittin, Ruth V. "The Effect of Categorization on Preference for Popular Music Styles." Ph.D. Florida State University, 1989. *Dissertation Abstracts International* 50: 2417A.

Investigates the "effect of stylistic categorization on preference for popular music styles." Subjects were asked to categorize music selections using three different methods: prescribed classification (jazz, pop, or rock), unprescribed classification, and controlled without overtly classifying. Results showed no significant difference among the methods. Further testing using realtime classification methodology indicated significant differences from the first study, thus suggesting the benefit of using of realtime measurement in music preference studies.

560. Cartmell, Dan J. "Stephen Sondheim and the Concept Musical." Ph.D. University of California, Santa Barbara, 1983. *Dissertation Abstracts International* 44: 3208A.

Studies Stephen Sondheim's "contribution to a style of musical theatre termed the concept musical." Claims that Sondheim uses rock music, as well as other musical genres, to create feeling and mood by emphasizing rhythm and using "pastiche bases, dissonance and irony."

561. Darling, Dennis Lee. "The Construction of a Semantic Differential Scale Designed to Measure Attitude Toward Selected Styles of Music." Ed.D. University of Illinois at Urbana-Champaign, 1982. *Dissertation Abstracts International* 43: 716A.

Constructs and implements a "semantic differential instrument designed to measure attitude of undergraduate students toward selected styles" of music, specifically Renaissance, baroque, classical, romantic, contemporary art, country-western, hard rock, soft rock, Balinese, and modern jazz. Investigates "the extent to which attitude toward the selected styles was related to and affected by academic major, sex, grade classification, music experience, and scores on the Aliferis Music Achievement Test." Each variable was discovered to affect attitude toward one or more of the tested styles. Further, the "effect of tempo, performance medium, and familiarity and recognition" differed depending upon the style.

562. Emblidge, David Murray. "A Dialogue of Energy: Rock Music and Cultural Change." Ph.D. University of Minnesota, 1973. *Dissertation Abstracts International* 34: 7265A.

Explores rock music as a process of shifting aesthetics and cultural change. Claims that rock music moves society toward a new consciousness. Examines the rock styles of Janis Joplin, Jimi Hendrix, The Band, Blood Sweat & Tears, Bob Dylan, and the Rolling Stones.

563. Graffius, Karen O'Neal. "Music Preference: a Comparison of Verbal Opinions and Behavioral Intentions of Selected High School Students." Ph.D. Louisiana State University and Agricultural and Mechanical College, 1988. *Dissertation Abstracts International* 49: 3652A.

Compares high school students' opinions and behaviors in regard to music preference. One-hundred-two male and female, black and white adolescents enrolled in either gifted or regular curriculum programs were asked to select musicians from four categories "whose music they felt important enough to be passed on to future generations." The four categories were pop/rock/soul, jazz/blues/big-band, country-western, and classical. Subjects were then exposed to musical excerpts by the same musicians and asked whether they would purchase, or already owned, the music.

564. Harding, John Ralph. "A Survey of the Evolution of Jazz for the General Reader." D.M.A. University of Miami, 1981. *Dissertation Abstracts International* 42: 3341A.

Recounts the evolution of jazz music from its origins as a blend of European and African music in the late 1700s through various forms to its contemporary styles. Discusses the 1960s merge of jazz and rock music sounds that resulted in fusion.

565. Hicken, Leslie Wayne. "Relationships Among Selected Listener Characteristics and Musical Preference." D.Mus.Ed. Indiana University, 1991. *Dissertation Abstracts International* 43: 1089A.

Determines the relationship among musical training, familiarity with musical styles, musical aptitude, field dependence-independence, socio-economic status, gender, and musical preference. Subjects were 176 high school students. Utilized the following instruments: Musical Experience Inventory, Otis Dudley Duncan Socio-economic Index, Gordon Musical Aptitude Profile, and Group Embedded Figures Test. Presented twelve musical genres: jazz combo, jazz vocal, jazz big band, symphonic, chamber literature, opera, band, show-instrumental, show-vocal, rock, country & western, non-western. Finds that musical experience and aptitude, familiarity, socio-economic status, field independence, and gender are significantly correlated with preference.

566. Hoffman, Alan Neil. "On the Nature of Rock and Roll: An Enquiry Into the Aesthetic of a Musical Vernacular." Ph.D. Yale University, 1983. *Dissertation Abstracts International* 44: 2618A.

Examines three "principal stylistic and aesthetic criteria" of rock music. The first criterion is that rock music is recorded music and many of its characteristics are derived from this aspect. The second criterion is that rock music is a genre with unique styles embedded as "structural facets." The third criterion is that rock music is dance music, which also impacts on its rhythm and structure. Notes that the three criteria are not intended to be mutually exclusive.

567. Hoover, John Gene. "The Warner Brothers Film Musical, 1927-1980." Ph.D. University of Southern California, 1985. *Dissertation Abstracts International* 46: 2468A.

Discusses Warner Brothers film musicals from 1927 to 1980 "in terms of their socio-cultural context, generic conventions, and studio ideology and style." As for rock music, Warner Brothers Studios have sought to capitalize on the youth market since the mid-1950s by focusing on the production of rock musicals and Broadway adaptations during this period.

568. Horn, Barbara Lee. "Hair: Changing Versions." Ph.D. City University of New York, 1982. *Dissertation Abstracts International* 43: 2832A.

Studies the evolution of the rock musical *Hair* from its original Public Theater staging in 1967, through its Broadway production, to the 1978 film version. Investigates how the "dramatic form, thematic content, and theatrical techniques" illuminated and reflected the 1960s counterculture. Places *Hair* in the historical context of American musicals. Notes that the ongoing revision of the content changed *Hair* from an anti-war musical to an "explicit assault on the conventions of the Broadway musical comedy." Includes interviews and an analysis of critiques. Concludes that *Hair* is a legitimate extension of the counterculture and that its popularity is due to relevance, adaptability, and appeal.

569. Jumpeter, Joseph Anthony. "The Utilization of a Personalized System of Instruction in a Specific Area of a Music Appreciation Course." D.Ed. Pennsylvania State University, 1980. *Dissertation Abstracts International* 41: 4323A.

Investigates whether utilization of the a Personalized System of Instruction (PSI) would, for teaching about jazz and rock music, positively affect an increase in factual knowledge when compared to a lecture-demonstration teaching method. Also tests whether a PSI would affect music preference differently than a lecture-demonstration method. A PSI is characterized by five elements: mastery learning, self-pacing, emphasis on the written word, lecture-demonstration for purposes of motivation and enrichment, and student proctors. Subjects were thirty-five college students enrolled in a music appreciation course assigned randomly to two groups (test and control). Results indicate no difference between the groups in regard to increased factual knowledge or music preference.

570. Kealy, Edward Robert. "The Real Rock Revolution: Sound Mixers, Social Inequality, and the Aesthetics of Popular Music Production." Ph.D. Northwestern University, 1974. *Dissertation Abstracts International* 35: 6818A.

Focuses on the "sound mixer," or the occupation of mixing recorded music for mass reproduction, in relation to the "sound makers" (i.e., musicians) and the "sound marketers" (i.e., record producers). Identifies three models: Bureaucratic, Entrepreneurial, and Craft. Explores the sound mixers' loss of control over the aesthetic production of rock music to the musicians and producers. Demonstrates shifts in control over recording studio technology and the consequential change in status for the sound mixer from artisan to technician.

571. May, William Vernon, Jr. "Musical Style Preferences and Aural Discrimination Skills of Primary Grade School Children." Ph.D. University of Kansas, 1983. *Dissertation Abstracts International* 44: 1016A.

Examines the music genre preferences of grade school children based on grade level, gender, and race. Subjects were 577 children in grades one through three tested using the Music Preference Reaction Index (MPRI) instrument. Results indicate that the subjects preferred rock music and country music with more pronounced preferences in higher grades.

572. Ramaglia, Bellino Benedetto. "The Transcription, Analysis and Study of Representative Recordings of Rock Music 1954-1969." Ed.D. Columbia University Teachers College, 1980. *Dissertation Abstracts International* 42: 5052A.

Stresses the lack of scores and other instructional materials available for incorporating and utilizing rock music in the music education curriculum. Pulls together selected pieces of rock music as examples to be used in music education. Transcribes stylistic representations from recordings into scores.

Analyzes each score in order to illustrate the important and relevant features, including instrumentation, orchestration, form, melody, harmony, and rhythm. Identifies three stylistic eras of rock music and comments on the musical characteristics of each period. The first era is defined as "the early years" (1954-1957) in which rock music became the most popular genre. The second era is called "the expansion period" (1958-1963) in which rock music grew into a national phenomenon. The third era is labeled "the maturation period" (1964-1969) in which the Beatles rose and fell. Also includes discussions of the recording techniques used in each era.

573. Stewart, Richard E. "A Comparison of Music Preferences of Students in Three Educational Systems: Seventh-Day Adventist, Public, and Private Independent Schools." Ph.D. University of Miami, 1984. *Dissertation Abstracts International* 45: 1066A.
 Compares the music genre preferences of 1,508 students from three types of school systems: Seventh-Day Adventist, public, and private. Looks at the effects of musical background and grade levels on music preference. Subjects were grouped into three categories by grade level: fourth and fifth grades, seventh and eighth grades, and eleventh and twelfth grades. Utilized ten musical genres: classical, country, disco, easy listening, jazz, new wave, reggae, religious, rock, and soul music. Results indicate that rock music was ranked high in terms of preference among all three grade categories and country music was ranked lowest. Musical background was relevant in the listening preferences for some of the genres, including rock music.

574. Tamm, Eric Alexander. "Brian Eno, Electronic Musician: Progressive Rock and the Ambient Sound, 1973-1986." Ph.D. University of California, Berkeley, 1987. *Dissertation Abstracts International* 48: 2191A.
 Chronicles the musical development of Brian Eno. Covers Eno's musical influences, "artistic intent," and styles. Discusses and analyzes Eno's progressive rock albums and ambient music albums. Concludes with an examination of Eno's work from "ontological, historical, and aesthetic" perspectives.

575. Valdez, Stephen Kenneth. "The Development of the Electric Guitar Solo in Rock Music, 1954-1971." D.M.A. University of Oregon, 1992. *Dissertation Abstracts International* 53: 3407A.
 Articulates the development of the electric guitar as the most prominent instrument in rock music between 1954 and 1971. Notes that many rock groups during this period had two guitarists. One guitar was used to play rhythm, working with the bass and drums. The second guitar was used to play lead with "melodic embellishments." Observes that the basic structure of rock music is a twelve-bar blues style that permits the lead guitarist to perform improvised solos. Focuses on the evolution of the guitar solo in rock music and highlights

the work of Danny Cedrone (Bill Haley & The Comets), Frank Beecher (Bill Haley & The Comets), Scotty Moore (Elvis Presley), Chuck Berry, George Harrison, Keith Richards, Eric Clapton, Jimmy Page, and Jimi Hendrix.

576. Walser, Robert Anton. "Running with the Devil: Power, Gender, and Madness in Heavy Metal Music." Ph.D. University of Minnesota, 1991. *Dissertation Abstracts International* 52: 2319A.
   Studies heavy metal music of the 1980s and presents a history of the genre. Focuses on the Van Halen song *Running with the Devil* to explore how the music, in addition to the lyrics, produces meaning. Claims that heavy metal guitarists have appropriated "rhetorical models and musical materials from classical composers and performers." In doing so, heavy metal musicians have laid claim to "power and artistry" for a different social class. Explores gender issues in heavy metal music by examining the construction of masculinity in the music. Criticizes the stereotyping of heavy metal music as "adolescent deviance" by arguing that it is used by fans to cope with, and give meaning to, American society.

FILMS AND VIDEOS

577. *The Big T.N.T. Show.* Larry Peerce, dir. American International Pictures, 1966.
   Presents Joan Baez, the Byrds, Ray Charles, Bo Diddley, Donovan, the Lovin' Spoonful, Roger Miller, the Ronettes, and Ike and Tina Turner in concert. Captures the transitional mid-1960s music scene on film.

578. *The Concert For Bangladesh.* Saul Swimmer, dir. Twentieth Century Fox.
   Documents one of the first large-scale benefit rock concerts. Held in New York City in 1971. Performers include Bob Dylan, George Harrison, Billy Preston, Leon Russell, Ravi Shankar, and Ringo Starr. Other contributing musicians include Eric Clapton, Klaus Voorman, and Jim Keltner.

579. *Fillmore.* Richard T. Heffron, dir. Twentieth Century Fox, 1972.
   Commemorates the closing of the Fillmore West in San Francisco. Offers an array of rock groups representing the San Francisco sound.

580. *Let The Good Times Roll.* Robert Abel and Sid Levin, dirs. Columbus Pictures, 1973.
   Captures and documents many performers from the 1950s.

581. *Monterey Pop.* James Desmond, Barry Feinstein, D. A. Pennebaker, Albert Maysles, Roger Murphy, Richard Leacock, Nick Proferes, dirs. Leacock-Pennebaker Films, 1969.

Presents segments of the historic Monterey International Pop Festival from 1967. Numerous landmark performances by such artists as The Who, Janis Joplin, and Jimi Hendrix.

582. *Rock Music of the Eighties.* Merit, 1990.

Explores various rock music styles of the 1980s. Reports on the impact of new technologies.

583. *Sympathy for the Devil.* Jean-Luc Godard, dir. New Line Pictures, 1970.

Captures the Rolling Stones in the studio recording the song *Sympathy for the Devil.*

Politics

ARTICLES

584.   Berry, Cecelie, and David Wolin. "Regulating Rock Lyrics: A New Wave of Censorship?" *Harvard Journal on Legislation* 23 (1986): 595-619.

Explores the "leading cases in First Amendment jurisprudence to determine if objectionable music falls within the scope of protected expression." Considers the clear and present danger test and the obscenity doctrine, the "impact of variable obscenity on the First Amendment rights of minors," and due process constraints. Reviews the issues surrounding censorship, parental sovereignty, and industry self-regulation. Concludes that even if the government can legally restrict objectionable music, such power would be "so burdened by process constraints" that a threat to the music industry would not be realized.

585.   Bright, Terry. "Soviet Crusade Against Pop." *Popular Music* 5 (1985): 123-148.

Describes the Soviet Union's 1983 campaign by the Ministry of Culture to "destroy" rock music groups through excessive censorship. Explains the differences between amateur rock groups and the official Vocal Instrumental Ensembles. Discusses the rise of rock music groups in the Soviet Union and the eventual, but few, punk groups. Notes the biggest threat to the authorities was the rise of new wave bands due to the "sharp irony and accurate realism of everything they sang, said or did."

586.   Cooper, B. Lee. "Lyrical Commentaries: Learning from Popular Music." *Music Educators Journal* 77, no. 8 (1991): 56-59.

Argues that popular music lyrics, including those of rock music, serve to challenge commonly held beliefs and examine our social heritage. Includes a chart ranging from 1962 through 1987 of political events (e.g., the 1970 shootings of students by the Ohio National Guard at Kent State University), personalities (e.g., Spiro Agnew, Richard Nixon), song titles (e.g., *Ohio*), and artists (e.g., Crosby, Stills, Nash & Young). Illustrates various uses of nursery rhymes and children's tales as lyrical commentaries. Discusses issues of free speech and censorship.

587.   Cushman, Thomas. "Rich Rastas and Communist Rockers: A Comparative Study of the Origin, Diffusion and Defusion of Revolutionary Musical Codes." *Journal of Popular Culture* 25, no. 3 (1991): 17-61.
   Traces the history of two musical genres or styles (codes), reggae and Soviet rock, in order to understand the "ironic process" of how revolutionary musical codes become central elements of the social systems that they oppose. Compares and contrasts the development and evolution of the above two musical codes in order to present a model of cultural appropriation. Structures the cultural appropriation of musical styles into a "social career" model defined by three stages: creation-articulation, diffusion-appropriation, and defusion-immobilization. Concludes that the existence of similar patterns in the cultural appropriation of reggae and Soviet rock music demonstrates that cultural appropriation "serves hegemonic functions" in both capitalist and socialist environments. Notes that while the model of the process holds true for both types of societies, the mechanisms that drive the process are different.

588.   Denisoff, R. Serge. "Fighting Prophecy with Napalm: *The Ballad of the Green Berets.*" *Journal of American Culture* 13, no. 1 (1990): 81-93.
   Details the rise of folk rock music in the 1960s, giving particular attention to anti-war themes in the works of Bob Dylan and, specifically, Barry McGuire's *Eve of Destruction*. Focuses on the history behind the patriotic song recorded by Barry Sadler, *Ballad of the Green Berets*. Considers the political motives behind the song and the role of RCA.

589.   Eriksen, Neil. "Popular Culture and Revolutionary Theory: Understanding Punk Rock." *Theoretical Review* 18 (1980): 13-35.
   Articulates the complex relationship between ideology and culture in order to define the ways in which punk rock music fulfills a "revolutionary cultural function." Discusses class and cultural hegemony, subcultures, countercultures, and the youth culture. Explores in detail the punk rock movement, the musicians, and the political nature of the themes of sex and violence. Highlights the punk group Gang of Four. Concludes that punk rock is an ideology that expresses a "critical realism" as opposed to the traditional escapism of rock music. Notes that punk music serves as a restructuring element in popular culture. Acknowledges the tentative nature of punk rock music, but claims it still serves to validate a particular ideology.

590. Fox, William S., and James D. Williams. "Political Orientation and Music Preferences Among College Students." *Public Opinion Quarterly* 38, no. 3 (1974): 352-371.

Studies the political relationship of popular music genres to the "political orientations, music involvement, and musical preferences of college students." Contends there are two opposite approaches to thinking about the political nature of popular music. The first is that popular music does not convey strong political messages to its audience, regardless of the intent of the performers. Popular music serves as an "opiate of the young" by reducing or ignoring the political consciousness of the audience, thus implicitly supporting the status quo. The second approach is that popular music challenges traditional values, asserts new ideologies, and calls for social and political change. Notes that a content analysis methodology for studying popular music may be essential but is insufficient. Content analysis focuses on the lyrics and ignores the influences of rhythm, melody, and other musical connotations. Content analysis also does not address audience perceptions. Therefore, the authors utilized survey methodology to study 730 undergraduate college students enrolled in sociology classes. Results indicate that political orientation is associated with music involvement and musical preferences. Liberals attend more concerts, buy more records, and listen to more music. Conservatives listen to the radio more often. Interestingly, rock music (high appeal) and country music (low appeal) were not strongly associated with political orientation. Liberals favored folk, blues, and protest music more than conservatives did. Conservatives favored pop and easy listening more than liberals did. Concludes that the widespread appeal of rock music among liberals and conservatives demonstrates its limited political value.

591. Frith, Simon. "Rock and Popular Culture." *Socialist Revolution* 7, no. 1 (1977): 97-112.

Questions contemporary analysis of rock music as mass communication with a political significance. Uses three books as a means of raising important theoretical issues: *Any Old Way You Choose It* by Robert Christgau, *It's Too Late To Stop Now* by Jon Landau, and *Mystery Train* by Greil Marcus. Concludes that rock music is first and foremost a commodity designed to generate profits through production, marketing, and sales. Also, rock music's status as commodity does not determine its meaning. Rock music can, as art, convey contrary ideological messages.

592. Grossberg, Lawrence. "Rock, Territorialization and Power." *Cultural Studies* 5, no. 3 (1991): 358-367.

Claims that rock music has never been a true political force, despite its influences on social and cultural conditions. Argues that rock has not challenged the dominant social systems. This is not to say that rock music has not attempted to challenge the status quo, but it has not been concerned with "the organization of political consensus and economic relations." The political nature of rock music has been defined mainly by those who oppose it. Rock music does not address political realities, only the impact of those realities on everyday life (e.g., rock music can address the suffering from apartheid, but not "the international political economic system which sustains apartheid").

593. Kanzer, Adam M. "Misfit Power, the First Amendment and the Public Forum: Is There Room in America for the Grateful Dead?" *Columbia Journal of Law and Social Problems* 25, no. 3 (1992): 521-565.

Addresses First Amendment issues raised by city council decisions to ban the Grateful Dead from municipally-owned arenas. Analyzes "the current state of First Amendment doctrine regarding access to public forums" and concludes that the law does not provide for targeting specific groups such as the Grateful Dead. Examines why Deadheads (referred to as the "Haight-Ashbury on wheels") are often found to be offensive to communities. Presents examples of specific Grateful Dead performance bannings. Reviews several court cases that may support the constitutionality of banning the Grateful Dead. Discusses issues of content-neutral versus content-based bans and valid time, place and manner regulations. Supreme Court rulings "delegate the authority to balance interests to the local lawmakers."

594. Kennedy, David. "Frankenchrist Versus the State: The New Right, Rock Music and the Case of Jello Biafra." *Journal of Popular Culture* 24, no. 1 (1990): 131-148.

Details the trial of Jello Biafra after his arrest for distribution of "harmful matter to minors." The matter was a poster included with the album by his rock group, the Dead Kennedys. The poster is from a work titled *Landscape #20, Where Are We Coming From?* by artist H. R. Giger. Discusses the formation of the Parents Music Resource Center (PMRC) and related efforts to censor rock music. Biafra was acquitted. Concludes that a legal precedent was not established, but the case was "a tactical draw and a strategic victory for free speech in its battle against censorship."

595. Kurti, Laszlo. "Rocking the State: Youth and Rock Music Culture in Hungary, 1976-1990." *East European Politics and Societies* 5, no. 3 (1991): 483-513.

Stresses that the political, economic, and cultural crises of Eastern Europe in the early 1980s were best demonstrated in the "emergence of alternative youth and rock music cultures." Argues that the new music culture facilitated an atmosphere of glasnost and was vital in altering the political structure. Concludes that the fusion of traditional folk music with rock music created a dangerous, politically dynamic music that "embodied new ideas and values, challenging possibilities for an alternative culture and future."

596. Laing, Dave. "'Sadeness', Scorpions and Single Markets: National and Transnational Trends in European Popular Music." *Popular Music* 11, no. 2 (1992): 127-140.

Suggests the possibility that there is a shifting of power from Anglo American control over popular music to the European community. Explores the strategies of European multinational companies that control the European music industry and describes the cultural policies of the European Community. Offers that dance music, heavy metal music, and adult oriented rock may provide opportunities for greater participation by European and Eastern European musicians in the international popular music scene.

597. McDonald, James R. "Politics Revisited: Metatextual Implications of Rock and Roll Criticism." *Youth & Society* 19, no. 4 (1988): 485-504.

Expresses the view that rock music can be political without generating an immediate active response. Contends that if a rock song creates "an awareness," or consciousness, then a potential for empowerment has been established. Observes that the rock music of the 1980s is not necessarily apolitical simply because it has not produced political action. Describes rock music as being metatextual in that similar aspects of the same text have their own "fragmented construct." Uses the Bruce Springsteen composition *Born in the U.S.A.* as an example. The song has been interpreted as, and has evoked the audience reactions of, a statement of patriotism as well as political protest. Concludes that the political interpretation of rock music is dependent on the extent to which it reinforces various existing individualized audience perspectives.

598. Ramet, Pedro. "Rock Counterculture in Eastern Europe and the Soviet Union." *Survey* 29, no. 2 (1985): 149-171.

Considers the elements of political socialization in rock music and the differing reactions to it in various Eastern European countries. Notes that rock music expresses youth alienation and promotes contact with the West through the imitation and glorification of styles and fashions. Observes that rock music has emotional effects and psycho-cultural effects that influence perceptions of society. It also has socio-cultural effects that influence peer group associations and identifications, plus political effects that influence orientations. Details the responses to these effects in the Soviet Union, Poland, Czechoslovakia, East Germany, Yugoslavia, Romania, Bulgaria, and Hungary.

599. Robinson, John P., Robert Pilskaln, and Paul Hirsch. "Protest Rock and Drugs." *Journal of Communication* 26, no. 4 (1976): 125-136.

Studies the relationship between the political messages of rock music during the 1960s and the drug culture of the same era. Discovers that rock music was influential in portraying drug use as generational behavior, whereas political rock music was "less effective in conveying a consistent or enduring leftward political orientation." Suggests that rock music never appropriated a Marxist perspective and it may have actually "served to channel social unrest into a more politically passive direction." Protest rock music allowed a token, rather than active, political opposition to the mainstream. The portrayal of a drug culture in rock music may have also dissipated any political impact of the music in the minds of members of society at-large.

600.   Tillman, Robert H. "Punk Rock and the Construction of 'Pseudo-Political' Movements." *Popular Music and Society* 7, no. 3 (1980): 165-175.

Characterizes as flawed theories of mass culture that view punk rock as a political force challenging the form and content of both popular music and the dominant social order. Argues historical realism that attempts to link art and politics "inevitably fails because it misapprehends the complexities" of the relationships. Uses perceptions of the Sex Pistols as an example of the critical theoretical errors derived from not realizing that while social structures can create cultural phenomena, they cannot dictate content. Concludes that rock music is an art that is inherently apolitical. Speculates that rock is "too sensual and aesthetic and lacks the purpose-rational orientation" required for serious political consequences.

601.   Ullestad, Neal. "Rock and Rebellion: Subversive Effects of Live Aid and *Sun City*." *Popular Music* 6, no. 1 (1987): 67-92.

Presents a framework of social and political structures around which rock music can be seen to operate. Notes that most rock music resides within the dominant culture, a hegemony that encourages pleasure and consumerism, yet adapts to change, discontent, and rebellion. Claims that the flexibility of hegemonic structures allow the expression of discontent without enduring significant change, ensuring that the dominant power structures to remain. Looks at Live Aid as an event that operated within contemporary hegemonic structures, urging charity, philanthropy, and cooperation. Observes that one result was an internal shift toward social concerns and, more radically, disruptive openings of the usual order that allowed additional challenges to the existing structures, such as the *Sun City* events. Distinguishes *Sun City* from the USA for Africa events by noting the strong educational campaign regarding apartheid that accompanied *Sun City*.

602.   Weinstein, Deena. "Rock: Youth and Its Music." *Popular Music and Society* 9, no. 3 (1983): 2-15.

Notes that rock music is usually observed from the perspective of cultural intent or social effect. Claims that the debate as to whether rock music is "an authentic creative expression or merely a commodity for sale" can be better approached if a distinction is made between popular music (commodity) and rock music (authentic). States that in times of economic expansion, rock music becomes more political and confrontational, while in times of economic restraint rock music supports the status quo. Concludes that the continuing existence of rock music is best understood in the context of the continuing and expanding existence of a distinctive youth culture. Also published in the book *Adolescents and Their Music: If It's Too Loud, You're Too Old*, edited by Jonathon S. Epstein.

603. Winders, James A. "Reggae, Rastafarians and Revolution: Rock Music in the Third World." *Journal of Popular Culture* 17, no. 1 (1983): 61-73.
Suggests that the revolutionary potential of rock music was only a brief glimmer in the history of the United States. However, there is greater potential for it to act as a force of political and social change in underdeveloped countries such as Jamaica. Reviews the growth in popularity of reggae music, which is uniquely Jamaican but contains roots of American black music (i.e., rock music). Discusses in detail the history of, and strong ties between, reggae music and the Rastafarian movement. Concludes that perhaps the future of rock music resides in underdeveloped countries where it can be fused with native music to "become the voice of previously voiceless people."

CHAPTERS

604. Brace, Tim, and Paul Friedlander. "Rock and Roll on the New Long March: Popular Music, Cultural Identity, and Political Opposition in the People's Republic of China." In *Rockin' the Boat: Mass Music and Mass Movements*, edited by Reebee Garofalo, 115-127. Boston: South End Press, 1992.
Observes that the youth of the People's Republic of China have turned to rock music. Claims that their particular form of rock music challenges traditional musical forms in the culture and the "hegemony of the government as the legitimate arbiter of Chinese culture." Describes the genre of Chinese rock music known as "yaogun yinyue" and its use as a tool for political opposition. Argues that the political and cultural meaning of rock music cannot be reduced to the effect. States that meaning is an act that is negotiated and relational.

605. Christgau, Robert. "Rah, Rah, Sis-Boom-Bah: The Secret Relationship Between College Rock and the Communist Party." In *Microphone Fiends: Youth Music & Youth Culture*, edited by Andrew Ross and Tricia Rose, 221-226. New York: Routledge, 1994.
Articulates some thoughts on the historical relationship between politics and rock music. Concentrates on, but is not limited to, discussing the politics of 1960s rock music in terms of black and white performers. Touches on punk rock and rap music.

606. Coreno, Thaddeus. "Guerrilla Music: Avant-Garde Voice as Oppositional Discourse." In *Adolescents and Their Music: If It's Too Loud, You're Too Old*, edited by Jonathon S. Epstein, 189-224. New York: Garland, 1994.

Suggests that rock music offers little in terms of oppositional discourse, although it is attacked frequently as a threat to society and the status quo. Asserts that music can socialize, but not indoctrinate. Claims that rock music, as a capitalist commodity, permits and promotes rebellion, alienation, individualism, and political protest, as long as it is profitable. Musically "authentic counterideologies" that would radically change the status quo are not to be found. In fact, rock music channels "oppositional adolescent energy away from organized political activity towards domesticated leisure rituals." Offers that the unpredictable nature, lack of stratification, and musical conformity in avant-garde music "expose the architecture of domination."

607. Cushman, Thomas. "Glasnost, Perestroika, and the Management of Oppositional Popular Culture in the Soviet Union, 1985-1991." In *Current Perspectives in Social Theory*, 25-67. Greenwich, Conn.: JAI Press, 1993.

Offers an explanation of glasnost and perestroika in which the relationship between culture and politics is explored. Argues that the emergent cultural openness during this period represents a sophisticated management of oppositional culture. Draws upon the critical theories of Herbert Marcuse, Antonio Gramsci, and Jurgen Habermas. Focuses on rock music because of its historic role as one form of oppositional culture in the Soviet Union and as a means of empowerment. Reviews the evolution of selective tolerance in the 1970s through official Vocal Instrumental Ensembles and the development of an underground infrastructure for the production and distribution of rock music. Contends that Mikhail Gorbachev initiated glasnost and perestroika in order to coopt oppositional cultural values for the purpose of rejecting previous Soviet regimes and for consolidating support. The result was a decline in the status of rock musicians as dissenters. Consequently, glasnost and perestroika maintained the status quo by presenting it as progressive.

608. Douglas, Louise, and Richard Geeves. "Music, Counter-culture and the Vietnam Era." In *From Pop to Punk to Postmodernism: Popular Music and Australian Culture from the 1960s to the 1990s*, edited by Philip Hayward, 101-112. North Sydney, Australia: Allen & Unwin, 1992.

Discusses Australian rock music in relation to the counterculture politics of the late 1960s and early 1970s. Characterizes the political mood of the Australian recording industry as parsimonious and conservative. Covers the nature of media outlets for rock music during this period. Argues that Australian rock music was stunted during this period due to the music industry, the media, and a lack of creativity on the part of Australian musicians.

609. Frith, Simon, and John Street. "Rock Against Racism and Red Wedge: From Music to Politics, from Politics to Music." In *Rockin' the Boat: Mass Music and Mass Movements*, edited by Reebee Garofalo, 66-80. Boston: South End Press, 1992.

Studies two movements is Great Britain designed to politically and socially mobilize youth: Rock Against Racism (founded in 1976) and Red Wedge (founded in 1986). Discusses the political changes in music in the decade between the founding of these two movements. Explores the changing political nature of the youth culture and the "aesthetics of protest." Notes that people feel the most "passionately" about music when it has the "power to mark boundaries" (e.g., punk music).

610. Garofalo, Reebee. "Nelson Mandela, the Concerts: Mass Culture as Contested Terrain." In *Rockin' the Boat: Mass Music and Mass Movements*, edited by Reebee Garofalo, 54-65. Boston: South End Press, 1992.

Reviews two concerts held to benefit Nelson Mandela and the anti-apartheid movement. The first concert was on June 11, 1988, at Wembley Stadium in London, England. The second concert was held on April 16, 1990 at the same location. Discusses the implications of rock music mega-events for political causes.

611. Garofalo, Reebee. "Understanding Mega-Events: If We Are the World, Then How do We Change It?" In *Rockin' the Boat: Mass Music and Mass Movements*, edited by Reebee Garofalo, 14-35. Boston: South End Press, 1992.

Describes mega-events such as *Live Aid* as celebrations of technology. Uses culture theory to explain the relationships between rock music, social issues, and the impact on other cultures. Discusses the role of technology and the power of rock stars. Analyzes mega-events in terms of fund raising, consciousness raising, and mobilization. Concludes that mega-events are useful for "priming the political pump."

612. Gray, Herman. "Popular Music as a Social Problem: A Social History of Claims Against Popular Music." In *Images of Issues: Typifying Contemporary Social Problems*, edited by Joel Best, 143-158. New York: Aldine de Gruyter, 1989.

Uses three case-studies to illustrate a "broader social and political debate over the moral order" of society. Jazz music, in the 1920s, was denounced as eroding traditional values due to elements of immigration, the "celebration of consumption," and increasing industrialization and urbanization. In the 1950s, rock music was denounced as being anti-religious and pro-Communism, and as originating from African American culture. In the 1980s, the Parents Music Resource Center (PMRC) utilized feminism, children's rights, and anti-pornography issues and symbols to denounce rock music, thus giving their goals broader appeal and greater support than previous assaults on popular music. Presents an overview of the U.S. Senate hearings that resulted from PMRC pressure. Discusses the music industry's response. Concludes that to assert control over production and consumption of rock music is difficult because the content, meaning, and experience is in the hands of the consumer. Periodic attempts to do so can be viewed in a larger context of desiring to bring "moral control over a world thought to be out of control."

613. Grossberg, Lawrence. "The Political Status of Youth and Youth Culture." In *Adolescents and Their Music: If It's Too Loud, You're Too Old*, edited by Jonathon S. Epstein, 25-46. New York: Garland, 1994.

Contends that youth are linked to a commodity status of economics either as a market or as an audience. Challenges assumptions regarding their political status, especially the notion that youth is a subordinate other. Argues that youth is "not an identity but a distribution of practices and affects." Traces the formation of the youth culture during the post-World War II era. States that rock music served to map the boundaries of the youth culture, transforming it from a "transitional culture" into a "culture of transitions." Rock music created a culture based on creating identity through "refusing identities." Explores the issues surrounding the contemporary struggle over youth, popular culture, and the political state.

614. Hayes, Nick. "The Dean Reed Story." In *Rocking the State: Rock Music and Politics in Eastern Europe and Russia*, edited by Sabrina Petra Ramet, 165-178. Boulder: Westview Press, 1994.

Profiles the life of Dean Reed, an American entertainer who embraced socialism as a rejection of United States imperialism. Discusses how Reed met and fulfilled certain needs for communist countries (e.g., ex-patriot popular culture figure who rejected western ideology). Reports that Reed died suspiciously in the German Democratic Republic on June 12, 1986.

615. Herman, Gary. "The Struggle for Song: A Reply to Leon Rosselson." In *Media, Politics and Culture: A Socialist View*, edited by Carl Gardner, 51-60. London: Macmillan Press, 1979.

Counters the arguments made in a chapter by Leon Rosselson from this same volume. Contends that the production of rock music can be accessed by the masses. Points out the struggle within the music industry between capitalistic motivation and ideological control over production.

616. Kurti, Laszlo. "'How Can I be a Human Being?' Culture, Youth, and Musical Opposition in Hungary." In *Rocking the State: Rock Music and Politics in Eastern Europe and Russia*, edited by Sabrina Petra Ramet, 73-102. Boulder: Westview Press, 1994.

Explores the relationship between rock music and the ideological context in which it is "created and consumed." Contends that Hungary's political new wave music was caused by government stagnation. Updates a previous article by the author that appeared in *East European Politics and Societies* (v. 5, no. 3, Fall 1991).

617. Leitner, Olaf. "Rock Music in the GDR: An Epitaph." In *Rocking the State: Rock Music and Politics in Eastern Europe and Russia*, edited by Sabrina Petra Ramet, 17-40. Boulder: Westview Press, 1994.
   Provides a political history of rock music in the German Democratic Republic (GDR). Discusses the significant role of GDR rock musicians in the fall of the communist government. Explores the relationship between rock music and the GDR mass media. Notes that GDR rock musicians were concerned about maintaining an identity in the reunified Germany.

618. Ramet, Sabrina Petra. "Rock: The Music of Revolution (and Political Conformity)." In *Rocking the State: Rock Music and Politics in Eastern Europe and Russia*, edited by Sabrina Petra Ramet, 1-14. Boulder: Westview Press, 1994.
   Demonstrates that rock music is not just a cultural phenomenon, but also a political one. Discusses rock music's role in the former Soviet Union and Eastern Europe. Mentions the cult of personality that developed around John Lennon's death. Notes that Lennon represents a symbol of hope and peace. Covers the various political treatments given rock music in communist countries, from "taboo to conformity." Concludes that the political nature of rock music is not limited to that of Eastern European countries.

619. Ramet, Sabrina Petra. "Rock Music in Czechoslovakia." In *Rocking the State: Rock Music and Politics in Eastern Europe and Russia*, edited by Sabrina Petra Ramet, 55-72. Boulder: Westview Press, 1994.
   Comments on the history of rock music in Czechoslovakia. Observes that until the late 1960s, it was common practice to sing rock music in English. Discusses the role of politics in the historical eras of Czechoslovakian rock music. Highlights the accomplishments of the rock group Plastic People of the Universe. Notes that the 1989 collapse of communism resulted in a depoliticization of rock music which was accompanied by a loss of interest in the musical arts. Contends that greater freedoms resulted in less of a need for rock groups to serve as outlets for expressing political rebellion.

620. Ramet, Sabrina Petra. "Shake, Rattle, and Self-Management: Making the Scene in Yugoslavia." In *Rocking the State: Rock Music and Politics in Eastern Europe and Russia*, edited by Sabrina Petra Ramet, 103-132. Boulder: Westview Press, 1994.
   Presents the history of rock music in Yugoslavia and its relationship to government. Notes the influences on rock music from western culture. Observes that in Yugoslavia rock music has a somewhat depoliticized history in that the government did not view it as a "dissident force." Discusses the effects

on, and varying responses by, rock musicians to the war that started in 1991. Updates an earlier article by the author (under the name Pedro Ramet) that appeared in *Eastern European Politics and Societies* (vol. 2, no. 2, Spring 1988). This chapter is followed by an interview between the author and Goran Bregovic, leader of the rock group Bijelo Dugme, from Sarajevo.

621. Rosselson, Leon. "Pop Music: Mobiliser or Opiate?" In *Media, Politics and Culture: A Socialist View*, edited by Carl Gardner, 40-50. London: Macmillan Press, 1979.

Contends that the song is the "most powerful emotional force of all." Discusses the way in which the potential political aspect of music is diminished by its capitalistic conversion into commodity. Demonstrates how this has occurred from the early 1900s to the present, focusing on folk music and rock music. Claims that rock music is limited in its concerns and expresses adolescent emotions. Suggests that folk music may offer a possibility of creating community through self-expression.

622. Steggels, Simon. "Nothing Ventured, Nothing Gained: Midnight Oil and the Politics of Rock." In *From Pop to Punk to Postmodernism: Popular Music and Australian Culture From the 1960s to the 1990s*, edited by Philip Hayward, 139-148. North Sydney, Australia: Allen & Unwin, 1992.

Focuses on the Australian rock group Midnight Oil as being musicians who "consistently engage in the sphere in which the musical and political processes intersect." Examines the group as providers of political critique through promotion and popularization within a cultural form. Claims that Midnight Oil attempts to challenge the social establishment from within. Examines the various recordings of Midnight Oil from a socio-political perspective and places them within that context.

623. Szemere, Anna. "The Politics of Marginality: A Rock Musical Subculture in Socialist Hungary in the Early 1980s." In *Rockin' the Boat: Mass Music and Mass Movements*, edited by Reebee Garofalo, 93-114. Boston: South End Press, 1992.

Explores how rock music may have contributed to the undermining of political order by creating "alternative social and cultural space" where the "dramatization" of the overall crisis in Hungary was made possible. Studies punk and new wave music in Hungary in comparison to similar movements in Great Britain. Argues that the music was politically successful because it was able to exist in the margins between the tolerated and the forbidden, between popular and high art, "thus subverting traditional frontiers."

624. Ullestad, Neal. "Diverse Rock Rebellions Subvert Mass Media Hegemony." In *Rockin' the Boat: Mass Music and Mass Movements*, edited by Reebee Garofalo, 36-53. Boston: South End Press, 1992.

Probes the ability of rock music to mobilize individuals for social action. Notes that rock music serves as rebellion which, in turn, can be empowering. Contends that this aspect of rock music has been coopted for the benefit of social issues. Discusses the *Live Aid* and *Farm Aid* concerts, the *Sun City* record, the Nelson Mandela tribute concert, the Amnesty International concerts, the AIDS benefit album *Red, Hot & Blue*, and other efforts.

625. Vila, Pablo. "Rock National and Dictatorship in Argentina." In *Rockin' the Boat: Mass Music and Mass Movements*, edited by Reebee Garofalo, 208-229. Boston: South End Press, 1992.

Asserts that the years of dictatorship in Argentina (1976 to 1983) gave rise to a form of rock music known as "rock nacional." Claims that across time rock nacional has come to constitute a counterculture. Breaks the time period into four segments in which rock music: 1) became politicized as a channel of subversion, 2) went through a period of crisis as a music genre, 3) experienced a renaissance, and 4) became tied to the peace movement. Concludes that rock nacional is an oppositional tool that has functioned as a means of resistance and participation within an authoritarian society.

626. Wicke, Peter. "The Times They Are A-Changin': Rock Music and Political Change in East Germany." In *Rockin' the Boat: Mass Music and Mass Movements*, edited by Reebee Garofalo, 81-92. Boston: South End Press, 1992.

Emphasizes the role of rock music in contributing to the fall of the Berlin Wall in 1989. Claims that rock music can convey meaning and values that "shape patterns of behavior imperceptibly over time." States that in the German Democratic Republic, the repression of rock music made the genre a "medium of resistance." Details the events of September and October 1989 when rock musicians articulated a strong political stance.

BOOKS

627. Denisoff, R. Serge. *Sing a Song of Social Significance*. Bowling Green, Ohio: Bowling Green University Popular Press, 1972.

Covers a wide spectrum of songs of persuasion, including rock music and folk rock. Claims that little is known about the protest song genre although music is increasingly used for social commentary and political statements. The extent to which music has any political power remains in question. Although it is a form of propaganda, protest music is not a determinant of power. Examines the use of protest songs to promote religious ideals, American communism, and commercial interests. Attempts to relate Karl Mannheim's notion of relationism to counterculture politics.

628. Denisoff, R. Serge, and Richard A. Peterson, eds. *The Sounds of Social Change: Studies in Popular Culture*. Chicago: Rand McNally, 1972.

Collects numerous previously-published essays on the use of music as a tool for social change. Devotes the third chapter to rock music. Observes that rock music facilitated the development of the 1960s counterculture. Presents essays expressing views from the New Left as well as the Radical Right. Asserts that rock music is subjective and its political interpretation is dependent more upon the audience than on the performer.

629. London, Herbert I. *Closing the Circle: A Cultural History of the Rock Revolution*. Chicago: Nelson-Hall, 1984.

Contends that rock music reflects sociopolitical and cultural values, probably more than it influences them. Claims that the history of rock music has followed a predictable revolution pattern of rebellion, revolt, and social reaction. Also notes that revolutions are not defined by their successes. Asserts that rock music highlights the paradoxical nature of a modern society that "cannot live without traditions," yet "cannot live contentedly with traditions." States that rock has symbolized both revolt and tranquility in its brief history. Identifies stages of rock music's revolutionary and cyclical pattern: accession (1957-1963), germinal (1964), fructidor (1965-1972), thermidor (1973-1978), and restoration (1979-present).

630. Orman, John. *The Politics of Rock Music*. Chicago: Nelson-Hall, 1984.

Identifies implications of rock music to the political system. Notes that rock music has influenced, and has been influenced by, politics since its early beginnings in the 1950s. Observes that the political struggles surrounding rock music have implications "for rock as art and as politics." Defines rock music politics as the attempt to propagandize through music in order to support a specific social movement, establish a particular worldview, or to accomplish an "expressive function." Surveys the responses by the political elite to rock music. Assesses the actual power of rock music to affect political attitudes and behaviors. Explores such issues as racism, sexism, capitalism, the electoral process, student activism, and marijuana policies. Devotes entire chapters to Bob Dylan, the Rolling Stones, John Lennon, and Phil Ochs. Also discusses Crosby, Stills, Nash, & Young and the Byrds. Dedicates one chapter to reviewing the contents of F.B.I. files, obtained through the Freedom of Information Act, on Janis Joplin, Jimi Hendrix, Jim Morrison, and Elvis Presley. Concludes that rock music has rarely had any political influence on audiences. Rather, rock music is a leisure activity used for escapism, relaxation, or entertainment. Further, rock music "reflects racism and sexism in its songs and its institutional practices." Rock music is "conspicuous consumption."

631.	Philbin, Marianne, ed. *Give Peace a Chance: Music and the Struggle for Peace.* Chicago: Chicago Review Press, 1983.

Represents the catalog of the Peace Museum (Chicago) exhibition on music and peace. Features artifacts from musicians (e.g., John Lennon, Harry Chapin, Bob Marley, Holly Near, Malvina Reynolds, Almanac Singers) who have worked for peace. Includes essays by Yoko Ono, Pete Seeger, and Joan Baez, as well as other essays written by scholars. Contains a dedication by Yoko Ono.

632.	Pratt, Ray. *Rhythm and Resistance: Explorations in the Political Uses of Popular Music.* New York: Praeger, 1990.

Explores the political uses of popular music. Covers spirituals, gospel music, the blues, folk music, and rock music. Discusses rock music in terms of expressing sexuality (e.g., Elvis Presley) and rebellion. Devotes a chapter to the role of women performers by touching on their limited role in the 1960s' counterculture, the women's music movement, and oppositional images of the 1980s (e.g., Debbie Harry, Cyndi Lauper, Madonna). Considers the significance of Bruce Springsteen's work. Contends that throughout his career, Springsteen has articulated "the cultural contradictions of life in the backwash of postindustrial capitalism."

633.	Street, John. *Rebel Rock: The Politics of Popular Music.* Oxford: Basil Blackwell, 1986.

Attempts to explain why rock music means so much to so many people. Asserts that rock music forms a part of how people interpret their lives. Explores the relationship between the public world and the private experiences of individuals. Organizes the discussion into three segments. The first section deals with the way popular music is used by the power elite. The second section discusses how "political choices are made and expressed in the production of popular music" by the music industry and musicians. The third section concerns the methods by which rock music acquires meaning. Concludes that rock music cannot politicize audiences to the point of action or turn "musicians into politicians," but it can help people come to know more about themselves and their desires.

634.	Wicke, Peter. *Rock Music: Culture, Aesthetics and Sociology.* Cambridge: Cambridge University Press, 1990.

Investigates the "social and cultural origins of rock music." Attempts to identify and explain the social functions of rock music and how they give meaning and value to the audience. Argues that the aesthetics and sociology of rock music are the very elements that give it significance. Contends that rock music "imposes conditions and cultural consequences which allow it to become a symptom of much more far-reaching and fundamental changes." Explores in detail the social aesthetics of rock music as it developed historically. Includes an extensive bibliography. Translated by Rachel Fogg.

DISSERTATIONS

635.   Cary, Michael DeWitt. "The Rise and Fall of the MC5: Rock Music and Counterculture Politics in the Sixties." Ph.D. Lehigh University, 1985. *Dissertation Abstracts International* 46: 1724A.
   Follows the counterculture political endeavors of the rock group MC5. Finds that "the music industry functioned as an adjunct to the political regime to suppress the deviant politics of the MC5." As a result, the MC5 "assumed a militant posture" which alienated them from the 1960s counterculture and contributed to their career demise.

636.   Johnson, Mary Jane Earle. "Rock Music as a Reflector of Social Attitudes Among Youth in America During the 1960s." Ph.D. Saint Louis University, 1978. *Dissertation Abstracts International* 39: 1680A.
   States that by the 1960s, rock music was synonymous with youth and rebellion. Members of the counterculture used rock music to communicate political ideologies to the establishment and among themselves. Emphasizes that beyond the lyrics, the sensual sound, rhythm, and beat of rock music contributed to its political appeal among "dissident youth." Concludes that the music of the 1960s did, in fact, reflect social unrest, but the political agendas were not realized. Claims that the social upheaval of the 1960s can be viewed as a logical extension of a "youth-conscious affluent society" and not as an aberration in America's history.

637.   Levine, Stephen Irving. "Political Socialization, Student Radicalism, and American Political Science: An Analysis of Folk and Rock Music and Changing Radical Attitudes at the Florida State University." Ph.D. Florida State University, 1971. *Dissertation Abstracts International* 32: 5309A.
   Contends that the relationship between university instruction and the development of political attitudes has received inadequate attention. Socialization theory does not account for the role of personality development and thus cannot account for radicalization among college and university students. Examines radical themes in contemporary folk and rock music and argues that such themes are contributing factors in the socialization process of students. Also explores other radicalization factors such as teaching techniques, familiarity with literary, intellectual and cultural personalities, alienation, sexual activity, and drug use.

638.   Murphy, B. Keith. "A Rhetorical and Cultural Analysis of the Protest Rock Movement, 1964-1971." Ph.D. Ohio University, 1988. *Dissertation Abstracts International* 49: 2862A.
   Labels the protest music of the 1960s and early 1970s as a "social-capital" movement because it developed from the profit motive of the music industry. Protest rock music evolved as a result of stress on the American ideology of the time period, an attempt to reject the status quo, an ability to mobilize, and an

inability of the power brokers to halt collective behavior. Concludes that in the United States it is necessary for a social movement to utilize the mass media. Notes that one option for doing so is to articulate the rhetoric by means that are profitable.

639.   Weller, Donald J. "Rock Music: Its Role and Political Significance as a Channel of Communication." Ph.D. University of Hawaii, 1971.
   Determines, from a content analysis of rock music lyrics, that there are two types of audiences: 1) Top 40, and 2) underground. Contends that audiences will prefer to listen to rock music with lyrics that reinforce existing values and beliefs. Concludes that there is an increasing number of people who listen by choice to lyrics expressing "counterculture" values.

FILMS AND VIDEOS

640.   *Rock Around the Kremlin.* Filmmakers Library, 1985.
   Documents the underground influences of rock music on Soviet culture.

Psychology

ARTICLES

641. Aebischer, Verena, Miles Hewstone, and Monika Henderson. "Minority Influence and Musical Preference: Innovation by Conversion not Coercion." *European Journal of Social Psychology* 14, no. 1 (1984): 23-33.

Starts with the premise that it is difficult to change strongly held beliefs and opinions or to introduce new norms. Proposes a possible methodology that would integrate concepts of minority influence (versus majority influence) and social categorization (in-groups and out-groups). Focuses on behavioral style, situational norms, and predispositions of influence targets. Studies 186 French adolescents concerning musical preferences. Supports "the effect on an indirect measure (i.e., conversion), but finds no corresponding effect on a direct measure."

642. Arnett, Jeffrey. "Adolescents and Heavy Metal Music: From the Mouths of Metalheads." *Youth & Society* 23, no. 1 (1991): 76-98.

Explores the attitudes and social characteristics of adolescent males who favor heavy metal music. Investigates the appeal of heavy metal music, behavioral characteristics, effects of the music, self-perceptions, and attitudes toward society. Subjects were 175 male adolescents between the ages of fourteen and twenty, interviewed by the author. Among the subjects who liked heavy metal music, it was discovered that this genre of music is more than a preference, it is "an intense avocation." Heavy metal music affects worldviews, consumer behavior, moods, friendships, and self-perceptions. Identifies the major attraction to heavy metal music as being the artistic talents of the performers and the themes contained in the social issues of lyrics to the songs. Concludes that heavy metal music reflects, rather than causes, "recklessness and despair among adolescents." The rising popularity of heavy metal music is a symptom of increasing alienation.

643. Attig, R. Brian. "The Gay Voice in Popular Music: A Social Value Model Analysis of *Don't Leave Me This Way*." *Journal of Homosexuality* 21, no. 1-2 (1991): 185-202.

Focuses on homosexuality in popular music as having the potential for creating "positive social change regarding societal values about homosexuality." Reviews the history of the "gay voice" in popular music. Utilizes a modified version of the Social Value Model to analyze the Communards' video *Don't Leave Me This Way* on the basis of narrative content, narrative symbols, and lyrical content. Concludes that the video "effected a dialectical synthesis" of mainstream and homosexual values because it both expressed a homosexual perspective and was commercially successful.

644. Baumeister, Roy F. "Acid Rock: A Critical Reappraisal and Psychological Commentary." *Journal of Psychoactive Drugs* 16, no. 4 (1984): 339-345.

Probes the impact of LSD usage in the actual musical composition and performance of acid rock music. Claims that it has been problematic for researchers to explain the creative process in terms of mental states. Indicates that musicians who used LSD and produced acid rock "significantly affected the evolution of rock music." References the works of the Beatles, the Grateful Dead, and Jefferson Airplane to illustrate concepts of sound, structure, emotion, and lyrics. Concludes that acid rock was definitely derived from the following traits associated with the use of LSD: short attention spans, emotional ambiguity, heightened interests in novel sensations, unbiased fascinations with just about everything, and desires to explore complex and subtle musical elaborations. Points to a positive aspect of acid rock as representing the beginning of experimentation with instrumental sophistication. Points to the exhaustion of guitar solo possibilities as a negative result.

645. Belsham, Richard Lee, and David W. Harman. "Effect of Vocal vs Non-Vocal Music on Visual Recall." *Perceptual and Motor Skills* 44 (1977): 857-858.

Studies the effects of vocal versus non-vocal background music on visual recall. Subjects were forty college students (twenty males and twenty females) provided with a photograph and a twenty item questionnaire regarding the photograph. One group of subjects observed the photograph for sixty seconds while listening to the composition *The Weight* with both instrumental and vocal tracks. They then completed the questionnaire. A second group listened to the same instrumental track of *The Weight* without a vocal track before completing the questionnaire. Results show that the group listening to the instrumental-only version of the piece made fewer errors on the questionnaire. Concludes that the use of music with vocal tracks should be differentiated from music with instrumental-only tracks for the purposes of experimentation.

646.   Brown, Elizabeth F., and William R. Hendee. "Adolescents and Their Music: Insights into the Health of Adolescents." *JAMA (Journal of the American Medical Association)* 262, no. 12 (1989): 1659-1663.

Studies the literature on the influences of rock music on adolescents. Indicates that total immersion into a subculture such as heavy metal music may be an indication of alienation. Claims that extreme identification with heavy metal may signal a risk of drug abuse or satanic practices. States that physicians should be aware of the importance of rock music to adolescents. Asserts that music preference can be used as an indication of adolescent emotional and mental health.

647.   Corhan, Cynthia M., and Beverley Roberts Gounard. "Types of Music, Schedules of Background Stimulation, and Visual Vigilance Performance." *Perceptual and Motor Skills* 42, no. 2 (1976): 662.

Studies the "effects of different types of music on performance on a signal detection task." Argues that on the basis of arousal theory and previous research, rock music will be more closely associated with better performance than will background instrumental music. Concludes that vigilance performance is better when the background stimulation is "discontinuous and contains elements of uncertainty" as with rock music, which is more vigorous.

648.   Cripe, Frances F. "Rock Music as Therapy for Children with Attention Deficit Disorder: An Exploratory Study." *Journal of Music Therapy* 23, no. 1 (1986): 30-37.

Hypothesizes that rock music can serve to decrease activity levels and increase attention spans among children with Attention Deficit Disorder (ADD). Suggests that if the hypothesis is true, then rock music could be used as an "adjunctive therapy which could be administered without training." Subjects were eight ADD children, all males, between the ages of six and eight. All subjects were tested individually. Results show a significant decrease in motor activities with the introduction of rock music. Results do not indicate any significant changes in attention spans.

649.   Cross, Herbert J., and Randall R. Kleinhesselink. "The Impact of the 1960s on Adolescence." *Journal of Early Adolescence* 5, no. 4 (1985): 517-531.

Raises questions regarding the impact of stress from the social and cultural events of 1960s on adolescents. Surveys the radicalization effects of protest as related to the civil rights and anti-war movements, the pervasive societal stress created by the Vietnam War (e.g., distrust, political divisiveness, death, the draft), the drug culture, and changes in sexual attitudes and behavior. Discusses the role of rock music as an outcome and as a contributing factor to stress. Notes that the movements in the 1960s towards simplified lifestyles and humanized educational systems failed to materialize because of the rapid pace of technological developments coupled with increasing demand on resources.

States certain implications for today's youth who must have good skills and not allow themselves to be distracted by "the available means to indulge themselves," if they wish to be successful.

650.   Cupchik, Gerald C., Martin Rickert, and Julie Mendelson. "Similarity and Preference Judgments of Musical Stimuli." *Scandinavian Journal of Psychology* 23, no. 4 (1982): 273-282.
   Studies the effects of "technical-structural and personal-affective processes on judgments of musical stimuli." Operationalizes "technical-structural" as judgments about stylistic similarity between pairs of musical stimuli. Operationalizes "technical-affective" as forced choice preference judgments. Uses the genres of classical, jazz, and rock music. Results indicate that tempo as a structural property is least important in similarity and preference judgments. Finds similarity and preference judgments to be different processes.

651.   Danenberg, Mary A., Margaret Loos-Cosgrove, and Marie LoVerde. "Temporary Hearing Loss and Rock Music." *Language, Speech, and Hearing Services in Schools* 18, no. 3 (1987): 267-274.
   Investigates the effects of live rock music on adolescent and adult hearing. Twenty students (seven males, thirteen females), twelve to seventeen years of age, and seven adults were pre- and post-tested. Results indicate that nineteen students and six adults experienced at least a 5 dB threshold shift at one or more of the tested frequencies. Fifteen students and "all of the adults who experienced shifts also reported tinnitus." Six subjects were randomly selected for additional post-testing three days after hearing the live rock music, with four of these subjects experiencing only partial recovery to pre-test levels. Speculates that because music can be damaging at levels below the thresholds for discomfort, it "may not be perceived as harmful and will not be avoided."

652.   Daoussis, Leonard, and Stuart J. McKelvie. "Musical Preferences and Effects of Music on a Reading Comprehension Test for Extroverts and Introverts." *Perceptual and Motor Skills* 62, no. 1 (1986): 283-289.
   Studies extroverts and introverts to determine the effects of background music on reading comprehension. Subjects were divided into to reading groups: no music, and rock music at a low volume. Notes no difference in reading comprehension scores between the two groups for extroverts, but introverts who listened to the rock music scored significantly lower than the introverts in the no music group. Concludes that extroverts and introverts are affected differently by music. Suggests support for the "contention that the effects of music on cognitive performance are partly mediated by individual differences."

653. Dollinger, Stephen J. "Personality and Music Preference: Extroversion and Excitement Seeking or Openness to Experience?" *Psychology of Music* 21, no. 1 (1993): 73-77.

Tests the relationships of music preference to extroversion, excitement seeking, and openness to experience among college students. Results indicate that openness to experience is positively associated with preference for a variety of musical genres, particularly less conventional genres such as new age, classical, jazz, reggae, folk, and soul. Extroversion is positively related to a preference for jazz music. Excitement seeking is positively related to a preference for rock music.

654. Epstein, Jonathon S., and Robert Sardiello. "The Wharf Rats: A Preliminary Examination of Alcoholics Anonymous and the Grateful Dead Head Phenomena." *Deviant Behavior* 11, no. 3 (1990): 245-257.

Studies the fans of the Grateful Dead (Deadheads) who have formed a group known as Wharf Rats, with membership comprising recovering alcoholics who follow the twelve step program of Alcoholics Anonymous. Compares the Wharf Rats with Alcoholics Anonymous "in terms of intergroup communications, public information and spirituality, which is central to 12 steps programs." Concludes that the two groups are very similar, but questions how the Wharf Rats can be successful if they do not change their surroundings or disassociate themselves from the rest of the Deadhead community. Hypothesizes that their success may be explained by the Deadhead value system, which respects individual choices and autonomy.

655. Fidler, James R., Eugene B. Zechmeister, and John J. Shaughnessy. "Memory for Frequency of Hearing Popular Songs." *American Journal of Psychology* 101, no. 1 (1988): 31-49.

Examines memory for situational frequency using rock songs. Memory was also related to subjects' (college students) knowledge of song titles and artists used. Results were similar to those for memory frequency of verbal stimuli. Provides support for "automatic processing view of frequency encoding," but also indicates that meaningful elaboration of the stimuli can be a determinant of memory frequency.

656. Finnas, Leif. "A Comparison Between Young People's Privately and Publicly Expressed Musical Preferences." *Psychology of Music* 17, no. 2 (1989): 132-145.

Compares the music preferences of adolescents when self-reported publicly versus privately. Subjects were Finnish adolescents between the ages of twelve and fourteen. Results show that subjects expressed less preference for traditional types of music when reporting preferences publicly than when reporting privately. Results did not show that subjects expressed greater preference for rock music when reporting preferences publicly than when reporting privately. Contends that publicly expressed preferences are influenced by the estimation of peer preferences and by the extent that music preference is related to variables such as social status, popularity, and peer group membership.

657.   Finnas, Leif. "Do Young People Misjudge Each Others' Musical Taste?" *Psychology of Music* 15, no. 2 (1987): 152-166.

Probes the extent to which adolescents misjudge the musical tastes of their peers. Subjects were 302 Finnish ninth grade adolescents. Self-reported musical preferences were compared to estimates of peer preferences. Results indicate an overestimation of peer preference for rock music and an underestimation of peer preference for classical music. Concludes that adolescents' false beliefs regarding peers' musical preferences may have undesirable consequences, such as conformity to unreal social norms.

658.   Fontaine, Craig W., and Norman D. Schwalm. "Effects of Familiarity of Music on Vigilant Performance." *Perceptual and Motor Skills* 49, no. 1 (1979): 71-74.

Questions previous research on vigilance performance that suggests rock music is associated with better performance due to its discontinuity and uncertainty. Uses thirty-five undergraduate college students (twenty-seven males, eight females) as subjects to examine the effects of familiarity on vigilance performance. Tests five conditions: familiar rock music, familiar easy listening music, unfamiliar rock music, unfamiliar easy listening music, and no music. Results show that musical genre had no effect, but familiarity did significantly increase arousal. Demonstrates the importance of the psychological condition of familiarity on physiology.

659.   Fucci, Donald, Daniel Harris, Linda Petrosino, and Molly Banks. "The Effect of Preference for Rock Music on Magnitude-Estimation Scaling Behavior in Young Adults." *Perceptual and Motor Skills* 76, no. 3 (1993): 1171-1176.

Tests the relationship between preference for a particular music genre and estimates of how loudly the music is played. Supports previous research that suggests preferred music is perceived as less loud than unpreferred music when both are played at the same level of sound.

660.   Greenfield, Patricia M., Lisa Bruzzone, Kristi Koyamatsu, Wendy Satuloff, Karey Nixon, Mollyann Brodie, and David Kingsdale. "What Is Rock Music Doing to the Minds of Our Youth? A First Experimental Look at the Effects of Rock Music Lyrics and Music Videos." *Journal of Early Adolescence* 7, no. 3 (1987): 315-329.

Reports on three studies on the "cognitive effects of rock music lyrics and videos." The first study used Bruce Springsteen's *Born in the U.S.A.* and Madonna's *Like A Virgin* to examine the comprehension of lyrics. The second study used fifth and sixth grade students as subjects to test whether music videos limit the imagination. The third study was similar to the second, but used college students as the subjects, producing similar results. Concludes that the influences of rock music lyrics on elementary school-age children are minimal because lyric comprehension "follows rather than leads general development," especially in regard to themes of sexuality. Music videos detract from song lyrics and reduce the emotional response to a song. Also, rock music songs heard without visuals are more stimulating to the imagination.

661. Greer, R. Douglas, Laura G. Dorow, and Andrew Randall. "Music Listening Preferences of Elementary School Children." *Journal of Research in Music Education* 22, no. 4 (1974): 284-291.

Attempts to determine music preferences and attention spans of grade school children. Subjects were 134 children from preschool through sixth grade. Subjects were exposed to rock music, non-rock music, and white noise. Concludes that as children advance in age or through grade levels, they will increasingly prefer rock music. Notes that the transition between the third and fourth grades seems to be pivotal with regard to music preference.

662. Greeson, Larry E. "Recognition and Ratings of Television Music Videos: Age, Gender, and Sociocultural Effects." *Journal of Applied Social Psychology* 21, no. 23 (1991): 1908-1920.

Reports on a study in which young adults and adolescents rated three types of music videos (explicit, neutral, Christian) according to theme recognition and favorability. Results indicate that, unlike previous findings, subjects are capable of accurately recognizing themes. Also, older subjects and female subjects rated explicit videos less favorably than younger subjects and male subjects did. Finally, subjects who watch MTV regularly or who seldom attend church were more likely to rate music videos favorably. Concludes that when given the opportunity, youth are able to recognize and evaluate those media presentations designed to influence their behavior, attitudes, and values.

663. Hansen, Christine Hall. "Priming Sex-Role Stereotypic Event Schemas with Rock Music Videos: Effects on Impression Favorability, Trait Inferences, and Recall of a Subsequent Male-Female Interaction." *Basic and Applied Social Psychology* 10, no. 4 (1989): 371-391.

Demonstrates the effects of sex-role stereotype priming through rock music videos. Subjects, 178 male and female undergraduate students, viewed rock music videotapes that portrayed two different sex-role schemas. Male and female actors were then observed interacting either consistently or inconsistently with the schemas. Behavior that was schema consistent "resulted in a positive enhancement of traits." Results indicate that portrayal of sex-role stereotypic behavior in rock music videos can have a predictable effect on appraisal, impressions, and memory of similar real life interactions. Therefore, rock music videos may act as priming stimuli with "strong, predictable, and nonconscious cognitive effects on viewers."

664. Hansen, Christine Hall, and Ranald D. Hansen. "Constructing Personality and Social Reality Through Music: Individual Differences Among Fans of Punk and Heavy Metal Music." *Journal of Broadcasting & Electronic Media* 35, no. 3 (1991): 335-350.

Discovers several "intriguing links between rock music preferences and individual differences in both personality attributes and social perceptions." Surveyed ninety-six undergraduates (thirty males, sixty-six females) between the ages of eighteen and twenty-five, to examine the relationships among musical preference, social judgments, and personality characteristics. Preference for heavy metal music was associated less with need for cognition and more with Machiavellianism and machismo. Subjects who preferred heavy metal music also provided higher estimates of consensus for antisocial behavior and attitudes. Preference for punk rock music was associated with being less accepting of authority. Subjects who preferred punk rock music provided higher estimates of frequencies of anti-authority behavior. Concludes that music preferences can be meaningful indicators of social attitudes and personality characteristics.

665. Hansen, Christine H., and Ranald D. Hansen. "How Rock Music Videos Can Change What is Seen When Boy Meets Girl: Priming Stereotypic Appraisal of Social Interactions." *Sex Roles* 19, no. 5-6 (1988): 287-316.

Examines the effects of mass media priming of sex role stereotypes and subsequent appraisal of interpersonal behavior. Subjects were 221 undergraduate college students. Subjects were shown rock music videos that depicted either sex role stereotypic behavior of men and women or contained no stereotypic behavior. Subjects then observed and appraised an interaction between a man and woman. Results indicate that priming via rock music videos did influence appraisal of interactions. When the woman reciprocated the man's sexual advances, she was appraised as "more nonthreatening, submissive, skilled, competent, sexual, sensitive, and sympathetic" than when she did not. When the man praised the woman, he was evaluated as "more nonthreatening, sexual, assertive, and dominant." These effects were not present when priming had not occurred. Concludes that priming of sex role stereotypes through the mass media can be extended into reality, even when the audience recognizes the priming media as fantasy.

666. Hansen, Christine Hall, and Ranald D. Hansen. "Rock Music Videos and Antisocial Behavior." *Basic and Applied Social Psychology* 11, no. 4 (1990): 357-369.

Tests the effects of rock music videos on interpretations of observed antisocial behavior. Determines that exposure to antisocial rock music videos results in "more favorable impressions of someone who engaged in antisocial behavior." Indicates that positive attitudes become associated with antisocial behavior through this visual medium because of reinforcement from "strong, positive, emotional responses generated by the music." Social learning, excitation-transfer, cognitive priming, social psychological, and information-processing theories are all utilized to explain the effects and consequences.

667. Harris, Clarke S., Richard J. Bradley, and Sharon K. Titus. "A Comparison of the Effects of Hard Rock and Easy Listening on the Frequency of Observed Inappropriate Behaviors: Control of Environmental Antecedents in a Large Public Area." *Journal of Music Therapy* 29, no. 1 (1992): 6-17.

Studies the effects of music genres on the frequency of inappropriate behavior at a state-supported mental health hospital. Compares rock music and rap music to easy listening and country music as factors affecting behavior of adult patients in a public area of the hospital. Lyric content and rhythm variations were not controlled. Results indicate that a greater number of inappropriate behaviors were observed when rock music or rap music was played than when easy listening or country music could be heard. Discusses possible reasons for the results.

668. Johnson, Norris R. "Panic at 'The Who Concert Stampede': An Empirical Assessment." *Social Problems* 34, no. 4 (1987): 362-373.

Reviews the events of the December 3, 1979, concert by The Who at the Cincinnati Riverfront Coliseum. Notes that eleven persons were killed in a crush by the crowd entering the concert. The disaster was quickly labeled a stampede. Discusses previous research and theories related to the concept of panic. Makes distinctions between "panics of acquisition and of escape." Argues that the theory of panic as a cause of the deaths is not a satisfactory explanation. Discovers that there was not unregulated competition for limited resources and that cooperative behavior was evident throughout the situation. The nature of the competition that did exist was that of wanting to escape the crush of the crowd rather than wanting to enter the arena for the better seats. Concludes that instances of complete "ruthless competition" are rare because most crowds are comprised of smaller social groups that constrain totally selfish behavior.

669. Joseph, Catherine, and A. K. Pal. "Effect of Music on the Behavioural Organization of Albino Rats Using the Operant Conditioning Technique." *Indian Journal of Applied Psychology* 19, no. 2 (1982): 77-84.

Contends that animal research may inform the study of the effects of background music on learning behavior. Twelve albino rats were separated into three groups receiving different auditory stimuli: no music, classical music, and rock music. Hypothesizes that musical stimulation will affect organizational behavior "in different orders and sequences." Results indicate that the effect of music was positive in the early learning stages but detrimental in the later stages. Rock music specifically was shown to reduce initial random activity more than the other music-type exposures.

670. Kellaris, James J., and Anthony D. Cox. "The Effects of Background Music in Advertising: A Reassessment." *Journal of Consumer Research* 16, no. 1 (1989): 113-118.

Replicates the 1982 experiment by Gerald Gorn that showed subjects to be more likely to select a particular item based on selected background music associated with an item. Conducted three experiments. The first experiment essentially reproduced Gorn's work with some slight modifications to address previous criticisms of Gorn's study. Results indicate that music had no effect on product selection. The second experiment was a "nonexperiment" that replicated the first experiment's procedures except for the actual treatment. This was designed to test whether subjects were reacting to the situation or the actual treatment. Results suggest that subjects did react to the "demands of the procedure rather than the experimental stimuli." The third experiment was a replication of Gorn's study using rock music. Results demonstrate no significant relationship between item selection and music appeal. Concludes that the hypothesis that product selection can be conditioned simply through background music is not supported.

671. Kilpatrick, William. "The Demythologizing of Love." *Adolescence* 9, no. 33 (1974): 25-30.

Uses the noticeable change in rock music lyrics from the 1950s to the early 1970s to illustrate the demythologizing of romance. The author views the change in the lyrical content of songs to be reflective of a transformation in the youth culture and not the catalyst.

672. Kuras, Janet E., and Robert C. Findlay. "Listening Patterns of Self-Identified Rock Music Listeners to Rock Music Presented via Earphones." *Journal of Auditory Research* 14, no. 1 (1974): 51-56.

Measures the sound levels of rock music and of speech as preferred by listeners of rock music. Subjects were seven females and eighteen males between the ages of eighteen and twenty-five. Results indicate that listeners may select lower levels for music that they favor. Also, in all cases rock music was preferred at a higher level than was speech, but no typical level for rock music could be identified.

673. Leitner, Michael J. "The Representation of Aging in Pop/Rock Music of the 1960s and '70s." *Activities, Adaptation and Aging* 3, no. 2 (1982): 49-53.

Draws conclusions about the images of old age and aging as portrayed in nine popular songs from the 1960s and 1970s. Content analysis indicates that a common theme is "that of loneliness and sadness in old age." Acknowledges that it is difficult to assess the influence of rock music's lyrical content on adolescents' attitudes. Artists examined include George Harrison, John Prine, John Lennon, Paul McCartney, Cat Stevens, Brian May, Paul Simon, and Art Garfunkel.

674.	Litle, Patrick, and Marvin Zuckerman. "Sensation Seeking and Music Preferences." *Personality and Individual Differences* 7, no. 4 (1986): 575-577.

Correlates the scales from the Sensation Seeking Scale form V with a devised Musical Preference Scale. Factors on the Musical Preference Scale are: rock, classical, electronic, jazz, soul/rhythm and blues, popular, country and western, folk/ethnic, religious, and Broadway/TV/soundtrack music. Subjects were eighty-two undergraduate college students. Results indicate a positive correlation between total sensation seeking and preferences for rock music. Concludes that high sensation seekers "have a high optimal level of stimulation" and thus a high tolerance for music intensity.

675.	Locke, Eric L. "The Vance Decision: The Future of Subliminal Communication." *Law and Psychology Review* 15 (1991): 375-394.

Reviews the court case in which the heavy metal rock group Judas Priest was sued for intentionally placing subliminal messages in a song on their album *Stained Glass* that resulted in two individuals attempting suicide. Argues that the use of subliminal messages is an intentional practice by the media, that there is evidence it is potentially effective, and that such practice should be prohibited. Observes that regardless of a lack of understanding about the complete effect on behavior modification, there should be a law that would regulate the use of subliminal communication. Notes that the judge's decision in the Judas Priest case states that subliminal messages are not protected by the First Amendment and are a violation of privacy. Contends that a law governing this practice would not affect First Amendment protection of speech designed for the "conscious observer."

676.	Lynn, Steven Jay, and Bruce W. Carlson. "Comment on *Absorption and Enjoyment of Music* by Rhodes, David, and Combs." *Perceptual and Motor Skills* 67, no. 2 (1988): 522.

Contends that the authors of the article mentioned did not test their hypothesis as they claimed. Provides several reasons for this assertion.

677.	Mainprize, Steve. "Interpreting Adolescents' Music." *Journal of Child Care* 2, no. 3 (1985): 55-62.

Provides illustrations of how adolescent orientation to rock music can be used therapeutically. Offers that rock music can "provide a point of entry for therapeutic engagement" and act as a resource for better understanding the "psychodynamic, cognitive, affective, psychosocial and behavioural regularities and processes." Discusses certain behaviors in terms of self-expression, skill development, and social recognition.

678.	Mark, Arlene. "Adolescents Discuss Themselves and Drugs Through Music." *Journal of Substance Abuse Treatment* 3, no. 4 (1986): 243-249.

Summarizes a technique utilizing rock music lyrics as an enabling device for addicted adolescents to understand their dependency on drugs and alcohol.

Argues that rock music lyrics are an effective means of getting adolescents to communicate because of the intrinsic interest in music. Rock music lyrics are a familiar medium for expressing feelings. Discussions are invoked in which adolescents explore lyrics in relation to the stages of addiction: means of relief, increased dependence, loss of control, remorse, loss of interests, and physical deterioration.

679. Mark, Arlene. "Metaphoric Lyrics as a Bridge to the Adolescent's World." *Adolescence* 23, no. 90 (1988): 313-323.

Discusses the use of rock music lyrics to assist alienated adolescents with communication skills. Specifically, guided discussion about the issues expressed in popular lyrics can result in adolescents offering their opinions, listening to others, and constructively disagreeing. Typical themes include feelings, fear, family relationships, security, emotional pressure, and independence. Anticipated results are that alienated youth can begin to consider alternative coping strategies, learn possible ways to gain control over their lives, and function in society.

680. Martin, Graham, Michael Clarke, and Colby Pearce. "Adolescent Suicide: Music Preference as an Indicator of Vulnerability." *Journal of the American Academy of Child and Adolescent Psychiatry* 32, no. 3 (1993): 530-535.

Investigates the possible relationship between music preference and psychological health among adolescents. Surveyed adolescents on the measures of family closeness, suicidal thoughts and behavior, depression, delinquency, risk taking, drug and alcohol use, and music preference (popular music, rock music, metal/punk, jazz/blues, and Christian or classical). Results indicate that the majority of males prefer rock music and metal/punk music and the majority of females prefer popular music. Explores the association between preference for rock and metal/punk music and the above measures, especially among females. Proposes that adolescents with certain personal and family traits prefer rock and metal/punk because "the style or the themes and lyrics resonate with their own feelings of frustration, rage, and despair." Concludes that a preference for rock or metal/punk music among females may be an indication of vulnerability. Suggests that future studies seek to determine whether musical preference is predictive of behavior.

681. May, James L., and Phyllis Ann Hamilton. "Effects of Musically Evoked Affect on Women's Interpersonal Attraction Toward and Perceptual Judgments of Physical Attractiveness of Men." *Motivation and Emotion* 4, no. 3 (1980): 217-228.

Reports on an experiment in which thirty undergraduate females evaluated photographs of attractive and unattractive males while listening to affect-evoking "positive" rock music, "negative" avant-garde music, or no music. Results replicate previous research in which the attractive males were rated more positively on a number of traits. Further, the rock music resulted in more positive ratings than the avant-garde music, including interpersonal attraction and physical attractiveness. Supports the idea that "extraneous or irrelevant stimuli simply present in the situation influences interpersonal evaluations of character and preference."

682. McCarthy, Donna O., Mary E. Ouimet, and Jane M. Daun. "The Effects of Noise Stress on Leukocyte Function in Rats." *Research in Nursing and Health* 15, no. 2 (1992): 131-137.

Studies the effects of increased levels of noise on selected biological functions concerned with the healing of wounds. Exposed rats to 60 dB to 80 dB of rock radio programming for ninety minutes of every two hour period for a duration of twenty-four hours. Concludes that the exposure to noise stress did alter "some of the biological functions of leukocytes."

683. McIlwraith, Robert D., and Wendy L. Josephson. "Movies, Books, Music, and Adult Fantasy Life." *Journal of Communication* 35, no. 2 (1985): 167-179.

Explores the relationships between fantasy styles and particular media, as well as between fantasy styles and media content. Subjects were 176 college students (59 males and 117 females). With regard to rock music, males reported a "need for external stimulation and hostile-guilty-failure fantasies" while females reported only a need for external stimulation.

684. Metzger, Lois Kay. "A Study of the Musical Preference of Psychiatric Patients in a Short-Term Treatment Center." *Arts in Psychotherapy* 18, no. 4 (1991): 357-358.

Investigates a possible relationship between music preference, as defined by diagnosis, and behavior among persons with psychiatric disabilities. Twenty-five inpatients, ages twelve to forty-seven, were tested. Seven males and eighteen females diagnosed with schizophrenia, depression, attention deficit disorder, dysthymic, bipolar, and conduct disorder listened to, and rated, musical style (country, rock, jazz, classical, and new age) and preference. Results indicated that music style preferences could not be associated with specific diagnoses.

685. Newman, A. "Planetary Death." *Death Studies* 11, no. 2 (1987): 131-135.

Identifies selected songs as examples of adolescent preoccupation with omnicide. The thrust of the article is to draw attention to a possible heightened fear of planetary annihilation, primarily as a result of nuclear war, among adolescents. Suggests actions to counter this phenomenon.

686. Palmer, Lyelle L. "Auditory Discrimination Development Through Vestibulo-cochlear Stimulation." *Academic Therapy* 16, no. 1 (1980): 53-68.

Reviews adaptive level skills and passive level skills. Demonstrates that auditory discrimination abnormalities can be improved by use of sensorimotor stimulation methods. Twenty remedial learning subjects between the ages of six and seventeen who possessed auditory discrimination abnormalities were exposed to short periods of vestibular stimulation and sound (i.e., march or rock music) stimulation. Discrimination ability did improve and, in some cases, was completely normalized. Instrument used was the Wepman Auditory Discrimination Test.

687. Peretti, Peter O., and Heidi Kippschull. "Influence of Five Types of Music on Social Behaviors of Mice: Mus Musculus." *Psychological Studies* 35, no. 2 (1990): 98-103.

Investigates the extent to which five genres of music influence social behavior in mice. The genres tested were classical, country/bluegrass, jazz and blues, easy listening, and rock music. Classical music increased social activity, aggression, attraction, huddling, and sexual behaviors. Country/bluegrass music increased social activity and aggression. Jazz and blues music decreased aggression and competition. Easy listening increased huddling. Rock music decreased sexual activity and huddling while increasing aggression.

688. Peretti, Peter O., and J. Zweifel. "Affect of Musical Preference on Anxiety as Determined by Physiological Skin Responses." *Acta Psychiatrica Belgica* 83, no. 5 (1983): 437-442.

Investigates the effect of music on emotional state, specifically the effect of musical preference on anxiety. Two groups (music majors and nonmusic majors) of college students consisting of twenty-one males and nineteen females each were studied. Physiological skin response was measured before and during the introduction of anxiety, and then during the introduction of preferred music (i.e., classical, country/bluegrass, jazz/blues, easy listening, and rock music). Determines that musical preference does affect "anxiety differentially between males and females and between music and nonmusic majors." Speculates that music acts to reduce conflict between emotional and rational states. The type of preferred musical style did not affect outcomes, suggesting that no one style is either stimulative or sedative.

689. Peterson, Dena L., and Karen S. Pfost. "Influence of Rock Videos on Attitudes of Violence Against Women." *Psychological Reports* 64, no. 1 (1989): 319-322.

Examines the effects of rock music videos on male attitudes toward violence against women. Subjects were 144 male undergraduate college students exposed to music videos containing one of four conditions: erotic and violent, nonerotic and violent, erotic and nonviolent, and nonerotic and nonviolent. Results support previous research that indicates exposure to the nonerotic and violent condition results in greater aggressive attitudes toward women. Suggests that extended viewing of televised violence can result in increased aggression toward females.

690. Pfeil, Fred. "Rock Incorporated: Plugging into Axl and Bruce." *Michigan Quarterly Review* 32, no. 4 (1993): 534-571.

Presents Axl Rose and Bruce Springsteen as examples of how audiences are primed for rock performers. Discusses the ways in which rock performers are presented to the public already prepared with histories and assumptions. Tackles the issue of what constitutes the rock music phenomenon and how its meaning is to be assessed. Explores how the physical bodies of these performers deliver "complex messages of racial and social differentiation."

691. Prerost, Frank J. "The Influence of Sex Guilt on Mood State Following Exposure to Sexual Stimuli." *Psychological Reports* 73, no. 1 (1993): 201-202.

Studies the relationship between the level of sex guilt and exposure to rock music videos. Subjects were ninety male undergraduate college students shown one of three video conditions: sexual content, rock concert, or travelogue. Music videos with sexual content affected subjects with both high and low sex guilt scores by increasing their aggressive mood. Speculates that subjects with high sex guilt scores may have been angered by the video while subjects with low sex guilt scores may have associated the sexual content with aggressiveness.

692. Protinsky, Howard, and Rita Popp. "Irrational Philosophies in Popular Music." *Cognitive Therapy and Research* 2, no. 1 (1978): 71-74.

Speculates that the lyrical content of popular songs and country and western songs contain "irrational philosophies, and thus may be a source of reinforcement of irrational thinking in adolescents and adults." Uses rational-emotive theory to explore the notion that song lyrics encourage an innate tendency to practice self-defeating thinking. Performs a content analysis of 194 country and western songs and 166 rock songs to catalog the presence of any one of the eleven irrational beliefs developed by Maultsby: 1) unavoidable anger, 2) self-acceptance through approval by others, 3) absolute competence, 4) outside forces determine one's feelings, 5) task avoidance, 6) only one correct way to accomplish tasks, 7) one must achieve greatness, 8) one's actions reflect oneself, 9) absence of a loved one should result in depression, 10) dependency on stronger others, and 11) ignoring reality. Results indicate that the three most prevalent irrational beliefs in both musical genres are unavoidable anger, outside forces determine one's feelings, and dependency on stronger others.

693. Rhodes, Larry A., Daniel C. David, and Allan L. Combs. "Absorption and Enjoyment of Music." *Perceptual and Motor Skills* 66, no. 3 (1988): 737-738.

Hypothesizes that there is a "positive relationship between the trait of absorption and the ability to enjoy music" and that the relationship is stronger for certain genres of music. Subjects were thirty-five college students (twenty-three females, twelve males) between the ages of eighteen and twenty-four. Subjects completed the Tellegen Absorption Scale and then listened to musical excerpts from classical new age, rock, and country music. Results support the hypothesis and the findings suggest the relationship is strongest with classical music.

694.   Rosenbaum, Jill, and Lorraine Prinsky. "Sex, Violence and Rock 'n' Roll: Youths' Perceptions of Popular Music." *Popular Music and Society* 11, no. 2 (1987): 79-89.

Analyzes the results of surveying 121 male and 116 female adolescents regarding their favorite songs. Respondents were from a variety of academic performance backgrounds. Results indicate that adolescents find or understand few references to sex, drugs, and satanism in their favorite songs. Suggests that lyrics are not the primary reason that adolescents are attracted to a particular song, but rather the music or overall sound are attractive. Notes that subjects tended to interpret lyrics literally, ignoring symbolism and metaphors.

695.   Ruedrich, Stephen L., Robert J. Bishop, and Chung-Chou Chu. "Rock and Roll Music in Delusion Formation." *Journal of Operational Psychiatry* 14, no. 2 (1983): 115-117.

Presents three case-studies of persons hospitalized for suffering from grandiose delusions involving personalities from the rock music world. The first patient believed that John Lennon was speaking to him (after Lennon's death) or that he was John Lennon. The second patient believed that Bob Dylan was threatening her with harm through black magic. The third patient's delusions concerned Elton John sending agents to murder him. The authors think that these cases may "represent a more esteemed psychodynamic, cognitive/perceptual, or socio-cultural position" that rock music performers hold in American society. The seriousness with which rock music personalities are taken in this culture may increase the potential for these individuals to be victims as well as heroes.

696.   Schierman, Michael J., and Guy L. Rowland. "Sensation-Seeking and Selection of Entertainment." *Personality and Individual Differences* 6, no. 5 (1985): 599-603.

Explores the relationship between sensation seeking and preference for selected entertainment activities. Subjects were forty-two undergraduate college students (twenty males, twenty-two females). Utilizing the fifty-two item Entertainment Preference Inventory (EPI), finds that high sensation seeking (HSS) females "reported preferences for activities centered about alcohol, sexually-explicit materials and 'rock' music." Explains the HSS females' preference for rock music events in terms of "novel auditory and visual stimulation" and associated activities of substance abuse. HSS males preferred sexually-explicit materials and news/documentary reports. Also reports the preferences of low sensations seeking (LSS) individuals.

697.   Schreiber, Elliott H. "Influence of Music on College Students' Achievement." *Perceptual and Motor Skills* 66, no. 1 (1988): 338.

Tests the influence of background music on the academic achievement of college students. Subjects were sixty-four psychology students between the ages of eighteen and twenty-four. Thirty of the subjects were exposed to rock music for the first twenty minutes of each class session and thirty-four were not exposed to the music. Results indicate that those subjects exposed to rock music earned higher grades.

698.   Smith, Carol A., and Larry W. Morris. "Differential Effects of Stimulative and Sedative Music on Anxiety, Concentration, and Performance." *Psychological Reports* 41 (1977): 1047-1053.

Tests the differential effects of stimulative and sedative music on anxiety, concentration, and test performance. Subjects were thirty music majors and thirty psychology majors. Used three treatment conditions (stimulative music, sedative music and no music) and five types of music (classical, jazz/blues, country/bluegrass, easy listening, and rock). Results indicate that stimulative music increased anxiety, reduced concentration, and lowered subjects' test performance expectancies. Actual test performance was affected positively under the sedative condition of easy listening music for psychology majors and negatively for music majors. Under the stimulative condition of rock music, the effect was negative for music majors. Concludes that the effects of music are better understood based on "cognitive processes rather than on the basis of physiological-affective responses to musical stimuli."

699.   Smith, Carol A., and Larry W. Morris. "Effects of Stimulative and Sedative Music on Cognitive and Emotional Components of Anxiety." *Psychological Reports* 38 (1976): 1187-1193.

Investigates the effects of "stimulative and sedative music on the physiological and cognitive components of test anxiety." Subjects were sixty-six college students enrolled in a psychology course. Used three treatment groups (stimulative music, sedative music, and no music) and five types of music (classical, jazz/blues, country/bluegrass, easy listening, and rock). Results indicate that stimulative music maintained physiological arousal at an elevated state throughout an examination. Sedative and no music conditions resulted in decreasing physiological arousal as the examination progressed. Notes that musical genre preference did not affect the physiological effects of the music type. Suggests that the effects of stimulative music can be negative (e.g., worry) and positive (e.g., alertness, attentiveness) in helping sustain cognitive activity.

700.	Taylor, Marlene M. "Music in the Daily Experience of Grade Six Children: An Interpretive Study." *Psychology of Music* 13, no. 1 (1985): 31-39.

Explores the ways in which grade school children experience music. Subjects were eighteen sixth-grade students (twelve females, six males). Subjects were observed, interviewed, and administered Gordon's Musical Aptitude Profile. Results indicate that rock music was the preferred musical genre because it is socially acceptable due to adolescents thinking they are suppose to prefer it. Suggests that music education emphasizes learning through performance over the teaching of musical concepts. Recommends greater attention to individual learning needs.

701.	Thompson, Margaret, Suzanne Pingree, Robert P. Hawkins, and Carrie Draves. "Long-Term Norms and Cognitive Structures as Shapers of Television Viewer Activity." *Journal of Broadcasting & Electronic Media* 35, no. 3 (1991): 319-334.

Utilizes the Madonna video *Papa Don't Preach* to study the relationships among audience family communication patterns, sex and pregnancy experience, music video viewing motivation, and cognitive processing. Subjects were 186 high school students (108 females, 78 boys) ranging in age from thirteen to eighteen. Results indicate that the family communication pattern was one of the most "important predictors of cognitive activities."

702.	Thorne, Stephen B., and Philip Himelstein. "The Role of Suggestion in the Perception of Satanic Messages in Rock-and-Roll Recordings." *Journal of Psychology* 116, no. 2 (1984): 245-248.

Approaches the topic of hidden satanic messages in rock music recordings by exploring the power of suggestion. Sixty-five subjects were divided into three groups. All three groups listened to three rock songs that had been recorded backwards for the purposes of the experiment. The songs were the Beatles *Revolution No. 1*, Led Zeppelin's *Stairway to Heaven*, and Black Sabbath's *Black Sabbath*. The first subject group (control) was simply asked to listen to the recordings. The second group was given the suggestion that words could be heard on the recordings. The third group was given the suggestion that satanic messages could be heard on the recordings. Results show that the second group reported hearing more words than the other two groups. The third group reported hearing more satanic messages than the other two groups. Information was also collected from the subjects regarding their knowledge and beliefs about rock music recordings containing backward messages.

703.	Trostle, Lawrence C. "Nihilistic Adolescents, Heavy Metal Rock Music, and Paranormal Beliefs." *Psychological Reports* 59 (1986): 610.

Surveys sixty-six adolescents (forty-eight males, eighteen females; ages twelve to twenty) in Los Angeles, California, to determine the extent that preference for heavy metal music is correlated with the performance of satanic rituals. One-half of the subjects identified themselves as "stoners" (i.e., nihilistic adolescents engaged in satanic rituals). Results show that self-identification as a "stoner" is directly correlated with a preference for heavy metal music.

704.   Trzcinski, Jon. "Heavy Metal Kids: Are They Dancing with the Devil?" *Child and Youth Care Forum* 21, no. 1 (1992): 7-22.
Reviews the history of adult reactions to rock music in an attempt to give perspective to adult reactions to heavy metal music. Argues that banning heavy metal music would be unenforceable, would increase its popularity, and would not allow adolescents to make reasoned choices. Rather, a recommended solution is proposed in which adults become aware of the types of music that are of interest to adolescents. Adults should assist adolescents in developing critical listening skills. Further, adults and adolescents should communicate about the meanings being derived from heavy metal music, including "values, ethics, and morality."

705.   Tucker, Alexander, and Brad J. Bushman. "Effects of Rock and Roll Music on Mathematical, Verbal, and Reading Comprehension Performance." *Perceptual and Motor Skills* 72, no. 3 (1991): 942.
Demonstrates the effects of rock music on several types of academic performance. Subjects were 151 college students divided into two conditions: rock music, and no music. Measured mathematical, verbal, and reading comprehension performance. Instruments were the American College Test (ACT) and the Scholastic Aptitude Test (SAT). Results show that rock music decreased performance on mathematical and verbal measures, but not reading comprehension.

706.   Ulrich, R. F., and Marilyn L. Pinheiro. "Temporary Hearing Losses in Teen-agers Attending Repeated Rock-and-Roll Sessions." *Acta Oto Laryngologica* 77, no. 1-2 (1974): 51-55.
Investigates hearing loss among adolescents who listen to loudly amplified rock music. Over an eight week period, fourteen subjects (four boys and ten girls between the ages of thirteen and seventeen) were exposed to several hours of sound levels between 110 dB and 115 dB per session. Differential effects on the two ears were noted. Hearing returned to pre-exposure levels although significant temporary post-exposure shifts were found in all subjects. Other research suggests that hearing recovery after exposure does not preclude permanent damage.

707.   Walker, Michael W. "Backward Messages in Commercially Available Recordings." *Popular Music and Society* 10, no. 1 (1985): 2-13.
Details numerous examples of backward messages and related references to satanism and Aleister Crowley found on rock music recordings, including works by the Beatles (*White Album*), Eric Clapton (*Layla*), Led Zeppelin (*Stairway to Heaven*), the Electric Light Orchestra (*Eldorado*), Black Oak Arkansas (*When*

Electricity Came to Arkansas), Styx (*Snowblind*), Queen (*Another One Bites the Dust*), and Klaatu (*Silly Boys*). Discusses the phenomenon in terms of phonetical, acoustical, and phonemical experiences. Argues that there is "no evidence to support the theory of a separate speech perception mechanism operating at an unconscious level." Notes that there is also no biological reason why one should perceive backward messages because it would be a useless capability. Tested the notion that backward messages are not perceptible using thirty subjects. Results show that "subjects scored no better than chance." Concludes that individuals cannot understand backward messages either consciously or unconsciously and that subliminal stimulation does not cause behavior changes.

708.   Wanamaker, Catherine E., and Marvin Reznikoff. "Effects of Aggressive and Nonaggressive Rock Songs on Projective and Structured Tests." *Journal of Psychology* 123, no. 6 (1989): 561-570.

Studies the effects of listening to aggressive and nonaggressive rock music on hostility scores using the Thematic Appercention Test and the Buss-Durkee Hostility Scale. College students (thirty-nine females, fifty-one males) were divided into three groups. The first group was exposed to nonaggressive music with nonaggressive lyrics (Moody Blues). The second group listened to aggressive music with nonaggressive lyrics (Stryper). The third group heard aggressive music with aggressive lyrics (Motley Crue). Results show that hostility scores did not differ among the three groups, supporting the hypothesis that audiences do not attend to the content of rock music lyrics and that music apart from the lyrics does not affect aggression. Offers a variety of reasons as to what may have affected the results, including music preference, music familiarity, and the instruments used. Nevertheless, concludes that the results "argue against precipitously labeling rock songs as likely to stimulate violent behavior."

709.   Wass, Hannelore, M. David Miller, and Robert G. Stevenson. "Factors Affecting Adolescents' Behavior and Attitudes Toward Destructive Rock Lyrics." *Death Studies* 13, no. 3 (1989): 287-303.

Studies rock music preferences, listening behaviors, and attitudes regarding lyrics. Assumes that destructive themes in rock music contribute to destructive behavior in some adolescents. Concentrates on adolescents who are fans of music that promotes homicide, suicide, or satanism (HSSR). Surveyed 894 high school students in rural, suburban, and urban public and private schools. Results indicate that 17.5% of the sample could be considered HSSR fans. Data analysis shows that the significant variables in determining HSSR fan status are parents' marital status, student's gender and race, and school environment. HSSR status also predicted other attitudes and behaviors, such as believing that children under ten years of age should be permitted to listen to HSSR music and that HSSR music does not promote self-destructive behavior.

710. Weiler, Ernest M., Emily Mortimer, Roger C. Stuebing, and Chris Pavlakos. "A Further Study of Described Context Effect and Noise Annoyance Ratings." *Journal of Auditory Research* 21, no. 3 (1981): 155-158.

Demonstrates the "value of a noise annoyance-rating scale which depends on context within which the noise is heard." Twenty-four undergraduates were asked to rate twelve common sounds, including rock music, on a nine-point annoyance scale in two situations, work or recreation environments. Shows that relative values of noise levels can be measured rather than absolute values.

711. White, Arden. "Meaning and Effects of Listening to Popular Music: Implications for Counseling." *Journal of Counseling and Development* 64 (1985): 65-69.

Surveys the literature in order to establish major changes in popular music across time and the effects of rock music on adolescents. Contends that knowledge of popular music can assist counselors working with adolescents. Explores the dominant lyrical themes, the social and cultural changes that led to the rise of rock music, and the significance of radio. Concludes that popular music is used by adolescents as a diversion from stress and to establish an identity in contrast to the establishment.

712. Wilson, Claire V. "The Use of Rock Music as a Reward in Behavior Therapy with Children." *Journal of Music Therapy* 13, no. 1 (1976): 39-48.

Suggests modifying the behavior of preschool special education children with the use of rock music as a reinforcement device. Rock music was introduced to subjects and then withdrawn in response to inappropriate behavior. Subjects were six children (five boys and one girl) with behavioral or emotional problems, enrolled in a therapeutic preschool program. Used music by Traffic, the Beatles, and the Rolling Stones. Discusses the use of peer pressure and rewards.

713. Wooten, Marsha A. "The Effects of Heavy Metal Music on Affects Shifts of Adolescents in an Inpatient Psychiatric Setting." *Music Therapy Perspectives* 10, no. 2 (1992): 93-98.

Studies the effects of heavy metal music and rock music on affect shifts of adolescents in a psychiatric facility. Subjects were thirty-five patients who were mostly diagnosed with major affective disorder, disruptive behavior disorder, and psychoactive substance use disorder. Subjects were pre- and post-tested for fluctuations in moods. Those subject who indicated a preference for heavy metal music had significant increases in positive affect after listening to heavy metal music. Specifically, the subjects were more calm, relaxed, attentive, and energized.

CHAPTERS

714. Hearn, Jeff, and Antonio Melechi. "The Transatlantic Gaze: Masculinities, Youth, and the American Imaginary." In *Men, Masculinity, and the Media*, edited by Steve Craig, 215-232. Newbury Park, Calif.: Sage, 1992.

Argues that the international scope of the United States mass media results in a global Americanization of gender images. The American Western film genre and rock music are used to illustrate "two particularly significant moments in the construction of the American Imaginary." Defines American Imaginary based on the theories of Jacques Lacan regarding the Symbolic (the realm of language), the Imaginary (the realm of the ego), and the Reality (the realm onto which the other two are "grafted"). Notes in particular the impact of the film *Blackboard Jungle* as a defining moment in 1955 for the youth of Great Britain with regard to black culture and American fashion.

715. Richardson, James T. "Satanism in the Courts: From Murder to Heavy Metal." In *The Satanism Scare*, edited by James T. Richardson, Joel Best, and David G. Bromley, 205-217. New York: Aldine de Gruyter, 1991.

Reviews four types of legal cases that link illegal or antisocial activities with satanic rituals: murder, child abuse, brainwashing, and heavy metal music. Describes heavy metal cases as those in which musicians or record companies are charged with influencing or causing antisocial behavior (e.g., suicide). Satanism is used to help justify such accusations. Reviews the attempted suicide case involving the heavy metal group Judas Priest and the alleged subliminal messages on their album *Stained Glass*. The case explored the issue of whether subliminal messages were protected under the First Amendment. Focuses on the references to satanism made during the Judas Priest trial. Points to other satanic court cases related to brainwashing that "depend on simplistic psychological theory." Projects that because there is wide belief that heavy metal music exposes adolescents to satanic messages there will be more heavy metal legal cases. Concludes that more detailed research reveals alternative theories for many of these antisocial actions. Warns that basic legal rights may evaporate if the public comes to believe that satanism is a real cause of social problems.

BOOKS

716. Fuller, John G. *Are the Kids All Right?: The Rock Generation and Its Hidden Death Wish.* New York: Times Books, 1981.

Utilizes The Who's 1979 concert in Cincinnati, Ohio, as a point of departure for exploring crowd behavior at rock concerts. Suggests that the youth culture has a death wish. Offers explanations as to why behavior patterns change in a rock concert situation.

717.   Quarrick, Gene. *Our Sweetest Hours: Recreation and the Mental State of Absorption.* Jefferson, N.C.: McFarland, 1989.

Explores the various means of psychological escapism and diversion created when one becomes absorbed in recreational activities such as entertainment (e.g., films, television), recreational drugs, social interactions, the arts, meditation, and music. Chapter Nine discusses the "motion and emotion in music," focusing on rock and classical music. Describes music as exceeding everyday sounds with its rhythm, melody, harmony, and tempo so as to be qualitatively different, thus drawing more of one's attention. The emotions experienced when listening to music are reflective actions. Further, music has "an unlimited ability to arouse the entire range of human feeling." Rock music serves as a means of absorption because it is the antithesis of conventional musical styles. Also, "absorption in amplified sound is an inherent aspect of rock" and rock concerts encourage the abandonment of social standards in order to become absorbed in the music. Contends that rock music absorbs because its very nature forces a "hypnotic takeover of attention."

718.   Wills, Geoff, and Cary L. Cooper. *Pressure Sensitive: Popular Musicians Under Stress.* London: Sage, 1988.

Explores the causes and effects of stress on musicians working in popular music, including rock music. Looks at numerous factors related to stress in musicians, including performance anxiety, physical stress, poor working conditions, work overload, career development, and relationships. Reports the results of a survey on stress that was administered to musicians. Concludes that musicians' biggest stress factor is the worry about performing at their very best and to their own high standards. Notes that musicians do not smoke, drink, or use drugs more than the general population. However, musicians do suffer from above normal levels of anxiety. States that the most common coping mechanism is the use of humor. Reproduces the survey questionnaire.

DISSERTATIONS

719.   Apramian, Lisa Rose. "Qualitative Reconstruction of the Adolescent Self and the Meanings and Selfobject Functions of Rock Music: Eight Case Studies." Ph.D. University of Southern California, 1991. *Dissertation Abstracts International* 52: 2860A.

Considers "the meanings, modes of interaction, and psychological functions served by rock music through an exploration of adolescents' subjective experiences during primary solitary rock music engagement." Interviewed eight adolescents who listen to rock music for at least three hours per day. Suggests that by exploring how rock music is experienced and organized by adolescents, one may discover aspects of "conflict, shame, and emerging struggles for self-delineation." Proposes a qualitative methodology for further research.

720. Bartha, Robert Edward. "Personality Variables and Musical Preference." Ph.D. The Ohio State University, 1982. *Dissertation Abstracts International* 43: 2700B.

Studies musical listening preference in relation to personality and gender variables. Subjects were 150 graduate students. Concludes that there is a relationship between personality type and musical listening preference, but not between gender and preference.

721. Blackburn, William David. "The Relationship of Self-Concept to Adolescent's Musical Preferences and Level of Involvement with Music Listening." Ph.D. The Ohio State University, 1983. *Dissertation Abstracts International* 44: 3549B.

Contends that it has not been demonstrated that popular music is a causal element in terms of attitudes, values, and personality variables. Studied ninety-seven adolescents (fifty boys and forty-seven girls) in regard to "self-concepts, musical preferences, and level of involvement with music." Results indicate that males with preferences for hard rock music have "significantly higher self-satisfaction scores that the males in the pop rock group." The females who prefer pop rock have "significantly better overall self-concept and self-satisfaction scores than the females in the hard rock preference group."

722. Gunderson, Robin C. "An Investigation of the Effects of Rock Music Videos on the Values and Self-Perceptions of Adolescents." Ed.D. United States International University, 1985. *Dissertation Abstracts International* 46: 1875A.

Measures the association between the amount of time spent watching rock music videos and variables related to values and self-perception. Sampled 179 adolescents utilizing the Rokeach Value Survey and the Piers-Harris Self-Concept Scale. Results indicate no significant differences among adolescents who watch music videos very little, moderately, or heavily, and instrumental values or self-concepts. However, subjects who watch videos moderately or heavily ranked "mature love" higher on terminal values than those who watch few music videos.

723. Hansen, Christine Hall. "The Impact of Rock Music Video Priming on Appraisal of a Stereotyped Male-Female Interaction." Ph.D. Michigan State University, 1987. *Dissertation Abstracts International* 48: 3726B.

Reports on an experiment that explores the impact of exposure to rock music videos on appraisals of male-female interactions. Two types of videos were used to prime sex-role stereotypic schemas: socially harmonious (boy-meets-girl) and socially disharmonious (boy-dumps-girl). After priming, subjects viewed videotapes of scripted interactions that reflected one of the two stereotypic schemas. Results show that, contrary to predictions, the schema-consistent priming "enhanced favorability of both interactions." Positive impressions of harmonious interactions were enhanced by harmonious video priming and negative impressions of disharmonious interactions were reduced by disharmonious video priming.

724. Heindel, Sydney Clark, III. "The Creativity of James Douglas Morrison." Ph.D. University of Georgia, 1986. *Dissertation Abstracts International* 47: 2662B.

Focuses on the creativity of Jim Morrison. Studies thirteen psychological explanations centered on self-destructiveness as related to creativity and the dynamics of the relationship between the performer and the audience. Determines that none of the theories are mutually exclusive. Suggests a recognition of "inherent elements of the creative process such as solitude, ego-diffusion, and the need for mentors."

725. Hugonnet, Mitchell Henry. "An Experimental Study of Rock Video's Impact Upon the Attitudes and Values of Normal and Emotionally Disturbed Adolescents." Ph.D. American University, 1986. *Dissertation Abstracts International* 47: 5056B.

Tests three populations with regard to the effects of music videos on the attitudes and values of adolescents. The populations were forty-seven college students, sixty-seven high school students, and twenty-six emotionally disturbed male high school students. Subjects viewed thirty-five minutes of either "porn rock" videos or "soft rock" videos. Several instruments were used to measure attitudes and values. Results indicate that the videos had no effect on attitudes toward sexual activity and interpersonal aggression. Discusses specific population and gender differences. Concludes that harmful effects of music videos were not demonstrated.

726. Litle, Patrick Alan. "Effects of a Stressful Movie and Music on Physiological and Affect Arousal as a Function of Sensation Seeking Trait." Ph.D. University of Delaware, 1986. *Dissertation Abstracts International* 47: 3962B.

Measures the effect of music on stress in relation to traits of sensation seeking, sex, and musical preferences. Tests whether recovery after a stressful event (i.e., watching a stressful film) "would be enhanced by listening to preferred music." Results show that high scores for sensation seeking were significantly related to preferences for rock music and that low sensation seeking scores were associated with preferences for easy listening music. Concludes that listening to music does enhance recovery from a stressful event, but the influence of preferred music is undetermined. Speculates that non-preferred music "may provide sufficient distraction from stress."

727. Marks, Julie Ellen. "'On the Road to Find Out': Adolescent Development and Rock Music Preferences." Ph.D. California School of Professional Psychology, 1972. *Dissertation Abstracts International* 34: 861B.

Looks at the sociological influences of rock music on adolescent development. Argues that a lack of parental models for the purposes of identification can result in peer groups and subcultures becoming important role models. Hypothesizes that adolescents will prefer rock music with lyrical content relevant to their particular stage of development. Results indicate that adolescents are dealing with developmental issues at earlier ages than prevailing adolescent theory would suggest. Attributes this to an increased rate of maturation among adolescents. Concludes that rock music is not providing solutions to adolescent developmental crises.

728. Parker, Eric Scott. "Adolescent Musical Preference and Key Aspects of Personality." Ph.D. Adelphi University, 1986. *Dissertation Abstracts International* 47: 4309B.

Questions the relationship between the music preferences of adolescent males and sex and aggression. Subjects were 100 male college students, ages eighteen to nineteen. Utilized an original music preference scale that focuses on a dichotomy between heavy metal music and other rock music. Results indicate no relationship between preference for heavy metal music and sexual stimuli, but a significant relationship between preference for heavy metal music and aggression stimuli. Discovered significant negative relationships between preference for heavy metal music and "sex guilt, moral conflict guilt, and total guilt scores." Concludes that preference for heavy metal music is an indication of higher aggression and lower guilt. Offers that heavy metal music is used as "symbolic mastery" of anger and anxiety as part of the "development of the independent ego identity." Lower guilt scores are attributed to the "a lessening of superego functioning" during this period.

729. Raeburn, Susan Downing. "Occupational Stress and Coping in Professional Rock Musicians." Ph.D. Wright Institute, 1984. *Dissertation Abstracts International* 45: 1052B.

Identifies sources of occupational stress and coping processes among professional rock musicians. Interviewed ten professional musicians three times over a six month span. Examines variables such as demographics, behavior, physical status, health attitudes, social support, and psychological factors (e.g., self-esteem). Results show high levels of stress due to financial concerns, job insecurity, lack of peer recognition, pressure to do quality work, and "conflicts between career and other social roles." Notes that all subjects utilized both "problem-focused" and "emotion-focused" coping. Also looks at the use of chemical substances in the coping process. Discovered that fifty percent of the subjects "used substances in two-thirds of all episodes and twenty percent used substances in all episodes."

730. Reeve, Edward M. "Brain Electrical Activity Assessment of Concurrent Music and Event-Related Potential Cognitive Tasks." Ph.D. The Ohio State University, 1986. *Dissertation Abstracts International* 47: 3714A.

Explores the notion that information processing abilities may be affected by listening to music. Specifically addresses concerns about new technologies such as miniature headphones that allow for the listening of music while at work and at leisure. Subjects were fifteen males, between the ages of eighteen and twenty-four years, tested doing a visual identification task while listening to either rock music or classical music. Concludes that rock music "appears to influence an individual's decision making ability when he is listening to it at his preferred sound level." Speculates about music familiarity and listening habits.

731. Smith, Sheila Ann. "A Study of Personality Factors and Music Preference, Involvement, and Use Among Youth." Ed.D. Western Michigan University, 1989. *Dissertation Abstracts International* 50: 2181B.

Assesses the relationship between personality characteristics of introversion, norm-acceptance, and self-realization, and "music preferences, level of music involvement, and music uses among young people." Subjects were 200 college students (63 females, 137 males) between the ages of eighteen and twenty. Results indicate that subjects less involved in music tended to be more introverted and more norm-accepting. Females who preferred soft rock were more norm-accepting than other females. Discovered several significant relationships between the music variables. Concludes that the relationships among the personality and music variables are complex.

Religion

ARTICLES

732. Cooper, B. Lee. "Rock Music and Religious Education: A Proposed Synthesis." *Religious Education* 70, no. 3 (1975): 289-299.

Notes the conflict between religious purists who disdain rock music as being a tool of Satan and those who see fundamental Christian tenets in much of rock music. Claims that a result of this conflict is an increasing drift of youth from "church choir traditionalism" toward the "new religiosity" of the drug culture and rock music. Proposes a technique for incorporating rock lyrics into religious education, arguing that the key to success is in the selection of appropriate lyrical themes. States that the ultimate goal for synthesizing rock music into religious education must be to "produce behavioral as well as attitudinal change." Asserts that rock music represents one of the best forms of social and political commentary for adaptation into the curriculum. Concludes by presenting a recommended lesson plan organized by weekly themes, scriptural quotations, discussion questions, and suggested musical resources.

733. Cooper-Lewter, Nicholas. "Keep on Rollin' Along: The Temptations and Soul Therapy." *Black Sacred Music* 6, no. 1 (1992): 218-223.

Relates the personal experiences of racism faced by black athletes at a midwestern Christian college during the 1960s. African American students attempted to use soul music to realize a feeling of empowerment. Specifically, the music of the Temptations addressed this need. Contends that music can serve to inform and cultivate a system of core beliefs among members of a social group. Concludes that music is "unlimited in its potential to influence the well-being of human beings when it is symbiotically connected to healthy core beliefs."

734. Dudley, Roger L., Patricia B. Mutch, and Robert J. Cruise. "Religious Factors and Drug Usage Among Seventh-Day Adventist Youth in North America." *Journal for the Scientific Study of Religion* 26, no. 2 (1987): 218-233.

Attempts to identify factors that will predict drug usage by Seventh-Day Adventist adolescents. Surveyed 801 youths between the ages of twelve and twenty-four regarding frequency and type of drug use, attitudes and behaviors, and religious practice. Discovers that Seventh-Day Adventist youth as a group "report considerable less frequency in the usage of alcohol, tobacco, and marijuana" than found among the general population of high school students. Watching R-rated films and listening to hard rock music, recreational activities strongly discouraged by the church, were "both predictive of more frequent use." Results support previous research that indicates religious commitment is a factor in limiting drug usage.

735. Dyson, Michael Eric. "Rap Culture, the Church, and American Society." *Black Sacred Music* 6, no. 1 (1992): 268-273.

Asserts that rap music affirms the vitality of black oral tradition and reflects the culture of consumption and an obsession with sexual desire. Argues that rap music offers escapism from the drug culture, expression of social criticism, and reflects the sexism of the poor black community.

736. Dyson, Michael Eric. "Rights and Responsibilities: 2 Live Crew and Rap's Moral Vision." *Black Sacred Music* 6, no. 1 (1992): 274-281.

Examines the obscenity trial surrounding the rap group 2 Live Crew and the implications regarding First Amendment issues and issues of sex, race, and class. Touches on cultural attitudes toward black male sexuality. Argues that freedom of expression must be protected, but there is also a responsibility to criticize offensive social expressions.

737. Earl, Riggins R., Jr. "Family Violence and Youth Culture: Troubling Sounds at the Corner." *A.M.E. Zion Quarterly Review* (1983): 22-27.

Demonstrates the ways in which lyrics from selected rock songs illustrate a culture of violence and abuse. Gives special attention to the family unit. Argues that parents and children "must reassess what constitutes mutual moral obligation." Concentrates on Pat Benatar's *Hell is for Children* (child abuse), AC/DC's *The Problem Child* (violent children), and Stevie Wonder's *Village Ghetto Land* (violent society). Concludes that the youth culture uses electronic media to communicate messages about cultural violence and that "lyrics of many rock songs are pleas of despairing children." Insists that the issue is not whether humans are violent by nature or by nurture, but rather one of acknowledging the existence of violence and overcoming it.

738. Evans, J. Claude. "Pop Festivals and Pentecost." *Christian Century* (1969): 1303-1305.

Editorializes that the rock festivals of the late 1960s had religious significance. Suggests these festivals represent a "new vision of man and community." Argues that specific experiences in the Judeo-Christian tradition, which can be found in both the Old and New Testaments, speak to the religious significance of rock music and its manifestation through rock festivals. Refers to a New York Times Magazine article by Benjamin De Mott in which he claims that rock music serves to provide both escapism from, and confrontation with, the daily realities of life.

739. Gill, Jerry H. "The Fleshpots of Jersey: Bruce Springsteen and the Imagery of Bondage." *Encounter* 44, no. 4 (1983): 395-401.

Reviews the Bruce Springsteen album *The River* and its existential themes grounded in Biblical images, specifically Old Testament bondage. Examines several themes which converge in the title song. The river serves as "the confluence of Old Testament and New Jersey experience." In his lyrics, Springsteen uses the river to signify both cleansing and life as well as estrangement and death.

740. Gill, Jerry H. "The Gospel According to Bruce." *Theology Today* (1988): 87-94.

Contends that the lyrics of Bruce Springsteen represent gospel. Focuses on the songs from the albums *The River, Nebraska, Born in the U.S.A.*, and *Tunnel of Love*. Claims that Springsteen laments the lower socio-economic status of many Americans while affirming certain values and the possibility of renewal. Identifies a strong theme of bondage of place and time in Springsteen's work. Despite images of bondage, Springsteen "still expresses hope and affirms redemptive values." He celebrates the human spirit and emphasizes the power of individual responsibility. Illustrates these points with examples of Springsteen's lyrics. States that his strongest use of religious imagery is in the song *The River* where various forms of bondage converge and where one is cleansed by the river. Concludes that Springsteen's songs are an "authentic expression of the limitations and possibilities of human existence."

741. Greeley, Andrew M. "The Catholic Imagination of Bruce Springsteen." *Black Sacred Music* 6, no. 1 (1992): 232-243.

Suggests that there is a link between religious imagery and artistic and literary works. Analyzes the works of Bruce Springsteen to argue that Springsteen's work is profoundly Catholic because "his creative imagination is permeated by Catholic symbolism he absorbed" from the Sacraments. Focuses on the songs from the album *Tunnel of Love*. Concludes that: 1) "grace" can be found in popular culture, 2) the failure of the Catholic church to embrace Bruce Springsteen demonstrates the profoundness of the alienation of the church from the arts, 3) Springsteen, as a minstrel, is a true sacrament maker because of his use of religious metaphors, and 4) if religious imagery holds Catholics to the church, then church officials should give imagery more attention. Originally published in *America* (February 6, 1988).

742.	Greeley, Andrew M. "Like a Catholic: Madonna's Challenge to Her Church." *Black Sacred Music* 6, no. 1 (1992): 244-249.

Discusses the religious theme found in the Madonna music video *Like A Prayer*. Claims the criticisms of the video are due to Madonna being "a sexually attractive woman who dares to link her sexuality with God and religious images." Touches on the issue of guilt as a central theme in contemporary Catholicism and the antipathy by church leaders toward sexuality. Originally published in *America* (May 13, 1989).

743.	Howard, Jay R. "Contemporary Christian Music: Where Rock Meets Religion." *Journal of Popular Culture* 26, no. 1 (1992): 123-130.

Presents a view of contemporary Christian music as combining the Gospel message with rock music. Claims that Christian rock music can act as a social critic of society at-large and as a challenge to the Church and its role in society. Provides examples of Christian rock lyrics to illustrate certain central themes of the music. Offers that Christian rock music has the potential for "a radical critique of the Church and society." Observes that some Christian rock artists are challenging capitalistic ideology and hierarchical authority.

744.	Mellers, Wilfrid. "God, Modality and Meaning in Some Recent Songs of Bob Dylan." *Popular Music* 1 (1981): 142-157.

Examines selected works of Bob Dylan as a folk artist. Focuses in detail on the songs from three Dylan albums: *Street Legal*, *Slow Train Coming*, and *Saved*. Notes that Dylan's music and lyrics are "an intuitive reassessment of philosophical as well as social values."

745.	Mountford, Richard D. "Does the Music Make Them Do It?" *Christianity Today* (1979): 20-23.

Questions whether rock music actually causes one to be unable to resist temptation. Reviews the theoretical ability of music to affect character, starting with Plato. States that the Greek philosophers believed that music could affect one's will positively or negatively. Considers research from psychological and sociological fields. Notes that persons do respond physically and emotionally to music, but responses are dependent on numerous other factors. Concludes that the degree to which rock music will affect someone is dependent upon how much one desires to be affected.

746.	Pollard, Alton B., III. "Religion, Rock, and Eroticism." *Journal of Black Sacred Music* 1, no. 1 (1987): 47-52.

Explores the erotic music of Prince, as presented on the album *Purple Rain*, in an attempt to understand rock music's presentation of sexuality as "the only hope for some form of transcendence, liberation, freedom." Contends that the message of Prince is religious and that he promotes the idea that this world will not be perfect until there is divine intervention. Argues that Prince embodies the "many contradictions of modern life" and, therefore, is a metaphor awaiting a religious response.

747. Poole, Thomas. "Tracy Chapman: Jedermann, Prophet, or Cultural Narrator?" *Black Sacred Music* 6, no. 1 (1992): 253-261.
Puts forth an argument for a theological approach to music. Expresses the need to move beyond musicology by also considering performance. Focuses on Tracy Chapman who, through her songs, serves as more than a cultural narrator because she expresses a vision of justice for the individual and for society as a whole.

748. Preus, Klemet. "Contemporary Christian Music: An Evaluation." *Concordia Theological Quarterly* (1987): 1-18.
Examines contemporary Christian music in terms of its five major themes: the human predicament, Jesus Christ, coming to faith, the nature of faith, and Christianity. Illustrates with examples of song lyrics. Claims that most contemporary Christian rock music expresses the evangelicalism of Baptists. Contrasts the typical views conveyed in each of the five themes with Lutheran beliefs. Concludes that Lutherans should not advocate contemporary Christian music because the music's theology is "deficient."

749. Romanowski, William D. "Roll Over Beethoven, Tell Martin Luther the News: American Evangelicals and Rock Music." *Journal of American Culture* 15, no. 3 (1992): 79-88.
Provides a history of the development of contemporary Christian music (CCM). Notes that CCM is an attempt to merge evangelicalism with rock music. Discusses how CCM developed into an entire music industry. States that CCM emerged as religious propaganda with no historical ties, differing from other religious and secular musical genres. Recounts various reactions to CCM, especially once it had spawned a heavy metal context that gives mixed signals to the audience. Observes that the major audience for CCM are those who are already converted, thus reinforcing the notion that popularity is determined by the degree to which an artifact reinforces existing values.

750. Rotundo, E. Anthony. "Jews and Rock and Roll: A Study in Cultural Contrast." *American Jewish History* 72, no. 1 (1982): 82-107.
Contends that the overall influence of Jews on rock music has not been significant. Attempts to determine why rock and roll as an art form has not attracted creative Jews. First, the nature of rock music is reviewed to determine if its cultural roots differ from Jewish culture. Second, the careers of successful rock music Jews, including Bob Dylan, are examined to test ideas about the rock

music subculture. Concludes that "the Jewish cultural emphasis on verbal meaning, on restraint, on planning and 'scripting,'" have kept rock music from being appealing to Jewish musicians.

751.   Sandau, Jerry. "Here Comes the Knight: Rock 'n Roll Reflections on Kierkegaard." *Philosophy Today* 30 (1986): 265-268.

Utilizes the Dire Straits recording *Walk of Life*, written by Mark Knopfler, to illustrate a Kierkegaard belief that "music has a potential for enlightenment that the intellect cannot comprehend." Observes that rock music expresses the sublime in the "pedestrian." Rock music is pedestrian because it is simple, accessible, everywhere, and physical. Claims that when rock music is both pedestrian and sublime it is less complex and "maintains a stripped-down, unadulterated adherence to that absolute object."

752.   Sullivan, Mark. "'More Popular than Jesus': The Beatles and the Religious Far Right." *Popular Music* 6, no. 3 (1987): 313-326.

Traces the history of religious conservativism, especially the writings of David Noebel, and the attacks on the Beatles and John Lennon for being anti-religion and pro-communism.

753.   Tiger, Lionel. "Sacred Music in the Garden of Madison." *Worldview* (1976): 47-48.

Describes a 1976 performance by the Rolling Stones at Madison Square Garden in terms of a religious, anthropological experience.

754.   Turner, William C., Jr. "Keep on Pushing: The Impressions." *Black Sacred Music* 6, no. 1 (1992): 206-217.

Uses the songs of the Impressions to symbolize the themes of post-World War II African Americans. The Impressions' lyrics contain radical political elements. Compares the progression of political content in their songs and the progression of political awareness among a generation of African-Americans to the birth of a child. A period of gestation is followed by an irrepressible moment of delivery.

755.   Walters, James. "The Cultural Swing to JC." *Momentum* 3, no. 3 (1972): 27-32.

Comments on three theatrical works concerning the topic of Christianity: *Jesus Christ Superstar*, *Godspell*, and *Mass*. *Jesus Christ Superstar* is characterized as presenting the humanity of Christ in his struggle with his divinity. *Godspell* is discussed as a strict presentation of biblical parables. Leonard Bernstein's *Mass* is critiqued as an interpretation of the purpose and function of the Roman liturgy. Concludes that *Godspell* is more knowledgeable and sensitive than *Jesus Christ Superstar* which is an "orgy of sensation," and that *Mass* is appealing to the intellect. Notes that all three works are reflective of current social conditions and movements.

756. West, Cornel. "In Memory of Marvin Gaye." *Black Sacred Music* 6, no. 1 (1992): 224-226.

Notes that Marvin Gaye was a Christian artist, first and foremost. Focuses on his album *What's Going On* which is considered to be the "greatest album in Afro-American popular music." Originally published in *Christianity and Crisis* (June 11, 1984).

757. West, Cornel. "Sex and Suicide." *Black Sacred Music* 6, no. 1 (1992): 250-252.

Articulates the challenges facing Christianity in an age where youth respond to materialism and banality by embracing sex, drugs, and suicide. Questions whether cultural and religious resources are adequate to sustain the youth culture. Originally published in *Christianity and Crisis* (June 10, 1985).

758. Yamin, George Y., Jr. "The Theology of Bruce Springsteen." *Journal of Religious Studies* 18 (1990): 1-21.

Observes that the appearance of Christian rock music suggests that rock can be an appropriate means of articulating theology. Argues that the music of Bruce Springsteen contains a theology less superficial than that found in Christian rock music. Springsteen's music has a running theme of religious dilemmas. Notes that the religious aspects of Springsteen's work connect to the very fundamental characteristics of symbolic space and time in religion. Through symbolic images and themes embedded in urban America, Springsteen puts forward a "theological vision of redemption and salvation." Illustrates various themes by reproducing and analyzing the lyrics to *Adam Raised a Cain*, *Independence Day*, *Thunder Road*, *Born to Run*, *The River*, *Born in the U.S.A.*, *Nebraska*, and *Badlands*. Concludes that Springsteen's music continues a Hebrew-Christian religious tradition "that is both intellectually acceptable and emotionally relevant to contemporary listeners."

CHAPTERS

759. Cray, Graham. "Justice, Rock and the Renewal of Worship." In *In Spirit and in Truth: Exploring Directions in Music Worship Today*, edited by Robert Sheldon, 1-27. London: Hodder & Stoughton, 1989.

Argues that Christian worship must be contextual and that there is a "deficiency in the spirituality" among composers of contemporary music used in worship. Working from the premise that the music used in worship must be both contemporary and culturally relevant, concludes that rock music must be included. The gospel must be expressed in a form that is understood by the audience being addressed. Notes that rock music serves as a unifying catalyst in Western culture by linking private emotions to shared experiences, but it can also reinforce social divisions.

760.   Edgar, William. "The Message of Rock Music." In *Art in Question*, edited by Tim Dean and David Porter, 28-51. Basingstoke, England: Marshall Pickering, 1987.

Proposes a Christian approach to rock music. Begins by reviewing both the "Manichean" response (e.g., the material world is evil) and the relativist response (e.g., music is neutral) to rock music, then advances a three-part moderate approach. First, a language of "popular music aesthetics" is required. Second, there is a need for a "principle of redemption" regarding rock music. Third, the "social background" of rock music must be considered, because art is cultural and not just a source of amusement or luxury.

761.   Morrow, Patrick. "Sgt. Pepper, Hair, and Tommy: Forerunners of the Jesus-Rock Movement." In *Mystery, Magic and Miracle: Religion in a Post-Aquarian Age*, edited by Edward F. Heenan, 155-167. Englewood Cliffs, N.J.: Prentice-Hall, 1973.

Considers the anticipation of the Jesus-rock movement through an analysis of the Beatles' *Sgt. Pepper's Lonely Hearts Club Band* album, the musical *Hair*, and The Who's rock opera *Tommy*. The Beatles' album promotes achieving "spirituality through drugs." *Hair* dramatizes and satirizes such a lifestyle with a Christ-like tragic hero character, Claude Bukowski. The main character in *Tommy* is portrayed as a Christ-like figure who is ultimately rejected by his followers. The rise of a Jesus-rock movement is attributed to the process of legitimizing a search for spirituality and the presentation of an alienated youth as the ultimate tragic figure.

762.   Reich, K. Helmut. "Rituals and Social Structure: The Moral Dimension." In *Current Studies on Rituals: Perspectives for the Psychology of Religion*, edited by Hans-Gunter Heimbrock and H. Barbara Boudewijnse, 121-134. Amsterdam: Rodopi, 1990.

Uses the July 1985 *Live Aid* concerts to illustrate the effects of rituals on morality. Contends that it is possible to generate a vision of alternative moral worlds through the experience of ritual. Discusses the theoretical moral aspects of ritual and the mechanisms behind ritual as an agent of moral change. Argues that an effective ritual with symbolic aspects will evoke "engendering moods and motivations." Reviews the ways in which rock music festivals are ritualistic, with a spiritual connection of community among the participants. Notes that the Live Aid concerts (London, Philadelphia) were planned to be a "demonstration of moral and material solidarity" and were broadcast to 500 million television worldwide. Concludes that symbolic rituals can provide opportunities in the industrialized world for moral development.

763.   Scharlemann, Robert P. "Tillich and the Religious Interpretation of Art." In *The Thought of Paul Tillich*, edited by James Luther Adams, Wilhelm Pauck, and Roger Lincoln Shinn, 156-174. San Francisco: Harper & Row, 1985.

Traces Paul Tillich's ideas regarding the interpretation of religion in art as symbolic of a theology of culture. Notes that a key element in Tillich's thinking was the conceptual distinction between that which is represented by art and that which art may express. Religion is expressed through art regardless of the subject matter. Offers the rock opera *Jesus Christ Superstar* as an illustrative example. In the opera, technological reason or calculated means to an end is overcome by a religious dimension.

764.   Young, Bill. "Contemporary Christian Music: Rock the Flock." In *The God Pumpers: Religion in the Electronic Age*, edited by Marshall Fishwick and Ray B. Browne, 141-158. Bowling Green, Ohio: Bowling Green State University Popular Press, 1987.

Surveys the Christian-oriented contemporary rock music scene, also known as evangelical pop. Explores the history of the genre, focusing on the rock groups Petra, the Resurrection Band (Rez Band), Stryper, A.D., and artist Steve Taylor. Concludes by discussing the importance of Christian rock videos in bringing "their message to the common guy on the street" and thus opening the genre to a large new audience.

BOOKS

765.   Krug, Gary. *Rock - the Beat Goes On: A Christian Perspective on Trends in Rock Music*. Milwaukee: Northwestern, 1987.

Focuses on rock music from a Christian perspective. Chapters include: Music and the Word, The History of Rock, Let the Buyer Beware, Religious Symbols in Rock, Rock and Satanism/Occultism/Witchcraft, Hard Rock and Hard Drugs, Rock and Sex, Backmasking and Subliminal Messages, and Christian Rock.

766.   Lawhead, Steve. *Rock of This Age: The Real and Imagined Dangers of Rock Music*. Downers Grove, Ill.: InterVarsity Press, 1987.

Updates and expands substantially a previous book by the author, *Rock Reconsidered*. Discusses the relationship between rock music and Christianity and the influences of rock music throughout modern culture. Also touches on issues surrounding music videos and backward masking of messages in rock recordings. Covers the problematic nature of using rock music as a means of evangelism. Contends that rock music is just one of many aspects of contemporary society that has been "contaminated by secular humanism" which is described as a disease.

767. Lawhead, Steve. *Rock Reconsidered: A Christian Looks at Contemporary Music.* Downers Grove, Ill.: InterVarsity Press, 1981.

Articulates a Christian defense of rock music. Considers the nature of rock music. See entry number 766 for the updated version.

768. Peck, Richard. *Rock: Making Musical Choices.* Greenville, S.C.: Bob Jones University Press, 1985.

Presents a Christian perspective on rock music and contemporary Christian rock music.

769. Peters, Dan, Steve Peters, and Cher Merrill. *What About Christian Rock?* Minneapolis: Bethany House, 1986.

Offers some observations about Christian rock music in terms of its value to Christians.

770. Seidel, Leonard J. *Face the Music: Contemporary Church Music on Trial.* Springfield, Va.: Grace Unlimited, 1988.

Professes that contemporary Christian music is "fueled by the misguided belief in the neutrality of music." Contends that the rock music serves as a "vehicle for shallow theology." Labels the cause as "innocence," the effect as "complacence," and the responsibility as "obligation." Argues that music is not neutral and explains the absorption in rock music as a form of religion. Claims the problem with rock music is that it gives the audience what it wants, not what it needs.

DISSERTATIONS

771. Drum, Gary Richard. "The Message in the Music: A Content Analysis of Contemporary Christian and Southern Gospel Song Lyrics." Ph.D. University of Tennessee, 1987. *Dissertation Abstracts International* 48: 2762A.

Performs a content analysis "of twenty-seven Christian rock songs and thirty-one country gospel songs." Hypothesizes that Christian rock songs would contain an "evangelical-pentecostal-charismatic doctrinal perspective and that the country gospel songs would reflect a Calvinist, fundamentalist perspective." Results indicated that Christian rock songs were essentially lacking any doctrinal perspective and that country gospel songs were elementarily orthodox, "leaning toward Calvinism."

FILMS AND VIDEOS

772. *Rock My Religion.* Electronic Arts Intermix, 1983.

Explores the relationship between the development of rock music and its impact on Shakers.

Sociology

ARTICLES

773. Anderson, Bruce, Peter Hesbacher, K. Peter Etzkorn, and R. Serge Denisoff. "Hit Record Trends, 1940-1977." *Journal of Communication* 30, no. 2 (1980): 31-43.
   Analyzes the relationships among the hit record trends of market concentration, genre, performance mode, and lyric content. Attempts to illustrate stability and change in popular music. Divides the period from 1940 to 1977 into three epochs (1940-1958, 1959-1969, and 1970-1977).

774. Arnett, Jeffrey. "Heavy Metal Music and Reckless Behavior Among Adolescents." *Journal of Youth and Adolescence* 20, no. 6 (1991): 573-592.
   Delineates characteristics of adolescents who favor heavy metal music, with particular attention to reckless behavior. In comparing subjects who like heavy metal music to those who do not, differences were noted by gender. Males who prefer heavy metal music indicated higher rates of reckless behavior with regard to driving, sex, and drug use. Females who prefer heavy metal music indicated higher rates of reckless behavior with regard to shoplifting, vandalism, sex, and drug use. The same group of females also reported lower self-esteem. Both of these groups of males and females reported greater sensation seeking and were more self-assured with regard to sexuality and dating. Measurements used included the Sensation Seeking Scale, the Offer Self-Image Questionnaire, and the Rosenberg Self-Esteem Scale. Concludes by noting that while heavy metal music is associated with these behaviors, it does not necessarily cause them. American socialization "encourages creativity and autonomy, but may exact a cost in the form of higher rates of reckless behavior."

775.   Arnett, Jeffrey. "The Soundtrack of Recklessness: Musical Preferences and Reckless Behavior Among Adolescents." *Journal of Adolescent Research* 7, no. 3 (1992): 313-331.
   Surveys 248 high school students (113 boys, 135 girls) from middle-class socio-economic conditions regarding reckless behavior and musical preferences. Those adolescents who indicated preference for hard rock or heavy metal music also reported higher rates of reckless behavior. Types of reckless behavior included driving while intoxicated, driving at high rates of speed, unprotected sex, casual sex, drug use, shoplifting, and vandalism. Notes that preference for hard rock or heavy metal music was also associated with "higher levels of sensation seeking, negative family relationships, and, among girls, low self-esteem." Regression analysis indicated sensation seeking was the key factor in that adolescents who were high in sensation seeking behavior were also attracted to reckless behavior and were attracted to hard rock or heavy metal music. Results suggest that neither hard rock nor heavy metal music causes reckless behavior, rather both are symptoms of sensation seeking behavior.

776.   Baron, Stephen W. "The Canadian West Coast Punk Subculture: A Field Study." *Canadian Journal of Sociology* 14, no. 3 (1989): 289-316.
   Presents the results of field-study interviews among thirty-five members of Canada's punk rock subculture. Uses both functionalist and neo-Marxist theory to analyze the data. Organizes the discussion of findings into categories of background, goals, family, political attitudes, subculture style, and alternative status. Results show the subculture as being a reaction to socio-economic conditions, but notes that participation was not limited to members of any particular socio-economic class. Resistance to the dominant culture varied by gender. Alternate status was obtained through participation in violence.

777.   Bennett, H. Stith, and Jeff Ferrell. "Music Videos and Epistemic Socialization." *Youth & Society* 18, no. 4 (1987): 344-362.
   Conceptualizes epistemic socialization as having to do with events that "establish first principles." Claims that popular culture is an agent of espistemic socialization manifested in music videos. Explores themes of politics, romance, motion, conversion, and persona shift.

778.   Bleich, Susan, Dolf Zillmann, and James Weaver. "Enjoyment and Consumption of Defiant Rock Music as a Function of Adolescent Rebelliousness." *Journal of Broadcasting & Electronic Media* 35, no. 3 (1991): 351-366.
   Assesses the preference for defiant rock music among adolescents in terms of the trait rebelliousness. Subjects were eighty-two (fifty-one males, thirty-one females) adolescents between the ages of sixteen and nineteen. Subjects completed personality questionnaires and viewed rock music videos. Notes that "highly rebellious students did not enjoy defiant rock videos more than their less rebellious peers." Highly rebellious students also did not consume more defiant

rock music than their peers. Fails to support the idea that rebellious students "selectively engross themselves in defiant rock music." Also, nonrebellious students found defiant rock music to be appealing.

779.   Buxton, David. "Rock Music, the Star-System and the Rise of Consumerism." *Telos* 57 (1983): 93-106.
Analyzes the relationships among rock music, rock stars, and consumerism. Observes that rock music is expected to be a means of rebellion, yet is a capitalist commodity. Notes that the process of absorption through advertising makes objects, such as records, symbolic images that convey messages beyond their inherent value. Contends that the rock star image is a lifestyle symbolic image. Discusses the association of the rock lifestyle to the constitution of the modern self using as frameworks the work of Marshall McLuhan and the psychedelic era. Asserts that rock music "plays a role in product design, creating enhanced use values in abstract form which can subsequently be transferred to other products." Concludes that rock music is rebellious only on a symbolic level and remains "one of the last bastions of laissez-faire capitalism." Calls for "cultural intervention" that will permit musical aesthetics beyond the control of commodity-driven capitalism. Also published in the book *On Record: Rock, Pop, and the Written Word*, edited by Simon Frith and Andrew Goodwin.

780.   Clarke, Peter. "Teenagers' Coorientation and Information Seeking About Pop Music." *American Behavioral Scientist* 16, no. 4 (1973): 551-556.
Studies the information seeking behavior of adolescents in regard to popular music. Concludes that adolescents seek print information about performers for one of two reasons: 1) to address a social function of exchanging information among peers, or 2) to address cognitive needs.

781.   Cole, Richard. "Top Songs in the Sixties: A Content Analysis of Popular Music." *American Behavioral Scientist* 14, no. 3 (1971): 389-400.
Conducts a content analysis of top hits for each year of the 1960s as reported in *Billboard* magazine. Explores the themes of love/sex, religion, violence, and social protest. Contends that more research is needed because popular music entertains, informs, and may influence adolescents.

782.   Cooper, B. Lee. "Audio Images of the City: Pop Culture in the Social Sciences." *The Social Studies* 72, no. 3 (1981): 129-136.
Notes that contemporary lyrics (i.e., popular, soul, country) can be a "rich source of social commentary." Suggests the use of popular music to study the following themes: the urban troubadour, urban culture, images of specific cities, and the urban female.

783. Cooper, B. Lee. "'Nothin' Outrun My V-8 Ford': Chuck Berry and the American Motorcar, 1955-1979." *JEMF Quarterly* 16, no. 57 (1980): 18-23.

Observes that Chuck Berry is a contemporary minstrel, describing in song the experiences of young urban Americans. Focuses on Berry's use of automobile imagery in his lyrics "to depict issues of freedom, mobility, sexual relationships, prosperity, and authority." Discusses the following specific songs: *Maybellene, Come On, Nadine, No Money Down, Too Much Monkey Business, No Particular Place to Go, Move It, Almost Grown, Wuden't Me, Carol, If I Were, You Never Can Tell,* and *Back in The U.S.A.* Concludes that Berry is an oral historian who chronicles the impact of technology on everyday situations.

784. Cooper, Virginia W. "Women in Popular Music: A Quantitative Analysis of Feminine Images Over Time." *Sex Roles* 13, no. 9/10 (1985): 499-506.

Performs a content analysis of 1,164 songs from 1946, 1956, 1966, and 1976 in order to determine changes in the portrayal of women in popular song lyrics. Studies eleven stereotypic images of women: evil, physical appearance, need for a man, possession of a man, mother, sex object, delicate, child, pedestal, attractiveness, supernatural. Discovers significant changes across time for eight of the eleven images. Notes increased emphasis on the images of physical appearance and evil and a decreased emphasis on the images of delicate and need for a man.

785. Curtis, James M. "Toward a Sociotechnological Interpretation of Popular Music in the Electronic Age." *Technology and Culture* 25, no. 1 (1984): 91-102.

Applies and tests Marshall McLuhan's theories on mass media as applied to rock music and technology. Identifies three distinct periods in the development of rock music. Discusses each period in terms of media, sociology of the implied listener, enhancement, obsolescence, retrieval, and reversals. In the first period, 1954-1964, the media were the 45 rpm record and AM radio. In the second period, 1964-1974, the media were FM radio and record albums. In the third period, the medium was 12-inch extended play single records (i.e., disco).

786. Cutietta, Robert. "Rock Music Gets a Label." *Music Educators Journal* 72, no. 8 (1986): 36-38.

Outlines several problems with the warning labels for records proposed by the Parents Music Resource Center (PMRC). First, warning labels do not provide enough detail about the nature of specific lyrics. Second, warning labels on art require value judgments. Third, warning labels require interpretations of lyrics that may differ from the composer's intent. Fourth, warning labels address a symptom of social problems and not the causes. Fifth, warning labels impose undue burdens on the music industry. Argues that a better solution is to simply make printed lyrics available with the records for preview prior to purchase.

787. Dancis, Bruce. "Safety Pins and Class Struggle: Punk Rock and the Left." *Socialist Review* 8, no. 3 39 (1978): 58-83.

Argues that at its best, punk rock is "an energetic aesthetic attack" on, and protest against, authoritarianism and class. At its worst, punk rock is a "manifestation of cultural despair and decadence." Compares and contrasts the significant differences between the punk movements in Great Britain and the United States. Focuses on the Sex Pistols to illustrate the political significance of punk rock in Great Britain. Discusses the punk movement and its relationship to socialism in terms of class struggle, authoritarianism, violence, sexism, and racism. Notes that punk rock lacks a meaningful alternate vision.

788. Dee, Juliet Lushbough. "Media Accountability for Real-Life Violence: A Case of Negligence or Free Speech?" *Journal of Communication* 37, no. 2 (1987): 106-138.

Reviews fifteen cases in United States courts regarding child or adolescent victims of violence induced by media. Suggests that the courts have "hesitated to hold media organizations accountable for inciting the violent acts of individuals." One of the cases associated with rock music is McCollum v. Osbourne in which an individual committed suicide after listening to two recordings by Ozzy Osbourne, *Suicide Solution* and *Paranoid*. The case was dismissed on First Amendment grounds. Another case is Vance and Roberson v. Judas Priest in which two individuals attempted suicide after listening to the Judas Priest album *Stained Glass*. Concludes that these types of cases are attempts to find direct solutions to the problem of violence in society.

789. Dotter, Daniel. "Growing Up Is Hard to Do: Rock and Roll Performers as Cultural Heroes." *Sociological Spectrum* 7, no. 1 (1987): 25-44.

Describes the changing role of rock stars as cultural symbols, from anti-heroes to heroes. States that rock stars have emerged as cultural symbols due to the increasing acceptability and use of rock music to communicate social commentary. Traces the nature of the hero and anti-hero as embodied in Elvis Presley and explores the transitional nature of the Beatles. The Beatles and Bob Dylan started as anti-heroes but became heroes. Notes that rock musicians can become heroic when their music combines with elements of mass media promotion and audience responses and, thus, symbolizes a collective experience. Rock music heroes reinforce cultural values, present alternative "modes of expression," and assist in "the development of new cultural forms."

790. Durant, Alan. "Rock Revolution or Time-No-Changes: Visions of Change and Continuity in Rock Music." *Popular Music* 5 (1985): 97-121.

Addresses the polarized issues surrounding the interpretations of change and repetition in rock music. Attempts to review the three agencies of change most associated with rock music: technology, musical form, and political (e.g., economic, institutional, ideological) forces. Describes each agency's explanatory power, appeal, consequences, and limitations. Uses albums, synthesizers, and video as examples of technology. Considers radio, vocal accent, and lyrical address as examples of musical form. Discusses political forces in terms of leisure and rebellion. Concludes that cultural analyses of rock music typically fail because "the detailed conditions of the music's production, distribution and interpretation remain insufficiently acknowledged in formulations of position and purpose."

791. Endres, Kathleen L. "Sex Role Standards in Popular Music." *Journal of Popular Culture* 18 (1984): 9-18.

Examines the lyrical content of thirty-six songs, twelve songs each from 1960, 1970, and 1980, in order to determine sex roles projected in popular music. Determines that there are two elements most influential in establishing sex roles in popular music. The first element is that male performers dominate popular music. The second element is that songs are typically written in the first person. Thus, sex roles are usually male defined. Notes that current trends suggest that sex roles will be portrayed in less traditional terms than in earlier years.

792. Epstein, Jonathon S., and David J. Pratto. "Heavy Metal Rock Music, Juvenile Delinquency and Satanic Identification." *Popular Music and Society* 14, no. 4 (1990): 67-76.

Conducts a participatory observational study of delinquent adolescents to determine the relationship between heavy metal music, juvenile delinquency, and satanism. Subjects were fourteen students (eight males, six females) who attended a court-assigned middle school and participated in heavy metal music listening sessions. Observes that listening to heavy metal music did not affect negatively the behavior of the subjects. Although behavior such as self-mutilation was observed, there was no indication that such behavior was motivated by satanic beliefs. States that more research leading to a better understanding of heavy metal music as a genre would provide greater insight into adolescent attitudes and values.

793. Epstein, Jonathon S., David J. Pratto, and James K. Skipper Jr. "Teenagers, Behavioral Problems, and Preferences for Heavy Metal and Rap Music: A Case Study of a Southern Middle School." *Deviant Behavior* 11 (1990): 381-394.

Examines the relationship between adolescent behavioral problems, music preference, and commitment to music. Hypothesizes that music preference is related to race, and that music preference can predict behavior problems as can commitment to music. Surveyed eighty adolescents and used participant observation and school records. Results indicate that race is an indicator of music preference, but music preference and commitment to music cannot serve to predict behavior problems.

794. Fornas, Johan. "Moving Rock: Youth and Pop in Late Modernity." *Popular Music* 9, no. 3 (1990): 291-306.

Describes "moving" as being the meanings and functions of music. Explores the use of rock music in the external world of materialism, the social world of relations, and the internal world of subjective forces such as identity. Discusses rock music as a cultural form, used as communication through styles and symbols.

795. Friedenberg, Edgar Z. "Current Patterns of a Generational Conflict." *Journal of Social Issues* 25, no. 2 (1969): 21-38.

Casts the alienation of the 1960s counterculture as a truly unique generational conflict, different from any previous experiences. Attempts to explain the novelty of the situation. Claims that if adults want to understand the new generation's perspectives, then they need to listen to folk rock music. Identifies specific artists, divided into high art (Bob Dylan, the Beatles, Simon and Garfunkel, Donovan, Jefferson Airplane) and low art (Mothers of Invention, the Rolling Stones). Argues that these artists speak "for themselves of the patterns of generational conflict in which they are involved."

796. Frith, Simon. "Anglo-America and its Discontents." *Cultural Studies* 5, no. 3 (1991): 263-269.

Questions the extent to which the Anglo-American domination of popular music worldwide is secure or even real. Explores the concept of Great Britain as both a talent pool and a test market for popular music. Suggests that Europe is replacing the United States as the "mythical space" from which global music arises.

797. Frith, Simon. "'The Magic That Can Set You Free': The Ideology of Folk and the Myth of the Rock Community." *Popular Music* 1 (1981): 159-168.

Concentrates on the effects of the "ideology of folk" on the interpretation of rock music by members of the rock music culture. Delineates the folk argument that rock music is an authentic expression of community experience. Contends that the myth of community is central to all notions regarding rock music's cultural significance. Describes in detail how the idea of community has been created and developed in the rock music context.

798. Frith, Simon. "The Punk Bohemians." *New Society* 43, no. 805 (1978): 535-536.

Challenges the notion that punk music was a reaction to high unemployment and other economic conditions. Claims that it was actually a phase "in the history of radical British art." Defines punk rock as a "deliberate artistic exploitation of the media's own symbolic and visual language." Discusses the relationships among punk rock's promoters (e.g., Malcolm McLaren) and the bohemian art culture.

799. Frith, Simon, and Angela McRobbie. "Rock and Sexuality." *Screen Education* 29 (1978-79): 3-19.

Uses the film *Saturday Night Fever* as an entry into discussing the relationship between sexuality and rock music. States that rock music is the mass medium "most explicitly concerned with sexual expression." Claims that rock music is a complex mode of expression, combining music, lyrics, performance, and image. Understanding the sexual messages of rock music usually cannot be accomplished by examining just form or content. Rock music is used as a means of both sexual expression and sexual control. Describes representations of masculinity and femininity in rock music as well as the contradictions in these representations. Contends that sexuality is a construct of rock music. Concludes by looking at dance as the "most public setting for music as sexual expression." Also published in the book *On Record: Rock, Pop, and the Written Word*, edited by Simon Frith and Andrew Goodwin.

800. Garofalo, Reebee. "How Autonomous is Relative: Popular Music, the Social Formation and Cultural Struggle." *Popular Music* 6, no. 1 (1987): 77-92.

Explores the debate in neo-Marxist thinking about the utility of the "economic base/superstructure" metaphor to describe and analyze cultural production and consumption. Reviews the history of the American music industry. Examines the character and relative power of musicians, record companies, audiences, and music. Analyzes the cultural Marxist and classical Marxist theoretical frameworks and suggests a "post-Marxist" cultural theory. Uses events such as record sales, *Billboard* magazine charts, television broadcasts, pricing decisions, and censorship to challenge the validity and logic of Marxist theories.

801. Gold, Brian D. "Self-Image of Punk Rock and Nonpunk Rock Juvenile Delinquents." *Adolescence* 22, no. 87 (1987): 535-544.

Tests personality differences between "punk rock" and "nonpunk rock" juvenile delinquents. Subjects (two groups of twenty adolescents each, fifteen boys and five girls) held at a California juvenile hall were administered a series of personality tests. No significant differences were discovered between the groups, although results suggest the possibility of differences with regard to family dynamics. Claims that the distinguishing looks of punk rockers do not indicate significant self-image differences from other adolescent groups.

802. Goldberg, Herb. "Rock Music & Sex: A Exploration of Sex in the Rock Music Culture." *Sexual Behavior* 1, no. 5 (1971): 25-31.

Discusses the increase during the 1960s of sexual consciousness as conveyed in rock music. Notes an increasing acceptance of erotic and provocative sexual behavior on stage at rock concerts. Concludes that rock performers of the late 1960s and early 1970s are self-indulgent and deluded, and repress anger and destructiveness. Calls it a "sickness" of intimacy-anxiety and alienation.

803. Goldthorpe, Jeff. "Interview with Maximum Rock and Roll." *Radical America* 18, no. 6 (1984): 8-24.

Presents an interview conducted with the editors of *Maximum Rock n Roll*, an international punk magazine. Attempts to provide insight into the "politics, styles, and culture of the American hard core" punk scene.

804. Goodwin, Andrew. "Popular Music and Postmodern Theory." *Cultural Studies* 5, no. 2 (1991): 174-190.

Reviews the literature on postmodern theory and its relationship to rock music. Explores the confusion surrounding postmodernism when being interpreted as a theory or as a cultural condition. Offers three definitions for postmodern rock: 1) music that is outside the mainstream of popular music and is to be taken seriously, 2) music that is created by musicians who come chronologically after "modern rock," and 3) music that has evolved from punk rock. Because postmodernism is conceptually used to define theory, culture, and practice, "further analysis of its relation to music will have to take account of this epistemological feedback loop."

805. Gray, J. Patrick. "Rock As a Chaos Model Ritual." *Popular Music and Society* 7, no. 2 (1980): 75-83.

Explores the concept of rock music as a ritual and how it relates "to the existing power structure in the United States." Claims that societies permit chaos rituals in order to demonstrate that freedom from structure results in greater unhappiness, thus validating the current social system. Identifies three motifs by which rock music functions as chaos ritual. First, rock groups come in and out of existence, illustrating that rock music is unsuccessful in sustaining organization. Second, individual creativity is associated with personal destruction (e.g., Janis Joplin, Jimi Hendrix, Jim Morrison). Third, rock music is associated with violence.

806. Groce, Stephen B. "Occupational Rhetoric and Ideology: A Comparison of Copy and Original Music Performers." *Qualitative Sociology* 12, no. 4 (1989): 391-410.

Interviewed twenty-five local-level rock musicians (seventeen to forty years of age) in order to establish the differences between occupational rhetoric and ideology among copy and original musicians. Copy musicians are those who perform music written and made successful by others. Original musicians are those who perform original compositions. Discovers that copy musicians view themselves as technically competent and play music for economic reasons. Original musicians view themselves as creative and play music for artistic reasons. Concludes that the "structure and function of local-level musicians ideological orientations" are based on perceptions of themselves, their audiences, and the music industry.

807. Groce, Stephen B. "What's the Buzz?: Rethinking the Meanings and Uses of Alcohol and Other Drugs Among Small-Time Rock 'n' Roll Musicians." *Deviant Behavior* 12, no. 4 (1991): 361-384.

Raises the issue of the meaning and use of alcohol and drugs among rock musicians. Interviewed thirty-five local-level musicians to investigate "the relationships between the social organization of musicians' workplaces, the nature of musicians' work, and the meanings and uses of various mood-altering substances." Concludes that musicians use substances to relax, achieve a particular mood, increase creativity, and relieve boredom. Suggests a connection between group cohesiveness and ideology and the use of alcohol and drugs. Argues that the use of substances is a rational act reflective of "functional normative frameworks."

808. Gross, Robert L. "Heavy Metal Music: A New Subculture in American Society." *Journal of Popular Culture* 24, no. 1 (1990): 119-130.

Describes heavy metal music as a subculture which is "a provocative new force on the American cultural scene." Examines five aspects of heavy metal music and the related subculture: 1) the origins of the music, 2) the musical structure of heavy metal, 3) the cult or subculture structure, 4) the messages transmitted through heavy metal music, and 5) the economics. Concludes that, through marketing practices, a subculture has been created that allows the commercialization of youthful rebellion.

809. Harmon, James E. "The New Music and Counter-Culture Values." *Youth & Society* 4, no. 1 (1972): 61-82.

Applies Harold Lasswell's "scheme of universal values" to a content analysis of popular music. Lasswell's eight values for use in content analysis are: power, well-being, enlightenment, rectitude, respect, affection, wealth, and skill. Examines over 1,000 songs appearing between 1945 and 1969. Concludes that the youth movement of the late 1960s and the resulting "generation gap" were more cultural and lifestyle based than politically motivated.

810. Harrah-Conforth, Bruce. "Rock and Roll, Process, and Tradition." *Western Folklore* 49, no. 3 (1990): 306-313.

Uses the counterculture movement of the 1960s to explore the role of process and tradition in the definition of folklore. Contends that mass culture products, such as rock music recordings, can be "traditionalized by communities in order that they function as folk items." The performance of rock music at "ballrooms" or concert halls such as the Fillmore auditorium was one aspect of a larger communal ritual. Concludes that the counterculture "molded its resources" into a folklore process, even when those resources were mass-produced commercial artifacts.

811. Herman, Andrew. "You're in Suspicion: Punk and the Secret Passion Play of White Noise." *Canadian Journal of Political and Social Theory* 14, no. 1-3 (1990): 47-68.

Reviews and analyzes the book *Lipstick Traces* by Greil Marcus. Draws deeply upon Herman's own experiences with the punk rock movement in order to thoroughly critique *Lipstick Traces*. Praises Marcus for having "fewer theoretical crosses to bear" and for avoiding the scholars' trap of allowing theory to "all but silence the sound they are trying to understand." Observes that Marcus fails to understand the difference between transcendence and transformation. Criticizes his stance for being that of "a passive consumer rather than as engaged social critic or organic intellectual."

812. Hirsch, Paul M. "Sociological Approaches to the Pop Music Phenomenon." *American Behavioral Scientist* 14, no. 3 (1971): 371-388.

Explores four sociological approaches to studying rock music: content analysis, audience impact, technological change, and organizational analysis of the entertainment industry. Content analysis assumes that messages contained in rock music either induce or reflect attitudinal change in the audience. Audience impact assumes that values contained in rock music songs are understandable to the audience, agreed to by a majority of the audience, and influence attitudes and behavior among the audience. Technological change assumes that new technology forces old technology to redefine its market, in this case television forcing radio to develop subculture markets such as "Top 40" and "Underground" radio stations. Organizational analysis assumes that market forces drive the organizational structure which impacts on the nature and scope of rock music available to consumers.

813. Hyden, Colleen, and N. Jane McCandless. "Men and Women as Portrayed in the Lyrics of Contemporary Music." *Popular Music and Society* 9 (1985): 19-26.

Focuses on the portrayal of men and women in the lyrics from 106 popular songs between 1972 and 1982. Compiles lists of the adjectives used to describe men and to describe women. Results suggest that women are portrayed in traditional stereotypical sex roles. Finds that men are portrayed as possessing both masculine and feminine characteristics. Concludes that the results suggest possible implications for sex role socialization, but notes the limitations of lyrical content analysis methodology.

814. Jones, Kevin E., and Patricia Atchison Harvey. "Modeling the Rock Band and Audience Interaction." *Free Inquiry in Creative Sociology* 8, no. 2 (1980): 131-134,138.

Attempts to model the relationships between audiences and rock groups in a typical bar setting so that researchers will have a "framework to classify components of interaction." Offers a typology of bar patrons (hustler, romancer, escaper, obliged, facilitated, converser, listener, and follower) in relation to rock groups. Theoretically based on collective behavior and symbolic interaction.

815.   Kamin, Jonathan. "Taking the Roll Out of Rock 'N' Roll." *Popular Music and Society* 2 (1972): 1-17.

Demonstrates that early rock music illustrates one example of the white culture representing a deprived group in relation to the black culture. Notes that one result of the rise of rock music was that black cultural standards became the norm. Details how this transformation occurred as a result of cover version recordings. Observes that as a result rock music audiences are committed to the music and the associated dances are expressive and not formal.

816.   Kealy, Edward R. "Conventions and the Production of the Popular Music Aesthetic." *Journal of Popular Culture* 16, no. 2 (1982): 100-115.

Explores from a sociological perspective the processes involved in the production of rock music. Indicates two levels on which the rock music aesthetic is created. First is the music industry's massive distribution and promotion mechanism designed to personalize the impersonal medium of recorded music. Second is the music industry's support of the social network required for the complex technological effort to produce the music product. Focuses on the shifting power structures in the music industry from the corporations to the musicians.

817.   Kealy, Edward R. "From Craft to Art: The Case of Sound Mixers and Popular Music." *Sociology of Work and Occupations* 6, no. 1 (1979): 3-29.

Traces the history of the nature of recording technicians or "sound mixers." Notes that the creation of rock music has three major components: music (e.g., musicians, composers), technology (e.g., recording engineers and producers), and marketing (e.g., record promoters). Studies the effects on the process when the musicians become interested in the technology "as a new medium for artistic expression." Notes that sound mixing has been transformed from a craft to an art as a result of technological developments and increasing artistic control over the entire process. The occupation of sound mixer has evolved from a union craft mode to that of entrepreneurial and art modes. Also published in the book *On Record: Rock, Pop, and the Written Word*, edited by Simon Frith and Andrew Goodwin.

818.   Kohl, Paul R. "Looking Through a Glass Onion: Rock and Roll as a Modern Manifestation of Carnival." *Journal of Popular Culture* 27, no. 1 (1993): 143-161.

Uses the concept of the medieval European carnival as characterized by Mikhail Bakhtin to study rock music of the 1960s. Carnival is described as the place where juxtapositions are eliminated, where anything goes, and where social status and political hierarchy are removed. Claims that the major consequence of carnival is a positive degradation and debasement. Notes that the closest manifestation of carnival in this century is rock music. Argues that the Beatles contributed more to this realization than any other music group or performer. Illustrates with the following examples: 1) the Beatles on *The Ed Sullivan Show*, 2) the hysteria surrounding the Beatles' concerts, 3) their disregard for social hierarchies, exemplified when John Lennon claimed that the Beatles were more popular than Jesus Christ. Concentrates on the album *Sgt. Pepper's Lonely Hearts Club Band* as the apex of the Beatles as carnival. Continues by focusing on the dialectic response to the Beatles by Frank Zappa and the Mothers of Invention with their album *We're Only in It for the Money*. Gives the Captain Beefheart album *Trout Mask Replica* as an extreme example of the grotesque in carnival and the Velvet Underground's song *Heroin* as a sympathetic vision of the grotesque. Presents the Monterey International Pop Festival, Woodstock, and Altamont concerts as the most literal examples of the "carnivalesque tradition."

819. Korzenny, Felipe, Joyce McClure, and Barbara Rzyttki. "Ethnicity, Communication, and Drugs." *Journal of Drug Issues* 20, no. 1 (1990): 87-98.

Explores the "degree to which different patterns of communication media exposure are associated with attitudes and behaviors related to drug usage." Examines four ethnic groups: Whites, Blacks, Hispanics, and Asians. Subjects were 171 individuals (forty-five Whites, forty-two Hispanics, forty-three Asians, and forty-one Blacks) interviewed in San Francisco. Tests whether differential social information processing exists among ethnic groups by studying the association of media habits and drug usage and attitudes. Shows that television, rock music, print, and interpersonal communication yield different results across ethnic groups. Demonstrates that rock music exposure is "correlated with positive attitudes towards drugs and drug consumption." These particular associations were found to be less pronounced for Whites.

820. Kotarba, Joseph A., and Laura Wells. "Styles of Adolescent Participation in an All-Ages, Rock 'n' Roll Nightclub: An Ethnographic Analysis." *Youth & Society* 18, no. 4 (1987): 398-417.

Presents the results of a four month period of ethnographic observations and interviews conducted at an all-ages rock club in Houston, Texas. Identifies four distinct styles used by adolescents: metal heads, punkers, yuppies, and posers. Each style is defined by music preference, fashion, interactions, and life philosophy. Observes that there is relatively easy movement between styles, suggesting adolescent experimentation with self-identity.

821. Kotarba, Joseph A., Mark L. Williams, and Jay Johnson. "Rock Music as a Medium for AIDS Intervention." *AIDS Education and Prevention* 3, no. 1 (1991): 47-49.

Stresses two methods by which rock music can serve as a vehicle for AIDS intervention. One method is to utilize rock music as a conversational device during interviews in order to maintain the attention of respondents. The second method is to use the music as "a medium for transmitting preventive care messages."

822. Koval, Howard. "Homogenization of Culture in Capitalist Society." *Popular Music and Society* 12, no. 1 (1988): 1-16.
Seeks to test the theory put forward in *Dialectics of Enlightenment* by Theodor Adorno and Max Horkheimer that capitalism leads to a homogenization of culture. Adorno and Horkheimer contended that capitalism results in a systematic reduction of new ideas, messages, and values being introduced into the culture. The mass media repeat old ideas and thus trivialize meaning. Examines rock music in order to determine if a selected cultural form confirms or contradicts this idea of capitalist culture. Chooses rock music because it is a dominant element of popular culture and it is believed to be an expression of rebellion and dissent. Argues that if the themes in rock music are not very diverse and are repeated frequently, then the theory of Adorno and Horkheimer is supported. Suggests that the music industry is able to negate the rebellious messages of rock music through repetition until the messages have no meaning. Looks at the *Billboard* magazine weekly charts of Top 100 records from 1958 to 1982. Notes the total number of songs on the charts, the number of new artists, and the length of time on the charts. Concludes that since about 1964, audiences have been exposed to "a narrower range of music, with its impact and meaning (at least potentially) diluted through constant repetition." Attributes this to the development of the music industry and its emphasis on mass production, marketing, and consumption. Confirms the predictions of Adorno and Horkheimer.

823. Kurtz, Howard. "Differences in Themes in Popular Music and Their Relationship to Deviance." *Popular Music and Society* 8, no. 2 (1982): 84-89.
Investigates the possibility that lyrical themes and criminal behavior are associated. Assumes that certain musical genres are appealing to specific racial groups (i.e., the majority of the soul music audience is black, the majority of the popular music audience is white). Examines the lyrical content of songs listed in *Billboard* magazine's soul and pop charts between 1970 and 1978. Identifies six deviant themes; drink, sex, automotive, taking, violence, and gambling. Concludes that popular music (whites) deviant themes involve sex, drinking, and automobiles, while soul music (blacks) deviant themes involve taking.

824. Lance, Larry M., and Christina Y. Berry. "Has There Been a Sexual Revolution? An Analysis of Human Sexuality Messages in Popular Music, 1968-1977." *Journal of Popular Culture* 15, no. 3 (1981): 155-164.
Examines the lyrics of popular music from 1968 to 1977 in an attempt to verify the occurrence of a "sexual revolution." Contends that rock music "provides daily communication of sex roles, sexual behaviors, and sexual relationship to Americans." Provides a brief history of changing sexual attitudes

as reflected in other media. Performs a content analysis of hit rock songs with lyrics which address sexuality. Discovers that an increasing number of songs deal with sexual activity and that the lyrics "indicate a more liberal attitude toward sexual activity in general, and more sexual freedom for women in particular." Notes a shift in lyrics from casual sexual relationships to more emotionally involved relationships. Contends that the sexual behavior presented in rock music lyrics both reflects and influences socially acceptable behavior. Concludes that there is support for the notion that a sexual revolution has occurred.

825. Leming, James S. "Rock Music and the Socialization of Moral Values in Early Adolescence." *Youth & Society* 18, no. 4 (1987): 363-383.

Explores the links between rock music and adolescent values. Specifically examines the extent to which rock music is salient to adolescents, the extent to which adolescents think that rock music has negative values, and the extent to which adolescents accept and incorporate the values of rock music. Surveyed fifty-eight adolescents between the ages of eleven and fifteen (twenty-five males and thirty-three females). Results suggest that "simple explanations for complex social phenomena seldom stand up under close scrutiny." Concludes that adolescents are not "passive receptors" of rock music's value content.

826. Levine, Edward M. "The Role of Cultural Values in the Etiology of Psychopathologies: An Inter-Disciplinary Approach." *International Journal of Sociology of the Family* 12, no. 2 (1982): 189-200.

Claims that current cultural values are impulse-gratification, self-centeredness, and present-orientation. These values are generated and reinforced through sex and aggression themes in rock music and through increasing acceptance of deviant sexual behavior. The result is a modified effect on child-rearing behavior which is "to the detriment of children's emotional development and socialization."

827. Levine, Harold G., and Steven H. Stumpf. "Statements of Fear Through Cultural Symbols: Punk Rock as a Reflective Subculture." *Youth & Society* 14, no. 4 (1983): 417-435.

Studies the punk rock scene in Los Angeles, California, to articulate elements of a particular type of subculture. Explores the subculture in terms of "its own identity, values, and cohesion." Focuses on the issues of subculture self-preservation and relationships to the dominant culture. Concludes that the punk rock movement in Los Angeles embodies those "crucial elements by which a subculture may be defined." Includes elements of style, issues that give the style meaning, and a "private code" through which meaning is articulated. Self-preservation is achieved through intimidation that sets the subculture apart from the dominant culture. Specifically, the theme of fear is embodied by the subculture through fashion, music, and symbols, thus reflecting the subculture's perception of fear in the dominant culture. Contrasts the reflective subculture of the punk movement with the outlaw subculture of motorcycle gangs and the alternative subculture of hippies.

828. Levine, Mark H., and Thomas J. Harig. "The Role of Rock: A Review and Critique of Alternative Perspectives on the Impact of Rock Music." *Popular Music and Society* 4 (1975): 195-207.

Notes that there are two basic, but opposing, models that have been applied to the study of rock music in regard to the effects of mass media. The first model suggests that rock music manipulates a passive audience and can affect attitudes and behaviors. The second model suggests that rock music only reinforces existing beliefs and values to an extent that is audience determined. Reviews and critiques the literature written under both models.

829. Lewis, George H. "The Creation of Popular Music: A Comparison of the 'Art Worlds' of American Country Music and British Punk." *International Review of the Aesthetics and Sociology of Music* 19, no. 1 (1988): 35-51.

Examines the process of creating art and, in particular, popular music. Contends that it is not an individualistic process, but rather is a social one of production and consumption. Claims that the production of art is market oriented and therefore art must be presented in a form that can be understood and appreciated. Uses country music and punk music to illustrate the very different forms that these processes may take under different social conditions. Concludes that the creation of culture is a social process that can be understood only "within the social environment within which it is created and consumed."

830. Lewis, George H. "This Bitter Earth: Protest and Style in Black American Music." *National Forum* 62, no. 3 (1982): 26-28.

Remarks on the study of protest themes in black music. Contends that music is the primary mode of communication regarding a shared perspective within the black community and that rock music provides symbols for rebellion. Places black music into five categories: retreatist, pluralistic, assimilationist, secessionist, and militant. Describes retreatist as existing in the gospel tradition. Pluralistic music emerged as a reflection of urbanization among African Americans. Assimilationist describes cross over music (e.g., Motown sound). Secessionist is a rejection of the dominant cultural styles (e.g., James Brown). Militant has a goal of domination. Also discusses disco music within the context of these categories.

831. Lull, James. "Popular Music: Resistance to New Wave." *Journal of Communication* 32, no. 1 (1982): 121-131.

Surveys 375 college students to assess the impact of new wave music. Argues that new wave music is faced with two sources of resistance. The first is the music industry that is inclined to only introduce safe commodities into the marketplace. The second source of resistance is the personal, social, and cultural predisposition of the audience. Summarizes students attitudes toward new wave music in terms of mood, history, confusion, lifestyle, social function, emotional discomfort, and frivolity.

832.   Lumer, Robert. "American Popular Music and American Values." *Zeitschrift fur Anglistik und Amerikanistik* 29, no. 1 (1981): 59-69.

Comments on themes found in American popular music, particularly rhythm and blues, country music, and rock music. Debates the extent to which rock music can be described as art. Argues that rock music performers fail to "understand the forces that created their own emotional world" and the results were desperate and destructive musical statements. Blames the commercialization of rock music for confining and controlling the extent to which the genre can articulate meaningful issues.

833.   Martin, Bernice. "The Sacralization of Disorder: Symbolism in Rock Music." *Sociological Analysis* 40, no. 2 (1979): 87-124.

Demonstrates that the rock music culture illustrates paradoxically the use of symbols by youth to articulate "anti-structure" and to create "communitas." Symbols and symbolic behavior are used by the youth culture to achieve identity. Contends that the relationship between anti-structure and communitas can be both symbiotic and contradictory.

834.   Mashkin, Karen Beth, and Thomas J. Volgy. "Socio-Political Attitudes and Musical Preferences." *Social Science Quarterly* 56, no. 3 (1975): 450-459.

Investigates "the relationship between socio-political attitudes and musical preferences of college students." Further examines if popular music reflects or shapes audience attitudes or does both. Subjects were 232 college students (131 males, 101 females) enrolled in either psychology or political science courses. Results indicate that there are significant relationships between musical preferences (i.e., rock, folk, country) and socio-political attitudes, but the direction of the relationships is undetermined. Concludes that the relationships are not due to any one factor. Speculates that because college students reject conventional agents of socialization, popular music should be "highly salient" at least as a reinforcing agent.

835.   Meade, Marion. "Does Rock Degrade Women?" *Sexual Behavior* 1, no. 5 (1971): 28-29.

Observes the widespread sexism existing in the culture of rock music. Criticizes the lyrics of the Rolling Stones and Bob Dylan. Notes the virtual absence of any women in the film *Woodstock*. Comments on the existence of groupies and the lack of women in the music industry.

836. Meade, Marion. "Women and Rock: Sexism Set to Music." *Women: A Journal of Liberation* 2, no. 1 (1970): 24-26.

Comments on the ways in which rock music presents a "consistently degrading image of women" and celebrates male supremacy. Notes that the sexual revolution of the 1960s resulted in the transformation of the image of women in rock music lyrics. Whereas women were portrayed as goddesses or girls next door, they are now treated as sex objects. Provides numerous examples from rock music lyrics, but focuses on the works of Bob Dylan and the Rolling Stones.

837. Miletich, Leo N. "Rock Me with a Steady Roll." *Reason* 18 (1987): 20-27.

Presents the issue of rock music censorship in the context of a much longer history of attempts to ban selected music.

838. Mitsui, Toru. "Japan in Japan: Notes on an Aspect of the Popular Music Industry in Japan." *Popular Music* 3 (1983): 107-120.

Discusses the growth and internationalization of the record industry in Japan. Uses the British rock group known as Japan as a case-study of music industry marketing in Japan.

839. Morse, Margaret. "Postsynchronizing Rock Music and Television." *Journal of Communication Inquiry* 10, no. 1 (1986): 15-28.

Discusses the production of rock music videos and the status of rock music as a commodity. Analyzes music videos as discourse, directed from a source to an audience. Argues that rock music is becoming less a formation of culture and audience and more a formation of the corporate advertising world. Contends that the current youth culture must deal with "the massive penetration by advertising culture" into all aspects of life.

840. Mullen, Patrick B. "Hillbilly Hipsters of the 1950s: The Romance of Rockabilly." *Southern Quarterly* 22, no. 3 (1984): 79-92.

Discusses the similarities between the nature of 1950s rockabilly music and the beat generation. Characterizes rockabilly music as "rebellion against societal controls, excess, hedonism, and a sense of community among outsiders." Notes that most studies of rockabilly emphasize its regional development and the influences of Protestant fundamentalism. Outlines common themes found in the rockabilly and beat cultures, using Jack Kerouac's book *On the Road* as a point of reference. Observes that both rockabilly musicians and beatniks sought to emulate styles of black culture through a romanticized and stereotypical perspective (e.g., hedonism). Also points out the adolescent excess and sexism of beatniks and rockabilly musicians. Both subcultures forged a "unity of life and art." Concludes that both the beat generation and rockabilly music represented an ambivalent rebellion against the middle-class values to which members actually aspired.

841. Plopper, Bruce L., and M. Ernest Ness. "Death as Portrayed to Adolescents Through Top 40 Rock and Roll Music." *Adolescence* 28, no. 112 (1993): 793-807.

Acknowledges rock music as an important communicative source about the image of death in society. Conducted a content analysis of popular death-theme songs from 1955 through 1991, focusing on cause of death, gender, relationships among characters, attitudes, and coping. Observes distinct content changes across time.

842. Politis, John. "Rock Music's Place in the Library." *Drexel Library Quarterly* 19, no. 1 (1983): 78-92.

Begins with a brief history of rock music and an overview of contemporary rock music. Proposes that libraries need to concentrate on the aural culture, in addition the traditional print culture, because it represents a record of post-war artistic expression and historical commentary. Concludes that libraries traditionally reflect middle-class values, but in a time of cultural plurality resources should be allocated to providing the public with access to rock music. Notes that for many persons rock music is the "dominant form of artistic and cultural expression."

843. Prinsky, Lorraine E., and Jill Leslie Rosenbaum. "'Leer-ics' or Lyrics: Teenage Impressions of Rock 'n' Roll." *Youth & Society* 18, no. 4 (1987): 384-397.

Reviews the literature regarding the interpretations of rock music lyrics by adolescents. Argues that interpretation is based on life experiences and knowledge base. Therefore, adults are more likely than adolescents to interpret lyrics as having references that are explicitly sexual, violent, or satanic. Ties this concept directly to the notion that metaphor perception is dependent upon metacognitive knowledge. Concludes that the idea of warning labels or ratings for records, as promoted by the Parents Music Resource Center (PMRC), may be counterproductive. Labels or ratings may educate adolescents about themes of which they were previously unaware or may make the recordings more desirable to a rebellious youth culture.

844. Rosenbaum, Jill Leslie, and Lorraine Prinsky. "The Presumption of Influence: Recent Responses to Popular Music Subcultures." *Crime & Delinquency* 37, no. 4 (1991): 528-535.

Presents a study of twelve hospitals in California with adolescent care programs which were provided a hypothetical situation of parents complaining about a child's taste in music, clothes, and posters. The majority (ten) of the hospitals recommended mental health treatment. Labeling theory suggests that the labeling of adolescents as delinquents or as mentally ill based on musical or fashion tastes may result in pushing them into deviant roles.

845. Ruffner, Marguerite Anne. "Women's Attitudes Toward Progressive Rock Radio." *Journal of Broadcasting* 17, no. 1 (1972-73): 85-94.

Studies the attitudes of fifty-one women between the ages of eighteen and thirty-four years toward progressive rock music radio stations. Focuses on subjects' decision-making processes and motivational influences. Discovers some evidence that progressive rock music is "positively associated with the fulfillment of audience needs." Suggests strategies for attracting "non-listeners" into the progressive rock audience.

846. Santino, Jack. "Rock and Roll as Music; Rock and Roll as Culture." *World and I* 5 (1990): 494-505.

Comments on rock music from several perspectives. Attributes early rock music's popularity to the fact it divided generations and provided an opportunity for the younger generation to articulate an independent aesthetic. Observes that now several generations belong to, and share, rock music culture. Notes that the synthesis of rhythm and blues and country music that gave birth to rock music was only the beginning of a "dynamic process" of merging and diverging musical styles within rock music. Also focuses on rock music as a capitalistic enterprise with the single purpose of making money. Sociologically, the rebellious image of rock music is described as a contradiction between artistic expression and an intentional design to increase profits. Contends that the most important aspect of rock music is its cultural impact and that the most relevant element of rock music as a social force is the individual listener. The rock audience identifies with music that then reinforces existing attitudes. One positive aspect about rock music is that it can assist adolescents to "gain a sense of their identity." Concludes that rock music is no different from other forms of popular culture in articulating social evils and, therefore, should not be singled out for censorship.

847. Scudder, David F. "On Buxton: Structuralist Logic and the Conspiracy of Latent Functions." *Telos* 59 (1984): 167-171.

Counters the assertions made in David Buxton's article *Rock Music, the Star-System and the Rise of Consumerism*. Claims that the relationships among the aesthetics of rock music, the counterculture, and consumerism were not based on "insidious latent functions and conspiracies." Notes that the counterculture movement was decidedly anti-consumerism and the rock stars of the era were seen as aesthetic and intellectual leaders, not agents of consumerism. States that although record companies marketed rock music through the mass media which in turn spread counterculture values, this was "simple opportunistic profit logic, not consumer discipline and consciousness."

848. Shepherd, John. "A Theoretical Model for the Sociomusicological Analysis of Popular Musics." *Popular Music* 2 (1982): 145-177.

Defines a theoretical model for identifying "the musical articulations of different cultural realities" in industrialized societies. Notes that rock music exists in a traditional working-class reality. Punk rock emits from alienation seeking to rebel by forcing society to examine itself. Progressive rock music reflects a desire to re-order society from a more humane perspective. Common to all subgenres of rock music is the emphasis on "the inherent potential of people to exist fully in the world."

849. Sherman, Barry L. "A Decade of Decadence: The First Ten Years of Music Video." *World and I* 5 (1990): 482-493.

Shows that MTV "celebrates social anomie, cultivates hedonism, and reinforces" sexism and racism. Provides a history of MTV that describes a "classic product life-cycle curve" in that an initial period of novelty was followed by rapid growth and maturation, then decline, and finally repositioning through marketing. Labels MTV audiences as television's second generation, the first being the post-World War II baby-boomers. Explores MTV's sexist gender portrayals, racist images, and violence. Notes the association of sex and violence in music videos. Observes a politically leftist stance in many videos, but also a capitalistic orientation that celebrates materialism. Raises the issue of the extent to which MTV images are being internalized by audiences, especially through the adolescent socialization process.

850. Stratton, Jon. "Beyond Art: Postmodernism and the Case of Popular Music." *Theory, Culture and Society* 6, no. 1 (1989): 31-57.

Proclaims that "bourgeois aesthetic theory" has defined art in such a way that it is separate from the "domain of material production." In doing so, the possibility of a "working-class aesthetic" is denied. Argues that there is, in fact, a working-class aesthetic based on pleasure as opposed to reason. Identifies three stages in rock music history in which aesthetics are reconstructed within the context of capitalism's shift from production to consumption.

851. Straw, Will. "Systems of Articulation, Logics of Change: Communities and Scenes in Popular Music." *Cultural Studies* 5, no. 3 (1991): 368-388.

Discusses the logics of change typical of different musical genres. Argues that the significant processes for analysis are those in which specific social differences (e.g., gender, race) are expressed within the audience. Musical genres will evolve as a result of social institutions and organizations of the audience.

852. Stringer, Julian. "The Smiths: Repressed (but Remarkably Dressed)." *Popular Music* 11, no. 1 (1992): 15-26.

Uses the group the Smiths as a case-study of the social and political tensions invested in star images. Discusses the contradictions in the image and songs of the Smiths.

853. St. Lawrence, Janet S., and Doris J. Joyner. "The Effects of Sexually Violent Rock Music on Males' Acceptance of Violence Against Women." *Psychology of Women Quarterly* 15, no. 1 (1991): 49-63.

Studies the effects of sexually violent music on seventy-five undergraduate males and their attitudes toward women, violence against women, and sexual arousal. Results show that exposure to heavy metal music increased sex-role stereotyping and negative attitudes toward women. Sexually violent lyrics did not produce significant elevations of scores beyond those of heavy metal music in general. Nonreligious orientations were associated with greater prejudicial attitudes toward women.

854. Tanner, Julian. "Pop Music and Peer Groups: A Study of Canadian High School Students' Responses to Pop Music." *Canadian Review of Sociology and Anthropology* 18, no. 1 (1981): 1-13.

Probes variables such as gender, age, social class, commitment to school, and delinquency as factors influencing musical preferences among adolescents. Focuses on the genres of heavy metal, progressive rock, and Top 40. Finds that females are more likely than males to favor Top 40 music. Older adolescents are more likely to favor progressive rock music. Top 40 is favored by the working-class, while progressive rock music is favored by the middle-class. Heavy metal music "provides a symbolic rejection of the prevailing values" for those working-class adolescents who have a lower commitment to school. Concludes that music preferences reflect various social experiences of adolescents.

855. Tanner, Julian. "Youth Culture and the Canadian High School: An Empirical Analysis." *Canadian Journal of Sociology* 3, no. 1 (1978): 89-102.

Tests two propositions regarding the relationship between adolescent cultures and commitment to school as an institution of learning. The first proposition states that there is an association between either of two adolescent subcultures, "street culture" (delinquency) and "pop-media culture," and a low commitment to school. The second proposition is that involvement in the two subcultures is differentiated by gender and socio-economic background. Commitment to school was measured using an attitude scale. Self-reports of behavior were used to determine subculture membership. Attitude toward rock music was also used to determine pop-media culture membership. Socio-economic background was based on father's occupation. Results indicate that gender is a significant factor, but socio-economic status is not, in both the commitment to school and subculture membership.

856. Thaxton, Lyn, and Charles Jaret. "Singers and Stereotypes: The Image of Female Recording Artists." *Sociological Inquiry* 55 (1985): 239-263.

Studies ninety-one album covers of female performers in order to determine stereotyping of images. Album covers were organized into four categories: country music, rhythm and blues music, rock music, and pop music.

Determines that rock singers are perceived as being less traditional than pop singers. Concludes that female performers are not presented in the same way as women in other media.

857. Vaught, Charles, Kenneth B. Perkins, and Mary Ann Sheble. "Southbound: Migration Themes in Southern Music." *Free Inquiry in Creative Sociology* 8, no. 1 (1980): 67-70,76.

Explores the theme of migration in southern popular music in order to support a "frontier" hypothesis explaining the occurrence of migration. The frontier hypothesis articulates migration based on a desire to escape oppressive social conditions, as opposed to economic and ecological motivations. Hypothesizes that southern music will "express discontent with social conditions in areas outside the South." Sampled 344 song lyrics from 1965 to 1978 and created an inventory of migration themes. Results show 22 percent of the songs contained migration themes, with odyssey and escapism being primary. Concludes that the "aesthetic creations of man may be a good index to the human condition in society."

858. Vila, Pablo. "Rock Nacional and Dictatorship in Argentina." *Popular Music* 6, no. 2 (1987): 129-148.

Articulates the phenomenon of "rock nacional" that developed in Argentina between 1976 and 1983 as an oppositional cultural expression of the youth culture. Claims that rock nacional functioned to create values in opposition to the political regime, strived to maintain autonomy in order to avoid cooption, and provided an "ideology of everyday life." Contends that as a result it has come to constitute a political counterculture. Describes the rock concert as the principal channel for participation.

859. Wass, Hannelore, Jana L. Raup, Karen Cerullo, Linda G. Martel, Laura A. Mingione, and Anna M. Sperring. "Adolescents' Interest in and Views of Destructive Themes in Rock Music." *Omega* 19, no. 3 (1988-89): 177-186.

Studies 694 adolescents from twelve to nineteen years of age with regard to preferences for rock music songs with themes of homicide, satanism, and suicide (HSS). Results show that HSS rock music fans were more likely to know all of the lyrics to their favorite songs and to believe that young children should be allowed to listen to HSS music. Results also indicate that HSS music fans were less likely to think that adolescents would commit acts of HSS as a result of listening to HSS rock music, even if the adolescents were "depressed, in trouble, or drug abusive." Over sixty percent of the non-HSS adolescents thought that young children should not be allowed to listen to HSS music and that adolescents would be likely to commit HSS acts after listening to HSS rock music. Concludes that, in spite of popular belief, adolescents do understand and know the lyrics to rock songs.

860. Wass, Hannelore, M. David Miller, and Carol A. Redditt. "Adolescents and Destructive Themes in Rock Music: A Follow-Up." *Omega* 23, no. 3 (1991): 199-206.

Reports on a follow-up study regarding preferences among adolescents for rock music containing themes of homicide, suicide, and satanism (HSSR). Subjects were 120 juvenile offenders (ages thirteen to eighteen) in two detention centers. Notes that a larger percentage of these subjects, compared to the previous study of at-large adolescents, prefer HSSR rock music. Studies whether destructive lyrics combined with other social factors leads to antisocial behavior. Speculates that HSSR themes in rock music may serve as a "trigger for such behavior impacting those who are already 'at risk.' Suggests that because a larger percent of the subjects in this study prefer HSSR rock music, there is a strong relationship between antisocial behavior and HSSR music preference. Observes that the juvenile offenders were more similar than different in terms of their music preferences, whether or not they were HSSR music fans.

861. Weinstein, Deena. "The Sociology of Rock: An Undisciplined Discipline." *Theory, Culture and Society* 8, no. 4 (1991): 97-109.

Presents an extensive review essay of four books on popular music. Criticizes these works and most other scholarship on the sociology of rock music for lacking methodological rigor. Attributes the absence of a paradigm to the "postmodernist freedom to study anything in any way."

862. Wells, Alan. "Popular Music: Emotional Use and Management." *Journal of Popular Culture* 24, no. 1 (1990): 105-117.

Surveys college students in order to measure their use of rock music. Subjects were asked about dancing, emotions, and moods. Results indicate that music is an important part of the lives of college students. Students may judge peers based on musical preference. Music also has emotional meaning associated with personal experiences. Subjects reported using music to alter moods and manipulate emotions as a "self administered psychotherapy."

863. Wells, Alan. "Women in Popular Music: Changing Fortunes from 1955 to 1984." *Popular Music and Society* 10 (1986): 73-85.

Evaluates the amount and degree of success of female popular music performers over the thirty year period of rock music. Looks at top selling singles and albums. Discovers that female performers are under-represented. Attributes the greatest increase in women's success as occurring in disco music.

864. Westley, Frances. "Bob Geldof and Live Aid: The Affective Side of Global Social Innovation." *Human Relations* 44, no. 10 (1991): 1011-1036.

Uses Bob Geldof and Live Aid as a case-study of the relationship between "visionary leadership and global social innovation." Analyzes four aspects of visionary leadership: 1) the personal history of the visionary, 2) the skills required to enact a vision, 3) the structure in which the visionary acts, and 4) the historical period in which the visionary acts. Further, music is discussed in terms of its ability to mobilize. Concludes that Geldof was successful because he was able to connect the affective aspects of rock music and famine imagery to create global social innovation.

865. Wicke, Peter. "Rock Music: A Musical-Aesthetic Study." *Popular Music* 2 (1982): 219-243.

Calls for a completely new theoretical approach to understanding the development of self within the context of society through the assimilation of rock music. Claims that new notions of art and music can be obtained only by studying their practice among the masses. Discusses paradigms related to the development of rock music. Argues that the aesthetics of rock music are based on elements different from those of traditional art. Rock music is directed at the collective experience and not "bourgeois individualism." Notes that rock music "is not rational, like music in the European art tradition." Rock music is seen as an art product of the contradicting elements of mass culture and creativity.

866. Wolfe, Arnold S. "Review Essay." *Journal of American Culture* 7, no. 4 (1984): 85-88.

Challenges a number of assertions made in Simon Frith's book, *Sound Effects*. Argues that rock music today does not represent an ideological community of youth, but rather "a shadow sold with considerable success as substance."

CHAPTERS

867. Abel, Marjorie R. "'I Know It's only Rock & Roll. . .': Patriarchy, Culture, and Rock Music." In *Research in American Popular Music*, edited by Kenneth J. Bindas, 61-75. Carrollton, Georgia: West Georgia College, 1992.

Looks at rock music within the context of American culture and argues that the music cannot be explained in terms of sociological functions. Rather, there is patriarchy and cultural meaning "encoded in the description and positioning of rock music" in American culture. Examines the concept of culture and the problems associated with defining it. Notes that rock music functions as a dialectic mechanism that exchanges power and conformity. Observes that rock music has been marginalized by the dominant culture thus minimalizing its role in the construction and definition of culture. However, through the predominance of audience participation, rock music challenges these patriarchical notions. Contends that elements of American culture which do not emulate the European tradition are viewed as anti-culture. The result is a lack of recognition for rock music, with its African American heritage, as a contributing factor to American culture. Instead, rock music is seen as culturally deviant. Concludes that social hierarchies contribute to maintaining certain cultural dominances.

868. Bradby, Barbara. "Do-Talk and Don't-Talk: The Division of the Subject in Girl-Group Music." In *On Record: Rock, Pop, and the Written Word*, edited by Simon Frith and Andrew Goodwin, 341-368. New York: Pantheon Books, 1990.
   Examines selected recordings of girl groups from the early 1960s in order to reassess their meaning from a positive feminist perspective. Focuses on the significance of pronoun sequence and the relationship between the lead singer and the "contradictory" chorus.

869. Denisoff, R. Serge, and Mark H. Levine. "The One Dimensional Approach to Popular Music: A Research Note." In *American Popular Music: Readings from the Popular Press*, edited by Timothy E. Scheurer, 9-15. Bowling Green, Ohio: Bowling Green State University Popular Press, 1989.
   Observes that scholarly research into popular music usually takes one of two directions: 1) surveying adolescents about musical preferences, or 2) content analysis of lyrics. Notes that the focus on lyrics is a one dimensional approach that ignores the importance of musical aesthetics. Comments that a strictly lyrical analysis of the works by Elvis Presley would not reveal much about his social significance, which was visual and tied to the rockabilly music genre. Provides examples of similar lyrics from selected songs by Bob Dylan, Chuck Berry, and Eddie Cochran to illustrate how various musical styles can address different audiences although the lyrics themselves could be grouped together. Recommends addressing entire recordings as gestalt: lyrics, musical style, and performance. Originally appeared as an article in the *Journal of Popular Culture* (vol. 4, no. 4, Spring 1971).

870. Dotter, Daniel. "Rock and Roll is Here to Stray: Youth Subculture, Deviance, and Social Typing in Rock's Early Years." In *Adolescents and Their Music: If It's Too Loud, You're Too Old*, edited by Jonathon S. Epstein, 87-114. New York: Garland, 1994.
   Documents the relationship between rock music and deviant behavior in the early years of the genre. Explores the role of mass media in the facilitation of this relationship and the resulting social construction of deviance. Observes that the deviant behavior of rock music performers in the 1950s nearly destroyed the genre and led to an expectation that the 1960s would be more conventional. In reality, the 1960s produced not only lifestyle deviance, but also political deviance. Discusses the Woodstock festival as the zenith of 1960s deviance. Analyzes how deviant rock music lifestyles and politics were made commercial commodities through positive social typing in the mass media.

871. Dyer, Richard. "Teenage Dreams." In *On Record: Rock, Pop, and the Written Word*, edited by Simon Frith and Andrew Goodwin, 410-418. New York: Pantheon Books, 1990.
   States that disco is more than music, it is a "certain sensibility" that is "economically, technologically, ideologically, and aesthetically determined."

Discusses disco music in relation to capitalism. Identifies the major characteristics of disco as eroticism, romanticism, and materialism.

872. Edwards, Emily D. "Does Love Really Stink?: The 'Mean World' of Love and Sex in Popular Music of the 1980s." In *Adolescents and Their Music: If It's Too Loud, You're Too Old*, edited by Jonathon S. Epstein, 225-249. New York: Garland, 1994.

Conducted a content analysis of the *Billboard* Top 20 songs between 1980 and 1989 in order to determine if consistent messages were present. Argues that popular music is a central socializing agent for adolescents who are beginning to develop romantic relationships. Discusses the results in terms of love and sex themes, stages of relationships, and the roles of lovers. Observes that lyrics portray love as unstable and rarely mention marriage as a goal. Notes that love is often equated with "mental illness, addiction, black magic, regret, and heartache." Suggests that popular music lyrics may contribute to a worldview that is negative and pessimistic.

873. Friesen, Bruce K. "Powerlessness in Adolescence: Exploiting Heavy Metal Listeners." In *Marginal Conventions: Popular Culture, Mass Media and Social Deviance*, edited by Clinton R. Sanders, 65-77. Bowling Green, Ohio: Bowling Green State University Popular Press, 1990.

Probes heavy metal music as an adolescent subculture which is often perceived as deviant. Reviews traits of the heavy metal music subculture, including the role of music, existential pleasures, and gender expectations. Determines that such a subculture does exist, with participants sharing a collective definition of the subculture. However, close scrutiny of the shared values reveals that "heavy metal participants do not adhere to values that are contrary to those of society." Although the symbols used to represent the values do, in fact, deviate from traditional symbolic communication, the implied messages do not. Concludes that the temptation to consider the heavy metal subculture as deviant is a classic example of labeling.

874. Frith, Simon. "Afterthoughts." In *On Record: Rock, Pop, and the Written Word*, edited by Simon Frith and Andrew Goodwin, 419-424. New York: Pantheon Books, 1990.

Follows up on some thoughts regarding a previously published article titled *Rock and Sexuality*, co-authored with Angela McRobbie. Contends that it is more important to demonstrate how "sexuality is constructed by the performing conventions themselves" as opposed to how "performers articulate a predefined ideology."

875. Frith, Simon. "Towards an Aesthetic of Popular Music." In *Music and Society: The Politics of Composition, Performance and Reception*, edited by Richard Leppert and Susan McClary, 133-149. Cambridge: Cambridge University Press, 1987.

Suggests a relationship between the sociological production and consumption of rock music and its aesthetic value. Identifies four social functions of popular music. Popular music is used: 1) by the audience for identity formation, 2) to manage our public and private lives by providing internal meaning and external expression of emotions, 3) to organize time and memory, and 4) to provide a sense of cultural possession. Discusses an aesthetics of popular music based on sociological functions.

876. Frith, Simon. "Video Pop: Picking Up the Pieces." In *Facing the Music: A Pantheon Guide to Popular Culture*, edited by Simon Frith, 88-130. New York: Pantheon Books, 1988.

Describes the changes in the production and consumption of rock music during the 1980s. Argues that these changes can no longer sustain the following assumptions. First, it has been assumed that musical needs of the masses are not met very well by the industry, thus resulting in periodic changes. In reality, technology has driven the marketplace and the music-producing industry (e.g., record companies) does not survive by contriving consumer behavior, but rather by ensuring that whatever consumers are doing will result in a financial return. Second, it has been assumed that commercialization of rock music happens after the music has existed as a human expression. In reality, music does not ever exist as an independent art form free from technological and economic conditions. Third, is the assumption that rock music styles represent various subcultures in which popular culture is only realized through consumption.

877. Frith, Simon. "Why do Songs have Words?" In *Lost in Music: Culture, Style and the Musical Event*, edited by Avron Levine White, 77-106. London: Routledge & Kegan Paul, 1987.

Discusses the history of the sociological study of song lyrics. Notes that simple content analysis of lyrics is an insufficient means of studying popular songs because "actual performance and musical setting" are not taken into account in the analysis. Observes that one of rock music's claims to art is the poetry of the lyrics. Criticizes that "rock poetry is a matter of planting poetic clues." Uses Bob Dylan's work to illustrate that his lyrics are poetic because the images he creates are both personal and obscure as opposed to common. Contends that popular songs, as opposed to rock music, are popular not because their lyrics are exceptionally poetic, but rather because they present a romantic ideology in common language. Argues that sociologists have been too concerned about "lyrical content, truth, and realism."

878. Garrett, Sheryl. "Teenage Dreams." In *On Record: Rock, Pop, and the Written Word*, edited by Simon Frith and Andrew Goodwin, 399-409. New York: Pantheon Books, 1990.

Recounts the author's own experiences and the experiences of other women as fans of rock groups. Concludes that the identity of the female fan is derogatory and that female fans are treated with contempt.

879. Gendron, Bernard. "Theodor Adorno Meets the Cadillacs." In *Studies in Entertainment: Critical Approaches to Mass Culture*, edited by Tania Modleski, 18-36. Bloomington: Indiana University Press, 1986.

Argues that the theoretical work on popular music by Theodor Adorno (from 1941) has been dismissed too quickly by critical theorists of rock music. Recasts Ardorno's attempt "to expose the political and aesthetically destructive ways in which the capitalist mode of production affects popular music," which is done through standardization. Applies this central issue to the creation of meaning in rock music.

880. Grossberg, Lawrence. "Is Anybody Listening? Does Anybody Care?: On 'the State of Rock'." In *Microphone Fiends: Youth Music & Youth Culture*, edited by Andrew Ross and Tricia Rose, 41-58. New York: Routledge, 1994.

Questions the meaning of the death of rock music. Discusses the problems of conceptualizing rock music production, consumption, and effects. Notes that rock music is effective through the production of moods, passions, and the "organization of will." Rock music is different in that it struggles with authenticity. It also defines a "politics of fun" by rejecting boredom and celebrating energy. Connects the concepts of the death of rock music to the death of liberalism in America, the fragmentation of the youth culture struggling for identity, and the lack of rebellion.

881. Hall, Stuart, and Paddy Whannel. "The Young Audience." In *On Record: Rock, Pop, and the Written Word*, edited by Simon Frith and Andrew Goodwin, 27-37. New York: Pantheon Books, 1990.

Attempts to define a method of identifying standards by which popular music can be judged. Discusses the commercial entertainment nature of rock music balanced against its spirit of rebelliousness.

882. Hayward, Philip. "Charting Australia: Music, History and Identity." In *From Pop to Punk to Postmodernism: Popular Music and Australian Culture from the 1960s to the 1990s*, edited by Philip Hayward, 1-8. North Sydney, Australia: Allen & Unwin, 1992.

Discusses the history of rock music in Australia and its relationship to popular culture in general. Notes that Australian rock music is primarily adapted from other cultures, drawing comparisons to the development of rock music in the United States.

883.   Jarvis, Bob. "The Truth is Only Known by Guttersnipes." In *Geography, The Media & Popular Culture*, edited by Jacquelin Burgess and John R. Gold, 96-122. New York: St. Martin's Press, 1985.
   Identifies several themes useful for geographical research using rock music: mobility, the automobile, the quest for the promised land, urbanization, and alienation. Raises several issues that need to be addressed when examining the influences of environment on culture. Warns against analyzing entertainment too seriously. Includes numerous lyrical examples from rock music to illustrate the various concepts presented.

884.   Johnson, Vivien. "Be My Woman Rock 'n' Roll." In *From Pop to Punk to Postmodernism: Popular Music and Australian Culture From the 1960s to the 1990s*, edited by Philip Hayward, 127-138. North Sydney, Australia: Allen & Unwin, 1992.
   Argues that an important role of women in the history of Australian rock music is that of audience participant. Claims that women as the audience of rock music has been "a vital factor in its power as a medium of cultural expression." Discusses various interpretations of women's association with rock music in terms of oppression and liberation.

885.   Lewis, George H. "Who Do You Love? The Dimensions of Musical Taste." In *Popular Music and Communication*. 2nd ed., edited by James Lull, 134-151. Newbury Park, Calif.: Sage, 1992.
   Suggests that music should be considered as "a system of symbolic meaning to individuals and members of social groups." When members of these groups act politically to gain or maintain position in society, they create meaning through their internal and external communication. Discusses music as a system of meaning (i.e., symbolic communication). Rock music preference is used to determine social group membership, especially among adolescents. Explores the connections between musical culture and social structure and the connections between postmodernism and "taste cultures." Taste cultures describe historical adolescent communities of common characteristics. Taste cultures are constructed of three elements: demographics, aesthetics, and politics.

886.   Lewis, Jerry M. "Crowd Crushes at Two Rock Concerts: A Value-Added Analysis." In *Adolescents and Their Music: If It's Too Loud, You're Too Old*, edited by Jonathon S. Epstein, 251-281. New York: Garland, 1994.
   Studies two rock concerts in which crowd crushes resulted in death: the 1979 concert by The Who in Cincinnati, Ohio, and the 1991 concert by AC/DC in Salt Lake City, Utah. Applies the Smelser model of collective behavior to these events. Notes that all five elements of the Smelser model were present at each event: structural conduciveness, structural strain, growth of a generalized belief,

mobilization for action, and social control. Discusses policy implications and responsibilities related to ethics, fan culture, social control agents, mass media, and the scholarly community.

887. Lull, James, and Roger Wallis. "The Beat of West Vietnam." In *Popular Music and Communication*. 2nd ed., edited by James Lull, 207-236. Newbury Park, Calif.: Sage, 1992.
Describes Vietnamese culture in the United States and its contradictions. The Vietnamese music culture is derived from American influences during the Vietnam War. Uses the San Jose, California, Vietnamese community as a case-study. Observes the cultural adaptation, with specific attention given to music adaptation through traditional Vietnamese music, varied musical genres, and new wave styles. The club culture and associated dancing play an important role in the cultural adaptation.

888. Marcus, Greil. "Corrupting the Absolute." In *On Record: Rock, Pop, and the Written Word*, edited by Simon Frith and Andrew Goodwin, 472-478. New York: Pantheon Books, 1990.
Raises the issue of authenticity in contemporary rock music and whether the genre continues to have meaning.

889. Markson, Stephen L. "Claims-Making, Quasi-Theories and the Social Construction of the Rock'n'Roll Menace." In *Marginal Conventions: Popular Culture, Mass Media and Social Deviance*, edited by Clinton R. Sanders, 29-40. Bowling Green, Ohio: Bowling Green State University Popular Press, 1990.
Focuses on the Parents Music Resource Center (PMRC) and its efforts to label selected rock music as a "social problem." Demonstrates the ways in which rock music is presented as a social problem through the use of quasi-theories which are collective constructions of reality. Quasi-theories are not necessarily consistent with empirical data because they seek to explain phenomena from a particular perspective. Concludes that the "imagery and symbolism that claims evoke" will determine the fate of public issues more than the authenticity of the claims.

890. Mohan, Amy B., and Jean Malone. "Popular Music as a 'Social Cement': A Content Analysis of Social Criticism and Alienation in Alternative-Music Song Titles." In *Adolescents and Their Music: If It's Too Loud, You're Too Old*, edited by Jonathon S. Epstein, 283-300. New York: Garland, 1994.
Describes alternative music "in terms of the value system it communicates to its audience." Studies selected alternative music song titles from 1990, 1991, and 1992. Notes that song titles point the audience to "the most important lyric elements." Categorizes the value content of song titles into the following variables: negative event, social commentary, positive event, violence, humor, imperatives, sex, music/dancing, love/romance, and miscellaneous. Results indicate that alternative music titles articulate greater "social criticism,

pessimism, and alienation" than mainstream popular music. Supports Theodor Adorno's concept that music is a "social cement" that communicates and maintains values among the audience.

891. Murphie, Andrew, and Edward Scheer. "Dance Parties: Capital, Culture and Simulation." In *From Pop to Punk to Postmodernism: Popular Music and Australian Culture From the 1960s to the 1990s*, edited by Philip Hayward, 172-184. North Sydney, Australia: Allen & Unwin, 1992.
   Comments on the large dance parties held in Sydney, Australia. Notes the work of the Recreational Art Team (RAT) in developing the dance events. Discusses the events in terms of their sociological significance and power.

892. Peterson, Richard A. "Five Constraints on the Production of Culture: Law, Technology, Market, Organizational Structure and Occupational Careers." In *American Popular Music: Readings from the Popular Press*, edited by Timothy E. Scheurer, 16-27. Bowling Green, Ohio: Bowling Green State University Popular Press, 1989.
   Identifies five factors that influence the development of culture: law, technology, market, organizational structure, and occupational careers. Illustrates these factors by focusing on the evolution of rock music. Law was a factor in the formation of BMI as a royalties collecting agency to compete with ASCAP in the music publishing business. This ended the monopoly on popular music publishing and greatly expanded opportunities for songwriters in the music genres that formed rock music (e.g., country music, rhythm and blues). Technology was a major factor in the form of television, forcing radio stations in the 1950s to seek cost-effective means to fill airtime. The solution was to play records. Market was a factor to the extent that increased segmentation facilitated seeking diverse music genres. Organizational structure was significant in that independent record companies were formed to compete for increasing market segments. Finally, occupational careers affected rock music as singer-songwriters took greater artistic control over the entire production of records. Originally appeared as an article in the *Journal of Popular Culture* (vol. 16, no. 2, Fall 1982).

893. Phillips, Dennis D. "Meddling in Metal Music." In *Research in American Popular Music*, edited by Kenneth J. Bindas, 77-94. Carrollton, Georgia: West Georgia College, 1992.
   Studies the genre of heavy metal music. Interviewed 177 subjects in order to arrive at a definition of heavy metal music based on the social and cultural aspects of the genre. Traces the history and evolution of heavy metal music with a specific focus on *Billboard* magazine's charts and exposure through music videos. Identifies primary gratifications associated with heavy metal audiences. Contends that heavy metal music is both a positive and negative variable associated with socialization and contributes to, as well as suffers from, stereotyping. Reproduces the survey instrument used to interview subjects.

894. Reid, Scott A., Jonathon S. Epstein, and D. E. Benson. "Living on a Lighted Stage: Identity Salience, Psychological Centrality, Authenticity, and Role Behavior of Semi-Professional Rock Musicians." In *Adolescents and Their Music: If It's Too Loud, You're Too Old*, edited by Jonathon S. Epstein, 301-328. New York: Garland, 1994.

Measures among musicians the "magnitude of role identification via three related sociological concepts," identity salience, psychological centrality, and role authenticity. Results indicate that semi-professional musicians have a high level of identity associate with the musician role.

895. Savage, Jon. "The Enemy Within: Sex, Rock, and Identity." In *Facing the Music: A Pantheon Guide to Popular Culture*, edited by Simon Frith, 131-172. New York: Pantheon Books, 1988.

Suggests that adolescence, the primary market of rock music, has always been an ideological construct. Traces the rise of consumerism following World War II and the critical role the adolescent market played. Contends that the Beatles represented a maturation process of the power among adolescent consumers. Concludes that as popular music becomes more integrated with advertising, it has "nothing left to offer those out-groups that it once enfranchised."

896. Shank, Barry. "'In Your Eyes:' Identification, Consumption, and Production in Austin Rock 'n' Roll." In *Consumption and American Culture*, edited by David E. Nye and Carl Pedersen, 59-70. Amsterdam: VU University Press, 1991.

Provides a case-study of musician Kim Longacre as a personified representation of the Austin, Texas music scene in which "reciprocally constitutive effects" can be observed. Consumed and being consumed, she is a product of the music scene and a contributor as well. Traces the history of Longacre's career in order to illustrate the artist as consumer and as facilitator of consumption. Concludes that "although the motivations of desire remain unconscious and the structures of identification are constituted before the arrival of the subject, identification is an active process."

897. Shepherd, John. "Music and Male Hegemony." In *Music and Society: The Politics of Composition, Performance and Reception*, edited by Richard Leppert and Susan McClary, 151-172. Cambridge: Cambridge University Press, 1987.

Asserts that the majority of Western music articulates "male hegemonic process." Notes that the qualities of sound (i.e., timbre) found in rock music reinforce traditional gender roles and a masculine worldview, but that these notions can be negotiated by performers and audiences. Explores gender relations, social stratification, and cultural reproduction in classical and popular music.

898. Straw, Will. "Characterizing Rock Music Culture: The Case of Heavy Metal." In *On Record: Rock, Pop, and the Written Word*, edited by Simon Frith and Andrew Goodwin, 97-110. New York: Pantheon Books, 1990.

Describes in detail the environment in which heavy metal music was able to emerge. Discusses issues of masculinity and iconography. Concludes that among young males, rock music is "perhaps the most useful index" of competence and sexuality.

899. Turner, Graeme. "Australian Popular Music and its Contexts." In *From Pop to Punk to Postmodernism: Popular Music and Australian Culture from the 1960s to the 1990s*, edited by Philip Hayward, 11-24. North Sydney, Australia: Allen & Unwin, 1992.

Suggests ways in which Australian rock music has been integrated into the larger Australian culture. Discusses the music in terms of its geographical location while noting that Australian rock music does not adequately serve as a cultural narrative. Argues that one must examine rock music from the perspective of production and consumption in order to understand its relationship to Australian culture.

900. Weinstein, Deena. "Expendable Youth: The Rise and Fall of Youth Culture." In *Adolescents and Their Music: If It's Too Loud, You're Too Old*, edited by Jonathon S. Epstein, 67-85. New York: Garland, 1994.

Traces the creation and dissemination of various definitions of youth culture through the symbolic representations found in the history of rock music. Notes that during the early 1970s, the notion of youth culture became disassociated from a particular age group. The result was the creation of various youth subcultures that "exist by marginalizing themselves from the leisure culture's free-floating definition of 'youth.'" Thus, adolescents who want to reclaim youth as a culture of rebellion must engage in a cultural struggle with their peers as well as adults.

901. Wise, Sue. "Sexing Elvis." In *On Record: Rock, Pop, and the Written Word*, edited by Simon Frith and Andrew Goodwin, 390-398. New York: Pantheon Books, 1990.

Utilizes the images of Elvis Presley to demonstrate that women often accept "male accounts of the world at the expense of personal and subjective experiences." Concludes that feminists accept from men subjective ideas about rock music as objective fact without studying how women experience the phenomenon.

SOCIOLOGY

BOOKS

902.   Bradley, Dick. *Understanding Rock 'n' Roll: Popular Music in Britain 1955-1964*. Buckingham, England: Open University Press, 1992.

Probes numerous aspects of rock music, from musicological to sociological explorations. Discusses music as a cultural practice in terms of listening, semiological, communal, expressive, and iconic characteristics. Reviews the European musical tradition of classical and popular music that can be identified by "a certain hierarchy of musical parameters" and significance of the composer. Notes that the African American musical tradition is different from the European, but since about 1930 popular music demonstrates elements of both. Explores the significant impact on Great Britain of American performers such as Bill Haley, Buddy Holly, and Elvis Presley and the subsequent development of beat music. Places rock music in the context of Great Britain's social, economic, and cultural climate of the late 1950s and early 1960s. Discusses class, the youth culture, gender, and sexuality in the development of rock music in America and Great Britain. Shows that rock music functions "as a central part of rituals of resistance" within the youth culture. Contends that the central meaning and function of the use of rock music is that of communalization through which ritualized alienation is shared. Points to Elvis Presley as an example of the function of singing and audience responses in terms of identification.

903.   Cooper, B. Lee. *A Resource Guide to Themes in Contemporary American Song Lyrics, 1950-1985*. New York: Greenwood Press, 1986.

Starts with the premise that popular recordings are oral history which reflects American culture as an "audio collage." Provides an analysis of approximately 3,000 songs centered on cultural themes. Contends that because America is a pluralistic society, the content of popular songs reflects accurately "the conflicting social, political, and personal concerns" of individuals within society. Discusses the various lyrical themes in the same manner that a bibliographic essay would examine the printed literature on a given topic. The themes are organized into fifteen chapters: 1) Characters and Personalities, 2) Communication Media, 3) Death, 4) Education, 5) Marriage, Family Life, and Divorce, 6) Military Conflicts, 7) Occupations, Materialism, and Workplaces, 8) Personal Relationships, Love, and Sexuality, 9) Political Protest and Social Criticism, 10) Poverty and Unemployment, 11) Race Relations, 12) Religion, 13) Transportation Systems, 14) Urban Life, and 15) Youth Culture. Includes a selected discography, selected bibliography, song title index, and recording artist index.

904.   Cooper, B. Lee, and Wayne S. Haney. *Rock Music in American Popular Culture: Rock 'n' Roll Resources*. New York: Haworth Press, 1995.

Collects an array of essays, reviews, biographies, transcripts, and historical studies representing popular culture within a context of rock music. Designed to be a tool for librarians who wish to build popular culture collections. Includes a diverse range of topics, such as baseball songs, Christmas carols, food, medicine, bootleg recordings, dance fads, nursery rhymes, and disc jockeys.

905.   Denisoff, R. Serge. *Tarnished Gold: The Record Industry Revisited.* New Brunswick, N.J.: Transaction Books, 1986.

Traces in detail the "life cycle" of a record from artist to record company to radio to video to the press and publicity and finally to public reaction. Attempts to document and theorize about the production of culture. Begins by addressing the question of defining popular music. Discusses the critical importance of record companies in the creation of a market. Questions the value of the print media. Covers social issues surrounding rock music: sex, drugs, racism, satanism, censorship.

906.   Eisen, Jonathan, ed. *The Age of Rock: Sounds of the American Cultural Revolution.* New York: Vintage Books, 1969.

Collects journalistic writings by a variety of authors from the 1960s. Explores the role of rock music in the 1960s counterculture. Contends that rock music is a music of revolt and must not be viewed separately from the sociology of the youth movement culture.

907.   Eisen, Jonathan, ed. *The Age of Rock 2: Sounds of the American Cultural Revolution.* New York: Random House, 1970.

Gathers a number of writings, mostly from 1969, by a variety of journalists. Presents the culture of rock music as a representation of counterculture aesthetics.

908.   Epstein, Jonathon S., ed. *Adolescents and Their Music: If It's Too Loud, You're Too Old.* New York: Garland, 1994.

Presents sociological essays on the American youth culture and the central role of rock music [each essay is also listed as a separate entry in this volume]. States that rock music must continually change in order to be central to each new youth generation. Rock music functions within the youth culture to help define the self and create community. Includes, as a concluding chapter, a sixty-page selected annotated bibliography on recent theory and research in the sociology of popular music. The bibliography contains references to a variety of popular music styles, including rock music. It is organized into theoretical and methodological studies, historical and critical studies, and topical studies (i.e., production via performers, production via other means, consumption, women, content, music videos, and collected works).

909.   Frith, Simon. *Music for Pleasure: Essays in the Sociology of Pop.* New York: Routledge, 1988.

Brings together various writings by the author from the 1980s. Contends, as an overall theme, that the era of rock music is finished because the music and the music industry are too fragmented. Defines the rock era as beginning with Elvis Presley, peaking with the Beatles, and dying with the Sex Pistols. Attributes the death of the rock era to the commercialization process. Attempts to place rock music in a larger context of popular music by concentrating on the impact of technology, the errors of traditional subculture theory as applied to rock music, and the decoding of rock music conventions. Organized into six sections: 1) Money Changes Everything/That's Entertainment, 2) Working Class Heroes (and a Heroine), 3) Words and Pictures, 4) Screen Idols, 5) Playing with a Different Sex, and 6) Watching the Wheels Go By: Pop in the Eighties. Concludes with the chapter, *Making Sense of Video: Pop into the Nineties*.

910. Frith, Simon. *The Sociology of Rock.* London: Constable, 1978.
Organizes the sociology of rock music into three major sections: consumption, production, and ideology. Contends that the meaning of rock music is dependent upon its relationship to the youth audience. Begins with a discussion of consumption. Notes that rock music is a musical communication form from which ideology is derived from production, consumption, and aesthetics. Claims that the ideological impact of rock music is dependent upon the marketplace.

911. Frith, Simon. *Sound Effects: Youth, Leisure, and the Politics of Rock 'n' Roll.* New York: Pantheon Books, 1981.
Writes from the perspective that "rock is a crucial cultural practice and sociological analysis is needed to make sense of it." Argues that rock music is typically explored as a cultural phenomenon, but can be examined sociologically in terms of its production and consumption and in terms of ideology. However, rather than deriving meaning from the processes, one must look at "the meanings that are produced and consumed." Organizes the study into three general sections: meanings (rock music and its relationship to, and role in, mass culture), production (the making of music, records, money, and meaning), and consumption (by youth, and the ties to sexuality and leisure). Details the production of rock music through managing the market, deciding which musicians get to record, which songs get recorded, and which recordings reach the public (primarily through radio play). Analyzes consumption of rock music by a youth leisure culture with specific attention paid to "girl culture." Also observes the relationship between sexuality and rock music.

912. Frith, Simon, and Andrew Goodwin, eds. *On Record: Rock, Pop, and the Written Word.* New York: Pantheon Books, 1990.
Collects numerous previously-published essays representing "the most significant theoretical writings on rock and pop" [most of the essays are also included as separate entries in this volume]. Focuses on analytical studies as opposed to historical or critical treatments. Attempts to demonstrate the need to take an interdisciplinary approach to the serious study of popular music.

913. Grossberg, Lawrence. *We Gotta Get Out of this Place: Popular Conservatism and Postmodern Culture.* New York: Routledge, 1992.

Explores the "labyrinths of culture and power" through rock music. Starts by offering a theoretical model of cultural studies. Proceeds by defining rock music in terms of its significance and power in American culture. Studies the complex relationships among rock music, liberalism, and youth culture. Continues by addressing the reasons for new conservatism. Contends that the new conservatism is using the culture of rock music to "reconstitute the structure of authority and the configuration of everyday life." Concludes by considering why there is little opposition to the new conservatism and the implications for the meaning of capitalism.

914. Hutchinson, Sean. *Crying Out Loud: Life in a Sixties Rock Band.* Santa Barbara, Calif.: John Daniel, 1988.

Serves as a case-study relating the experiences of a rock group's attempt to gain fortune and fame during the 1960s. Traces the formation of the group, Far Cry, its evolution over a two year period, and its eventual demise. The musicians "lived together as a collective family" and exemplified the 1960s communal lifestyle.

915. Kaplan, E. Ann. *Rocking Around the Clock: Music Television, Postmodernism, and Consumer Culture.* New York: Routledge, 1987.

Concentrates on rock music videos as presented through MTV. Focuses on MTV as a televised commercial enterprise and the consequences of MTV within a postmodern context. Claims that MTV embodies in the extreme the use of television to keep audiences "endlessly consuming in the hopes of fulfilling our desire." Suggests that the linear history of rock music may have run its course as evident in MTV's indiscriminate use of "themes, motifs, and forms" that do not indicate reaction to, or foreshadowing of, popular culture. Concludes that MTV is consumption, selling everything from products to images. Discusses the implications from a feminist perspective. Includes textual analyses of selected music videos.

916. Lewis, Lisa A. *Gender, Politics and MTV: Voicing the Difference.* Philadelphia: Temple University Press, 1990.

Reveals a "historical moment in the making" with the beginning of MTV as "new terrain of ideological struggle over social inequality and subordinate status." Explores the origins of MTV marketing and audience targeting. Contends that by targeting the youth market with rock music, MTV reproduced and reflected the ideologies that function to maintain the power and dominance of white males. Outlines MTV's text designed to address an adolescent male audience by analyzing four videos from 1983: Jackson Browne's *Tender is the Night*, ZZ Top's *Sharp Dressed Man*, the Stray Cats' *Sexy and 17*, and Michael Jackson's *Beat It*. Presents case-studies of four female performers who have used MTV to reverse gender discrimination: Tina Turner, Pat Benatar, Cyndi

Lauper, and Madonna. Discovers a text of female address in their videos and explores the meaning and use of videos by the female audience. Concludes that the commercial process of production and consumption can serve as a "political arena capable of uniting" those with similar social concerns.

917.   Paglia, Camille. *Sex, Art, and American Culture: Essays.* New York: Vintage Books, 1992.
   Collects various essays and book reviews by the author. Includes discussions of Madonna's video *Justify My Love*, the symbolism of Madonna's persona, and a discussion of rock music as art.

918.   Pielke, Robert G. *You Say You Want a Revolution: Rock Music in American Culture.* Chicago: Nelson-Hall, 1986.
   Asserts that an American cultural revolution is exemplified in rock music. Notes that cultural revolutions are not just political or violent. Observes that rock music challenges existing values, produces strong reactions, and expands individual freedom. Argues that rock music rejects Judeo-Christian "convictions about destiny, inevitable progress, absolutist morality, fixed social positions, and eternal punishments and rewards." Provides a historical typology that compares and contrasts cultural and musical events. Explores the mass media used to convey rock music: radio, records, film, and television. Draws connections between rock music, religion, and philosophy. Examines the negation of the 1950s (Elvis Presley) and the affirmation of the 1960s (the Beatles).

919.   Weinstein, Deena. *Heavy Metal: A Cultural Sociology.* New York: Lexington Books, 1991.
   Presents an in-depth examination of heavy metal music from a sociological perspective. Claims that heavy metal music is affirming and not destructive, contrary to popular belief. Argues that critics often fail to understand the cultural roots of heavy metal music or its significance as an artistic expression of rebellion. Explores the relationships between heavy metal music and performers, audiences, and the music industry.

920.   Whiteley, Sheila. *The Space Between the Notes: Rock and the Counter-Culture.* London: Routledge, 1992.
   Explores the relationship between the 1960s counterculture and rock music. Studies the ways in which rock music, through such devices as instrumentation, style, and arrangement, provides both social and cultural meaning. Argues that rock music is a "symbolic act of self-liberation and self-realisation" in which reality and musical experience fuse. Articulates the use of musical coding to promote codes of behavior. Concentrates on the psychedelic musical works of Cream, Jimi Hendrix, Pink Floyd, the Beatles, and the Rolling Stones.

921. Williams, Paul. *Outlaw Blues: A Book of Rock Music.* New York: E. P. Dutton, 1970.
Presents some thoughts on rock music from the founder of *Crawdaddy!* magazine. Acknowledges that the book is not an explanation of rock music, but rather an expression. Discusses specific rock performers (e.g., the Byrds, Bob Dylan, Brian Wilson, the Doors) and selected recordings (e.g., *Pet Sounds*, *John Wesley Harding*) of the 1960s. Attempts to articulate how rock music communicates.

DISSERTATIONS

922. Aparin, Julia. "He Never Got Above His Raising: An Ethnographic Study of a Working Class Response to Elvis Presley." Ph.D. University of Pennsylvania, 1988. *Dissertation Abstracts International* 50: 179A.
Investigates working class audience response to Elvis Presley. Determines that responses to Elvis Presley by the working class and those that write about rock music are significantly different. Rather than seeing Elvis Presley as symbolic of youth and revolt, working class audiences view him as symbolic of traditional values. Provides explanation in terms of a pseudo-social relationship with a media figure who is considered to be a celebrated peer. Elvis Presley affirms the "dignity and worth of those generally ignored or despised in American society."

923. Cagle, Van Montgomery. "The Pop Art/Rock and Roll Connection: The Impact of Andy Warhol on Rock and Roll Style." Ph.D. University of Illinois, Urbana-Champaign, 1989. *Dissertation Abstracts International* 50: 1125A.
Provides a "case study and an analytical account of Andy Warhol's impact on rock and roll style." Focuses on Warhol's influence on glitter rock musicians of the 1970s and their subsequent influence on American and British youth. Attempts to reconceptualize common notions of cultural and subcultural studies.

924. Fogo, Fred Richard. "'Come Together, Over Me': Generational Memory and Social Drama in the Death of John Lennon." Ph.D. University of Utah, 1990. *Dissertation Abstracts International* 51: 4170A.
Considers the "cultural processes whereby symbolic meaning is attributed to a popular culture figure." Uses Victor Turner's paradigm of social drama and James Carey's ritual view of mass communication to study journalistic pieces on the death of John Lennon. Argues that the United States is in a "redressive phase of social drama" and that current events can be understood by examining how the generation of the 1960s articulates its collective experience by attributing symbolic meaning to a specific icon, John Lennon.

SOCIOLOGY

925. Harmon, James Elmer. "The New Music and the American Youth Subculture." Ph.D. United States International University, 1971. *Dissertation Abstracts International* 32: 4076A.

Examines the relationship between rock music and "cultural transformation." Provides a history of rock music, exploring reasons for the emergence of the genre in the 1950s. Describes the shifting values associated with rock music and the associated reactionary censorship issues. Discusses the function of rock music as communication.

926. Heitzeg, Nancy A. "The Solidarity of Self: Rock Subcultures and Societal Reaction." Ph.D. University of Minnesota, 1987. *Dissertation Abstracts International* 48: 2459A.

Addresses the sociology of rock music and deviance. Argues that rock music subcultures are viewed as providing social integration by incorporating a cult of the individual into their structures, thus permitting a social group based on the "primacy of the self." Examined variables such as demographics, family data, educational and occupational background, appearance, sexual activity, substance abuse, illegal activities, violence, and attitudes. Rock music subculture members differed greatly from a comparison sample "in terms of social psychology, interaction and deviation." Individuality was evidenced in subculture attitudes, organization, use of music, relationships, and deviant behavior.

927. Koval, Howard. "Unmaking of Subcultures: Maintenance of Hegemony in Capitalism." Ph.D. State University of New York at Stony Brook, 1989. *Dissertation Abstracts International* 50: 2673A.

Begins with the premise that capitalist societies promote the free exchange of ideas. Follows with the expectation that in this environment discontented groups will "transmit their radical beliefs into the traditional popular culture." Questions, then, how social stability is maintained or restored after social unrest. Considers two factors essential for maintaining stability: the influence of those controlling society's production and consumption (corporations), and the ideology of capitalism. Uses rock music as an example of a cultural element through which discontented groups can transmit radical beliefs. Three groups of songs are sampled to examine the influences of corporations and ideology: 1) hit popular songs, 2) radical rock music, and 3) Communist and Wobblie songs. Discovers through content analysis that the group of hit popular songs contains less "potentially disruptive elements than the songs in the other two samples."

928. Miller, Dale Susan. "Youth, Popular Music, and Cultural Controversy: The Case of Heavy Metal." Ph.D. University of Texas At Austin, 1988. *Dissertation Abstracts International* 49: 1864A.

Examines the cultural controversy of heavy metal music from the perspective of social ritual. Utilizes textual analysis to demonstrate how the subculture of heavy metal music serves as ritual and how it parallels anthropologically "some of the themes, symbols and practices of tribal initiation rites." Uses the work of Pierre Bourdieu to explain the heavy metal subculture as a means for its participants to create and exchange cultural power. Studies the 1985 Senate hearings and the Parents Music Resource Center (PMRC) as a social ritual and a forum for redefining social order. Concludes that the controversy over heavy metal music is a power struggle about the ownership of the authority to "redefine the boundaries of legitimate social and cultural practice." It is also a struggle over the power to assign value.

929. Whiteley, Sheila Margaret. "An Investigation into the Relationship Between Progressive Rock and the British Counterculture, 1967-1973." Ph.D. Open University, 1989. *Dissertation Abstracts International* 51: 2921A.
   Examines the relationship between progressive rock music and the British counterculture from 1967 to 1973. Explores the ways in which music creates meaning for an audience. One chapter deals specifically with the images of women in progressive rock music.

FILMS AND VIDEOS

930. *D.O.A.: A Right of Passage.* Lech Kowalski, dir. High Times Films, 1981.
   Presents a documentary of the punk rock movement, featuring many punk rock groups.

931. *Gimme Shelter.* Albert Maysles, David Maysles, and Charlotte Zwerin, dirs. Cinema, 1970.
   Captures on film the disastrous December, 1969, Altamont Concert. Features the Rolling Stones attempting to regain control over the rock festival from the stage while chaos reigns in the audience.

932. *Know Your Enemy.* Third World Newsreel, 1991.
   Explores the censorship issues surrounding the lyrical content of rap and hip-hop music.

933. *Punking Out.* Kossakowski, 1978.
   Documents the New York City punk scene at the nightclub CBGB.

934. *Rehearsal.* J. W. Morris, 1983.
   Studies rock groups as a means for an individual to overcome lower socio-economic conditions.

Author Index

Authors and editors of the items cited in this work are listed. Numbers after the names are citation entry numbers and not page numbers.

Abel, Marjorie R., 867
Aebischer, Verena, 641
Allan, Blaine, 242, 367
Amos, Alvin Emanuel, 557
Anderson, Bruce, 773
Anderson, Stephen, 156
Aparin, Julia, 922
Apramian, Lisa Rose, 719
Aquila, Richard, 157, 287
Arnett, Jeffrey, 642, 774-775
Ashley, Stephen, 276
Attig, R. Brian, 643
Aufderheide, Pat, 1

Bahry, Romana, 202
Baker-White, Robert, 368, 441
Ballantine, Christopher, 452
Bane, Michael, 288
Bangs, Lester, 523
Banks, Molly, 659
Barnes, Ken, 277
Baron, Stephen W., 776
Bartha, Robert Edward, 720
Baugh, Bruce, 453
Baumeister, Roy F., 644
Bayles, Martha, 243
Bayton, Mavis, 234, 501
Bell, Michael L., 85

Belsham, Richard Lee, 645
Belsito, Peter, 289
Belz, Carl, 290
Bennett, H. Stith, 524, 558, 777
Benson, D. E., 894
Bergenfeld, Nathan, 454
Berry, Cecelie, 584
Berry, Christina Y., 824
Berry, Venise, 2, 203
Bibliowicz, Azriel, 106
Bindas, Kenneth J., 244
Binkley, Robert, 86
Bird, Robert, 222
Bishop, Robert J., 695
Blackburn, William David, 721
Blanchard, B. Everard, 87
Bleich, Susan, 778
Bloomfield, Terry, 455
Bodinger-deUriarte, Cristina, 369, 442
Bordman, Gerald, 525
Boruszkowski, Lilly Ann, 44
Bourque, Darrell Jude, 443
Brace, Tim, 604
Brackett, David, 456
Bradby, Barbara, 868
Bradley, Dick, 902
Bradley, Richard J., 667

Branscomb, H. Eric, 370
Breen, Marcus, 278, 457
Breen, Thomas, 472
Brennan, Thomas, 463
Bright, Terry, 585
Brinkmeyer, Robert H., Jr., 371
Brittin, Ruth V., 458, 559
Broderick, Richard, 546
Brodie, Mollyann, 660
Brooks, Tilford, 526
Broven, John, 291
Brown, Charles T., 292, 527
Brown, Elizabeth F., 646
Brown, Jane D., 3-6
Brown, Mary Ellen, 7
Brown, William J., 444
Browne, David, 459
Bruchac, Joseph, 417
Bruzzone, Lisa, 660
Buchloh, Benjamin H. D., 372
Budds, Michael J., 293
Burchill, Julie, 294
Burk, Robert Eugene, Jr., 445
Burks, John, 245
Burnett, Michael, 502
Burns, Gary, 460
Burns, Gary Curtis, 68
Burton, Thomas L., 246
Bushman, Brad J., 705
Busnar, Gene, 295
Butchart, Ronald E., 88
Buxton, David, 779

Cagle, Van Montgomery, 923
Calder, Jeff, 158
Cameron, Dan, 373
Camp, Charles, 374
Campbell, Kenneth, 4, 6
Cantor, Joanne R., 8
Carlson, Bruce W., 676
Carson, Tom, 503
Cartmell, Dan J., 560
Cary, Michael DeWitt, 635
Castles, John, 204
Caywood, Carolyn, 89

Cerullo, Karen, 859
Chambers, Iain, 296
Chapple, Steve, 250, 297
Charlton, Katherine, 298
Chennault, Shirley A., 33
Chenoweth, Lawrence, 375
Chesebro, James W., 9
Chester, Andrew, 504
Chilcoat, George W., 90
Christenson, Peter, 10
Christgau, Robert, 528, 605
Chu, Chung-Chou, 695
Clark, Alan Randall, 69
Clarke, Michael, 680
Clarke, Paul, 461
Clarke, Peter, 780
Clifford, Mike, 529
Cohen, Sara, 228, 235
Cohn, Nik, 299, 430
Cole, Richard, 781
Collins, Betty R., 115
Combs, Allan L., 693
Comer, John, 505-507
Compton, Todd, 462
Conrad, Robert C., 376
Cooper, B. Lee, 88, 91-98, 140-141,
    159, 247, 537-538, 586, 732,
    782-783, 903-904
Cooper, Cary L., 718
Cooper, Laura E., 97-98
Cooper, Margaret, 165
Cooper, Virginia W., 784
Cooper-Lewter, Nicholas, 733
Coreno, Thaddeus, 606
Corhan, Cynthia M., 647
Cox, Anthony D., 670
Craig Houston, 244
Crandall, Dorothy Jean, 143
Crawford, Paul, 508
Cray, Graham, 759
Criner, Clyde, III, 144
Cripe, Frances F., 648
Cross, Herbert J., 649
Cruise, Robert J., 734
Cupchik, Gerald C., 650

AUTHOR INDEX

Curtis, James M., 785
Curtis, Jim, 300
Cushman, Thomas, 587, 607
Cuthbert, Marlene, 11
Cutietta, Robert, 99-100, 463, 786

Dallas, Karl, 326
Dancis, Bruce, 787
Danenberg, Mary A., 651
Danielou, Alain, 464
Dannen, Fredric, 301
Daoussis, Leonard, 652
Darling, Dennis Lee, 561
Daun, Jane M., 682
David, Daniel C., 693
Davidson, Charles W., 135
Davis, Bob, 289
Davis, Dennis K., 44
Dawson, Jim, 302
Decker, Jeffrey Louis, 205
DeCurtis, Anthony, 160, 229, 303, 377
Dee, Juliet Lushbough, 788
Degregoris, Christina Nicole, 145
Denisoff, R. Serge, 248-249, 266, 378, 465-466, 588, 627-628, 773, 869, 905
Denselow, Robin, 326
Denski, Stan, 12, 51-52, 70
Dery, Mark, 379
Desmond, Roger Jon, 13
Dinkelacker, James Walter, 71
Doerschuk, Bob, 530
Doherty, Thomas, 14
Doll, Susan M., 72
Dollinger, Stephen J., 653
Dominick, Joseph R., 36
Dorow, Laura G., 661
Doruzka, Lubomir, 467
Dotter, Daniel, 870
Doughty, Howard A., 380
Douglas, Ann, 381
Douglas, Louise, 608
Dowell, John A., 164
Downing, David, 531

Draves, Carrie, 701
Droke, Marilyn, 85
Drum, Gary Richard, 771
Dubin, Fraida, 101
Dudley, Roger L., 734
Duncan, Robert, 304
Dunne, Michael, 65
Durant, Alan, 532, 790
Duxbury, Janell R., 382
Dyer, Richard, 871
Dyson, Michael Eric, 735-736

Earl, Riggins R., Jr., 737
Edgar, William, 760
Edwards, Emily D., 872
Ehrenstein, David, 418
Eisen, Jonathan, 906-907
Eliot, Marc, 305
Emblidge, David, 161, 562
Endres, Kathleen L., 791
English, Helen W., 102
Ennis, Philip H., 306
Epstein, Jonathon S., 654, 792-793, 894, 908
Eriksen, Neil, 589
Errigo, Angie, 419
Escott, Colin, 307
Etling, Laurence W., 62
Etzkorn, K. Peter, 773
Evans, J. Claude, 738
Evans, Paul, 383
Ewen, David, 308

Farmer, Paul, 138
Felder, Rachel, 533
Fenster, Mark Andrew, 236
Ferrara, Lawrence, 468
Ferrell, Jeff, 777
Fidler, James R., 655
Findlay, Robert C., 672
Finnas, Leif, 656-657
Fiori, Umberto, 469
Fisher, Lynn, 6
Fiske, John, 7
Flanagan, Bill, 534

Fletcher, Peter, 535
Flores, Juan, 206
Flugrath, James M., 470-471
Fogo, Fred Richard, 924
Fontaine, Craig W., 658
Ford, Larry, 207
Fornas, Johan, 794
Foulger, Davis A., 9
Fowler, Charles B., 103
Fowlie, Wallace, 420
Fox, Sidney, 104
Fox, William S., 590
Franklin, James Leo, 146
Fransson, R. M., 384
Friedenberg, Edgar Z., 795
Friedlander, Paul, 162, 237, 604
Friesen, Bruce K., 873
Frith, Simon, 15, 279-280, 421, 591, 609, 796-799, 874-877, 909-912
Fromm, Mark Lawrence, 147
Fucci, Donald, 659
Fuller, John G., 716

Gaar, Gillian G., 309
Gaines, Donna, 208
Garofalo, Reebee, 209, 250, 297, 610-611, 800
Garrett, Sheryl, 878
Gass, Glenn, 105
Gay, Leslie Clay, Jr., 238
Geeves, Richard, 608
Gendron, Bernard, 879
George-Warren, Holly, 303
Geringer, John M., 472
Gerver, Robert, 148
Gill, Jerry H., 739-740
Gillett, Charlie, 310, 509
Glausser, Wayne, 16
Goertzel, Ben, 473
Gold, Brian D., 801
Goldberg, Herb, 802
Goldman, Albert, 251, 311
Goldsen, Rose K., 106
Goldstein, Richard, 312
Goldthorpe, Jeff, 803

Gonzalez, Juan-Pablo, 163
Goodwin, Andrew, 510-511, 804, 912
Gottlieb, Joanne, 210
Gounard, Beverley Roberts, 647
Gracyk, Theodore, 385
Graebner, William, 107
Graffius, Karen O'Neal, 563
Graham, David B., 108
Grandy, Larry Howard, 149
Grant, Barry K., 386
Gray, Herman, 612
Gray, J. Patrick, 805
Greeley, Andrew M. 741-742
Green, Archie, 211, 387
Greenfield, Patricia M., 660
Greer, R. Douglas, 661
Greeson, Larry E., 662
Gridley, Mark C., 474
Groce, Stephen B., 164-165, 806-807
Gross, Robert L., 808
Grossberg, Lawrence, 17-19, 53, 139, 592, 613, 880, 913
Grossman, Loyd, 313
Grushkin, Paul D., 422
Gunderson, Robin C., 722
Guralnick, Peter, 314

Hale, Tony, 109
Hall, Stuart, 881
Hamilton, Phyllis Ann, 681
Hamm, Charles, 166, 252, 315
Haney, Wayne S., 904
Hanna, Judith Lynne, 54
Hansen, Christine H., 20-21, 663-666, 723
Hansen, Ranald D., 20-21, 664-666
Harding, Deborah, 167
Harding, John Ralph, 564
Harig, Thomas J., 828
Harman, David W., 645
Harmon, James E., 22, 809, 925
Harrah-Conforth, Bruce, 810
Harris, Clarke S., 667
Harris, Daniel, 659
Harron, Mary, 512

AUTHOR INDEX

Harvey, John, 110
Harvey, Patricia Atchison, 814
Hatch, David, 316
Hawkins, Martin, 307
Hawkins, Robert P., 701
Hawkins, Stan, 475
Hayes, Nick, 213, 614
Hayward, Philip, 55, 882
Hearn, Jeff, 714
Hebdige, Dick, 212
Heindel, Sydney Clark, III, 724
Heitzeg, Nancy A., 926
Helfrich, David Charles, 150
Hendee, William R., 646
Henderson, Ian Clark, 73
Henderson, Monika, 641
Henk, William A., 126
Henke, James, 303
Henry, Lucy Patricia, 362
Henry, Tricia, 317
Herberger, Rainer, 111
Herman, Andrew, 811
Herman, Gary, 615
Hesbacher, Peter, 773
Heussenstamm, Frances K., 112
Hewstone, Miles, 641
Hey, Kenneth R., 476
Heyer, Margaret R., 124
Hibbard, Don J., 318
Hicken, Leslie Wayne, 565
Hill, Trent, 253
Himelstein, Philip, 702
Hinds, Elizabeth Jane Wall, 388
Hirsch, Paul 599, 812
Hoffman, Alan Neil, 566
Hoffman, Paul Dennis, 113
Hoffmann, Frank, 536-538
Hojris, Mikael, 477
Holden, Stephen, 168
Hoover, John Gene, 567
Hopkins, Jerry, 319
Horn, Barbara Lee, 568
Horne, Howard, 421
Horton, Donald, 56
Howard, Jay R., 743

Hughes, Walter, 513
Hugonnet, Mitchell Henry, 725
Hutchinson, Sean, 914
Hyden, Colleen, 813

Ingham, Peter, 254
Irwin, John A., 471

Jackson, John A., 320
Jahn, Mike, 321
James, David E. 389, 414
Jaret, Charles, 856
Jarrett, Michael, 255
Jarvis, Bob, 883
Johnson, Jackie Lavaree, 151
Johnson, Jay, 821
Johnson, Lawrence M., 28
Johnson, Mary Jane Earle, 636
Johnson, Norris R., 668
Johnson, Vivien, 884
Jones, Kevin E., 814
Jones, Steve, 66
Jones, Steven George, 74
Joseph, Catherine, 669
Josephson, Nors S., 478
Josephson, Wendy L., 683
Joyner, Doris J., 853
Jumpeter, Joseph Anthony, 569

Kaleialoha, Carol, 318
Kalis, Pamela, 23
Kamin, Jonathan, 479, 815
Kan, Alex, 213
Kanzer, Adam M., 593
Kaplan, E. Ann, 24, 415, 915
Kealy, Edward R., 570, 816-817
Kellaris, James J., 670
Keller, Susan Etta, 169
Kelly, Michael Bryan, 322
Kelly, William P., 256
Kemp, Jim, 25
Kennedy, David, 594
Kent, Jeff, 323
Keyes, Cheryl L., 214
Killian, Janice N., 480

Kilpatrick, William, 671
Kingsdale, David, 660
Kippschull, Heidi, 687
Kleinhesselink, Randall R., 649
Knight, Stewart, 514
Kohl, Paul R., 818
Korzenny, Felipe, 819
Kotarba, Joseph A., 215, 820-821
Koval, Howard, 822, 927
Kowieski, Richard E., 75
Koyamatsu, Kristi, 660
Kozak, Roman, 324
Krone, Betty, 471
Krug, Gary, 765
Kruse, Holly, 170, 515
Kuras, Janet E., 672
Kurti, Laszlo, 595, 616
Kurtz, Howard, 823
Kuwahara, Yasue, 171, 446
Kuzmich, John, Jr., 114

Laboissonniere, Barbara Rose, 447
Laing, Dave, 67, 325-326, 516, 596
Lampman, Richard A., 26
Lance, Larry M., 824
Landau, Jon, 539
Larkey, Edward, 172
Larrick, Nancy, 390
LaVoie, Joseph C., 115
Lawhead, Steve, 766-767
Leaning, Steve, 419
Leepson, Marc, 257
Leigh, Spencer, 327
Leitner, Michael J., 673
Leitner, Olaf, 617
Leming, James S., 825
Levine, Edward M., 826
Levine, Harold G., 827
Levine, Mark H., 828, 869
Levine, Stephen Irving, 637
Levy, Claire, 173
Lewis, George H., 174, 391, 829-830, 885
Lewis, Jerry M., 886
Lewis, Jon, 258

Lewis, Lisa A., 57, 916
Light, Alan, 175
Lindsay, Brian, 116
Linton, David S., 117
Lipsitz, George, 27, 216-217
Litle, Patrick, 674, 726
Little, Jim, 118
Locke, Eric L., 675
Loder, Kurt, 423
London, Herbert I., 629
Lont, Cynthia M., 218
Loos-Cosgrove, Margaret, 651
Love, Randolph D., 119
LoVerde, Marie, 651
Lull, James, 28-29, 41, 58, 219, 831, 887
Lumer, Robert, 832
Luskin, Bernard J., 120
Lydon, Michael, 328
Lynn, Steven Jay, 676
Lyons, Julie, 391

MacCluskey, Thomas, 121, 481
Madow, Stuart, 540
Mainprize, Steve, 677
Malm, Krister, 200
Malm, William P., 482
Malone, Jean, 890
Manuel, Peter, 176-177
Marcus, Greil, 30, 329-330, 392, 424, 541, 888
Mark, Arlene, 678-679
Markert, Louis Francis, 152
Marks, Julie Ellen, 727
Markson, Stephen L., 889
Marsh, Dave, 331, 425, 542
Martel, Linda G., 859
Martin, Bernice, 833
Martin, Graham, 680
Martin, Linda, 332
Mashkin, Karen Beth, 834
May, Chris, 233
May, James L., 681
May, William V., 483, 571
Mayer, Gunter, 178

AUTHOR INDEX

McAllester, David P., 179
McCaffery, Larry, 416
McCandless, N. Jane, 813
McCarthy, Donna O., 682
McClary, Susan, 281, 517
McClure, Joyce, 819
McConnell, Frank D., 393
McCourt, Tom, 60
McDonald, James R., 259, 597
McDonough, Jack, 333
McGilligan, Patrick, 260
McGregor, Craig, 282
McIlwraith, Robert D., 683
McKelvie, Stuart J., 652
McRobbie, Angela, 799
Meade, Marion, 835-836
Melechi, Antonio, 714
Mellers, Wilfrid, 543-544, 744
Meltzer, R., 426
Mendelson, Julie, 650
Merrill, Cher, 769
Metzger, Lois Kay, 684
Michie, J. Allen, 518
Middleton, Richard, 484
Milburn, Douglas, 394-395
Miletich, Leo N., 837
Miller, Dale Susan, 928
Miller, D. Merrily, 122
Miller, Jim, 334
Miller, M. David, 709, 860
Millward, Stephen, 316
Mingione, Laura A., 859
Mitchell, Tony, 180
Mitsui, Toru, 254, 838
Mohan, Amy B., 890
Mooney, Hugh, 261, 485
Moore, Allan F., 545
Morris, Larry W., 698-699
Morrow, Patrick, 761
Morse, David, 123, 396
Morse, Margaret, 839
Mortimer, Emily, 710
Mottram, Eric, 427
Mountford, Richard D., 745
Mowsesian, Richard, 124

Mueller, Jean W., 125
Mullen, Patrick B., 840
Mullikin, Colleen N., 126
Mundorf, Norbert, 50
Murphey, Tim, 127
Murphie, Andrew, 891
Murphy, B. Keith, 638
Murphy, Kevin, 448
Murray, James Briggs, 181
Mutch, Patricia B., 734
Mutsaers, Lutgard, 182

Nachman, Jay E., 9
Nassour, Ellis, 546
Neal, Charles, 428
Nehring, Neil, 397
Ness, M. Ernest, 841
Nett, Emily, 167
Neuendorf, Kimberly A., 23
Newland, Joseph N., 429
Newman, A., 685
Newman, Joyce, 519
Newsom, Sarah Duncan, 128
Nixon, Karey, 660
Nowell, William Robert, III, 76
Nugent, Stephen L., 31

Oglesbee, Frank W., 220
O'Grady, Terence J., 183, 486
Ohman, Marian M., 293
Orlova, Irina, 32
Orman, John, 630
Ouimet, Mary E., 682
Outwin, Christopher Maxwell, 77

Paddison, Max, 487
Paglia, Camille, 917
Pal, A. K., 669
Palmer, Lyelle L., 686
Palmer, Robert, 184, 335
Paraire, Philippe, 336
Parker, Eric Scott, 728
Parnell, Mike, 471
Parsons, Tony, 294
Pattison, Robert, 337

Patton, Nancy Dale Walker, 153
Pavlakos, Chris, 710
Pavletich, Aida, 547
Pearce, Colby, 680
Pearlman, Sandy, 488
Pearson, Anthony, 185
Peck, Richard, 768
Peellaert, Guy, 430
Pekacz, Jolanta, 186
Pembrook, Randall G., 489-490
Pendergast, Joseph S., 129
Peretti, Peter O., 687-688
Perkins, Kenneth B., 857
Perrone, Charles A., 187
Perry, Steve, 221
Perterson-Lewis, Sonja, 33
Peters, Dan, 769
Peters, Steve, 769
Peterson, Dena L., 689
Peterson, Richard A., 262, 628, 892
Petrosino, Linda, 659
Pfeil, Fred, 690
Pfost, Karen S., 689
Philbin, Marianne, 631
Phillips, Dennis D., 893
Pichaske, David, 338, 431-432
Pielke, Robert G., 918
Pilskaln, Robert, 363, 599
Pingree, Suzanne, 701
Pinheiro, Marilyn L., 706
Plasketes, George, 398, 491
Pleasants, Henry, 339
Plopper, Bruce L., 841
Podell, Janet, 548
Polan, Dana, 399
Politis, John, 842
Pollard, Alton B., III, 746
Pollock, Bruce, 340-341
Poole, Thomas, 747
Poovey, Mary, 130
Popp, Rita, 692
Potts, John, 283
Powe, Bruce W., 400
Powell, Neil, 401
Pratt, Ray, 632

Pratto, David J., 792-793
Prendergast, Mark J., 230
Prerost, Frank J., 691
Preus, Klemet, 748
Prinsky, Lorraine, 694, 843-844
Propes, Steve, 302
Protinsky, Howard, 692

Quarrick, Gene, 717

Raeburn, Susan Downing, 729
Ramaglia, Bellino Benedetto, 572
Ramet, Pedro, 188, 263, 598
Ramet, Sabrina Petra, 222, 618-620
Ramsey, Joseph, 131
Randall, Andrew, 661
Raup, Jana L., 859
Rauth, Robert, 264
Ray, Robert B., 402
Reading, Joseph Donald, 78
Redd, Lawrence N., 265, 342
Redditt, Carol A., 860
Reeve, Edward M., 730
Regev, Motti, 189
Reich, K. Helmut, 762
Reichardt, Jasia, 403
Reid, Jan, 343
Reid, Scott A., 894
Reitinger, Douglas W., 404
Rex, Idena, 59
Reznikoff, Marvin, 708
Rhodes, Larry A., 693
Richardson, James T., 715
Rickert, Martin, 650
Riley, Tim, 492
Riley, Vikki, 520
Rimler, Walter, 549
Robinson, Deanna Campbell, 132
Robinson, John P., 599
Roe, Keith, 34
Romanowski, William, 249, 266, 749
Roos, Michael E., 405
Root, Robert L., Jr., 493
Rorem, Ned, 550
Rose, Tricia, 551

AUTHOR INDEX

Rosenbaum, Jill, 694, 843-844
Rosenberg, Neil V., 267
Ross, Andrew, 551
Rosselson, Leon, 621
Rothenbuhler, Eric W., 60
Rotundo, E. Anthony, 750
Rouner, Donna, 35
Rowland, Guy L., 696
Rowland, Mark, 260
Roxon, Lillian, 552
Rubey, Dan, 190
Rubin, Nathan, 142
Ruedrich, Stephen L., 695
Ruffner, Marguerite Anne, 845
Russell, Ethan A., 433
Ryback, Timothy W., 231
Rzyttki, Barbara, 819

St. Lawrence, Janet S., 853
Saleh, Dennis, 434
Salzman, Eric, 494
Sandahl, Linda J., 436
Sandau, Jerry, 751
Sander, Ellen, 344
Santino, Jack, 191, 846
Santoro, Gene, 521
Sardiello, Robert, 223, 654
Satuloff, Wendy, 660
Savage, Jon, 345, 895
Savary, Louis M., 437
Schaefer, John, 553
Schafer, Carol A., 79
Schaffner, Nicholas, 346
Scharlemann, Robert P., 763
Scheer, Edward, 891
Scheibel, Dean Frederick, 80
Scherzer, Joel, 406
Schierman, Michael J., 696
Schmid, Randy, 407
Schmidt, Mathias R., 495
Schreiber, Elliott H., 697
Schultze, Helen Jacquin, 154
Schulze, Laurie, 5
Schwalm, Norman D., 658
Schwendener, Peter, 408

Schwichtenberg, Cathy, 61
Scudder, David F., 847
Sculatti, Gene, 347
Seay, Davin, 347
Segrave, Kerry, 332
Segreto, Anna, 133
Seidel, Leonard J., 770
Selvin, Joel, 348
Semmel, Keith David, 81
Shank, Barry, 232, 896
Shaughnessy, John J., 655
Shaw, Arnold, 268, 349-350, 554-555
Sheble, Mary Ann, 857
Shelton, Robert, 326
Shepherd, John, 848, 897
Sherman, Barry L., 36, 62, 849
Sholle, David, 52
Shore, Michael, 409, 438
Shrader-Frechette, K., 134
Shumway, David R., 192
Simpkins, John D., 37
Sinfield, Alan, 439
Singletary, Michael W., 38
Skipper, James K., Jr., 793
Skvorecky, Josef, 193
Smith, Ben A., 135
Smith, Carol A., 698-699
Smith, Jack A., 37
Smith, Martha Nell, 194
Smith, Paul, 195
Smith, Sheila Ann, 731
Smith, Stuart, 136
Snow, Robert P., 39
Sobul, Jeff, 540
Sorrell, Richard S., 269
Souster, Tim, 496
Sperring, Anna M., 859
Stambler, Irwin, 351
Stapleton, Chris, 233
Starr, S. Frederick, 270
Steggels, Simon, 622
Stevenson, Robert G., 709
Stewart, Alan D., 63
Stewart, Richard E., 573
Stigberg, David K., 196

Stockbridge, Sally, 64, 284
Stokes, Geoffrey, 358
Storm, Gary Bruce, 82
Stover, Sherri Elliott, 83
Stratton, Jon, 40, 850
Straw, Will, 851, 898
Street, John, 609, 633
Stringer, Julian, 852
Stuebing, Roger C., 710
Stuessy, Joe, 556
Stumpf, Steven H., 827
Sullivan, Henry W., 410
Sullivan, Mark, 752
Sun, Se-Wen, 41
Survilla, Maria Paula, 224
Sweeny, Carol E., 28
Szatmary, David P., 352
Szemere, Anna, 197, 623

Tamm, Eric Alexander, 574
Tankel, Jonathan David, 42
Tanner, Julian, 854-855
Taylor, Denis, 411
Taylor, Derek, 353
Taylor, Marlene M., 700
Taylor, Paul, 440
Taylor, Timothy D., 497
Thaxton, Lyn, 856
Theberge, Paul, 43
Thompson, C. Lamar, 131
Thompson, Dick, 137
Thompson, Margaret, 701
Thorne, Stephen B., 702
Thorton, Sarah, 271
Tiger, Lionel, 753
Tillman, Robert H., 600
Titus, Sharon K., 667
Tosches, Nick, 354
Troitsky, Artemy, 355
Trosset, Carol, 198
Trostle, Lawrence C., 703
Trow, Michael-Arthur, 356
Trzcinski, Jon, 704
Tucker, Alexander, 705
Tucker, Ken, 358

Tumas-Serna, Jane Anne, 84
Turner, Graeme, 899
Turner, William C., Jr., 754

Ullestad, Neal, 601, 624
Ulrich, R. F., 706

Valdez, Stephen Kenneth, 575
Vassal, Jacques, 357
Vaught, Charles, 857
Viera, Maria, 449
Vila, Pablo, 199, 625, 858
Vincent, Richard C., 44-45
Volgy, Thomas J., 834
Von Meier, Kurt, 272

Wald, Gayle, 210
Walker, James R., 46
Walker, Michael W., 707
Wallis, Roger, 200, 887
Walser, Robert, 498, 517, 522, 576
Walters, James, 755
Wanamaker, Catherine E., 708
Ward, Ed, 358
Wass, Hannelore, 709, 859-860
Weaver, James, 778
Weiler, Ernest M., 710
Weinstein, Deena, 602, 861, 900, 919
Weisskoff, Rita Seiler, 155
Welch, Richard, 273
Weller, Donald J., 639
Wells, Alan, 47, 862-863
Wells, John D., 412
Wells, Laura, 820
Wenner, Jann S., 359
West, Cornel, 274, 756-757
Westley, Frances, 864
Whannel, Paddy, 881
Whitcomb, Ian, 360-361
White, Arden, 711
White, Avron Levine, 285
Whiteley, Sheila, 499, 920, 929
Wicke, Peter, 48, 286, 626, 634, 865
Williams, James D., 590
Williams, Mark L., 821

AUTHOR INDEX

Williams, Paul, 921
Willis, Paul, 225
Wills, Geoff, 718
Wilson, Claire V., 712
Winders, James A., 603
Winn, James A., 500
Wise, Sue, 901
Wolfe, Arnold S., 49, 866
Wolfe, Basil N., Jr., 471
Wolin, David, 584
Wooten, Marsha A., 713
Worsley, John Ashton, 364

Yamin, George Y., Jr., 758
Yannelli, Andrew, 9
Yoffe, Mark, 226
Young, Bill, 764

Zamascikov, Sergei, 188, 222
Zechmeister, Eugene B., 655
Zillmann, Dolf, 8, 50, 778
Zion, Lawrence, 201, 275
Zook, Kristal Brent, 227
Zuckerman, Marvin, 674
Zweifel, J., 688

Subject Index

This is a detailed subject index to the contents of the works cited, not just to the annotations. Numbers after the subjects are citation entry numbers and not page numbers.

1930s, 549
1950s, 432, 556
1950s, and Education, 107
1950s, and History, 253, 269, 273, 280, 291, 293, 295, 308, 318-321, 350, 358, 366
1950s, and Sociology, 840, 870, 907, 918
1950s, and South Africa, 166
1960s, 427, 512, 541, 549, 556
1960s, and Education, 90, 107
1960s, and Ethnomusicology, 160
1960s, and History, 244-245, 269, 280, 292-293, 295, 304, 312, 318-319, 321-322, 338, 341, 344, 348, 356, 358, 361
1960s, and Mexico, 196
1960s, and Politics, 78, 599, 605, 628, 636
1960s, and Psychology, 649
1960s, and Sociology, 795, 802, 818, 870, 906, 914, 918, 921, 924
1960s, and Youth Culture, 398, 435
1967, 353
1970s, 107, 226, 245, 280, 292, 295, 304, 318, 358, 485, 556
1980s, 160, 304, 358, 556, 582, 872

1985, 423

A-Ha (music group), 7
Aboriginal Music, 204
Absolute Beginners (book), 397
Absorption, 676, 693, 717, 770
AC/DC (music group), 737, 886
Academic Performance, 124, 143, 697-699, 705
Acappella Music, 907
Acculturation, 246
Ace, Johnny, 354
Acid Rock Music (SEE ALSO: Psychedelic Rock Music), 292, 299, 308, 323, 352, 435, 486, 644
Acker, Kathy, 416
Acoustics (SEE: Sound)
Acquired Immune Deficiency Syndrome (AIDS), 25, 624, 821
Adam Raised a Cain (song), 758
Adler, Guido, 747
Adolescents (SEE ALSO: Youth Culture), 10, 13, 48, 57, 112, 143, 145, 147, 649, 679, 686, 694, 711, 719, 841, 843, 895
Adolescents, and Attitudes, 2, 112, 642, 662, 704, 709, 721, 725,

859-860
Adolescents, and Cognitive Processing, 35, 115, 701
Adolescents, and Culture, 53, 900
Adolescents, and Delinquency (SEE ALSO: Delinquency), 792-793, 800, 860
Adolescents, and Developmental Stages, 29, 727
Adolescents, and Emotionally Disturbed, 677, 725, 844
Adolescents, and Hearing, 471, 706
Adolescents, and Information Seeking Behavior, 780
Adolescents, and Literature, 131
Adolescents, and Music Preferences (SEE ALSO: Preferences, and Music Genres), 11, 34, 111, 563, 641-642, 656-657, 703, 713, 721, 728, 775, 793, 854, 859
Adolescents, and Music Skills, 502, 506, 508, 514
Adolescents, and Music Videos, 6, 41, 62, 83, 660, 662, 722, 849, 916
Adolescents, and Rebellion (SEE ALSO: Rebellion), 248, 273, 778
Adolescents, and Reckless Behavior (SEE ALSO: Reckless Behavior), 678, 709, 734, 774-775
Adolescents, and Styles, 820
Adolescents, and Subcultures, 58, 208, 855, 873
Adolescents, and Suicide (SEE: Suicide)
Adolescents, and Teaching, 133, 151
Adolescents, and Values, 35, 83, 89, 147, 704, 721, 725, 757, 825
Adolescents, and Worldviews, 88, 685, 872
Adorno, Theodor, 76, 325, 487, 510, 822, 879, 890
Advertising, 43, 670, 779, 839, 847, 895

Aesthetics, 690, 850, 885
Aesthetics, and Artworks, 409, 422
Aesthetics, and Music, 42, 103, 210, 337, 380, 426, 440, 453, 494, 511, 524, 528, 532, 545, 558, 562, 566, 570, 634, 816, 865, 869, 875, 906, 910
Aesthetics, and Music Videos, 438, 449
Affective Behavior, 8
Affective Disorder, 713
Africa, 233
African Americans (SEE ALSO: Black Musicians; Black Nationalism; Black Power), 2, 144, 205, 227, 274, 497, 733, 736, 754, 819, 823, 840, 867
African Music, 142, 181, 288
After Bathing at Baxter's (album), 375
Age Differences, 854
Aged (SEE: Elderly)
Aggression, 23, 687, 691, 708, 725, 728, 826
Album Covers (SEE: Sound Recordings, and Album Covers)
Alcohol, 77, 678, 696, 734, 807, 926
Alcoholics Anonymous (AA), 654
Alienation, 92, 112, 131, 143, 679, 795, 802, 834, 883, 890, 902
Aliferis Music Achievement Test, 561
Allman Brothers (music group), 334
Almanac Singers (music group), 631
Almost Grown (song), 783
Altamont Speedway Festival (1969), 311, 368, 427, 818, 907, 931
Alternative Music, 170, 298, 303, 533, 890
Ambient Music, 574
Ambivalence, 79
American Bandstand (television show), 308
American College Test (ACT), 705
American Hot Wax (film), 256

SUBJECT INDEX

Amnesty International, 624
Anarchy in the U.K. (song), 424
Anderson, Laurie, 379, 423, 444, 518, 553
Angels (music group), 341
Anger, 728
Animal Behavior, 687
Anna Stesia (song), 475
Another One Bites the Dust (song), 707
Anthrax (music group) 457
Anthropology, 198, 238, 753
Antisocial Behavior, 3, 664, 666
Anxiety, 688, 698-699, 718, 728
Apartheid, 601, 610
Apocalypse Now (film), 389, 404
Apollo Records, 291
Apollo Theater, 311
Appalachia, 207
Are You Experienced (album), 375
Argentina, 199, 625, 858
Arlen, Harold, 549
Armatrading, Joan, 534
Arousal Theory, 647, 652, 658
Art (SEE ALSO: Performance Art; Pop Art; Poster Art), 829
Art, and Culture, 1, 251, 385, 917
Art, and Politics, 591, 600
Art, and Punk Aesthetics, 392, 408-409, 424
Art, and Religion, 763
Art, and Sociology, 442, 865
Art, and Sound Recordings, 461
Art, and Videotapes, 372
Art History, 295, 403, 435
Art Music, 163, 561
Art Rock Music, 142, 298, 303, 315, 318, 334, 442, 453, 486, 545, 556
Art Schools, 421, 798
Articulation, 851
Artifacts, 42
Artists, 372, 387, 403, 428-429, 435, 442, 529
Artworks, 373, 387, 403, 409, 419, 422, 430, 435, 451

Asbury Park, New Jersey, 169, 378
ASCAP, 250, 892
Ashby, Hal, 389
Asian Americans, 819
Assimilation, 246
Attention Deficit Disorder (ADD), 648, 684
Attention Spans, 648, 661
Attitudes, 9, 15, 17-18, 30-31, 561, 666, 812, 819, 824, 926
Attitudes, and Adolescents (SEE: Adolescents, and Attitudes)
Attitudes, and College Students, 637, 689, 725, 831, 834, 853
Attitudes, and Teachers, 136
Attraction, 681, 687
Attribution Theory, 50
Audiences, 851, 902
Audiences, and Communication, 52-53, 65, 72
Audiences, and Concerts, 368, 668
Audiences, and Ethnomusicology, 165, 192, 228
Audiences, and Politics, 590, 597, 639
Audiences, and Radio, 28, 845
Audiences, and Sociology, 789, 812, 814, 828, 846, 893, 911, 929
Audiences, and Television, 5, 36, 61-62, 701, 849, 916
Auditory Research (SEE ALSO: Sound Levels; Hearing), 145, 651, 669, 672, 686, 710
Austin, Texas, 211, 232, 343, 387, 896
Australia, 520
Australia, and Communication, 55
Australia, and Ethnomusicology, 200, 204
Australia, and History, 275, 278, 282-284
Australia, and Politics, 608, 622
Australia, and Sociology, 882, 884, 891, 899
Austria, 172

Authenticity, 545, 880, 913
Authority, 92, 664, 743, 783, 787, 928
Authors, 382
Automobiles, 141, 783, 883
Avant-Garde Aesthetics, 317, 408, 424, 915
Avant-Garde Music, 142, 452, 478, 606
Avedon, Richard, 359
Awn, Kerry, 387
Axis Bold as Love (album), 375

Baby Boomers, 340, 924
Back in the U.S.A. (song), 783
Background Music, 37, 87, 115, 124, 126, 135, 645, 647, 652, 658, 674, 697
Backward Masking (SEE: Sound Recordings, and Backward Masking)
Badlands (song), 758
Baez, Joan, 239, 577, 631, 906-907
Bahaus, 442
Bakhtin, Mikhail, 818
Balazs, Bela, 69
Balin, Marty, 341
Balinese Music, 561
Ballad of the Green Berets (song), 588
Ballads, 196
Ballard, Hank, 906
Baltic Republics, 226
Band, The (music group), 161, 303, 329, 334, 398, 504, 539, 562, 907
Bandstand (television show), 284
Baptists, 557, 748
Baroque Music, 478, 561
Bars, 814
Barthes, Roland, 325, 399
Bartholomew, Dave, 335
Bass, 454, 463
Basso Ostinato, 454
Baudrillard, Jean, 473
Beach Boys (music group), 303, 334, 539
Beastie Boys (music group), 175
Beatlemania (musical), 256
Beatles (music group), 393, 405, 410, 417, 423, 426, 432-433, 462, 466, 492, 496, 500, 518, 527, 532, 540, 555-556, 907
Beatles (music group), and Communication, 81
Beatles (music group), and Ethnomusicology, 183, 200, 231
Beatles (music group), and History, 246, 251, 254, 257, 269, 290, 292, 299-300, 303, 311, 318-319, 322, 325, 334, 346, 353
Beatles (music group), and Psychology, 644, 702, 707, 712
Beatles (music group), and Religion, 752, 761
Beatles (music group), and Sociology, 97-98, 789, 795, 818, 895, 906, 918, 920
Beatniks, 840
Bebop Music, 274, 339
Beck, Jeff, 907
Bedford, David, 553
Beecher, Frank, 575
Behavior (SEE ALSO: Collective Behavior; Coping Behavior; Crowd Behavior; Deviant Behavior; Interpersonal Behavior), 62, 563, 662, 668, 709, 745, 792, 812, 819, 824, 828
Behavior, and Disorders, 713
Behavior, and Irrationality, 692, 716
Behavior Modification, 151, 667, 712
Belarus, 224
Beliefs, 35, 692, 828
Belushi, John, 359
Benatar, Pat, 220, 415, 737, 916
Benefits, 864
Benjamin, Walter, 510
Berlin, Irving, 549
Berry, Chuck, 497, 526, 534, 556, 575

SUBJECT INDEX

Berry, Chuck, and Ethnomusicology, 171, 237
Berry, Chuck, and History, 290, 295, 300, 303, 325, 328, 334, 364
Berry, Chuck, and Narrative, 446
Berry, Chuck, and Sociology, 783, 869
Berry, Richard, 331
Biafra, Jello, 594
Bible, 738
Bibliographies, 98, 116, 119, 247, 422, 440, 465, 486, 536-538, 556, 711, 903, 908
Big Band Music, 323, 563, 565
Bijelo Dugme (music group), 620
Biographies, 116, 351, 440, 465, 552
Birchall, Ian, 325
Bishop, Elvin, 579
Black Culture (SEE: Culture, and African Americans)
Black Entertainment Television (BET), 4
Black Music (SEE ALSO: Rhythm and Blues Music; Blues Music; Soul Music), 144, 181, 207, 221, 274, 288, 300, 308, 339, 349, 354, 542, 605, 815, 830, 911
Black Musicians (SEE: African Americans; Musicians, and African Americans)
Black Nationalism (SEE ALSO: African Americans), 205, 221, 227, 456
Black Oak Arkansas (music group), 707
Black Power (SEE ALSO: African Americans), 209, 308
Black Sabbath (music group), 702
Black Sabbath (song), 702
Blackboard Jungle (film), 264, 342, 714
Blackmore, Ritchie, 498, 522
Blondie (music group), 324, 423
Blood Pressure, 87
Blood Sweat and Tears (music group), 474, 539, 556, 562
Bluegrass Music, 85, 236, 267, 544, 687, 698-699
Blues Music (SEE ALSO: Black Music), 481, 486, 507, 521, 543, 545, 554-555, 563, 575
Blues Music, and Education, 85
Blues Music, and Ethnomusicology, 181
Blues Music, and History, 243, 288, 298, 303, 307, 311, 314, 316, 323, 334, 336-337, 352
Blues Music, and Politics, 590, 632
Blues Music, and Psychology, 680, 687, 698-699
BMI, 250, 892
Bohemianism, 798
Bondage, 740
Boney M (music group), 505
Bono, 534
Boomtown Rats (music group), 505
Bormann, Ernest, 81
Born in the USA (album), 367, 370, 740
Born in the USA (song), 414, 597, 660, 758
Born to Run (album), 367, 391
Born to Run (song), 194
Bosnia, 620
Boston, Massachusetts, 907
Boulding, Kenneth, 22
Bourdieu, Pierre, 928
Bowie, David, 300, 303, 317, 346, 423, 531-532
Brainwashing, 715
Branca, Glenn, 553
Brando, Marlon, 359
Brazil, 187
Brecht, Bertolt, 376, 394-395
Bregovic, Goran, 620
Brenston, Jackie, 354
Brighton Rock (book), 397
Brilliant Disguise (song), 194
British Invasion (SEE ALSO: 1960s), 527, 555

British Invasion, and Education, 142
British Invasion, and Ethnomusicology, 173, 207
British Invasion, and History, 98, 246, 280, 290, 293, 298-300, 303, 308, 313, 319, 322-323, 334, 336, 346, 352, 365
Brown, James, 303, 334, 456, 830, 906
Brown, Roy, 354
Brown Girl in the Ring (song), 505
Browne, Jackson, 534, 630, 916
Bubblegum Music, 303, 323, 338
Buddy Holly Story, The (film), 256
Buffalo Springfield (music group), 907, 921
Bulgaria, 173, 231, 276, 598
Burgess, Anthony, 397
Burnett, T-Bone, 534
Burroughs, William S., 82, 444
Bush, Kate, 515
Buss-Durkee Hostility Scale, 708
Butler, Jerry, 342
Bye Bye Birdie (musical), 525
Byrds (music group), 303, 334, 341, 577, 630, 921
Byrne, David, 423, 534

Cadence, 490
Cafferty, John, 378
Cage, John, 494
California Sound (SEE ALSO: Surf Music), 207, 521, 527, 555
California Sound, and History, 292, 299-300, 303, 315, 323, 352
Calvinism, 771
Camus, Albert, 248
Canada, 776, 855
Cancion Romantica Music, 176-177
Cannibal and the Headhunters (music group), 216-217
Capitalism, and History, 297, 305
Capitalism, and Politics, 591, 606, 630, 634, 638
Capitalism, and Sociology, 779, 812, 822, 846-847, 849-850, 865, 871, 905, 907, 927
Captain Beefheart, 423, 818
Careers (SEE ALSO: Occupations), 892
Careers, and Strategies, 152, 234
Carey, James, 924
Caribbean Music, 181
Carnival, 818
Carol (song), 783
Carroll, Lewis, 405
Carter Family (music group), 544
Cash, Johnny, 307
Catholicism, 132, 741-742
Cavaliere, Felix, 530
Cavern (nightclub), 327
CBGB (nightclub), 317, 933
Cedrone, Danny, 575
Censorship, 253, 584, 586, 594, 736, 843, 889, 905, 925, 932
Censorship, and Concerts, 593
Censorship, and History, 281, 332, 837
Censorship, and Sound Recordings, 10, 259, 786
Censorship, and Soviet Union, 585
Champaign, Illinois, 170
Chaos, 805
Chapin, Harry, 631
Chapman, Tracy, 747
Charles, Ray, 295, 303, 334, 539, 577
Cherish (song), 61, 489
Chess Records, 184, 291
Chicago, Illinois, 207, 295, 303, 334
Chicago (music group), 474, 556
Child Abuse, 715, 737
Children, 150, 483, 571, 648, 660, 686, 826
Children, and Preschool, 661, 712
Children's Literature, 586
Chile, 163
China (SEE: People's Republic of China)
Chords, 475, 502
Christ, Jesus, 755

SUBJECT INDEX

Christian Music, 680
Christian Rock Music, 748-749, 764, 768-769
Christianity, 746, 760, 765, 771
Christianity, and Baptists, 557, 748
Christianity, and Challenges, 743, 757, 759, 766-767, 770
Christianity, and Drama, 755, 761
Christianity, and Instruction, 732
Christianity, and Lutherans, 748
Christianity, and Music Videos (SEE ALSO: Music Videos), 662
Christianity, and Rock Festivals, 738
Christmas, 141
Chromaticism, 454
Chronologies, 67, 231
Cincinnati, Ohio, 668, 716, 886
Cinema, 25, 65, 308, 342, 360, 423, 554, 734, 918
Cinema, and African Americans, 181
Cinema, and Concerts, 241, 436, 451, 577-581, 931
Cinema, and Documentaries, 239, 398, 436, 583, 930-931
Cinema, and Exploitation Films, 69
Cinema, and History, 249, 256, 260, 266, 287, 303, 334, 336, 418
Cinema, and Musicals, 386, 436, 567
Cinema, and New Jersey, 378
Cinema, and Soundtracks, 436
Cinema, and War, 389, 404
Cinema, and Westerns, 714
City Across the River (film), 273
City Councils, 593
Civil Liberties, 594
Civil Rights Movement, 209, 308, 649
Clapton, Eric, 243, 334, 575, 707
Clark, Dave, 342
Clark, Dick, 253, 352
Clark, Guy, 211
Classical Music, 478, 498, 522, 535, 561, 563, 565, 573, 576
Classical Music, and Education, 87, 115, 124, 126, 135, 147, 472

Classical Music, and Psychology, 650, 653, 669, 674, 676, 680, 687, 693, 698-699, 717, 730
Classical Music, and Sociology, 897
Cleveland, Ohio, 207, 273
Clinton, George, 274
Clockwork Orange, A (book), 397
Clovers (music group), 354
Coasters (music group), 295
Cocaine (SEE ALSO: Drugs), 359
Cochran, Eddie, 299, 869
Cognition, 13, 20, 29, 35, 652, 664, 698-699, 701
Cohesion, 164
Cold Blood (music group), 579
Cold War, 313
Cole, Nat King, 354
Collective Behavior, 814, 886
College Students (SEE: Students, and College)
Come On (song), 783
Comedy, 525
Comics, 65
Coming Home (film), 389
Commerce, 228, 278, 301, 306
Commercialism, 21, 297, 319, 325, 466, 550, 602, 800, 839, 870, 876
Communards (music group), 643
Communes, 914
Communicative Competence, 607
Communism, 202, 332, 589, 612, 614, 617, 619, 927
Communitas, 198, 805, 833
Community, 43, 238, 593, 621, 797, 851
Community College, 120
Competition, 687
Composition, and Literature, 110, 402
Composition, and Music, 63, 66, 74, 100, 238, 453-454, 460, 469, 481, 493, 500, 502, 644
Comprehension, 13, 127
Concentration, 698
Concert Halls, 333
Concerts, 257, 376, 394-395, 496,

716, 886
Concerts, and Benefits, 610, 762
Concerts, and Politics, 593
Concerts, and Ritual, 223, 519, 717
Conditioning, 670, 745
Conformity, 92
Conklin, Lee, 435
Connery, Sean, 423
Conservatism, 590, 880, 913
Constitution of the United States (SEE: United States Constitution)
Consumerism, 60, 670, 779, 800, 847, 895, 915
Consumption, 612, 690, 735, 800, 822, 850, 875-876, 896, 899, 909-910, 927
Content Analysis (SEE: Lyrics, and Content Analysis; Music Videos, and Content Analysis; Song Titles, and Content Analysis)
Contract, 285
Conventionalization, 255
Conventions, 238
Conversion, 641, 777
Cooke, Sam, 295, 303, 334
Cooper, Alice, 359
Coping Behavior, 718, 729
Coppola, Francis Ford, 404
Copy Cats (music group), 164
Copyright, 66, 74, 285, 876, 911
Corporate Rock Music, 352
Cosmic Cowboy (song), 211
Costello, Elvis, 534
Counselors, 112, 711
Countdown (television show), 284
Counterculture (SEE ALSO: 1960s), 427
Counterculture, and Capitalism, 847
Counterculture, and Communication, 32
Counterculture, and History, 296, 300, 347, 353
Counterculture, and Music, 512, 568
Counterculture, and Politics, 589, 599, 608, 628, 630, 635-636, 638-639, 858
Counterculture, and Sociology, 795, 809-810, 906, 920, 929
Country Music, 282, 483, 527, 531, 543-544, 547, 554, 556, 561, 563, 565, 571, 573
Country Music, and Communication, 37-38, 65, 71
Country Music, and Education, 85, 90
Country Music, and Ethnomusicology, 161, 174, 207, 211
Country Music, and History, 243, 246, 252, 257, 267, 298, 308, 316, 319, 323, 336, 339, 354, 366
Country Music, and Psychology, 667, 674, 676, 687, 692-693, 698-699
Country Music, and Sociology, 829, 832, 834, 906, 911
Country Rock Music, 323, 343, 387
Cowboys, 211
Cox, Alex, 258
Cream (music group), 243, 496, 920
Creative Writing, 110
Creativity, 724
Credibility, 37
Creedence Clearwater Revival (music group), 303, 334, 539
Creem (publication), 542
Crikey It's the Cromptons (music group), 228
Criminal Activities, 926
Criticism, 40, 130, 461, 550
Croatia, 620
Crosby, David, 512
Crosby, Stills, Nash & Young (music group), 630
Crowd Behavior, 668, 886
Crowley, Aleister, 707
Crown of Creation (album), 375
Crudup, Arthur, 342
Cuba, 176-177
Cults, 715
Cultural Criticism, 130, 369

SUBJECT INDEX

Cultural Hearth, 207
Cultural Imperialism, 98
Cultural Practice, 192, 794
Culture (SEE ALSO: Mass Culture; Popular Culture), 105, 229, 562, 790, 822, 905, 912-913
Culture, and African Americans, 166, 273, 296, 310, 612, 714, 754, 840
Culture, and Appropriation, 587, 800
Culture, and Chile, 163
Culture, and Convergence, 207
Culture, and Cuba, 176-177
Culture, and Great Britain, 397, 439, 902
Culture, and Heroes, 789
Culture, and Hispanic Americans, 216
Culture, and Judaism, 750
Culture, and Latin Americans, 106
Culture, and People's Republic of China, 604
Culture, and Politics, 600, 629, 634
Culture, and Postmodernism, 804
Culture, and Production, 262
Culture, and Southern United States, 374
Culture, and United States, 9, 90, 140, 157, 171, 329, 337, 367, 427, 446, 544, 548, 576, 796, 846, 867, 902-903, 906-907, 917-918
Culture, and Values, 925, 928
Cumbia Music, 196
Curious Cargo (music group), 164
Curricula (SEE ALSO: Instructional Modules; Syllabi), 85, 95, 99, 114, 119, 137, 144, 149
Curtis, King, 539
Cygnus X-L (song), 129
Czechoslovakia, 180, 193, 231, 598, 619

Dada, 142, 392, 408, 424, 442
Dae, Sonny, 265
Dance, 6, 54, 153, 296, 317, 717, 815, 862
Dance, and Australia, 891
Dance, and Community, 851, 887
Dance, and Cuba, 176-177
Dance, and Empowerment, 58
Dance, and Sexuality, 799
Dance Music, 556, 566, 596
Dark Side of the Moon (album), 532, 920
Darkness on the Edge of Town (album), 367, 391
David, King, 738
Davis, Clifford, 285
Days of Future Past (album), 468
De Mott, Benjamin, 738
De Young, Dennis, 530
Dead Boys (music group), 324
Dead Kennedys (music group), 594
Deadheads, 185, 223, 593, 654
Death, 77, 141, 248, 685, 709, 716, 841, 859-860
Decision Making, 60, 442, 730, 845
Decline of Western Civilization, The (film), 258
Deconstruction, 139
Defiance (SEE ALSO: Rebellion), 778
Delillo, Don, 377
Delinquency (SEE ALSO: Adolescents, and Delinquency), 332, 680, 792-793, 854-855
Delusions, 695, 802
Democracy, 337, 510
Democratic Party Convention (1968), 90
Demographics, 28, 352, 662, 709, 885, 926
Depression, 680, 684
Desire, 839, 915
Despair, 375
Destri, Jimmy, 530
Detroit, Michigan (SEE ALSO: Motown), 207, 300
Deviant Behavior, 807, 823, 826, 844, 870, 873, 926

Devo (music group), 369, 530
Dialectics of Enlightenment (publication), 822
Diddley, Bo, 295, 577
Dido's Lament (song), 454
Differentiation, 164
Diffusion, 207
Digital Sampling, 510
Digital Technology, 66
Dionysus, 427
Dire Straits (music group), 751
Disco Music, 485, 513, 527, 532, 556, 573
Disco Music, and Education, 142
Disco Music, and Ethnomusicology, 181
Disco Music, and History, 252, 261, 264, 271, 292, 300, 303, 311, 315, 318, 349, 352, 365
Disco Music, and Psychology, 717
Disco Music, and Sociology, 785, 830, 863, 871, 911
Discographies, 98, 116, 140-141, 181, 295, 318, 486, 521, 529, 531, 556, 903
Discourse, 80
Dispatches (book), 389
Dissonance, 560
Divine Intervention, 746
Dixon, Willie, 534
Dolby, Thomas, 530
Domino, Fats, 237, 291, 295, 303, 334-335, 530, 556
Dominoes (music group), 354
Donovan, 239, 577, 795
Don't Leave Me This Way (song), 643
Doors (music group), 251, 303, 311, 334, 417, 427, 432, 906, 921
Downes, Geoff, 530
Dozier, Lamont, 549
Draft (SEE: Military, and Draft)
Drake, Bill, 906
Drama, 79, 198, 382, 400, 404, 445, 560, 755
Dreaming, The (album), 515

Dreams, 430
Drifters (music group), 295
Drug Abuse, 644, 678, 680, 734, 819
Drug Culture, 294, 318, 332, 338, 599, 644, 649, 765, 907
Drugs (SEE ALSO: Cocaine; Marijuana), 319, 599, 694, 757, 807, 819, 905, 926
Drunk Driving, 77
Due Process, 584
Dury, Ian, 461
Dyer, Richard, 72
Dylan, Bob, 417, 423, 426, 432, 466, 531, 534, 539, 544, 549, 555, 562, 578, 877, 907
Dylan, Bob, and Ethnomusicology, 174, 239
Dylan, Bob, and History, 246, 269, 290, 299-300, 303, 318, 325, 334, 352, 357, 359
Dylan, Bob, and Narrative, 446
Dylan, Bob, and Politics, 588, 630
Dylan, Bob, and Psychology, 695
Dylan, Bob, and Religion, 744, 750
Dylan, Bob, and Sociology, 789, 795, 835-836, 869, 906, 921
Dynamic Range, 472

Eastern Europe, 231, 596, 598, 618
Easy Listening Music, 28, 71, 135, 573, 590
Easy Listening Music, and Psychology, 647, 658, 667, 687, 698-699, 726
Ecology, 263, 857
Economic Conditions, 94, 352, 592, 857
Economics, 221, 257, 279, 297, 301, 305, 790, 876
Eddie and the Cruisers (film), 378
Educational Background, 926
Educational Systems, 88
Ego, 724, 728
Eisenhower, Dwight D., 125
Elderly, 673

Eldorado (song), 707
Electicism, 804
Elections, 630
Elections (1972), 359
Electric Flag (music group), 539
Electric Ladyland (album), 375
Electric Light Orchestra (music group), 707
Electronic Music, 555, 674
Elementary School Students (SEE: Students, and Elementary School)
Elvis (book), 374
Emerson, Keith, 530
Emotional Development, 826
Emotions, 8, 698-699, 713, 862, 875
Empowerment, 7, 15, 17-19, 30-31, 607, 733
Empty Places (performance art), 379
Enculturation, 62
Encyclopedias, 351, 440, 529, 552, 554
Engineers (SEE: Sound Recordings, and Engineers)
England (SEE: Great Britain)
English Language (SEE: Languages, and English)
Eno, Brian, 423, 574
Entertainment Preference Inventory, 696
Epistemology, 777
Eroticism, 243, 689, 742, 746, 871
Escapism, 857
Estonia, 226
Ethics, 886
Ethnicity, 3, 6, 200, 217, 221, 236, 252, 563, 819
Europe, 231, 596, 796
Evangelicalism, 749
Everly Brothers (music group), 237, 295, 303, 325, 334
Excellents (music group), 341
Excitation-Transfer Theory, 21, 50
Exercise, 153
Exertion, 153

Expectations, 80
Experimental Music, 582
Expressiveness, 453
Extroverts, 652-653

Fads, 295
Faithfull, Marianne, 63
Familiarity, 658
Family, 680, 701, 737, 775, 926
Famine, 864
Fans, 5, 878, 886
Fantasy, 81, 683
Fanzines, 208, 317, 362, 423, 533
Far Cry (music group), 914
Farm Aid (concerts), 624
Fashion, 57, 423, 512, 714
Fashion, and Communication, 6
Fashion, and History, 295, 313, 317, 359, 362
Fashion, and Sociology, 820, 827, 844, 923
Fashion (song), 532
Fear, 827
Females (SEE ALSO: Gender; Women), 6, 47, 50, 681, 683, 688, 791, 813
Feminism, and Communication, 7, 24, 57, 64, 415
Feminism, and Ethnomusicology, 167, 210, 234
Feminism, and History, 308
Feminism, and Sociology, 836, 868, 884, 901, 915-916
Fiction, 371, 377, 383, 393, 397, 416, 440, 444, 448
Fifty Ways to Leave Your Lover (song), 384
Film (SEE: Cinema)
Finland, 656-657
First Amendment, 584, 586, 593-594, 675, 715, 736, 788
Fleetwood Mac (music group), 285
Flying Burrito Brothers (music group), 907, 931
Folk Music, 466, 527, 543-544, 547,

554, 556
Folk Music, and Education, 85, 90, 101, 124, 134
Folk Music, and Ethnomusicology, 163, 200
Folk Music, and History, 269, 290, 293, 308, 325, 336, 352
Folk Music, and Politics, 414, 590, 605, 615, 621, 632
Folk Music, and Psychology, 653, 674
Folk Music, and Sociology, 834, 911
Folk Rock Music, 466, 486, 555-556
Folk Rock Music, and Education, 142
Folk Rock Music, and History, 269, 292-293, 298-299, 303, 315, 318, 323, 326, 334, 336-337, 357
Folk Rock Music, and Politics, 588, 627
Folklore, 810
Food, 141
Fountain of Salmacis, The (song), 384
Fragmentation, 246
France, 641
Frankenchrist (album), 594
Franklin, Aretha, 303, 311, 334, 539
Free Speech, 586, 593-594
Freed, Alan, 265, 273, 290, 320, 332, 342
Freedom of Information Act, 630
Freud, Sigmund, 484
Fried, Bob, 435
Friedman, Kinky, 211
Frith, Simon, 866
Fugs (music group), 341
Fulano (music group), 163
Full Metal Jacket (film), 404
Functionalism, 776
Fundamentalism, 734
Funk Music, 181, 274, 292, 298, 303, 349, 474, 527
Fusion Music, 181, 298, 564
Future, 91
Future Rock Music, 531

Gabler, Milton, 265
Gabriel, Peter, 469
Gang of Four (music group), 589
Gant, Cecil, 354
Garage Bands, 303
Garfunkel, Art, 673
Gaye, Marvin, 756
Geldof, Bob, 230, 864
Gender (SEE ALSO: Females; Feminism; Males; Masculinity; Sex Roles; Women), 45, 165, 190, 210, 236, 576, 665, 873
Gender, and Communication, 3, 5-6, 24, 52
Gender, and Differences, 23, 50, 70, 111, 480, 563, 565, 662, 709, 720, 731, 774, 776, 854-855
Gender, and Sociology, 897, 915-916
Generation Gap, 795
Generation X (music group), 930
Genesis (music group), 384
Genres, 388
Genres, and Argentina, 199
Genres, and Cinema, 260, 386
Genres, and Cuba, 176-177
Genres, and Literature, 79, 431
Genres, and Music, 85, 181, 191-192, 236, 246, 310, 485-486, 543, 561, 587, 650, 773, 851
Geography, 310
Geography Instruction, 207
George, Lowell, 534
George, Nelson, 221
German Democratic Republic, 48, 111, 178, 231, 286, 598, 617, 626
German Language (SEE: Languages, and German)
Germany, 178, 495
Gershwin, George, 549
Gestalt, 869
Ghana, 417
Gibson, Mel, 423
Giger, H. R., 594
Gimme Shelter (film), 311, 398

Ginsberg, Allen, 239, 427
Girl Groups, 220, 303, 334, 352, 868
Girls Just Wanna Have Fun (song), 438
Give My Regards to Broad Street (film), 410
Glasnost, 595, 607
Glitter Rock Music, 142, 296, 298, 317, 334, 362, 923
Glossaries, 440, 543
Go Betweens (music group), 55
Goals, 164
Godspell (musical), 755
Goldman, Albert, 374
Good Morning, Vietnam (film), 389
Gorbachev, Mikhail, 607
Gordon, Peter, 553
Gordon Musical Aptitude Profile, 565
Gordon Survey of Interpersonal Values, 147
Gordon Survey of Personal Values, 147
Gorn, Gerald, 670
Gospel Music, 181, 298, 303, 334, 349, 543, 554, 632, 674, 770-771
Gothic Novels (SEE ALSO: Novels), 388
Government, 90
Graham, Bill, 333
Graham, Dan, 372
Grammer, 101
Gramsci, Antonio, 607
Graphic Design, 413, 422, 434
Grateful Dead (music group), 539, 556, 579, 654
Grateful Dead (music group), and Ethnomusicology, 185, 223
Grateful Dead (music group), and History, 303, 328, 359
Grateful Dead (music group), and Politics, 593
Grateful Dead (music group), and Psychology, 644
Gratification, 35, 893
Grease (musical), 525

Great Britain, 397, 421
Great Britain, and Communication, 67
Great Britain, and Education, 138
Great Britain, and Ethnomusicology, 195, 200, 225, 228, 235, 239, 439
Great Britain, and History, 98, 243, 296, 299, 317, 345, 356, 362
Great Britain, and Politics, 609
Great Britain, and Psychology, 714
Great Britain, and Sociology, 796, 798, 811, 881, 902, 907, 929
Great Jones Street (book), 377
Green, Al, 303, 334
Greene, Graham, 397
Greenpeace (organization), 624
Greetings From Asbury Park, N.J. (album), 367
Griffin, Rick, 403, 435
Grotesque, 818
Group Cohesion, 238
Group Dynamics (SEE ALSO: Musicians, and Groups), 164, 654, 668, 806-807
Group Embedded Figures Test, 565
Groupies, 835, 878, 906
Growth, 489
Grunge Music, 142, 210, 303
Guilt, 691, 728
Guitar Slim, 184
Guitarists, 142, 575
Guitars, 184, 237, 280, 300, 463, 473, 521, 575
Guitars, and Sales, 257
Guns N' Roses (music group), 556
Gunter, Hardrock, 354
Guthrie, Woody, 357

Habermas, Jurgen, 607
Haight-Ashbury (SEE: San Francisco, California)
Hair (musical), 464, 525, 568, 761
Haley, Bill, 527, 555-556, 575
Haley, Bill, and Ethnomusicology, 237

Haley, Bill, and History, 249, 265, 290, 292, 295, 299, 325, 354
Haley, Bill, and Sociology, 902
Hall, Roy, 354
Hammer, 190
Hardcore Music, 208
Harmonica Frank, 329
Harmony, 104, 144, 460, 475, 481, 489-490, 505, 545, 572
Harris, Wynonie, 354
Harrison, George, 303, 549, 575, 578, 673
Hawkins, Jay, 354
Hawkins, Ted, 423
Headroom, Max, 423
Health, 87, 103, 153, 682
Hearing (SEE ALSO: Auditory Research; Sound Levels), 470-471, 651, 706
Hearst, Patty, 359
Heart Rate, 87, 153
Heavy Metal Music, 388, 457, 498, 522, 527, 556, 576
Heavy Metal Music, and Communication, 20, 52
Heavy Metal Music, and Education, 139, 142
Heavy Metal Music, and Ethnomusicology, 190, 215, 596
Heavy Metal Music, and History, 243, 298, 303, 315, 323, 334, 336, 349, 352
Heavy Metal Music, and Psychology, 642, 646, 664, 680, 703-704, 713, 715, 728
Heavy Metal Music, and Religion, 749, 770
Heavy Metal Music, and Sociology, 774-775, 792, 808, 853-854, 873, 893, 898, 919, 928
Hedonism, 313, 840
Hegemony, 163, 589, 601, 897
Hell is for Children (song), 737
Hello (song), 100
Hendrix, Jimi, 375, 496, 499, 521, 562, 575
Hendrix, Jimi, and Ethnomusicology, 174
Hendrix, Jimi, and History, 243, 245, 303, 311, 328, 334
Hendrix, Jimi, and Politics, 630
Hendrix, Jimi, and Sociology, 832, 920
Hero Figure, 78-79, 157, 211, 220, 695, 789
Heroes are Hard to Find (album), 285
Heroin (song), 818
Herr, Michael, 389
High School Students (SEE: Students, and High School)
Higher Education, 105, 121, 130, 831
Hippies, 226, 244, 338, 347-348, 353, 435, 512, 810
Hip-Hop Music, 932
Hispanic Americans, 174, 216-217, 819
Historical Realism, 600
Historical Revisionism, 256
History Instruction, 93-96, 107, 113, 125
Hit Records (SEE ALSO: Sound Recordings, and Sales), 68, 159, 351, 490, 773, 781, 822-823, 854, 863, 872
Holland, 182
Holland, Brian, 549
Holland, Eddie, 549
Holly, Buddy, 516, 556
Holly, Buddy, and Ethnomusicology, 157, 174, 237
Holly, Buddy, and History, 295, 300, 303, 325, 334
Holly, Buddy, and Sociology, 902
Home Taping, 279
Homicide, 709, 715, 859-860
Homosexuality, 194, 236, 513, 643, 895
Honecker, Erich, 286
Hooks, 460

SUBJECT INDEX

Hope, 375
Hopkins, Nicky, 907
Horkheimer, Max, 822
Horns, 463
Hostility, 708
Hot Tuna (music group), 579
Hounds of Love (album), 515
Huddling, 687
Hudson, Garth, 530
Human League (music group), 530
Humanities Instruction, 116, 120
Hungary, 197, 231, 595, 598, 616, 623
Hynde, Chrissie, 63

I Am the Walrus (song), 405
I Have the Touch (song), 469
I Wanna Hold Your Hand (film), 256
Icons, 72, 924
Idealism, 9
Identification, 896, 902
Identity, 35, 56, 170, 232, 794, 875, 894
Ideology, 414, 449
Ideology, and Education, 106
Ideology, and History, 337
Ideology, and Politics, 163, 227, 589, 591, 606, 616, 634
Ideology, and Religion, 743
Ideology, and Socialism, 615
Ideology, and Sociology, 790, 806, 834, 866, 877, 910-911, 913, 915
If I Were (song), 783
Illustrations, 430
Imagery, 741
Imagination, 660
Immigration, 612
Imperial Records, 291
Impressions (music group), 417, 754
Impulse Gratification, 826
In Concert (television show), 49
Independence Day (song), 758
Indian Music, 488
Individualism, 926
Indorock Music, 182

Industrialization, 612, 879
Information Processing, 666
Information Seeking Behavior, 780
Initiation, and Literary Themes, 131
Innovation, 255, 864
Institutions, 790
Instructional Modules (SEE ALSO: Curricula), 144
Instructional Resources, 140, 572
Instrumentation, 460, 505, 572
Instruments, 463, 907
Interactions, 926
Interpersonal Behavior, 663, 665, 725, 820
Interpersonal Communication, 679, 819
Interpersonal Values, 143, 147
Intervention, 677, 821
Interviewing Techniques, 821, 893
Interviews, 51, 238, 776
Introverts, 652, 731
Ireland, 230
Irons, Greg, 435
Irony, 9, 560
Israel, 189
It's a Beautiful Day (music group), 579

Jackson, Janet, 190
Jackson, Michael, 160, 274, 300, 303, 311, 359, 556, 916
Jackson, Wanda, 354
Jactars (music group), 228
Jagger, Mick, 359, 423, 534, 549, 906
Jamaica, 11, 587, 603
Japan, 838
Japan (music group), 838
Jazz Music, 464, 467, 474, 479, 486, 518, 527, 543, 554, 561, 563-565, 569, 573
Jazz Music, and Communication, 71
Jazz Music, and Education, 85
Jazz Music, and Ethnomusicology, 178, 193, 439
Jazz Music, and History, 274, 296,

308, 311, 323, 325, 334, 339, 360, 364
Jazz Music, and Politics, 612
Jazz Music, and Psychology, 650, 653, 674, 680, 687, 698-699
Jazz Music, and Sociology, 830, 906
Jazz Rock Music, 292, 298, 303, 556
Jedermann, 747
Jefferson Airplane (music group), 375, 432, 531, 556, 579, 931
Jefferson Airplane (music group), and Communication, 16
Jefferson Airplane (music group), and History, 303, 334, 341
Jefferson Airplane (music group), and Psychology, 644
Jefferson Airplane (music group), and Sociology, 795
Jefferson Airplane Takes Off (album), 375
Jefferson Starship (music group), 531
Jesus Christ Superstar (rock opera), 131, 226, 546, 755, 763
Jett, Joan, 220
Jewish Culture (SEE: Culture, and Judaism)
Jewish Musicians (SEE: Musicians, and Judaism)
Joel, Billy, 530
John, Elton, 292, 303, 334, 530, 695
John Wesley Harding (album), 906
Johnny B. Goode (song), 497
Johnson, Don, 423
Johnson, Robert, 329
Jones, Booker T., 530
Jones, Rickie Lee, 534
Joplin, Janis, 303, 539, 556, 562
Joplin, Janis, and Ethnomusicology, 220
Joplin, Janis, and History, 243, 245, 328, 334
Joplin, Janis, and Politics, 630
Joplin, Janis, and Sociology, 832, 906
Jordan, Louis, 354
Journalism, 12, 40, 76, 523, 924

Judas Priest (music group), 675, 715, 788
Junior High School Students (SEE: Students, and Junior High School)
Junk (song), 454
Justify My Love (song), 917
Justman, Seth, 530
Juvenile Delinquents (SEE: Adolescents, and Delinquency)

Kalninsh, Imant, 226
Kansas City, Missouri, 207
Kantner, Paul, 16, 333
Katzman, Sam, 249
Kent State University, 90, 359
Kern, Jerome, 549
Kerouac, Jack, 406, 840
Keyboardists, 557
Keyboards, 463, 530
Kierkegaard, 751
Kiev, Ukraine, 202
King, Albert, 311
King, B. B., 303, 328, 334, 342, 539
King, Carole, 539, 549
King Harvest (song), 161
Kingsmen (music group), 331
Kinks (music group), 285, 303, 334, 346
Kirshner, Don, 352
Klaatu (music group), 707
Knopfler, Mark, 534, 751
Kracauer, Siegfried, 69
Krashen, Stephen, 127
Kristofferson, Kris, 534
Kubrick, Stanley, 389, 404

Labeling Theory, 844, 873
Labs, 137
Lacan, Jacques, 445, 714
Lamb (music group), 579
Land of a Thousand Dances (song), 217
Lane, Robin, 63
Lane, Ronnie, 423

SUBJECT INDEX

Language Skills, 101, 155
Languages, 108, 118, 127
Languages, and English, 118, 127
Languages, and German, 495
Languages, and Spanish, 106
Lasswell, Harold, 809
Last Waltz, The (film), 256, 398
Latin America, 106
Latin American Music, 106, 506
Latvia, 226
Lauper, Cyndi, 57, 220, 415, 423, 438, 916
Law, 262, 285, 892
Layla (song), 707
Leadership, 864
Learning, 135, 669
Learning Disabilities, 686
Leave It (song), 100
Led Zeppelin (music group), 303, 334, 702, 707
Leisure (SEE ALSO: Recreation), 630, 696, 798, 910-911
Lennon, John, 405, 410, 433, 462, 500, 549
Lennon, John, and Communication, 79
Lennon, John, and Ethnomusicology, 160
Lennon, John, and History, 303, 359
Lennon, John, and Politics, 630-631
Lennon, John, and Psychology, 673, 695
Lennon, John, and Sociology, 818, 906, 924
Lennox, Annie, 220, 415
Lesson Plans, 93, 96
Leukocytes, 682
Lewis, Jerry Lee, 237, 273, 295, 303, 307, 314, 334-335, 530, 556
Lewisville, Texas, 738
Liberalism, 590, 880, 913
Libraries, 89, 181, 842, 904
Licensed to Ill (album), 175
Like a Prayer (video), 742
Like a Virgin (song), 660

Liliput (music group), 392
Linguistics, 316
Lipstick Traces (book), 408, 811
Listening Skills, 704
Literary Criticism, 393
Lithuania, 226
Little Richard, 237, 291, 295, 303, 334, 526, 530, 556
Live Aid (concert), 160, 230, 601, 611, 624, 762, 864
Liverpool, England, 228, 235, 327, 356
Logsdon, Jimmie, 354
London, England, 299
Lonesome Cowboy Bill (song), 444
Longacre, Kim, 232, 896
Lord, John, 530
Los Angeles, California, 217, 258, 289, 383, 827
Los Angeles Times (publication), 76
Los Lobos (music group), 174, 216
Loud Music, 332, 706
Loudness, 453, 659, 672
Louie Louie (song), 331
Love, 56, 112, 318, 531, 671, 781, 872
Love is the Drug (song), 384
Lovin' Spoonful (music group), 341, 577
LSD (Lysergic Acid Diethylamide), 644
Lucy in the Sky with Diamonds (song), 405
Lutherans, 748
Lviv, Ukraine, 202
Lyon, Johnny, 378
Lyrics, 6, 112, 128, 337, 437, 460-461, 482, 490, 505, 549, 556, 671, 679, 808, 877
Lyrics, and Acid Rock Music, 644
Lyrics, and Addiction Treatment, 678
Lyrics, and Beatles (music group), 81, 417, 432
Lyrics, and Berry, Chuck, 171, 783
Lyrics, and Censorship, 259, 332,

786, 843, 932
Lyrics, and Chapman, Tracy, 747
Lyrics, and Communards, 643
Lyrics, and Comprehension, 13, 660, 694
Lyrics, and Content Analysis, 56, 68, 88, 141, 162, 237, 414, 446, 590, 639, 673, 692, 727, 771, 773, 781, 791, 809, 812-813, 823-824, 841, 857, 869, 872, 877, 883, 903
Lyrics, and Deviant Themes, 20, 694, 709
Lyrics, and Doors (music group), 417, 432
Lyrics, and Dylan, Bob, 417, 432
Lyrics, and Gabriel, Peter, 469
Lyrics, and German Language, 495
Lyrics, and Hendrix, Jimi, 375
Lyrics, and Impressions (music group), 417
Lyrics, and Jefferson Airplane (music group), 375, 432
Lyrics, and Languages, 118
Lyrics, and Literary Allusion, 382
Lyrics, and Metaphors, 396, 407
Lyrics, and Ochs, Phil, 432
Lyrics, and Poetry, 102, 109, 123, 152, 390, 401, 417, 420, 431-432, 450, 877, 906
Lyrics, and Punk Rock Music, 362
Lyrics, and Rap Music, 175
Lyrics, and Reggae Music, 11
Lyrics, and Religion, 732, 746, 771
Lyrics, and Rolling Stones (music group), 432
Lyrics, and Sexual Content, 38, 694, 824, 835, 853
Lyrics, and Simon, Paul, 432
Lyrics, and Social Commentary, 38, 92, 94, 117, 586, 597, 903
Lyrics, and Springsteen, Bruce, 367, 370, 381, 391, 597, 739-740, 758
Lyrics, and Violence, 737
Lyrics, and Welsh Identity, 198
Lyrics, and Who, The (music group), 417, 432
Lyrics, and Women, 63, 167, 784, 813, 836

Mab Darogan (rock opera), 198
Machiavellianism, 664
Machismo, 664
MacInnes, Colin, 397
MacLean, Bonnie, 435
Madonna, 415, 489, 512, 556
Madonna, and Communication, 5, 7, 57, 61
Madonna, and Ethnomusicology, 190
Madonna, and History, 303
Madonna, and Psychology, 660, 701
Madonna, and Religion, 742
Madonna, and Sociology, 916-917
Magazines, 40, 43, 536-538
Magnetic Tape, 279
Magnitude Estimation Scaling Behavior, 659
Mailer, Norman, 82
Males (SEE ALSO: Gender; Masculinity), 6, 47, 50, 683, 688, 725, 791, 813, 853, 897
Malmsteen, Yngwie, 498, 522
Mandela, Nelson, 610, 624
Manichaeism, 760
Manipulation, 8
Mann, Carl, 307
Mannheim, Karl, 627
Manson, Charles, 300, 359
Manzarek, Ray, 530
Marcus, Greil, 408, 811
Marcuse, Herbert, 76, 607
Marginality, 623
Marijuana (SEE ALSO: Drugs), 630, 734
Marketing, 419, 512, 773
Marketing, and Cinema, 266
Marketing, and Communication, 14, 21, 25, 43
Marketing, and History, 305
Marketing, and Politics, 612
Marketing, and Psychology, 690

SUBJECT INDEX

Marketing, and Sociology, 808, 822, 831, 876, 892, 905, 911
Marley, Bob, 587, 631
Marxism, 176-177, 776, 800
Masculinity (SEE ALSO: Gender; Males; Men), 52, 576, 690, 714, 799, 813, 897-898
Mason, Bobbie Ann, 371
Mass (theatrical production), 755
Mass Culture, 866, 911
Mass Media, 236, 542
Mass Media, and Communication, 13, 25, 32, 48, 53, 58, 65, 71
Mass Media, and Education, 86, 117, 136
Mass Media, and Ethnomusicology, 207
Mass Media, and History, 226, 251, 342, 352
Mass Media, and Politics, 638
Mass Media, and Psychology, 675
Mass Media, and Sociology, 788-789, 819, 828, 886, 905, 910, 918, 922
Material Girl (song), 7, 415
Materialism, 871
Mathematics, 122, 148, 705
Maximum Rock n Roll (publication), 803
May, Brian, 673
Maybellene (song), 783
MC5 (music group), 635, 907
McCartney, Paul, 303, 410, 454, 462, 500, 505, 549, 673, 906
McDonald, Michael, 530
McDonald, Skeets, 354
McGhee, Brownie, 342
McGhee, Stick, 354
McGuinn, Roger, 341, 630
McLaren, Malcolm, 240, 317, 392
McLuhan, Marshall, 86, 300, 325, 779, 785, 798
Meaning, 133, 545
Meaning, and Communication, 59, 80
Meaning, and Culture, 199, 229, 551, 604, 822, 832

Meaning, and Politics, 604, 633-634
Meaning, and Punk Rock Music, 67, 212
Meaning, and Sociology, 576, 794, 879-880, 888, 929
Media Content, 683, 788
Media Types, 683
Melbourne, Australia, 520
Melody, 104, 144, 454, 460, 464, 481, 489-490, 502, 505, 572
Meltzer, Richard, 907
Memory, 13, 217, 655, 875
Memphis, Tennessee, 207, 288, 303, 307, 334-335, 349
Men (SEE ALSO: Males; Masculinity), 897
Mental Health (SEE ALSO: Mental Retardation), 646, 667, 844
Mental Retardation, 122
Mentors, 724
Merseybeat Sound, 327, 356
Messages, 37, 53, 707
Metallica (music group), 215, 457, 556
Metaphor, 396, 404, 694, 746, 843
Metaphysics, 26
Meter, 490
Mexican Americans (SEE: Hispanic Americans)
Mexico, 174, 196
Meyers, Jimmy, 265
Mice, 687
Michaels, Lee, 530
MIDI (Musical Instrument Digital Interface), 510
Midnight Oil (music group), 55, 204, 622
Midnighters (music group), 354
Migration, 207, 250, 857
Milburn, Amos, 354
Military, 92
Military, and Draft, 90
Miller, Roger, 577
Minogue, Kylie, 59
Minstrel Shows, 325

Mississippi Delta, 207
Mitchell, Joni, 534, 539
Mobility, 524, 777
Mode, 316
Models, 12, 479-480
Modernism, 449, 455
Modulation, 490
Mohawk, Essra, 341
Monkees (music group), 299, 341
Monroe, Bill, 267
Monterey International Pop Festival (1967), 353, 581, 818
Monterey Pop (film), 398, 581
Moods, 153, 691, 713, 862
Moody Blues (music group), 468, 708
Moon, Keith, 359
Moore, Merrill, 354
Moore, Scotty, 575
Morals, 103, 612, 762, 825
Morrison, Jim, 245, 420, 630, 724
Morrison, Van, 230, 303, 334, 534, 539
Morse, Ella Mae, 354
Moscoso, Victor, 435
Mother Earth (music group), 341
Mothers of Invention (music group), 325, 423, 487, 795, 818, 906
Motion, 777
Motivation, 34, 41, 128, 144, 155, 845
Motley Crue (music group), 708
Motor Activities, 648
Motown (SEE ALSO: Detroit, Michigan), 181, 274, 293, 303, 315, 334, 349, 352, 486, 527, 539, 556, 830, 906
Mouse Studios, 435
Move It (song), 783
Mroja (music group), 224
MTV (television), 23, 449, 457, 916
MTV (television), and Art, 399, 412
MTV (television), and Communication, 4, 14, 24, 29, 41, 46, 49, 61-62, 415
MTV (television), and

Ethnomusicology, 160, 190
MTV (television), and History, 284, 300, 303, 332, 352
MTV (television), and Sociology, 804, 849, 905, 909, 915
Mull of Kintyre (song), 505
Multidimensional Scaling, 71
Municipal Arenas, 593
Munsterberg, Hugo, 69
Murders (SEE: Homicide)
Murphey, Michael, 211
Music, and Background Noise, 151
Music, and Education, 85-86, 99-100, 103-104, 114, 119, 121, 136-138, 463, 468, 480, 489, 502, 505-506, 508, 514, 569, 572, 700, 907
Music, and Form, 104, 481, 502, 572, 790
Music, and Loudness, 672
Music, and Mood, 104
Music, and Therapy, 677, 679, 684, 713
Music Appreciation, 8, 142
Music Industry, 158, 236, 440, 465, 542, 548, 554, 773, 816, 864
Music Industry, and Australia, 275, 278, 608
Music Industry, and Great Britain, 228
Music Industry, and History, 245, 262, 297, 301, 305-306, 319-320, 800
Music Industry, and Hungary, 197
Music Industry, and Independents, 428
Music Industry, and Japan, 838
Music Industry, and Marketplace, 60, 363, 822, 831, 879
Music Industry, and Politics, 612, 633, 635
Music Industry, and Self-Regulation, 584
Music Industry, and Simulation, 148
Music Industry, and Sociology, 82, 905, 907, 911-912

Music Industry, and Wales, 200
Music Preference Reaction Index (MPRI), 483, 571
Music Publishing, 250, 306, 440, 892, 911
Music Videos, 415, 449, 532, 777, 790, 893, 905, 909, 916
Music Videos, and Art, 1, 399, 412, 429, 438, 917
Music Videos, and Censorship, 332
Music Videos, and Communication, 4-7, 14, 24, 27, 33, 39, 41, 44-45, 49-50, 55, 57-58, 61-62, 64-65, 73, 83, 190, 447, 839, 849
Music Videos, and Content Analysis, 3, 23, 36, 61, 194, 643
Music Videos, and Defiance Themes, 778
Music Videos, and Education, 100, 133
Music Videos, and History, 352
Music Videos, and Literary Allusion, 382
Music Videos, and Psychology, 660, 662-663, 665-666, 701, 722-723, 725
Music Videos, and Religion, 742, 764, 766
Music Videos, and Sex, 21, 689, 691
Music Videos, and Violence, 21, 23, 46, 689
Musical Equipment, 66, 74, 524
Musical Experience Inventory, 565
Musical Preference Scale, 674
Musical Structures, 316, 566
Musicals, 256, 525, 567-568, 674
Musicians, 47, 80, 158, 162, 333, 354, 360, 428, 433, 542, 554, 894, 911
Musicians, and African Americans, 4, 33, 241, 265, 297, 310, 349, 352, 526, 543, 756, 830
Musicians, and Communication, 43, 51, 66, 74
Musicians, and German Democratic Republic, 617
Musicians, and Great Britain, 327, 421
Musicians, and Groups, 148, 158, 164-165, 228, 235, 238, 303, 333-334, 524, 529, 806-807, 814, 914, 934
Musicians, and History, 308, 350, 430
Musicians, and Israel, 189
Musicians, and Judaism, 750
Musicians, and New Jersey, 169
Musicians, and Politics, 630
Musicians, and Record Production, 509, 570, 816-817
Musicians, and San Francisco, California, 348
Musicians, and Stress, 718, 729
Musicians, and Women (SEE: Women Musicians)
Musicology, 517, 545, 912, 920
My Generation (song), 532
Mysticism, 464
Mythology, 9, 27, 129, 211, 223, 430, 446, 497, 797

Nadine (song), 783
Narrative, 101, 399, 899
Narrative, and Band, The (music group), 161
Narrative, and Berry, Chuck, 446
Narrative, and Cinema, 398, 404
Narrative, and Dylan, Bob, 446
Narrative, and Music Videos, 7, 24, 643
Narrative, and Springsteen, Bruce, 367, 370, 381, 414, 446
Narrative, and Vietnam War, 389
Nashville, Tennessee, 207
Native Americans, 179
Near, Holly, 631
Nebraska (album), 367, 370, 740
Nebraska (song), 758
Nelson, Tracy, 341
New Age Movement, 761
New Age Music, 653, 676, 693

New Jersey, 169
New Music, 452, 518, 553
New Order (music group), 195
New Orleans, Louisiana, 207, 291, 295, 303, 334-335
New Testament, 738
New Wave Music, 485, 527, 573, 582
New Wave Music, and Education, 142
New Wave Music, and Ethnomusicology, 156
New Wave Music, and History, 252, 289, 292, 298, 303, 315-316, 318, 323-324, 336, 346, 365
New Wave Music, and Politics, 585
New Wave Music, and Sociology, 831
New York City, New York, 207, 238, 300, 303, 317, 324, 362, 933
New York Dolls (music group), 317
New York Magazine (publication), 312
New York Times (publication), 76
Newman, Randy, 311, 329
Newport Jazz Festival, 364
Nicholson, Jack, 359
Night They Drove Old Dixie Down, The (song), 161
Nightclubs, 169, 324, 327, 333, 887, 911
Nihilism, 24, 703
No Money Down (song), 783
No Particular Place To Go (song), 783
No Wave Music, 156
Noise (SEE: Sound Levels)
Norms, 164, 731
Nostalgia, 16, 168, 217, 907
Not Drowning Wave (music group), 55
Novels, 131, 377, 382, 388-389, 397, 448
Nuclear War, 685
Nueva Cancion Music, 163
Nueva Trova Music, 176-177

Nursery Rhymes, 586

Objectification, 165, 207
Obscenity, 584, 736
Occupations (SEE ALSO: Careers), 926
Ochs, Phil, 432, 630, 637, 907
Odyssey Theme, 857
Offer Self-Image Questionnaire, 774
Old Testament, 738-739
Oldfield, Mike, 553
Omnicide, 685
On the Road (book), 840
One Step Up (song), 194
Ono, Yoko, 309, 631
Open Your Heart (song), 5
Openness, 653
Opera, 565
Opinions, 563
Optimism, 81
Oral History, 92, 293, 783, 903
Orbison, Roy, 303, 307, 334
Orchestration, 572
Organizational Communication, 80
Organizational Structure, 812, 892
Orr, Norman, 435
Osbourne, Ozzy, 788
Otis Dudley Duncan Socio-Economic Index, 565
Outlaw Image, 78
Ovid, 384

Page, Jimmy, 575
Page, Larry, 285
Paglia, Camille, 385
Panic, 668
Pantheism, 337
Papa Don't Preach (song), 5, 701
Paradigms, 493, 861, 865
Paranoid (song), 788
Parental Advisory Labels (SEE: Sound Recordings, and Labeling)
Parental Sovereignty, 584
Parents Music Resource Center (PMRC), 13, 141, 160, 259, 332,

SUBJECT INDEX

584, 612, 786, 837, 843, 889, 928
Parks, Van Dyke, 907
Parsons, Talcott, 310
Participant Observation, 238
Patriarchy, 867
Payola, 257, 290, 303, 305, 308, 320, 332, 334, 350, 352, 911
Peace, 90, 631
Peace Museum (Chicago), 631
Peer Pressure, 712
Peers, 656-657
Pentecost, 738
People's Republic of China, 604
Percussion, 506
Perestroika, 607
Performance, 63, 84, 228, 453, 460, 493, 524, 549, 773, 869, 911
Performance Art, 409
Performers, 303, 319, 334, 480, 529, 695
Perkins, Carl, 273, 295, 307, 328, 335, 534
Personal Values, 35, 147, 704, 722, 725, 825
Personality, and Tests, 801
Personality, and Traits, 664, 681, 728, 731, 778
Personality, and Types, 396, 720
Personalized System of Instruction, 569
Personas, 777
Persuasion, 627
Pessimism, 890
Petty, Tom, 534
Philadelphia, Pennsylvania, 207, 300, 303, 334
Phillips, Sam, 184, 273, 307, 314, 335
Philosophy, 76, 134, 385, 744, 751, 820, 918
Phonetics, 707
Phonology, 101
Photographs, 362, 433
Physical Appearance, 926
Physicians, 646

Physiology, 698-699
Piano, 507
Pickett, Wilson, 539
Piers-Harris Self-Concept Scales, 722
Pink Floyd (music group), 133, 346, 531-532, 920
Plastic, 396
Plastic People (music group), 180, 619
Plato, 745
Platoon (film), 389
Platters (music group), 295
Play, 777
Pleasure, 15, 17-18, 30-31, 139
Poetry, and Education, 102, 109-110, 123, 152, 390, 401
Poetry, and Literature, 382, 417, 420, 431-432, 443, 450
Poetry, and Music Videos, 133, 447
Poetry, and Sociology, 877
Poland, 186, 213, 231, 598
Political Attitudes, 16, 54
Political Culture, 393, 531, 542, 777, 790, 870, 885, 907
Political Power, 297, 306, 927
Political Protest, 78, 209, 467, 599
Political Revolution, 286
Political Science, 92, 94, 295
Pop, Iggy, 423
Pop Art, 923
Popular Culture, 139, 296, 865, 904
Popular Literature, 536-538
Porter, Cole, 549
Poster Art (SEE ALSO: Psychedelic Posters), 333, 422, 435
Posters, 333, 362, 403
Postmodernism, 421, 449, 455, 511, 518, 533
Postmodernism, and Art, 399
Postmodernism, and Communication, 1, 15, 17-19, 24, 27, 30-31, 73
Postmodernism, and Education, 139
Postmodernism, and History, 304
Postmodernism, and Literature, 402
Postmodernism, and Sociology, 215,

804, 885, 909, 913, 915
Power, 576, 611, 633, 891, 928
Power, and Politics, 592
Pragmatism, 9
Preferences, 670, 885
Preferences, and Entertainment, 696
Preferences, and Music Genres (SEE ALSO: Adolescents, and Music Preferences), 34, 70, 111, 153, 458, 483, 559, 561, 563, 565, 571, 573, 590, 641, 650, 652-653, 656-657, 659, 661, 664, 674, 680, 688, 700, 709, 726, 728, 731, 834
Preferences, and Music Videos, 21, 778
Pregnancy, 701
Present Orientation, 826
Preservation, 181
Presley, Elvis, 527, 539, 544, 555-556, 575
Presley, Elvis, and Communication, 72, 76
Presley, Elvis, and Education, 125
Presley, Elvis, and Ethnomusicology, 192, 237, 374
Presley, Elvis, and History, 253, 257, 265, 267, 269, 273, 290, 292, 295, 299-300, 303, 307, 311, 318, 325, 329, 334-335, 342, 352
Presley, Elvis, and Politics, 630, 632
Presley, Elvis, and Sociology, 789, 869, 901-902, 906, 918, 922
Press, The, 297, 905, 911
Preston, Billy, 578
Pretenders (music group), 423
Prima, Louis, 354
Primary Education, 121
Priming, 663, 665-666, 723
Prince, 303, 423, 475, 746
Prine, John, 534, 673
Print Media, 236, 819
Prisioneros, Los (music group), 163
Private Dancer (song), 415
Private Schools, 573

Problem Child, The (song), 737
Proby, P. J., 299
Producers (SEE: Sound Recordings, and Producing)
Production, 612, 690, 800, 822, 850, 875, 896, 899, 910, 927
Professor Longhair, 335
Profits, 305, 911
Progressive Music, 531
Progressive Rock Music, 478, 499, 545, 574, 582, 848, 854, 929
Prosperity, 649, 783
Protean Model, 380
Protest Music, 466, 555, 588, 590, 599, 627
Protest Music, and Communication, 58, 78
Protest Music, and Education, 95
Protest Music, and History, 244, 308, 318, 338, 352
Protest Music, and Politics, 631, 638
Protest Music, and Sociology, 781
Psychedelic Posters (SEE ALSO: Poster Art), 333, 403, 422
Psychedelic Rock Music (SEE ALSO: Acid Rock Music), 142, 293, 298, 323, 336, 347, 499, 540, 555, 920
Psychiatric Patients, 713
Psychoactive Substance Use Disorder, 713
Public Enemy (music group), 175
Public Forums, 593
Public Policy, 13
Public Schools, 92, 573
Publications (SEE: Magazines; Print Media)
Puerto Ricans, 206
Pulitzer, Roxanne, 359
Punk Rock Music, 156, 168, 212, 455, 485, 503, 512, 527, 542, 545, 582
Punk Rock Music, and Art, 142, 392, 409, 424
Punk Rock Music, and Australia, 520

SUBJECT INDEX

Punk Rock Music, and Canada, 776
Punk Rock Music, and Communication, 15, 17-18, 30-31, 73
Punk Rock Music, and Czechoslovakia, 193
Punk Rock Music, and Eastern Europe, 231
Punk Rock Music, and Great Britain, 240, 294, 345-346, 362, 397, 787, 798, 811
Punk Rock Music, and History, 252, 280, 292, 294, 296, 298, 300, 303, 315-318, 323-324, 330, 332, 336, 352, 362, 365
Punk Rock Music, and Hungary, 623
Punk Rock Music, and Literature, 416
Punk Rock Music, and Los Angeles, California, 258, 289
Punk Rock Music, and New York City, New York, 362
Punk Rock Music, and Poland, 213
Punk Rock Music, and Politics, 585, 589, 600, 605, 634
Punk Rock Music, and Psychology, 664, 680
Punk Rock Music, and San Francisco, California, 219, 289
Punk Rock Music, and Sociology, 236, 787, 800, 803-804, 827, 829, 848, 911, 930, 933
Purcell, Henry, 454
Purple Rain (album), 746

Quasi-Theories, 889
Quatro, Suzi, 220
Queen (music group), 707
Quest, 883
Quicksilver Messenger Service (music group), 579

Racial Differences, 5-6, 75, 190, 268, 480, 793
Racism, 92, 221
Racism, and History, 297, 352
Racism, and Politics, 630
Racism, and Punk Rock Music, 787
Racism, and Religion, 733
Racism, and Sociology, 203, 815, 849, 905
Radicalism, 637, 927
Radio, 440
Radio, and AM, 785
Radio, and Audiences, 28
Radio, and College, 533
Radio, and Communication, 39
Radio, and Easy Listening, 28
Radio, and FM, 82, 785
Radio, and History, 250, 257, 262, 297, 300, 306, 308, 319, 334, 342, 360
Radio, and Marketing, 60, 277, 363
Radio, and News, 28
Radio, and Programming Formats, 26, 28, 71, 277, 283, 363
Radio, and Progressive Format, 28, 82, 845
Radio, and Sociology, 790, 892, 905-906, 911, 918
Radio, and Top 40 Format, 28, 303
Radio, and Underground Programming, 906
Rag Mama Rag (song), 161
Raga Music, 488
Ragtime Music, 325, 339, 360, 564
Railroads, 92, 141
Ramones (music group), 317, 324, 423, 503
Rap Music, 556, 582
Rap Music, and Communication, 2, 54, 73
Rap Music, and Ethnomusicology, 160, 175, 190, 203, 205-206, 214, 227, 236
Rap Music, and History, 274, 298, 303, 349, 352
Rap Music, and Politics, 605
Rap Music, and Psychology, 667
Rap Music, and Religion, 735-736
Rap Music, and Sociology, 932

Rastafarians, 587, 603
Rat Trap (song), 505
Rationalization, 510
Rational-Emotive Theory, 692
Rats, 669, 682
Raven, Genya, 63
RCA (company), 297, 588
Reading, 115, 126, 128, 145-146, 150, 154, 390, 652, 705
Rebel Without a Cause (film), 273
Rebellion (SEE ALSO: Adolescents, and Rebellion; Defiance), 112, 244, 246, 352, 420, 624, 632, 778, 808, 840
Recessions, 257
Reciprocally Constitutive Effects, 896
Reckless Behavior (SEE ALSO: Adolescents, and Reckless Behavior; Sensation Seeking Behavior), 774-775
Recoding, 42
Record (publication), 542
Record Companies, 440, 905, 907
Record Companies, and Africa, 233
Record Companies, and Australia, 278
Record Companies, and History, 257, 262, 291, 297, 301, 305, 320
Record Companies, and Independents, 278, 533, 892
Record Companies, and San Francisco, California, 333
Record Companies, and Wales, 200
Records (SEE: Sound Recordings)
Recreation (SEE ALSO: Leisure), 717
Red Hot & Blue (album), 624
Red Wedge, 609
Redding, Otis, 303, 334, 526, 539
Redemption, 739-740, 758
Reed, Dean, 614
Reed, Lou, 317, 531, 534
Reference Books, 459
Reggae Music, 11, 142, 296, 298, 303, 323, 349, 573, 582, 587, 603, 653
Relationships, 68, 531, 718, 926
Relevance in Education, 136
Religious Instruction, 732
Religious Music, 573
Religious Themes, 781, 918
Remedial Education, 128, 148, 150
Renaissance Music, 478, 561
Repetition, 484
Repo Man (film), 258
Representation, 7
Research Methods, 12, 116, 162, 861
Resources, 558, 649
Response, 493
Revolution (song), 702
Rewards, 712
Reynolds, Malvina, 631
Rhetoric, 16, 56, 68, 78, 81, 375, 493, 638
Rhodes, Randy, 498, 522
Rhythm, 104, 144, 453, 460, 464, 481, 489, 502, 505-507, 545, 566, 572
Rhythm and Blues Music (SEE ALSO: Black Music), 237, 479, 486, 526, 554-555-556
Rhythm and Blues Music, and Ethnomusicology, 181
Rhythm and Blues Music, and History, 246, 250, 252, 257, 265, 268, 272, 280, 287, 290, 299, 303, 308, 316, 319, 334-335, 339, 342, 349, 365-366
Rhythm and Blues Music, and Psychology, 674
Rhythm and Blues Music, and Sociology, 815, 832, 906
Rich, Charlie, 307
Richards, Keith, 423, 534, 549, 575
Riffs, 502
Rimbaud, 420
Risk Taking, 680
Ritchie, Lionel, 100
Ritual, 223, 519, 762, 805, 810, 924,

928
River, The (album), 367, 370, 391, 739-740
River, The (song), 739-740, 758
Rivers, Johnny, 159
Robinson, Bobby, 295
Robinson, Smokey, 328
Rock Against Racism, 609
Rock & Roll Confidential (publication), 425
Rock Around the Clock (film), 249, 342
Rock Around the Clock (song), 265
Rock Around the World (television show), 284
Rock Festivals, 226, 241, 303, 334, 581, 738, 762, 931
Rock in Rio (concert), 187
Rock Nacional, 199, 625, 858
Rock Operas, 198, 453, 525, 546
Rockabilly Music, 521, 527, 555, 840
Rockabilly Music, and History, 267, 290, 295, 303, 334, 352, 366
Rocket to Russia (album), 503
Rodgers, Jimmie, 544
Rodgers, Richard, 549
Rokeach Value Survey, 722
Role Models, 220, 480
Roles, 112, 894
Rolling Stone (publication), 423, 512, 542
Rolling Stones (music group), 393, 398, 426, 432-433, 539, 556, 562, 583, 907, 931
Rolling Stones (music group), and Communication, 76
Rolling Stones (music group), and Culture, 397, 427
Rolling Stones (music group), and History, 242-243, 245-246, 290, 292, 299-300, 303, 311, 318, 325, 328, 334, 346
Rolling Stones (music group), and Politics, 630
Rolling Stones (music group), and Psychology, 712
Rolling Stones (music group), and Religion, 753
Rolling Stones (music group), and Sociology, 97, 795, 832, 835-836, 906, 920
Rolling Stones (music group), and Theater, 368
Romance, 7, 777, 877
Romania, 231, 598
Romantic Music, 478, 561
Romanticism, 9, 24, 337, 385, 871
Ronettes (music group), 577
Ronstadt, Linda, 159
Rose, Axl, 690
Rosenberg Self-Esteem Scale, 774
Rosolato, Guy, 484
Roxy Music (music group), 384
Royalties, 253, 305
Rubber Soul (album), 183
Rubinson, David, 333
Running with the Devil (song), 576
Rush (music group), 129
Russell, Leon, 578
Russia (SEE ALSO: Soviet Union), 222, 618

Sacraments, 741
Sadler, Barry, 588
Sain Records, 200
Salsa Music, 176-177
Salt Lake City, Utah, 886
Salvation, 758
Sam the Sham, 907
Sampling (SEE: Sound Recordings, and Sampling)
San Francisco, California, 521, 556, 907
San Francisco, California, and Art, 422, 435
San Francisco, California, and Ethnomusicology, 207, 219
San Francisco, California, and History, 289, 303, 308, 315, 333-334, 347-348, 359

San Francisco, California, and Music, 466, 512, 579
San Francisco, California, and Sociology, 906
San Jose, California, 887
Santana (music group), 579
Satanism, and History, 243, 332
Satanism, and Psychology, 694, 702-703, 707, 709, 715
Satanism, and Religion, 765
Satanism, and Sociology, 457, 792, 859-860, 905
Saturday Night Fever (film), 799
Saved (album), 744
Saxophones, 237
Scaggs, Boz, 579
Scandinavia, 477
Schematic Processing, 20
Schema, and Music, 488
Schizophrenia, 684
Schnepf, Bob, 435
Scholastic Aptitude Test (SAT), 705
School, 88, 854-855
Science Fiction, 531
Scores, 572
Sebastian, John, 341
Secondary Education, 94, 121
Sedation, 698-699
Seeger, Pete, 631
Self-Destruction, 724
Self-Esteem, 774-775
Self-Expression, 677
Self-Help Techniques, 654
Self-Identity, 112, 820
Self-Image, 779, 800, 847
Self-Perception, 721-722, 826
Self-Realization, 731
Self-Reference, 65
Semantics, 101
Semiology, 67
Semiotics, 84
Senate Hearings (SEE: United States Senate Hearings)
Sensation Seeking Behavior (SEE ALSO: Reckless Behavior), 653, 674, 696, 726, 774-775
Sensation Seeking Scale, 674, 774
Sentimentality, 161
Sequencer, 510
Sequencing, 8
Sesame Street (television show), 106
Seventh-Day Adventists, 573, 734
Sex, 735, 757, 872
Sex, and Communication, 38, 50
Sex, and Psychology, 691, 694, 701, 728
Sex, and Religion, 765
Sex, and Sociology, 203, 781, 783, 905
Sex, and Television, 21, 36
Sex Differences (SEE: Gender)
Sex Education, 25
Sex Pistols (music group), 423, 512, 811
Sex Pistols (music group), and Communication, 76
Sex Pistols (music group), and Culture, 392, 397, 424, 600
Sex Pistols (music group), and Ethnomusicology, 240
Sex Pistols (music group), and History, 294, 345, 359
Sex Pistols (music group), and Sociology, 787, 798, 930
Sex Roles (SEE ALSO: Gender), 3, 23, 44-45, 663, 665, 714, 723, 791, 799, 813, 874
Sexism (SEE ALSO: Women, and Attitudes Toward), 44-45, 205, 630, 735-736, 787, 836, 840, 849
Sexual Activity, 725
Sexual Arousal, 853
Sexual Attitudes, 649, 824
Sexual Behavior, 649, 687, 824, 826
Sexuality, 736, 802
Sexuality, and Communication, 5, 35
Sexuality, and Ethnomusicology, 194, 236
Sexuality, and Politics, 632
Sexuality, and Psychology, 660, 714

SUBJECT INDEX

Sexuality, and Religion, 742, 746
Sexuality, and Sociology, 799, 874, 895, 897, 911-912
Sexually Explicit Materials, 332, 689, 696
Sgt. Pepper's Lonely Hearts Club Band (album), 98, 300, 353, 518, 532, 761, 818, 906, 920
Sgt. Pepper's Lonely Hearts Club Band (film), 256
Shakers, 772
Shankar, Ravi, 578
Sheet Music, 317, 362, 507
Shepard, Sam, 400, 441, 445
Shirelles (music group), 295
Shirts (music group), 324
Short Stories, 382
Show Tunes, 565
Sigue Sigue Sputnik (music group), 518
Silkwood, Karen, 359
Silly Boys (song), 707
Simon, Paul, 303, 341, 384, 432, 534, 539, 549, 673
Simon & Garfunkel, 341, 795
Simpson, Valerie, 539
Simulation Theory, 148
Singer, David, 435
Sisters are Doin' it for Themselves (song), 415
Situationist International, 424
Skill Development, 677
Skinheads, 219
Slang, 75
Slick, Grace, 16, 220
Slow Train Coming (album), 744
Sly and the Family Stone, 303, 334, 539
Smelser, Neil J., 886
Smith, Esau, 354
Smith, Patti, 63, 220, 317, 324, 400
Smiths (music group), 852
Snowblind (song), 707
Social Activity, 687
Social Categories, 641

Social Construction, 548, 889
Social Criticism, 78, 95, 735, 890
Social Drama, 924
Social Influences, 641
Social Innovation, 864
Social Interaction, 723
Social Mobility, 783
Social Models, 814
Social Psychology, 636, 664, 926
Social Reality, 185
Social Recognition, 677
Social Responses, 479
Social Stability, 927
Social Values, 584, 643
Socialism, 176-177, 615, 621, 787
Socialization, 29, 35, 58, 75, 219, 369, 774, 777, 813, 825-826, 834
Socio-economic Conditions, 217, 228, 235, 252, 776, 934
Socio-economic Status, 2, 11, 54, 565, 662, 787, 854-855, 922
Soft Rock Music, 318, 323, 485
Solitude, 724
Sondheim, Stephen, 560
Song Titles, and Content Analysis, 890
Songs, 159, 370
Songwriters, 298, 303, 334, 501, 534, 549
Songwriting, 440
Soul Music (SEE ALSO: Black Music), 526-527, 547, 555-556, 563, 573
Soul Music, and Communication, 38
Soul Music, and Education, 85
Soul Music, and Ethnomusicology, 181
Soul Music, and History, 274, 293, 298-299, 303, 308, 311, 323, 334, 336, 349, 352
Soul Music, and Psychology, 653, 674
Soul Music, and Religion, 733, 754, 756
Sound, 489, 707

Sound Effects (book), 866
Sound Foundations (START program), 148
Sound Levels (SEE ALSO: Auditory Research; Hearing), 150, 651, 672, 682, 710
Sound Preferences, 145
Sound Recordings, 140, 461, 496, 516, 566, 785, 790, 876, 911, 918
Sound Recordings, and Album Covers, 167, 413, 419, 434, 856
Sound Recordings, and Albums, 370
Sound Recordings, and Backward Masking, 13, 702, 707, 765-766
Sound Recordings, and Censorship, 10, 786
Sound Recordings, and Cover Versions, 159, 246, 265, 491, 815
Sound Recordings, and Crossovers, 221
Sound Recordings, and Engineering, 74, 460, 539, 570, 817
Sound Recordings, and History, 277, 280, 302, 308
Sound Recordings, and Literary Allusion, 382
Sound Recordings, and Producing, 74, 460, 494, 509, 539, 570, 816
Sound Recordings, and Ratings, 10, 612
Sound Recordings, and Remixing, 42
Sound Recordings, and Sales (SEE ALSO: Hit Records), 257, 773, 822
Sound Recordings, and Sampling, 876
Sound Recordings, and Soundtracks, 266
Sound Recordings, and Studios, 333, 555, 816-817
Sound Recordings, and Tribute Albums, 491
South Africa, 166
Southern Rock Music, 207, 303, 315, 476, 857
Soviet Union (SEE ALSO: Russia), 222, 270, 598
Soviet Union, and Communication, 32
Soviet Union, and Ethnomusicology, 188, 226, 231
Soviet Union, and History, 264, 355
Soviet Union, and Politics, 585, 587, 607, 640
Spanish Language (SEE: Languages, and Spanish)
Spare Parts (song), 194
Special Education, 122, 712
Specialty Records, 291
Spector, Phil, 299, 303, 334, 906
Speech, and Loudness, 672
Spheeris, Penelope, 258
Spiritual Music, 181, 632
Spirituality, 654
Sports, 295
Springsteen, Bruce, 423, 512, 556
Springsteen, Bruce, and Communication, 53
Springsteen, Bruce, and History, 300, 303, 352, 359
Springsteen, Bruce, and Narrative, 194, 367, 370, 381, 391, 414, 446
Springsteen, Bruce, and New Jersey, 169, 378
Springsteen, Bruce, and Politics, 597, 630, 632
Springsteen, Bruce, and Psychology, 660, 690
Springsteen, Bruce, and Religion, 739-741, 758
Spurgen, Nancy, 930
Stained Glass (album), 675, 715, 788
Stairway to Heaven (song), 702, 707
Star Club (music group), 55
Starr, Ringo, 303, 578
START (Simulations That Address Remedial Teaching), 148
Status, 217, 656, 776, 783, 818
Stereotypes, 3, 663, 665, 723, 784,

SUBJECT INDEX

813
Stevens, Cat, 673
Stewart, Rod, 334
Stimulation, and Music, 669, 674, 696
Stimulation Techniques, 8, 686, 698-699
Stimuli, 681
Sting, 359, 534
Stone, Jesse, 354
Stone, Sly, 329, 359
Stone Pony (nightclub), 169
Stray Cats (music group), 916
Street Legal (album), 744
Stress, 87, 649, 682, 718, 726, 729
Structures of Response, 139
Stryper (music group), 708
Students, and College, 20, 70, 75, 87, 590, 637, 645, 653, 655, 663, 665, 683, 688, 691, 697-699, 725, 731, 831, 834
Students, and Elementary School, 483, 571, 661, 700
Students, and High School, 41, 113, 115, 124, 148, 565, 701
Students, and Junior High School, 135, 146, 151, 480, 793
Students, and Non-Music Majors, 149, 472
Studio 54 (nightclub), 311
Study Habits, 146
Styx (music group), 707
Subconscious, 675
Subcultures, 58, 80, 397, 440, 589, 840, 851, 895, 902, 909, 911-912, 926, 928
Subcultures, and Countercultures, 32, 599
Subcultures, and Ethnomusicology, 170, 185, 208, 212, 223, 225, 551
Subcultures, and Heavy Metal Music, 646, 808
Subcultures, and Punk, 219, 827
Subliminal Messages, 675, 707
Suburbs, 208

Suicide, 675, 680, 709, 715, 746, 757, 788, 859-860
Suicide Solution (song), 788
Summer, Donna, 415
Sun City (album), 601, 624
Sun Records, 184, 273, 307, 314, 335
Superbad (song), 456
Superego, 728
Supreme Court (SEE: Unites States Supreme Court)
Surf Music (SEE ALSO: California Sound), 282, 290, 323, 556
Surrealistic Pillow (album), 375
Survey Methodology, 70, 590, 718
Surveys, 831
Sweden, 34
Sweet and Sour (television show), 411
Swimming Pool Q's (music group), 158
Swing Music, 339, 360, 564
Syllabi (SEE ALSO: Curricula), 149
Symbolic Interaction, 219, 814, 833
Symbolism, 29, 318, 694, 779, 794, 833, 885, 889
Symbolism, and Art, 413
Symbolism, and Heroes, 789, 924
Symbolism, and Religion, 765
Symbolism, and Subcultures, 67, 643, 827, 873
Sympathy for the Devil (song), 389, 583
Synthesizers, 66, 280, 530-532, 790
S/Z (literature), 399

T. Rex (music group), 346
Take On Me (song), 7
Talking Heads (music group), 324, 423, 451
Tanglewood Symposium, 99
Task Performance, 155
Tastes, 89, 236, 885
Taxes, and Great Britain, 195
Taylor, James, 534
Teachers, 85-86, 103, 149

Teaching Strategies, and History, 93, 97, 113, 298
Teaching Strategies, and Humanities, 116, 129
Teaching Strategies, and Languages, 108, 118
Teaching Strategies, and Music, 99-100, 103-104, 114, 119, 137, 149, 569
Teaching Strategies, and Philosophy, 134
Teaching Strategies, and Poetry, 102
Teaching Strategies, and Reading, 128
Teaching Strategies, and Religion, 732
Teaching Strategies, and Social Studies, 91, 94-96, 98, 117
Technology, 262, 461
Technology, and Communication, 39, 58, 66, 74, 447
Technology, and History, 250, 292, 304, 306, 313, 352
Technology, and Music, 465, 494, 496, 510-511, 519, 524, 555, 582
Technology, and Politics, 279, 611
Technology, and Psychology, 649
Technology, and Sociology, 783, 785, 790, 804, 812, 876, 892, 909
Teen Idols, 293, 298, 303, 352, 555
Teenagers (SEE: Adolescents; Youth Culture)
Telephones, 141
Television (SEE ALSO: MTV (television), 25, 701, 819, 905, 915, 918
Television, and Australia, 284, 411
Television, and Children, 106
Television, and Communication, 4, 14, 29, 41, 49, 62, 65, 415
Television, and History, 256, 287, 295, 308, 342
Television, and Public Service Announcements, 77
Television, and Sex, 36

Television, and Violence, 36, 689
Television (music group), 317, 324
Tellegen Absorption Scale, 676, 693
Tempo, 150, 460, 490, 650
Temptation, 745
Temptations (music group), 733
Ten Wheel Drive (music group), 474
Territorialization, 592
Texas, 303, 334
Theater, 368, 376, 394-395, 441, 525, 554, 560
Theberge, Paul, 510
Thematic Apperception Test, 708
Themes, 51, 101, 370
Therapy, 648
Thompson, Hunter S., 359
Thrashing, 219
Three Dog Night (music group), 539
Thriller (album), 160
Through the Looking Glass (book), 405
Thunder Road (song), 758
Tillich, Paul, 763
Timbre, 104, 897
Tin Pan Alley, 207, 252, 325, 350, 360
Tinnitus, 651
Tiny Tim, 311
Tobacco, 734
Tommy (rock opera), 131, 311, 417, 761
Tone, 316, 464, 490
Too Much Monkey Business (song), 783
Tooth of Crime, The (drama), 400
Tork, Peter, 341
Toto (music group), 530
Tougher than the Rest (song), 194
Touring, 319
Townshend, Peter, 359, 534
Traffic (music group), 712
Tragedy, 79
Treniers (music group), 354
Troggs (music group), 285
Trout Mask Replica (album), 818

SUBJECT INDEX

Troy, Doris, 8
Tunnel of Love (album), 370, 740-741
Tunnel of Love (song), 194
Turner, Ike, 184, 577, 931
Turner, Joe, 354
Turner, Tina, 415, 423, 577, 916, 931
Turner, Victor, 924
Tuten, Randy, 435
Twist, The (dance; song), 290, 299
2 Live Crew (music group), 736

U2 (music group), 230, 303, 556
Ukraine, 202
Underground Music, 298, 317, 362, 428
United States, and Southern Region, 857
United States Constitution, 584, 593
United States Senate Hearings, 259, 612, 786, 928
United States Supreme Court, 593
Upstage (nightclub), 169
Urbanization, 92-93, 96, 161, 203, 217, 612, 782, 883
Uses and Gratifications Model, 6

Valens, Ritchie, 174, 216-217
Validation, 238
Values (SEE ALSO: Interpersonal Values; Personal Values), 89, 662, 692, 828, 890, 925
Values, and Culture, 450, 634, 789, 809, 832
Van Halen (music group), 556, 576
Van Halen, Eddie, 498, 522
Van Ronk, Dave, 341
Velvet Underground (music group), 303, 317, 423, 444, 496, 531, 818
Verbal Skills, 705
Vestibular Physiology, 686
Veterans, 414
Vicious, Sid, 930
Victims, 695
Videotapes, 372
Vietnam War, 90, 244, 359, 389, 404, 414, 588, 649
Vietnamese, 887
Vigilance Performance, 647, 658
Village Ghetto Land (song), 737
Village Voice (publication), 312
Violence, 853
Violence, and Cinema, 69
Violence, and Communication, 3, 21, 36, 46, 50
Violence, and History, 249
Violence, and Psychology, 689, 695, 708
Violence, and Religion, 737
Violence, and Sociology, 203, 776, 781, 787-788, 849, 926
Visionaries, 864
Visual Recall, 645
Vocal Instrumental Ensembles, 202, 226, 231, 585, 607
Vocalization, 545, 790
Volume (SEE: Sound Levels)
Volunteers (album), 375
Volunteers of America (song), 16
Vulgarity, 332, 337

Waiting for Your Taxi (song), 461
Waits, Tom, 534
Wakeman, Rick, 530
Wales (SEE ALSO: Great Britain), 198, 200
Walk of Life (song), 751
Wall, The (film), 133
War, 90, 389
Warhol, Andy, 317, 423, 923
Warner Brothers Studios, 567
Warner-Reprise Records, 297
Watergate, 359
Waters, Muddy, 184, 539
Wattstax Festival, 241
We are the World (song), 480
WEA Records, 285
Weather, 407
Weber, Max, 510
Weight, The (song), 645
We're Only In It for the Money

(album), 818
Wharf Rats, 654
What's Going On (album), 756
When Electricity Came to Arkansas (song), 707
Whitaker, Jessie, 342
Whitcomb, Ian, 361
White Album, The, 300, 518, 707
Whites, 823
Whiz, The (musical), 525
Who, The (music group), 417, 423, 432, 532
Who, The (music group), and History, 292, 299, 303, 311, 325, 334, 346
Who, The (music group), and Psychology, 668, 716
Who, The (music group), and Religion, 761
Who, The (music group), and Sociology, 886
Who'll Stop the Rain (film), 389
Wild, the Innocent, and the E Street Shuffle, The (album), 367
Wild One, The (film), 273
Williams, Hank, 544
Williams, Raymond, 76
Wilson, Brian, 921
Wilson, Jackie, 303, 334
Wilson, Wes, 435
Winwood, Steve, 530
Wolfe, Tom, 359
Women (SEE ALSO: Females; Feminism; Gender), 7, 44-45, 167, 220, 228, 547, 632, 799, 845, 868, 878, 901
Women, and Attitudes Toward (SEE ALSO: Sexism), 62, 167, 531, 689, 736, 784, 813, 834, 836, 853, 929
Women, and Australia, 884
Women, and Exploitation, 69, 835
Women, and Literature, 415-416
Women Musicians, 63, 165, 210, 214, 218, 220, 234, 294, 297, 303, 309, 313, 501, 543, 547, 799, 856, 863, 916
Women's Music, 218, 632
Wonder, Stevie, 303, 334, 359, 737, 830
Woodstock (1969), 300, 359, 427, 818, 870, 907
Woodstock (film), 398, 835
Work Songs, 181
Working class (SEE ALSO: Socio-Economic Status), 922
World Cup Soccer (1990), 195
World in Motion (song), 195
World Music, 160, 303, 565
Wright, Gary, 530
Writing Composition (SEE: Composition, and Literary)
Wuden't Me (song), 783

X (music group), 258
X-Ray Spex (music group), 930

Yaogun Yinyue Music
Yes (music group), 100
Yothu Yindi (music group), 55
You Never Can Tell (song), 783
Young, Neil, 174, 303, 534
Your Own Thing (musical), 525
Youth (SEE: Adolescents)
Youth Culture, and Communication, 15, 17-18, 30-31, 39
Youth Culture, and Education, 132
Youth Culture, and History, 251, 281, 306, 364
Youth Culture, and Politics, 589, 613, 636
Youth Culture, and Psychology, 671
Youth Culture, and Sociology, 208, 551, 602, 833, 880-881, 900, 902, 908, 911, 913
Yugoslavia, 263, 598, 620

Zappa, Frank, 325, 423, 487, 795, 818, 906
ZZ Top (music group), 423, 916

About the Author

JEFFREY N. GATTEN is Assistant Professor in Libraries and Media Services, University Libraries, Kent State University. He holds an advanced degree in Sociology as well as in Library Science and is the compiler of *The Rolling Stone Index* (1993).

HARDCOVER BAR CODE

REF ML128.R6 G37 1995
Gatten, Jeffrey N
Rock music scholarship : an
interdisciplinary